More praise for *Megatrends for Women*

"I love *Megatrends for Women*. It's a powder keg! It is going to have an extraordinary impact. It brings such focus and clarity to where we are and where we are going. It is profoundly empowering."
—Barbara Grogan
CEO, Western Industrial Contractors

"Offers extraordinary insight into the future of women in America. *Megatrends for Women* is proof that we are beginning to break down the glass ceilings and give women the voice and the power that have for far too long been the exclusive privilege of men."
—Governor William F. Weld
Commonwealth of Massachusetts

"This book has great power . . . Full of fascinating data and the argument is engaging . . . Extremely useful for women . . . It prepares us for the final ascent."
—Mary Maples Dunn
President, Smith College

"I was overcome with emotion reading *Megatrends for Women*, as it embodies the very values for which I have been working for thirty years. Embodies and, even better, emblazons!"
—Susan Davis
CEO, Capital Missions Company

"Once again, Aburdene's and Naisbitt's strong combination of pre-science, clear thinking and stunning research will rivet the attention of the economic, political and social communities."
—Carol Anderson Tabor
Publisher, *Working Woman* magazine

"An eye-opener! Aburdene and Naisbitt show that the women of this country are the powerful resource necessary to keep our country competitive."
—Jack Kuehler
President, IBM Corporation

BOOKS BY **Patricia Aburdene and John Naisbitt**

Megatrends for Women
Megatrends 2000
Megatrends
Reinventing the Corporation

Megatrends for Women

Patricia Aburdene and John Naisbitt

FAWCETT COLUMBINE · NEW YORK

For Jennifer Jones. Having waited nearly eighteen years, it is your aunt's supreme pleasure to walk into the future with you woman to woman.

A Fawcett Columbine Book
Published by Ballantine Books

This edition published by arrangement with Villard Books, a division of Random House, Inc.
Villard Books is a registered trademark of Random House, Inc.

Library of Congress Catalog Card Number: 93-90038

ISBN: 0-449-90825-9

Cover design by David Stevenson

Manufactured in the United States of America

First Ballantine Books Edition: November 1993

10 9 8 7 6 5 4 3 2 1

Acknowledgments

Sometimes people say, "You must have quite a large staff to do all that research." No, we answer, we have Joy Van Elderen; she just *does the work of* a large staff. She is our treasure, the researcher other writers can only dream about. She takes mountains of newspaper clippings and other information and transforms them into digestible memos. She knows the Library of Congress like the back of her hand. She can track down just about anyone by phone and interview them or extract that last morsel of information we need to make our case. It is an understatement, but here it is anyway: there is no way we could have written *Megatrends for Women* without Joy.

Linda McLean Harned, who runs our office and itineraries, reviewed both manuscript and galleys, offered many important suggestions and helped with research and fact checking. Her unfailing and wonderfully competent support in many areas of our lives sustained us during the hectic period devoted to this book.

Our agent, the incomparable Ed Victor, played a decisive and early role in the conceptualization of this book. As the project's godfather, he saw it through every stage of growth. It used to be said, "Behind every successful man is a great woman." Behind *Megatrends for Women* there is a most supportive man.

Our experience with Villard has been an absolute pleasure. There is nothing Peter Gethers, Diane Reverand or Maureen McMahon would not do to assist and support us. How many writers can say that?

v

Corinne Kuypers-Denlinger's extensive memo on women's health issues became the substance for the first draft of the Menopause Megatrend chapter. Everett Rogers and Wendy Brooks helped us understand critical mass. Carolyn Long made substantial contributions to the Save the World chapter. Harriett Woods and Steve Schwadron reviewed the politics chapter. Sue Cobb and Donna and Jack Coombs reviewed the sports chapter. Claire Schwadron read the religion chapter. Elizabeth Sherwood, William Ury and Bill Leigh went through the entire manuscript. We are grateful to all of them for thoughtful suggestions and comments and their excitement about the project.

A small team with extensive knowledge about women's issues reviewed the entire manuscript. They were: Frances Lear, Barbara Grogan, Mary Rowe, Riane Eisler, Susan Davis and Carol Anderson Taber. Some made lengthy, detailed suggestions. That these busy, successful people would take the time to read our book could be interpreted as support for our work. It is and we are deeply grateful. But we also know it comes from their passionate caring about women and the challenges and issues before them.

Contents

Preface

Early in the next century, it will be clear that the women's movement reached a turning point in 1992 and 1993. After decades of slow progress and frustration, the movement reached critical mass (described at length on pages xx–xxiii). Simply put, women attained sufficient power in all spheres of public life. Their future progress became unstoppable.

Evidence of the movement's critical mass is everywhere:

- From the statehouse to the U.S. Senate, women have succeeded in raising millions of campaign dollars, casting 7.2 million more votes than men in 1992 and propelling a new administration to power.
- Women-owned firms have grown by 20 percent. At this dramatic rate, they may well employ twice as many people as the Fortune 500 companies in the near future.
- Anglicans have voted to ordain women, U.S. bishops have stood up to the Vatican's anti-female line and the U.S. military now has its first female rabbi as chaplain.
- The wage gap between men and women has narrowed to 74.5 cents to the dollar in 1992. In the first quarter of 1993, women were already earning 77 cents to every dollar men earned.
- Breast cancer research expenditures have hit $400 million, quadruple 1991 funding.

- A female goalie has played in the National Hockey League.
- Women pilots in the U.S. military are now training for combat missions.

And a collaborative couple resides in the White House.

One dramatic week in June 1993, the U.S. saw a new female senator, Kay Bailey Hutchison of Texas, and a woman Supreme Court justice nominee, Ruth Bader Ginsberg, while the world counted two new female prime ministers, Kim Campbell of Canada and Tansu Cilla of Turkey—a great moment in the women's movement and a powerful manifestation of critical mass.

It's 1993. Do You Know Where the Women Are?

Whether you are in business or politics, whether you are male or female, you cannot succeed today without substantive in-depth knowledge about the changing profile of women, their lifestyles, values, opinions and workstyles.

Hillary Rodham Clinton is the most visible metaphor for generational change. Like the First Lady, millions of women will move into power this decade as legislators, athletes, entrepreneurs, governors, physicians, fashion designers, executives, attorneys, clergy members and social activists.

Who are these women? If you are in business, they are your customers.

Did you know that

- 75 percent of household health decisions are made by women?
- Women buy 50 percent of automobiles, although Toyota recently discovered that women buy 60 percent of its vehicles?
- Women account for 80 percent of consumer spending?

Women are now responsible for a huge chunk of the spending on products we associate with male consumers. Women purchase

- 45 percent of the nation's tires.
- 40 percent of sports equipment.
- 75 percent of men's apparel.
- one fourth of trucks.
- one third of all beer.

Each trend that is documented in this book is empowering to women. In addition, each trend offers you and your company a new avenue, a new opportunity, a new vantage point from which to view, address and interact with women, the leaders of tomorrow.

A Question of Demographics

The first generation of women with lifelong, full-time careers is just entering its prime power years. These women, who came of age in the '70's and honed their careers in the '80's, are getting ready to shake up the world in the 1990's and beyond.

Many, perhaps most, are baby boomers, but their ranks also include those women in their late 40's, 50's, and 60's whose careers and lifestyles parallel those of younger women.

The Women's Movement: Phase Two

The time has come to change the strategic objectives of the women's movement.

In phase one of the women's movement, liberation meant raising consciousness, pioneering new roles and exposing sexism. That will continue for a long time. Just ask survivors of domestic violence, poverty, child abuse, breast cancer and inner-city strife if consciousness has been raised sufficiently about their causes.

Consciousness raising continues. Nevertheless, for millions of women, it is time to shift gears, to reorient their personal objectives.

It is time to shift from liberation to leadership.

That is the most appropriate description for the change many women are going through today. That is *the* megatrend for women.

Though the answer is clear to many, some might ask, why should women want to seek leadership? Isn't life stressful enough juggling careers, families, community life?

Women are already involved, they might argue. Women vote, hold office, start new companies, wield economic power as consumers, tackle such intractable issues as crime, drugs and teen pregnancy at the grass roots of society. What specific benefits will women reap by taking on the added burdens and responsibilities of leadership?

The answer is simple: the power to create, not just influence, the world in which they live.

Unless women assume leadership at every level of society and

integrate female sensibilities into the very fiber of the social and economic power structure, the ideal of equality and balance between
women and men will never be achieved.

Without attaining leadership, women will continue to live in a
world constructed and dominated by men. Women will keep responding to someone else's agenda, addressing the ills of a world they did
not create.

Ultimately it is impossible to achieve genuine liberation in a
male-dominated society. That is why the old-fashioned definition of
feminism—the *full* participation of women and the integration of their
values, concerns and opinions at every level of society—still holds.
That shift from liberation to leadership, phase two of the women's
movement, is the unifying theme of this book.

Defining Leadership

But what is leadership? Do women practice a different brand of
leadership from the traditional one that many, though not all, men
espouse? Won't women behave "exactly like men," some people suggest, once they achieve positions of power?

As a society, we are only beginning to appreciate the nuances of
questions like these. Meanwhile, the requirements of leadership have
evolved in the past decade, largely in response to the massive shifts we
described in *Megatrends* and *Megatrends 2000*.

We offer the following definition of leadership, which applies in
business, politics and the community. Though it would be unsuitable
in decades past, it works well for the 1990's:

**Leadership entails envisioning and articulating a new reality,
persuading others of its benefits and inspiring them to embrace
and actualize it.**

In changing times like ours, the ability to envision, persuade and
inspire is critical to leadership. Women possess these traits as much as,
or possibly more than, men. That was not always so.

Leadership: Old and New

In a stable era like the cold war industrial period, by contrast, a
leader's job was to maintain the status quo. So the key trait of leadership was to command and control: the leader emerged out of the

existing power structure, which gave him (it was usually a him) the authority to command people to carry out orders or face the threat of force, expulsion or punishment.

Command-and-control leadership was, and to a certain degree still is, characteristic of the military, old-line party politics, the former Communist party, unions, religious hierarchies, the industrial workplace and underworld crime organizations.

Historically, women were largely absent from such structures and therefore never "learned" the command-and-control model, which, as we argued in both *Megatrends* and *Megatrends 2000*, is completely ineffective in a high-tech, information-based economy. That means women now possess an ironic advantage over men schooled in the old ways: women need not "unlearn" the authoritarian leadership style.

Besides, throughout society the command-and-control model of leadership is being replaced by the inspire-and-communicate model. That opens the way for women to lead.

Today, old-line authority is undermined by the widespread belief in individual rights and participatory democracy. The authoritarian approach that saves lives in the military is unacceptable to the civilian population of a democracy. It is very difficult to coerce people in an information economy that employs skilled, educated workers who can find jobs elsewhere.

Similarly, recent changes in U.S. political life weaken the command-and-control model. So long as the United States and the former Soviet Union had nuclear weapons aimed at each other and were prepared to use them, Americans were more inclined to elect a leader with a background in military affairs or with the image of a superpatriot. A female leader (at least one not cast in the Margaret Thatcher mold) would be a highly unlikely choice as commander in chief.

But now Americans want a leader to address domestic concerns, build consensus and express a national vision. It is much easier to envision a caring, competent woman, especially one with vision and wit, as U.S. president.

In times of great change people are more open to new kinds of leadership, including women's leadership.

A Question of Role Models

Great leadership opportunity will abound for women. That is the admittedly optimistic subtext of *Megatrends for Women*. The question this book asks is, will women be ready to assume it?

Did Carol Moseley Braun or Patty Murray grow up thinking, "Someday I'm going to be a U.S. Senator!"

Neither did you.

Indeed, baby boom women had virtually no female role models—in politics, sports, commerce or any other public arenas. That lack of models is a real handicap in a world that is rapidly transforming itself and generating extraordinary new opportunities for women.

When you finish *Megatrends for Women*, you may still complain about not having known a lot of positive role models, but you will certainly have read about a lot of them.

Women's Leadership and the Global Megatrends

We have witnessed a period of deep-seated political, economic and technological change:

- At peace with the former Soviet Union, the United States must start tackling such issues as health care and the environment, areas in which women politicians have demonstrated expertise.
- The military is reinventing itself as a humanitarian force on call for natural disasters and relief efforts, thereby jeopardizing old-line macho definitions of leadership.
- Technology allows people to work as easily at home as in the most sophisticated office. Telecommuting, described in Chapter 8, is gaining increased acceptance. Women who want to work at careers at home during the child-rearing years have more options than ever before.
- U.S. and European firms have only begun to exploit new growth areas and will require more managers with language skills and cross-cultural sensitivity; that spells opportunity for women. Latin America, having stabilized politically in recent years, is surging economically. China now registers 10 percent growth a year and the next hothouse of economic growth will be Vietnam.

Meanwhile, old, male-dominated systems, born of the industrial age, "politics as usual" and the superpower conflict, no longer work.

People are seeking new formulas and with them a new style of leadership.

That spells opportunity for women, but only if they are willing to embrace the task of leadership. Most women in their prime career years are still operating under the set of goals they established as young women, goals that are probably too modest in light of today's opportunities. For many women it is time for a midlife, midcareer reassessment. The end result, in most cases, will be to create new, more ambitious goals.

This book will give you a lot of ideas about career and personal goals, but it was mainly designed to inspire you to seek and assume leadership in all areas of your life. We have gathered many of the breakthroughs and success stories together in one place to stimulate you to rethink your goals. It is our hope that *Megatrends for Women* inspires you to revise your goals upward and to answer the call of leadership.

Introduction

This is a book about powerful women transforming an imperfect world.

Megatrends for Women began with a simple question: what trends do women need to know about to be empowered now and in the future?

After sifting through mountains of information, we concluded that women need to know how *other women,* from every walk of life, are shaping social, political and economic trends, and that men, in order to function in today's world, need to know about it, too.

Teachers talk to teachers. The insurance people to other insurance people. The Baptists to Baptists. Leftists to leftists. You know what is going on in your company, church or political party. You rarely get the opportunity to see what is happening elsewhere.

When the subject is women, what is happening is awesome.

Women are transforming the world we live in.

By telling their stories, by describing the trends they are shaping, by showing how they are challenging the most sexist institutions from the medical establishment to organized religion, by offering example after example of women activists, entrepreneurs, politicians, CEOs and athletes, we will make the case that the time for women to embrace their power and set their creativity free has at long last arrived.

Whether you are female or male, the ways that women are changing the world will influence your education, career, marriage, recreation, next business venture, investments, election or advertising campaign.

If you are a woman, you need to know this is *not* the time to hold back; it is the time to go for it.

Megatrends for Men?

This book is addressed only to women—and to men who come in contact with them. So if you are not a husband, boyfriend or father, or if your work or business in no way involves women, then it is safe to say the megatrends women are involved in will not interest you very much. That probably represents about 2 percent of men.

As women and men re-sort out the issues that have divided them, and seek a deeper, more creative level of partnership, men will want and need to know about the trends shaping women's lives, about the new activities women engage in. "Believe me," said one man who read this book in manuscript, "I found it every bit as interesting as any woman would."

Fathers of girls and young women play critical roles in reinforcing their self-esteem, encouraging them to explore and take risks and supporting them in thinking through career and education options. By describing what some of the world's most active and powerful women are doing, this book will help a dad deliver state-of-the-art fatherly advice.

Suppose that after a string of male bosses, your new supervisor is a woman. The trend toward a Women's Leadership style is one you will want to know about to help decide what she expects of you and how to take advantage of possible career-growth opportunities under her watch.

Finally, as a businessman or professional, it is essential to keep up with your female market, population or clients. The business pages are filled with examples—from retailers in bankruptcy to athletic footwear makers whose $20 million ad campaign flopped—of businesses that ignored, underestimated or misunderstood the importance of a **changing women's market.** For venture capitalists, auto makers, pharmaceutical firms, food producers, advertisers, health-care, computer and electronics firms—to name just a few industries—**hundreds of billions of dollars** are at stake if you are ignorant or lazy enough to neglect women and the changes they are experiencing and precipitating.

The Quest for Women's Liberation

This book takes women's liberation as a point of departure and asks, What comes next?

That is not to say we think women's liberation has been achieved.

Those men who seek to dominate are not about to give up the abuse of power; sexual harassment, sexist institutions and the horrifying violence against women tell us the quest for women's rights will continue for some time.

Male-dominated institutions from the U.S. Senate to the hierarchy of the Roman Catholic Church will be dragged kicking and screaming into the 21st century. But alongside the dying past they symbolize, a host of new institutions are flourishing:

- The Arizona state legislature, 35.6 percent female;
- Six and a half million women-owned businesses that generate more jobs than the Fortune 500;
- India's Self-Employed Women's Association Bank, which makes loans to "questionable risks" and has a 96 percent repayment rate.

Women's liberation has not yet been achieved.

Nevertheless, women in various stages of freedom and autonomy have found the wherewithal within themselves to act, to succeed, to transform. They are doing so from politics to sports to health care. They are bishops and prime ministers, social activists and leaders of the environmental movement, athletes who sometimes triumph over men, anchorpersons, business leaders and professionals and 54 percent of the electorate.

Even though women are not yet fully liberated, they are transforming the different arenas described in this book by building a new reality, a new social order or paradigm that will eventually replace the old order based on the domination of the male sex, its values and power.

Two contradictory realities live together side by side. Some feminists look at the old and say, "See, nothing is changing." In our opinion, that is about the past. This book documents what we see looking at the new paradigm, and it is, we believe, about the future.

Critical Mass

The idea of "critical mass" is very important to this book.

"The notion of 'critical mass' originated in physics, which defined it as the [minimum] amount of radioactive material necessary to produce a nuclear reaction," writes Everett M. Rogers, professor of communication at the Annenberg School for Communication, University of Southern California, Los Angeles, in *The Information Systems Research Challenge: Survey Research Methods,* published by Harvard Business School.

The other key point is, once critical mass is reached, the process becomes self-sustaining.

The size of the reaction and when it happens depend on the *concentration and purity* of the material used and the geometry of the surrounding reaction system.

In other words, it's not just how much new matter is introduced—it is the quality of the input and the environment around it.

"Illustrations of 'critical mass'—situations in which a process becomes self-sustaining after some threshold point has been reached—abound in everyday life," Rogers continues. "It shows up in epidemiology, fashion, survival and extinction of the species, language systems, racial integration, jaywalking, panic behavior and *political movements*" (emphasis added).

Sociologists are also instructed by the idea of critical mass: how many people (what is the critical mass?) are necessary to adopt a new practice, product or belief system before it becomes a chain reaction that in time persuades most people to adopt the practice or product?

What was the critical mass for telephone answering machines? Was it 20 percent? Forty percent?

What was the critical mass for fax machines? What we do know is that it was much less than 50 percent.

In the context of this book, what is the critical mass needed

for women's liberation to become an unstoppable, accepted phenomenon?

Social change happens when critical mass occurs.

One metaphor for critical mass is an avalanche. Tiny snow crys-
tals move, and it looks like nothing at all is happening. Millions
become billions, and then there is a *turning point* and boom! A loud
explosion.

Critical mass is like a landslide; it is when a trend becomes a
megatrend; it is the point when one accepted social paradigm no
longer makes sense and is replaced by another.

It is an idea whose time has come.

What was the critical mass of women in the workplace before
"family issues" began to be taken seriously? We will raise questions
like that throughout this book.

In his landmark book *The Diffusion of Innovations* (The Free
Press), Everett Rogers demonstrated that when 13 percent of a population accept a new idea it is only a matter of time before at least 84
percent accept the idea, with time as the unknown. Rogers says that
in the sociological context the threshold for critical mass ranges *between 5 and 20 percent.*

"Once the 'critical mass' is achieved the rate of adoption of an
innovation becomes self-sustaining," says Rogers.

**We believe the critical mass of support among both women
and men to achieve all the objectives of the women's movement
is already in place.**

Critical mass alone is not enough, however. The next challenge
is to energize that critical mass and transform it into action. That
process, already initiated by millions of women, is what this book
describes.

Critical Mass for Democracy

The first modern democracy was set up in the United States in
1776. It has been a slow and tumultuous journey of more than 200
years, but most of the countries of the world will become democracies
by the year 2000. Once critical mass was achieved in the 1970's, the
number of democracies doubled in a single decade.

In 1900 there were only 13 democracies. By 1919, there were 25. The movement toward democracy continued in fits and starts: just after World War II, the count was back to 13. By the 1970's the figure had slowly climbed to 30 or so countries.

Looking back, in the 1970's critical mass appears to have been attained: the number of democratic countries in the world *doubled* in the decade of the 1980's to more than 60. In 1990 for the first time in history, more than 50 percent of the world's people lived in democracies. In the 1990's the fragile democracy in the former Soviet Union can be added. At the end of the decade, once the old men in China pass away, the stage will be set for China to join the ranks of democratic countries—at that point 90 percent of the world's people will live in a democracy.

A Question of Time

When it comes to critical mass, the question is always time. But the women in this book are not willing to wait. They have moved on; they are transforming society *now* because somehow, even though this remains an imperfect world, they have found the strength to act today to change the world or a small part of it.

One way to grossly misunderstand what we are saying here is to conclude, "Aburdene and Naisbitt say the critical mass has been achieved, so there is no further need for the women's movement, for activism, for working to demand equal rights for women. We can all sit back and wait for the avalanche."

No.

Critical mass is a very simple but tricky phenomenon. You can try to predict when it will happen—but you can never be sure until it does. Even though the critical mass is there, no one knows how much time it will take to become fully manifest. One thing is certain: the harder we work, the sooner the change occurs.

Sometimes a critical mass is in place, but it needs a spark to set it off. In the South in the '60's the critical mass of people necessary to create the civil rights movement was already there, but it took Rosa Parks's refusal to go to the back of the bus to ignite it. Indeed, it was not even known that a critical mass was present until the spark set it on fire. The civil rights movement had begun—but it certainly did not mark the end of racism.

The Senate hearings for the confirmation of Clarence Thomas was a similar situation. The all-male lineup of senators presuming to judge conduct that involved women will forever be an icon of the oppressiveness of male domination in government. It was burned into many women's brains and made women more angry than any event in recent memory. Then and there women decided to do something about it. Read about what they did in Chapter 1.

Critical Mass II

When it comes to the women's movement, critical mass cannot be measured simply in terms of opinions and behaviors. Say 40 percent of people believe in women's rights, so what? What are they *doing* about it? That is what this book describes. Not only does a critical mass of men and women embrace women's liberation—that has probably been the case for a decade or more—but a second critical mass of women and like-minded men is acting on that belief to shape society and the institutions within it.

Countervailing Forces

The achievement of critical mass for social change, of course, does not happen in a vacuum. In society, there are usually countervailing forces working against it and slowing down its achievement.

"I hate talking to answering machines." Most of us felt this way, but we got over it.

"How the hell do you pronounce 'Ms.'?" Sort of like "miss," with a *z*.

This is the small stuff.

When it comes to real social change, the countervailing forces are a lot more powerful. Incumbency. The Supreme Court. A justice system that is still steeped in a legal tradition of male dominance. The male-dominated leadership of the Fortune 500.

These are the kind of countervailing forces women bump up against in attempting to achieve true equality. In sum, the old power structure that does not particularly want to give way. But eventually, once critical mass is achieved, it does give way. Nothing stands in the way of an idea whose time has come.

Admittedly, we are optimists. But we believe that countervailing forces like these are on the verge of becoming *overrun* with an avalanche of support from both women and men to at long last create a new reality where women and men share power and equality—or at the very least to begin to build it.

Women and Their Power

This book asks: what have women *done* with the freedom and power they possess?

The answer is: a lot. Women are changing every sphere of life. This book addresses those changes chapter by chapter.

After the Clarence Thomas hearings, women, in their anger over sexual harassment, the abortion issue and the cruel insensitivity of their elected officials, were awakened to their political and financial power. Millions and millions of dollars poured into the coffers of women's PACs and campaign funds. In March 1992 came the first **stunning show of political power:** against all the odds, Carol Moseley Braun upset incumbent senator Alan Dixon of Illinois, one of the 11 Democrats to join Republicans to vote for Thomas's confirmation. Next came Democrat Lynn Yeakel's nomination and campaign to defeat GOP Senator Arlen Specter of Pennsylvania. It is only the beginning of a landslide that will see the **first woman president.**

In what has been considered the male arena of **sports,** women dominate most sports and fitness activities. Sports researchers predict women will beat men's times in the 26-mile marathon event by 1998. The 1992 Winter Olympics was the metaphor: U.S. women brought home **all 5 gold medals**—in total, 9 of 11 medals won by Americans.

What are the ten most promising careers and industries for women? Our candidates are listed. The next step for women in business is leadership. Over time women have evolved a successful leadership style that rejects the military model in favor of supporting and empowering people. Male management guru Peter Drucker endorses it—because **it works better** than the old ways. Meanwhile more than 5 million women-owned businesses, the Fortune 500 firms of the 21st century, generate more jobs than the big corporations on that overesteemed list.

Just as women achieve new heights in business and politics, modern women are fascinated with the mythology of the **"Goddess Reawakening."** Meanwhile feminist theologians reject the notion that divinity is somehow male and are reinterpreting Scripture to reclaim women's spiritual heritage.

As 40 to 50 million baby-boom women march toward menopause—and increased **health** risks—women activists are leading a movement to increase funding for breast-cancer research and expose the risk of heart disease, which kills more women than all cancers combined. Women who have not marched since Vietnam are hitting the pavement, banners in hand.

A new archetype has emerged in the work world: **collaborative couples**—wives and husbands who merge their talents in design and finance, administration and construction to create new family businesses. Their hard work brings the rewards of greater work satisfaction, autonomy, flexibility and multimillion-dollar assets.

In **fashion,** long thought of as a women's area, male designers dictated women's taste top-down for decades, but today the fastest-growing, most successful firms are Liz Claiborne and Donna Karan. A critical mass of working women is compelling the fashion/retail industry to reinvent itself to respond to their needs.

After decades of disruption and divorce, a new era is dawning for the **family.** Studies, surveys and polls all show its members, tired of overwork, want to spend time together. The question is how to make a living, too. That is what families, corporations and government will grapple with as a critical mass of women in the workplace has compelled companies to realize their employees are attached to husbands, wives and children.

As **activists,** environmentalists and new-wave volunteers, women are addressing today's social issues with a fury. It is through women in Third World villages and on inner-city streets that society will confront and solve its most intractable problems. Women have determined that the violence against them must stop and that the perpetrators, with the support of good men everywhere, will be exposed and prevented from harming again.

U.S. women are the first to admire how women the world over are emerging as political leaders. It gives new meaning to the term **New World Order.** Not only is Norway run by a woman, women lead all three Norwegian political parties. In northern Europe, women are setting the pace as presidents and prime ministers. Women are making stunning advances in developing countries from Panama, where the feisty mayor of Panama City hosts a two-hour daily talk radio show, to Myanmar (formerly Burma), where the jailed opposition leader, Daw Aung San Suu Kyi, is a woman and recently won the Nobel Peace Prize. The New World Order is happening around the globe.

What Comes Next for Women?

Our vision is a positive one.

What women have accomplished is by any standard extraordinary. There is just no way one can look at it and say, "This is all superficial. Deep down women are as oppressed as ever, even more so. The male power structures remain intact—it's just business as usual. **And it's never going to change.**"

That is simply not true.

In this imperfect world, where sexism, violence, sexual abuse and harassment are, tragically, still with us, powerful women are planting their feet and effecting change. This book documents their actions, chapter by chapter, in every sphere of life.

The remnants of male domination—from religious fundamentalism to the U.S. Supreme Court—may well be trying to set women back 200 years or 2,000. They will enjoy small, ill-gotten victories, but they will never succeed for long.

And the reason is critical mass—what it takes to get a movement going and self-sustaining. There are simply too many powerful women with too many male allies (younger men, yes, but older, too).

The balance has finally tipped in women's favor.

Alongside the decadent abuse of male power another reality grows stronger every day. Millions of women the world over are taking economic and political power, building new institutions, infusing them with new, more humanistic values, saving the world or a part of it.

Which Megatrend Is This?

This book is not about women "taking over" and imposing their own brand of oppression on men and other women, *not* a Patriarchy to Matriarchy megatrend. It is about partnership.

Riane Eisler, the author of *The Chalice and the Blade* (Harper & Row; see Chapter 9), describes two basic types of societies—dominator or partnership: "The dominator model is based on ranking, backed by fear or force. It starts at the core of society—the male half of humanity dominating the female."

If women (or any other wronged party) "seize power," you can still have the same old domination mode. Look at the "Reign of

Terror" in 18th-century France or Mao's Cultural Revolution in China. But there is another alternative.

"The partnership model is a way to structure human relationships based on *linking,* rather than force or fear," says Eisler.

"It is not about women taking over, but women and men together expressing their full potential—neither superior or inferior," Eisler says.

Now *that* is revolutionary.

"If we are ever to have a truly pluralistic society, where people's differences are freely expressed, celebrated—and utilized for everyone's benefit, it must begin with a partnership between women and men," she argues.

One early reader objected to our frequent use of the word "power" or "powerful" to describe women, because she associates the word with force (that certainly has echoes of Eisler's dominator model). "You mean spirit, or inner strength," she told us. "Not power."

But the *Random House Webster's College Dictionary*'s first definition of power is the "ability to do or act; capability of doing or accomplishing something." That is the sense in which we use the word, and it certainly describes the women in this book. Spirit and inner strength are frequently the source of their power.

An Attempt at Synthesis

In an age of analysis and specialization, we aspire to "bring it all together," to create an overview, a synthesis. But we know it is impossible to succeed completely. The subject of virtually every *subhead* within a chapter of *Megatrends for Women* could be a book; some could fill many bookshelves. We have not covered everything. There will be issues you will wish we had discussed—or said more about—and wonderful people we failed to acknowledge. This is a difficult part of being generalists that we have come to live with; we hope our readers can accept it, too.

Turning the Corner

For millennia, women have lived in repression and under male domination. Women have been tortured and raped and treated like cattle. After cycles when women's lives improved, there was even worse repression. But in the 20th century, the right combination of factors was finally present: critical mass clicked in.

Metaphorically, the Goddess has awakened. There may be hard days, but there is no going back. Women have never come this far before. The spark of women's power, beauty and creativity, long buried or forgotten, has never been reborn on such a mass level.

It is difficult to accept that reality, to really believe it. We shall be attacked for even suggesting it.

We are so used to thinking of women being minimized, of women fighting for liberation, that we are incapable of the next step: envisioning what the world will look like when women create institutions, collaborate as equal partners with men, when women change the male-dominated structures they can no longer live in. And then build a new world.

Yet we must begin.

Because women's liberation is not the end. Not by any means. It is the beginning of a lot of work. There is a whole world out there that needs to be totally transformed so that women and men can create, desire, build and play.

What comes next?

We hope this book begins to answer that question.

Megatrends for Women

1.
Women in Politics: The Road to the U.S. Presidency

Cynics still scoff at the "Year of the Woman" and, in a way, they are right: 1992 was a lot more than a media label; it launched a political power drive that will not let up until one third to one half of all representatives, senators and governors are women.

As far as 1992 goes, the political facts speak for themselves:

- Seven women now serve in the U.S. Senate and almost 50 women in the U.S. House.
- Money raised for women candidates broke all records and surpassed the most optimistic expectations.
- Unprecedented numbers of women now fill state legislatures and hold statewide elective office.

Said Harriett Woods, president of the National Women's Political Caucus: "I don't know what we're going to do for an encore."

Women elected Bill Clinton president by an eight-point margin over George Bush, according to the polling consortium Voter Research and Surveys. That set the stage for immediate executive action on family leave law and abortion rights.

President Clinton, by and large, won good marks for four female cabinet appointments:

- Donna Shalala, Department of Health and Human Services;
- Hazel O'Leary, Department of Energy;

• Carol Browner, Environmental Protection Agency (a position Clinton elevated to cabinet status); and
• Janet Reno, the first woman to head the Justice Department.

Several more women hold highly visible posts: Laura Tyson, chair of the Council of Economic Advisors; Alice Rivlin, deputy budget director; Dee Dee Myers, the youngest presidential press secretary; and Madeleine Kunin, deputy secretary of education.

But what will undoubtedly influence Clinton administration policy most is First Lady Hillary Clinton's "appointment" to the post of ex-officio presidential counselor. While some debate whether it is appropriate for the president's wife to hold what is tantamount to a cabinet post, America's working women, for the first time in U.S. history, have a First Lady who knows the pleasures and stresses of juggling home and career, marriage and professional standing. Equally important, the Clintons are a collaborative couple (see Chapter 6), who listen, talk things over, bounce ideas off each other and relate to each other intensely.

The positive role model of Hillary Clinton—energetic, intelligent, versatile, engaged—wins the hearts, minds and understanding empathy of working women the world over.

These recent developments follow two decades of grass-roots politicking from the school board to the statehouse. U.S. women today are winning the offices that will catapult them into top leadership. With the backing of female voters—now the majority of the American electorate—as well as men seeking new leadership, a new generation of women, today about 40 years of age, will assume top political posts over the next two decades. By 2008 U.S. women will hold at least 35 percent of governorships. A woman will be electable, or already elected, as U.S. president.

An impossibly rosy scenario? The authors can already hear feminists and chauvinists alike groaning under the very upbeatness of it all.

By any objective measure, women appear far from political equality. Before the 1992 election, women governed three U.S. states, two women served as U.S. senators, and a paltry 6.4 percent of the U.S. House of Representatives was female. The barren simplicity of those numbers represents a compelling argument *against* our optimistic thesis.

But those facts obscured a dynamic set of trends that had been quietly building for decades and that were set on fire by the 1991 confirmation hearings on the Supreme Court nomination of Clarence Thomas.

The avalanche of women's political power would have happened eventually. But Justice Thomas and the Senate Judiciary Committee became the dynamite, the catalyst that intensified the explosion and set it off in 1992.

They did not, however, cause it. An outside agent, even a powerful one, usually cannot provoke change unless the proper set of circumstances is already present. The 1992 political landscape owed itself to women's established political power base at the state and local levels and to voters, both male and female, who were tired of "politics as usual"—for the most part, "good ole boy" politics—and were ready for change.

That readiness was amply demonstrated in a *U.S. News & World Report* **poll published in April 1992. A stunning 61 percent of those surveyed thought "the country would be governed better" if more women held political office. In 1984 only 28 percent held that view.**

This chapter will analyze 10 powerful trends, which, taken together, make the case that women are on the verge of attaining *critical mass*—the turning point when women, and supportive male colleagues, have the power and numbers to bring their agenda to the forefront and start a self-sustaining megatrend that elects *more women to higher offices.*

Why Women Will Lead

The 10 trends described below prepared the groundwork for the surprising upsurge in women's political power in 1992 and for the decade ahead:

1. Year by year a *critical mass* of women has built a viable power base in state legislatures, as mayors and in statewide elective office.
2. A *record number* of women ran for office in 1992—and about one half won.
3. *New routes to power* that bypass the incumbent-ridden U.S. Congress are increasingly being discovered by women. As big-city mayors, state treasurers and secretaries of state,

women can mount successful races for the Senate and governorships.

4. *Term Limits.* Redistricting and retirements helped women
break the iron lock on congressional incumbency in 1992.
But in the longer run, the growing demand for term limits
will open hundreds of seats to women candidates.

5. *Money.* No longer can it buy a race. Today's voter is too
sophisticated to fall for a candidate whose main credential is
money. Paradoxically, women are becoming superb fund-
raisers; qualified women will not lack financial backing.

6. *Clarence Thomas.* The Thomas affair radicalized American
women. They ran for office and made political contributions
in record-breaking numbers in 1992—and will do so again in
1994.

7. *The Domestic Agenda.* Education, abortion, the environment, day care—what once were called "women's issues"
concern everyone now. This is where women have experience, confidence, strong feelings and clear positions.

8. *Women* now dominate the electorate—and consistently support their own. Men give women candidates high marks for
honesty and, with anti-incumbent sentiment running high,
are willing to give women a chance.

9. In the *Persian Gulf,* American women put their lives on the
line—even a diehard male chauvinist has to respect that.
Their sacrifice reinforces women's political legitimacy.

10. *Texas and California.* Women are making the greatest political headway in the largest, most powerful states, which also
historically produce presidents.

The media declared 1992 "the year of women in politics."
Women have won inspiring victories, but what happens when some
lose key races? For the most part, this chapter describes the long-term
change on which the politics of the future will be built.

**Long after women have profited from the House check-cash-
ing scandal, the anti-incumbency mood and the Thomas backlash, the underlying megatrends that will bring the first woman
U.S. president will still remain valid.**

1. Women's Grass-Roots Power Base Is Established

Power Base: State Legislatures

In the 1970's a new generation of women in their twenties looked at politics and saw a thoroughly male-dominated system. "Things ought to be different," they told themselves. "Women should hold half of those offices."

What is and what should be are two different things, they learned. Many did enter politics. But for the next two decades, most paid their political dues at the local level—on the school board or city council. Eventually they made it to the state legislature. Stars like Pat Schroeder, Nancy Kassebaum and Geraldine Ferraro won high elective office, but they were the exceptions. Most women in politics developed their power base by building critical mass in the statehouse.

Year after year, steady as clockwork, women increase their percentage in state legislatures. In 1993, 20.4 percent of U.S. *state legislators* were women. They hold 336 state senate and 1,180 house seats. The number of women in state legislatures has increased 500 percent since 1969, when women held only 4 percent of seats.

Washington State has the highest percentage of women legislators, with 39.5 percent. Arizona has 35.6 percent, Colorado 34 percent, Vermont 33.9 percent and New Hampshire 33.5 percent. Women reach a critical mass at around 20 percent. Then they are capable of building the coalitions that reinforce their power. Women hold 25 percent or more of legislative seats in 13 states: the five cited above, plus Connecticut, Idaho, Kansas, Maine, Minnesota, Nevada, Oregon and Wisconsin.

The five states with the lowest percentage (between 4.3 and 9.6 percent) of women legislators are Alabama, Arkansas, Kentucky, Louisiana and Oklahoma.

The Louisiana state legislature, which used to have the lowest percentage of women—2.1 percent—passed a restrictive antiabortion law in 1990 (subsequently vetoed by Governor Buddy Roemer, then overridden by the legislature, and finally struck down in the courts). State Treasurer Mary Landrieu, who was reelected without opposition and will hold office through 1995, predicted the process would serve as a wake-up call to Louisiana women. It did.

During 1991 six more women won seats in the Louisiana house, bringing the total number of women there to nine, triple the number in January 1991. Antiabortion incumbents lost five seats to women and several more to pro-choice men. Says campaign manager Harriet Trudell, "One of the sweetest victories was the trouncing of Representative Carl Gunter," who once said of incest victims, "That's how we get thoroughbred racehorses."

Louisiana pro-choice Democrat Melinda Schwegmann defeated incumbent Paul Hardy to become the state's first woman lieutenant governor.

America's Future

They may be unknown outside their districts, but America's state legislatures are full of future top leaders. Four women hold or recently held the top leadership positions in state senates: Ellen Craswell (R-Wa.); Bonnie Heinrich (D-N.D.); Jean Lloyd-Jones (D-Ia.), who lost the Iowa U.S. Senate race to incumbent Charles E. Grassley; and Gwen Margolis (D-Fla.). Two women serve as house speakers: Jane Hull (R-Ariz.) and Dee Long of Minnesota, a member of the Democratic Farmer-Labor party.

Democratic assemblywoman Jackie Speier was the first California lawmaker to be pregnant in office, bring her baby to work and set up a crib in the members' lounge. Elected in 1986, without her party's support, she became majority whip after just one year in office. Speier, who was reelected in 1992, is among the best and brightest on women's issues, says Kate Sproul, legislative advocate for the National Organization for Women's California chapter.

Nancy K. Kopp, five-term Democratic member of the Maryland house—and the state's first legislator to give birth in office—may become its first woman speaker. With the support of present speaker R. Clayton Mitchell, Jr., Representative Kopp became speaker pro tem in 1991. Kopp, a budget expert on education issues, is seen as a natural successor to Mitchell. "I have felt a special responsibility to address the problems of women and their families because of the opportunities I have been given," she says.

Power Base: Big-City Mayor

The job of big-city mayor is an ideal position for building a power base. The job requires administrative skill and generates the high visibility needed to run for higher office. Dianne Feinstein, former mayor of San Francisco, ran for governor in 1990—and narrowly lost, but won a Senate seat in 1992. Successful mayors can earn both respect and a track record for tackling intractable problems, from crime and drugs to housing and budget deficits.

Today there are women mayors in San Diego, San Jose and Washington, D.C., three of the 20 largest cities in the United States. In 1991 women held an even greater percentage of mayorships in the largest U.S. cities. Four of the 10 largest U.S. cities—Houston, San Diego, Dallas and San Antonio—were run by women.

In 1993:

• There are 176 women mayors in 974 cities with populations over 30,000.
• 19 of the 100 largest U.S. cities have women mayors.
• Women mayors govern 41 of the 202 U.S. cities with populations over 100,000.
• Two of California's three largest cities have women mayors.

Deedee Corradini, a Lebanese-born Presbyterian Democrat, became the first woman mayor of Mormon-dominated Salt Lake City. Corradini, who had not previously held office, won 55 percent of the vote. Businesspeople knew her as chair of the Utah Symphony. Corradini is an innovator: when state Republicans held their convention, she set up a booth to attract support. "The women of Salt Lake City feel a foot taller today," said Republican Bonnie Miller, who crossed party lines to vote for Corradini.

Washington, D.C.'s Sharon Pratt Kelly, 48, became the first black woman to lead a major U.S. city. Squeaky clean and the antithesis of her predecessor, former mayor Marion Barry, she won 87 percent of the vote on a pledge to "clean house with a shovel." Barry, who was videotaped smoking crack cocaine and eventually dropped out of the race, had bragged that Kelly would be the easiest candidate to beat. "It seemed obvious to me everybody wanted a change," she says.

A graduate of Howard Law School, Kelly was vice president of the local power company before running for mayor. A divorced mother of two, she remarried in 1991. Kelly faces a $300 million deficit, the nation's worst murder rate and poor morale since the Barry trial in 1990. Kelly, who is a volunteer Big Sister to a 16-year-old girl, convinced Congress to extend $100 million to keep the city solvent. Kelly sees public-private partnerships as key to turning the city around.

Not Just the Mayor: The Local Power Coalition

Houston, the largest city in Texas and the good ole boy capital of the universe, was a bastion of female power while Kathy Whitmire was mayor from 1981 through 1991. Said Whitmire, "If electing women runs counter to the macho image of Houston and the rest of the state, I'd say that image must be dead by now."

During her tenure Houston, the fourth-largest city in the United States, had women in the offices of police chief, district chief of county hospitals, superintendent of schools, president of the chamber of commerce and president of the University of Houston.

Houston is not the only concentration of female political power. In the great bellwether state of Colorado, three of the five statewide elected officials—treasurer, attorney general and secretary of state—are women. Eight of Denver's 13 city council chairs are held by women.

In Washington State women make up 40 percent of the legislature. Three of the state's nine members of the U.S. House of Representatives and four of its nine elected executive officers are women.

"You can't make a difference; you're just a mom in tennis shoes," a Washington State legislator told U.S. Senator Patty Murray (D-Wash.) back in 1979 when she campaigned to save a preschool program about to lose funding. Murray went on to serve four years in the state senate and two years in her party's statehouse leadership before her 1992 election to the Senate.

The New Girl Network

Former San Diego Mayor Maureen O'Connor, who was one of four women on the nine-member city council, says some of the mayor's most important support is from the private sector. She worked closely with Helen Copley, the area's foremost publisher, and with philanthropist Joan Kroc, a major stockholder in McDonald's. When something had to happen, this gang of three would swing into action.

In 1988 Mrs. Kroc wanted to donate $18 million to start a hospice for AIDS and other terminally ill patients. She talked to O'Connor, who asked then state assemblywoman Lucy Killea to sponsor the legislation. Incredibly, Governor Deukmejian vetoed the bill, until a letter from publisher Copley helped change his mind. He then reversed the veto.

In 1989 O'Connor, Copley and Kroc worked together to bring the Soviet Arts Festival to San Diego—earning the city $7 million.

"Every day I get up and thank God that we have Mrs. Kroc and Mrs. Copley in San Diego," said O'Connor. "They go not just the extra mile, but the extra hundred miles. What they do for this community—and they don't have to—goes beyond any mayor's wildest expectations of private-public partnership."

The new San Diego mayor, Susan Golding, was elected in 1992.

2. The More, the Better

The more women run, the more women win. That was already clear in 1990, when eight women ran for governor, compared with zero in 1980. In 1992 a record 2,376 women ran for state legislative seats, up 15 percent from 1990.

In 1990 a record 85 women won major party nominations for statewide office:

- 16 women ran for lieutenant governor.
- 17 women ran for secretary of state.
- 14 women ran for state treasurer.

Fewer of these offices were up for grabs in 1992, but between 1990 and 1992, women consolidated their gains and now hold about 20 percent of statewide elective offices.

"Most of them run for high office after working their way up the political ladder," says Ruth Mandel, director of the Center for the American Woman and Politics at New Jersey's Rutgers University, which extensively tracks numbers of women in state, local and national politics.

About 2,000 black women held office in 1990. Since 1970 the number of blacks elected to office has increased 400 percent, *but the number of black women has grown 1,400 percent.*

Once women run, they have a very respectable success rate. More than half—47 of the 85 who ran for statewide office in 1990—won.

Even before the great wave of women's political activity in 1992, the ground was being prepared.

In 1990 five of the six females elected to the post of lieutenant governor ran against other women; women were elected chief education official in eight states.

Iowa had the largest number of women—six—running for state-wide elective office in 1990. Iowa was the first to require that half of all state boards and commissions must be women. Appointments like those play a critical role in women's quest for power: they are often the stepping-stone to elected office.

"Women not only won key victories in 1990, from Connecticut to Missouri to Oregon, but the election was significant in positioning so many women to run for even higher office in the future," says Harriett Woods, president of the National Women's Political Caucus (NWPC).

All of that *before* the 1991 Clarence Thomas affair energized women to run for office, get more involved in politics and raise record campaign chests.

"My phones are ringing off the hook from women and men who are determined to elect more women in 1992," said Ellen Malcolm, head of EMILY's List (EMILY stands for Early Money Is Like Yeast). "The Judiciary hearings made visible the need to have more women in the Senate."

Immediately after the Thomas hearings, Ellen Malcolm had already spoken to 50 women interested in running for office in 1992.

In 1992 a record 11 women were nominated for the U.S. Senate; 5 won. A record 108 women won nominations for the U.S. House; 48 won, including 24 incumbents, 22 who ran for open seats and 2 challengers.

Redistricting gave Dallas its first African-American congressional district, won by Texas state senator Eddie Bernice Johnson, who is black. Lucille Roybal-Allard won a new minority district in central Los Angeles.

Just weeks after the Thomas hearings, Jane Danowitz, executive director of the bipartisan Women's Campaign Fund, predicted 10 new women could be sent to the U.S. Congress. At the time Washington insiders probably dismissed that estimate as overly optimistic, but 24 women actually won new House seats.

As noted, women won nearly half the political offices they ran for in 1990. In 1992 women won 44.5 percent of the U.S. House and Senate seats they ran for—a very respectable percentage, but consider the following: women won 54 percent of statewide elected offices and 57 percent of state legislative seats. All told, women's winning rate was better than half—55 percent.

3. New Routes to Power

In 1916, when some states did not allow women to vote, Jeannette Rankin, a Montana Republican, became the first woman in the U.S. Congress. More than seventy-five years later, it is clear that American women have *not* followed in her footsteps: in 1993 women held 47 or 10.8 percent, of the 435 seats in the U.S. House of Representatives. In addition, Eleanor Holmes Norton serves as the delegate from Washington, D.C. After the 1992 election, there were 35 Democrats and 12 Republicans. "It's one of the last locker rooms," says Margaret Roukema (R-N.J.).

But it will probably not be through Congress that women reach the Senate, governorships or the presidency.

Women have uncovered new routes to political power. The office of big-city mayor has already been discussed. Because it guarantees statewide name recognition, it may be a key step on the way to the U.S. Senate. A statewide elective office, such as state treasurer, can be a stepping-stone to the governorship.

Statewide Elective Executive Offices

In 1993, 72 women held statewide elective executive offices across the country—22.2 percent of the 334 available positions.

Three women, all Democrats, serve as governors in 1993: Joan Finney of Kansas, Barbara Roberts of Oregon and Ann Richards of Texas. But it may surprise you to learn how many women already hold important statewide elected offices that function as launch pads for higher office—especially governorships.

- *Eleven* women are lieutenant governors, in Connecticut, Delaware, Iowa, Louisiana, Michigan, Minnesota, Nebraska, Nevada, North Dakota, Utah and Vermont.
- *Nine* women are attorney generals, in Colorado, Indiana, Iowa, Nevada, North Dakota, Oklahoma, Utah, Virginia and Washington.
- In *16* states women serve as state treasurer: Arkansas, California, Colorado, Delaware, Idaho, Indiana, Kansas, Louisiana, Nebraska, North Dakota, Ohio, Oklahoma, Pennsylvania, Rhode Island, Texas and Wisconsin.

• *Eleven* states have women secretaries of state: California, Colorado, Connecticut, Iowa, Minnesota, Montana, Nevada, New Mexico, Rhode Island, South Dakota and Wyoming.

"We have been gradually building a base in city councils and county commissions and state legislatures, and now we have an immense pool from which to draw candidates for higher office," says Ruth Mandel. Today that growing pool includes scores of women with extensive experience as attorney general, state treasurer, secretary of state and lieutenant governor, women who will become governors later this decade and into the 21st century.

Incumbency

The problem with getting to Congress has always been incumbency. Officeholders seek reelection—and they win. Until quite recently, it has not been a promising picture for would-be legislators.

"Women basically still are playing a game of catch-up against the odds. It's tough for men or women to run as challengers. . . . The success rate of incumbents is over 90 percent, but women usually have little choice," says NWPC's Harriett Woods. In 1992, 39 women ran for open House seats, that is, new seats as a result of redistricting or seats where the incumbent did not run; 22 of them won.

Of course, incumbency helps women, too. Of the 28 women incumbents in the U.S. Congress who ran for reelection in 1992 (one successfully ran for a Senate seat), 24 won. Incumbency provides name recognition, a track record and an existing political network ready for fund-raising.

That leaves newcomers—including women—scanning the obituaries or studying the gossip column or the front page for members who have disgraced themselves enough to give the voters pause. Congress*men* have been known to oblige.

The next problem, of course, is money. Running for the U.S. Senate from a big state is a multimillion-dollar project. House seats require less funds, since you concentrate efforts within a smaller area.

"Women don't say, 'I think I want to be a U.S. senator, and I've got five million dollars and my daddy can provide the rest and I have lots of political friends,' " says Barbara Roberts, governor of Oregon. "They tend to come up through the ranks."

That, of course, is exactly what governors Roberts, Richards and

Finney did: built a track record of confronting and resolving state and local issues. Now that women are raising huge campaign chests (see point 6), all sorts of new approaches are possible.

The Bottom-Up Megatrend

In the long run, the political barriers to Washington may actually work in women's favor. At a time when state and local governments must learn to solve their problems without Washington, are people likely to elect a governor who has been sitting in hearings for two years or one who has rolled up her sleeves and walked among the people or battled it out in the statehouse?

As we said in *Megatrends,* Congress is an obsolete institution. (We did not win a lot of friends in Washington.) The action that really counts is at the state and local level—exactly where women have been for the last two decades.

Women have paid their dues and moved up through the ranks:

• The former school board president like Barbara Roberts who becomes secretary of state and then governor.
• The respected county commissioner like Ann Richards who is elected state treasurer and then governor.
• The high-profile mayor like Dianne Feinstein who stakes a claim to a Senate seat.

New Heroine in the House: State Treasurer

One of the most important stepping-stones is state treasurer. The person who balances the budget is a champion in people's eyes and has certainly earned one key credential for the governorship. As noted, women in 16 states are state treasurer.

When women build from the bottom up, a powerful local base of support is there when needed in the future. Political analysts point to the case of Texas governor Ann Richards, elected Travis County commissioner in 1976 and again in 1980. In 1982 she was elected treasurer of Texas and was reelected in 1986. "Over the years, she targeted women, and built a base of support that was rock solid," says Sharon Rodine, former president of the National Women's Political Caucus. "She didn't come to them a few months before election day, and say, 'I'm a woman, vote for me.' "

The offices of state treasurer, secretary of state and lieutenant governor are more viable routes to the governorship than serving in the U.S. Congress.

Joan Finney, governor of Kansas, was the first woman elected to the Kansas governorship, in November of 1990. In 1974 she was the first woman elected state treasurer and served five terms.

New Route: Secretary of State

The political career of Oregon governor Barbara Roberts began when her son was diagnosed as autistic. Oregon had no programs for children with special needs, and Roberts became a one-woman lobbying organization. She served on the Multnomah County Commission in 1978 and on the Parkrose School Board from 1973 to 1983.

"I basically took on all of the special interests of education and won," she recalls. She served on a series of boards, commissions and councils and wound up in the statehouse. Roberts was speaker for two terms and then won a statewide election for secretary of state, which became her springboard for the governorship.

First Woman Governor

Just 20 years ago, *no* woman had ever been elected governor of a U.S. state "in her own right." Three women—Nellie Ross (D-Wyo. 1925–27), Miriam "Ma" Ferguson (D-Tex. 1925–27 and 1933–35) and Lurleen Wallace (D-Ala. 1967–68)—were elected as surrogates for husbands who were deceased or could not run for reelection.

In 1974 Democrat Ella Grasso of Connecticut was the first woman elected governor in her own right in a landslide victory. She gave people toll-free access to her through the "Ella Phone" and was reelected in 1978. She championed a "sunshine" law that opened many functions of government to public scrutiny. A public figure for 28 years, she never lost an election. "Her name—simply 'Ella'—was a household word," says a Connecticut state document. She resigned from office on December 31, 1980, and passed away on February 5, 1981. Her legacy lives on in the new generation of women inspired by her example—grass-roots politics.

Eight states have elected women governors "in their own right."

Three of them serve now in Kansas, Oregon and Texas. In addition, Connecticut, Kentucky, Nebraska, Vermont and Washington have also elected women. A ninth woman, Governor Rose Mofford, who was secretary of state, assumed the governorship of Arizona from 1988 until 1991 after the impeachment and conviction of Evan Mecham.

More and more women are gaining state cabinet appointments. In 10 states a third or more of the cabinet are women. Republican governor William F. Weld of Massachusetts heads the list: 45.5 percent of his cabinet are women.

Power Base: Lieutenant Governor

There is nothing new about the lieutenant governorship as a springboard to higher office. It is a traditional training ground for the governor. What *is* new is the extent to which the office is coming to be associated with female candidates.

In 1990 an unprecedented number of male gubernatorial candidates chose women as running mates. Nineteen women ran for lieutenant governor.

In 1993, as noted, 11 women served as lieutenant governors. In the past women have served as lieutenant governors in Colorado, Hawaii, Kentucky, Massachusetts, Mississippi, Missouri, New York and South Carolina. Only 42 states have the office of lieutenant governor.

To date, 28 women have served as lieutenant governor in 19 states.

That means that in about 40 percent of all states, women have held the office generally considered an acceptable qualification for the governorship.

Democrat Madeleine Kunin became governor of Vermont, a predominantly Republican state. Kunin's route to power was from the statehouse to the lieutenant governorship, where she served two terms. In 1982 she was defeated in a bid for the governorship, but she was elected on her second try in 1984. In 1990 she decided not to seek a fourth term.

As governor, she doubled funding for public education; initiated a new public-school assessment program; revised vocational training; established kindergartens for all schools; created early education programs for three- and four-year-old low-income children; worked with the private sector to establish incentive grants for school restructuring.

After Governor Kunin committed herself to these "women's issues," Vermont was rated as the number-one state for children's services by the Children's Defense Fund and number one for environmental health. *Fortune* magazine called Kunin one of the top "education Governors."

"She'll be regarded fondly as the person who retired the deficit, as a person with a strong commitment to energy, environment, education," says Garrison Nelson, a political scientist at the University of Vermont.

Before joining the Clinton administration as deputy secretary of education, Kunin served as distinguished public policy visitor at Radcliffe College, working on ways to help women in politics and government in the future.

"You have to be resilient. . . . You have to not be easily discouraged," she advises women, who, she says, often underestimate their own abilities. She also tells women to "value your volunteer and community experience, because they demand the same skill as political organizing."

And what about the state office of attorney general? That's the job President Bill Clinton held before becoming governor of Arkansas. Virginia's attorney general Mary Sue Terry announced in 1993 her intention to run for governor, the first woman in her state to do so.

4. Redistricting, Retirements and Term Limits

Suppose you do not buy our notion that serving in Congress is not a critical entry on the résumé of the first woman president. Then the trend toward term limits, which would limit the time a congressperson (or other officeholder) can spend in office, will interest you. Limits provide "a window of opportunity for younger women," says former Washington representative Jean Marie Brough, a Republican.

Term limits are very controversial. Obviously, they can threaten women's hold on power, too. Term limits "would hurt the women of this country," says Ruth Mandel, director of the Center for the American Woman and Politics. "The few women's voices [in office] are the voices we need."

"This whole business of term limitations is wrong-headed," says Barbara Jordan, former congresswoman and special counsel on ethics to Texas governor Ann Richards. Jordan would prefer to see limits on how much you can contribute to a campaign.

We disagree. Americans are fed up with the congresspeople who make serving in Washington a career rather than a period of public service. But we also think that a two-year term is too short for Congress. What about changing the Constitution to give a congressperson two 3- or 4-year terms in Washington? Then it's on to other offices or back to the job she or he held before.

The grass-roots trend toward term limits is exploding in the 1990's. Colorado limits terms for Congress and statewide office. California and Oklahoma have term limits for state officeholders. In 1992 term limits were approved in 14 states. Since incumbency will remain at least somewhat of a barrier for women, term limits will be a boon to women who want to hold public office in general—and especially in Congress.

Redistricting

Redistricting in 1992 following the 1990 Census meant 19 new seats were up for grabs. The big winners were California (+ 7), Florida (+ 4) and Texas (+ 3). Arizona, Georgia, North Carolina, Virginia and Washington gained one each. In 1992 Florida women won three of those four new congressional seats.

Retirements

Twenty-five percent of the U.S. House retired, resigned or lost reelection in 1992. Unknown to most of the public, 167 congresspeople were eligible to retire and keep their PAC funds in 1992. By June 1992, 45 U.S. House members and seven senators had announced their intention to retire.

Democratic pollster Celinda Lake, 38, is a behind-the-scenes power broker who works only with pro-choice clients. She worked for two major women candidates seeking U.S. Senate seats: Geraldine Ferraro and Barbara Boxer.

Lake's polls and others showed a rise in anti-incumbency sentiment after the Thomas hearings. **As a result of newly created seats** and reapportionment, some observers accurately predicted that as many as 100 seats would be newly available to candidates. Added to that was the possibility of many retirements and the "throw the rascal out" mood of the country. In retrospect, it is easy to see how Lake could have predicted that women would make "historic gains" in 1992.

5. Money

Ask anyone who has run for public office: the big problem is almost always raising enough money to mount an effective campaign. Obviously, money remains a formidable factor in politics. But money alone can no longer be blamed as *the* factor blocking women from office, for two simple, but seemingly contradictory, reasons: 1) women are becoming dynamic political fund-raisers, and 2) voters are getting smarter about the role of money in campaigns.

Frank O'Brien, a direct-mail specialist, says female candidates today fare *better* than male counterparts at raising money through the mail. Women, he says, are protected against disillusionment with politics because they are "perceived by donors as a special breed."

Even before the Clarence Thomas nomination revolutionized political fund-raising among women (see point 6), there were already signs that younger women were ready to be big players on the political scene. Commissioned by Democratic fund-raiser Roger Craver, president of the direct-mail firm Craver, Matthews, Smith, pollster Peter Hart has identified women under 45 as the "most active and most generous donors to 'progressive' organizations."

The evidence is mounting that money cannot automatically "buy" a contest: women are winning even when they have had less money to make their case.

- Ann Richards spent $12 million in her winning campaign against Clayton Williams—who spent $22 million.
- Barbara Roberts raised about $2 million and won the Oregon governor's race against Dave Frohnmayer, who raised $3.5 million.
- Kansas governor Joan Finney raised less than $500,000 for her successful race against Mike Hayden—who raised nearly $2.5 million.

• Gloria Molina, daughter of an immigrant Mexican farm worker, was the first female and first Hispanic elected to the Los Angeles board of supervisors. She defeated her former boss, state senator Art Torres, in the race and was outspent *two to one.*

• Washington senator Patty Murray raised only 57 percent of what her opponent, Congressman Rod Chandler, had managed, yet she won by 10 percentage points.

Other women lose nobly, with a lot more votes than pundits predicted.

• New Jersey Republican candidate Christine Todd Whitman nearly beat popular incumbent senator Bill Bradley (D-N.J.), who *outspent her 12 to 1.*

• Lynn Yeakel raised less than half of what Pennsylvania senator Arlen Specter had accrued over a six-year period, yet she lost by only two points (51 to 49 percent).

Grossly outspending one's opponent clearly can backfire.

Women candidates used to complain they received smaller campaign contributions than men. But women have become far more sophisticated about how to raise money. There are 35 PACs (not counting state affiliates of national groups or issue PACs) that contribute primarily to women candidates or have a female donor base, says the Center for American Women in Politics.

The most important lesson is mining an important new source: women. Women raise billions for charity; they know exactly how to do it. The challenge for women candidates is channeling that tradition into politics.

"Women have the money. They're just not accustomed to giving it," said Dianne Feinstein before her coffers increased 25 percent after the Thomas hearings. "Politics has never been on their list of priorities."

It is now.

Who can close her pocketbook when Representative Patricia Schroeder asks, "How many of you have given as much money to a political candidate as you have for your last outfit?"

Do our two points about money seem to contradict each other? First we insist money cannot buy an election; then we show how much money women are raising (especially in point 6, which follows). Actually, there is no contradiction at all. Look at it this way: women have

won great victories with limited funds. How many more races will
competent women win when their finances are equal to or greater than
their opponents"?

6. Clarence Thomas

Supreme Court justice Clarence Thomas and the U.S. Senate may
have done more for feminist causes than *Ms.* magazine, the National
Organization for Women and Susan B. Anthony put together.

If you think we are getting carried away, listen to Eleanor Smeal,
former NOW president, currently head of the Fund for the Feminist
Majority: "The Senate has done more in one week to underscore the
critical need for more women in the Senate than feminists have been
able to do in 25 years."

So irate were women at the sight of a panel of middle-aged male
senators insensitively questioning Anita Hill on the delicate issue of
sexual harassment—and then voting to confirm Thomas—that they
vowed to get more involved in politics and to dig deep into their
pockets to elect more women.

• Ruth Mandel called women's response to the Thomas affair
  "unparalleled" and "a wake-up call all around the country."
• NOW signed up 13,000 new members in October and November,
  compared with its usual pace of 2,000 a month. Annual membership is $25.
• The Women's Campaign Fund in Washington received more
  than one check for $250 with a note saying, "This is for Clar-
  ence."
• Democratic fund-raiser Pamela Harriman told the Democrats
  she would not raise a dime for the 11 Democratic senators who
  voted for Thomas.

Women who had previously voted Democrat were particularly
incensed at Democrats who voted with Republicans for Thomas—and
vowed to try to unseat them with female candidates. That, of course,
will not be easy.

The 11 Democratic senators who voted with the Republicans for
Clarence Thomas were Boren (Oklahoma), Breaux (Louisiana),
DeConcini (Arizona), Dixon (Illinois), Exon (Nebraska), Fowler
(Georgia), Hollings (South Carolina), Johnston (Louisiana), Nunn

(Georgia), Robb (Virginia) and Shelby (Alabama). Women's groups said each of them would answer for their actions at the polls.

The first to do so was Senator Alan Dixon, 64, of Illinois. Undefeated in 43 years, he lost the March 1992 Democratic primary to Carol Moseley Braun, 44, a former state legislator and then Cook County recorder of deeds. Braun, who is an especially poised and articulate newcomer, was highly favored by women angry over the Thomas affair who vowed to work hard to bring out the votes for her. In that primary 42 percent of Republican women crossed party lines to vote for Braun. Braun's election in November of 1992 made her the first African-American woman to serve in the U.S. Senate.

The following month in the Pennsylvania primary, little-known founder and director of Women's Way Lynn H. Yeakel, 50, won the Democratic nomination for the Senate by beating Lieutenant Governor Mark Singel, who had the endorsement of the state party. Yeakel ran against Republican senator Arlen Specter, who was not a real popular guy among women. Janet Mason, secretary of Philadelphia's NOW chapter, called him "an affront to women. He is not fit to represent this state." Said longtime feminist Betty Friedan, author of the landmark *The Feminine Mystique,* "His behavior was inexcusable, unforgivable. The way he tried to destroy Anita Hill was a declaration of war against women." Yeakel lost in a close race, but a point had been made.

"We are going to fire up," says NWPC's Harriett Woods. "If necessary, we will find a woman to run against every one of these guys. They are going to have to learn. We don't expect them to vote with us all the time, but they should show a sensitivity to the concerns of more than half the population."

Fund-raiser Roger Craver told Senator Charles Robb (D-Va.), chairman of the Democratic Senatorial Campaign Committee, that his firm was terminating its contract with the committee. Craver called the way Senate Democrats dealt with the Thomas hearing *"an insurmountable obstacle to our ability to continue as the fund-raising consultant for the committee."*

In the weeks and months following the October 1991 hearings:

- EMILY's List raised $300,000 via direct mail two weeks after the hearings. After founder Ellen Malcolm appeared on *60 Minutes* on March 22, 1992—where it was reported that membership had doubled from 3,000 to 6,000—her office the next day got 2,000 more calls by 4:00 P.M.

• The National Women's Political Caucus raised $85,000 from one full-page newspaper ad picturing an all-female Senate Judiciary Committee and asking, "What if?"
• The Women's Campaign Fund saw direct-mail contributions increase by 50 percent.
• The Fund for the Feminist Majority and NOW saw contributions grow some 30 percent.

So encouraged was EMILY's List about its success, it aimed to double the $1.5 million it raised for women in 1990 to a 1992 goal of $3 million. But the group exceeded its goal and donated $6.2 million to women candidates, increasing its donor base to 24,000.

In 1992 the Women's Campaign Fund doubled membership and gave $1.2 million to 242 candidates.

Minnesota women have created the Minnesota Million campaign to raise $1 million to entice a strong Democratic woman candidate to challenge Republican senator Dave Durenberger in 1994. Before its first official meeting, the group, co-chaired by Nina Rothchild, had collected pledges of $122,000. "People have tracked us down," says Rothchild.

A group of prominent Republican women have started the WISH list: Women in the Senate and House. The group was established to help pro-choice Republican women get elected.

7. The Domestic Agenda

The environment, education, day care and abortion are no longer "women's issues." They have become mainstream. "There really are no women's and men's issues anymore," said March Fong Eu, California secretary of state, while running for her fifth term. "Everyone wants improvement of life."

Over the years women have amassed expertise on domestic issues. **As early as 1987, voters gave women higher marks than men in dealing with social and domestic issues such as day care, education and helping the poor,** according to a survey for the National Women's Political Caucus. (Men were seen as more effective on "technical issues"—such as arms control and trade. Hopefully, Congresswoman Pat Schroeder, who has made a name for herself on the House Armed Services Committee, and former Special Trade Representative Carla Hills are correcting these perceptions.)

But since then voters have come to consider foreign policy and defense, where women may be perceived as weak, to be *less important,* says a recent survey of 1,600 voters by pollster Celinda Lake. Domestic and social issues, where women are seen as strong, have become more important to voters. The study was conducted for the NWPC, EMILY's List and the Women's Campaign Fund.

Women in the statehouses are very actively promoting women's issues, says a 1991 survey of more than 1,000 state legislators by the Center for the American Woman and Politics (CAWP). Female Democrats are *most* likely to give high priority to issues such as child care and women's rights, but Republican women emphasized the issues *more than men of either party.*

"It's clear that without women sitting in our legislative bodies, there would be no child care, no family leave, no reproductive rights, no environmental concerns," says Jane Danowitz of the Women's Campaign Fund.

Women's issues have become political issues, but there is no denying that women have the edge in understanding them.

Women bring a fresh, nondogmatic approach. Oregon's governor, Barbara Roberts, calls herself an environmentalist, but also says, "I told environmental groups never to be smug when people are losing their jobs and their homes and their livelihood."

Abortion

On January 22, 1993, the 20th anniversary of *Roe v. Wade,* President Clinton eliminated the gag rule on abortion counseling and referrals at federally funded family-planning clinics. The rule, said the president, "endangers women's lives and health by preventing them from receiving complete and accurate medical information."

Women, regardless of their stand on abortion, consider it more important than men do, according to a study by the CAWP. When Minnesota Republican Mary Tambornino, a candidate for the state senate, lost the primary, she switched her allegiance to Democrat Judy Traub rather than support her own party's antiabortion candidate.

The National Abortion Rights Action League (NARAL) identified 2.4 million abortion-rights supporters and contributed more than $3 million to pro-choice candidates in the 1992 elections. "I feel very strongly that our nation has been wasting a great deal of time focusing on taking away the right to choose rather than focusing on reducing the need for abortion," says NARAL president Kate Michelman.

The U.S. Supreme Court's 1989 *Webster* ruling gave Missouri the power to restrict abortions and opened the door for other states to do so.

Roe v. Wade had said that a state could not interfere in a woman's right to an abortion. But in the 1992 *Planned Parenthood v. Casey* ruling, the Supreme Court affirmed Pennsylvania's (and, by extension, other states') right to restrict abortion. States can require a waiting period and reporting requirements or compel physicians to give a woman antiabortion information.

By April 1993, at least 100 bills restricting abortion had been introduced into the 1993 legislative session. Mississippi, North Dakota, Pennsylvania, South Dakota and Utah have restricted abortions. California, Connecticut, Florida, Maryland, Nevada and Washington have acted to protect abortion rights.

The Supreme Court's curbs on abortion increased membership in and contributions to pro-choice organizations. Philanthropist Peg Yorkin of Los Angeles gave $10 million, probably the largest gift to a women's rights organization, to the Feminist Majority Foundation. It will endow "a feminist brain trust," whose first project will be making RU-486, the "abortion pill," available to U.S. women. Says Yorkin, "I want to issue a wake-up call to feminists and women everywhere. All of us must give as much as we possibly can to prevent the impending destruction of women's rights."

"The Republican Party should look back and realize it has wasted its most valuable resource by not putting forward more pro-choice women," says Jane Danowitz, executive director of the Women's Campaign Fund. The fund supports candidates who favor abortion rights.

8. Women's Voting Power and the New Electorate

Today women's electoral power exceeds men's. Historically men voted in greater numbers than women. But beginning in 1980, the trend reversed itself. In the 1988 presidential election 6.8 million more women voted than men; in 1992, 7.2 million more voted. Women make up 54 percent of the electorate. Women who may have encountered prejudice and sexual harassment are devoted to giving competent female candidates a chance at the polling booth.

Political observers agree that both in 1990 and in 1992 women propelled women into office.

Women as well as men are revolted by "politics as usual." People are ready for a new breed of political leader, and women fit the profile. Most voters consider women candidates more honest and compassionate than their male counterparts, says a study by the NWPC.

According to a recent poll commissioned by the NWPC, the Women's Campaign Fund and EMILY's List, voters see women as incorruptible outsiders who seek change and try to make government work for ordinary people.

Republican pollster Linda Divall says, "There is a lot of information out there that indicates the environment is perfect for women candidates."

Pollster Celinda Lake agrees. "In an era when voters are strongly anti-incumbent and anti-political in their mood, women run as the ultimate outsiders, turning what was once a disadvantage at the polls to a strong advantage."

Furthermore, the U.S. electorate has gradually become more open to the idea of women in leadership. As early as 1987, half of U.S. voters said they believed a woman would lead just as well in the presidency as a male, according to a NWPC survey. Democrats, blacks, urban dwellers, younger voters, unmarried voters and most women considered women as capable of the presidency.

Men prefer voting for men, Celinda Lake found in a recent poll (no big surprise there). But men also view Republican women more favorably than any Democrat—male or female. Thirty-five percent of Democratic women said they would cross party lines to vote for a Republican woman over a Democratic man. Only 21 percent of Republican women said they would vote against party lines. **But a pro-choice Democratic woman running against an antiabortion Republican male has a 10-point lead among all voters surveyed.**

When respondents were asked to assess candidates' likelihood of winning, the women were rated an average of seven points lower than men.

Women in politics say they have a problem with the "toughness issue," convincing voters that, along with all that caring, they can also be tough on issues like drugs and crime. Geraldine Ferraro, a prosecutor before running for Congress, won her first election with the slogan "Finally a tough Democrat."

"To get anyone out of office, you have to explain to voters why they shouldn't be in office, and that means negative campaigning," says Jane Danowitz of the Women's Campaign Fund. And that can make women seem too tough or abrasive, some women politicians say.

Oregon governor Barbara Roberts, who has taken several controversial positions, tells women, "Demonstrate your courage very clearly . . . and stick to your position." She tells women to cite their credentials before declaring a position. When someone asks why she supports the sales tax, for example, she would say, "As a person who worked in business for 15 years and spent 4 years on the revenue and school finance committee, I'll tell you why I think this."

9. Operation Desert Storm

American women put their lives on the line to defend Saudi Arabia and free Kuwait. The Defense Department says 32,400 women, 6 percent of U.S. troops, served in the Gulf. The Women in Military Service for America Memorial Foundation, Inc., puts it higher: between 34,000 and 35,000. Women were armed and closer to the front lines than in any previous war.

Army women helicopter pilots flew supply missions into hostile fire in Iraq and Kuwait. In February 1991, 20 female pilots participated in the largest helicopter assault in history, airlifting men, fuel and ammunition 50 miles into Iraq. Army Major Marie Rossi, who had taken part in that mission, was killed soon after when her chopper crashed in Saudi Arabia.

Fifteen American women died in the Gulf. Two women, a truck driver and a flight surgeon, were among the 25 U.S. personnel held prisoner of war by Iraq; both received the Purple Heart for combat injuries. It was later revealed that the women were sexually assaulted as prisoners, a flagrant violation of all international, indeed human, standards. The constant danger to which women were exposed provoked new legislation removing in part the ban on women in combat.

- Women air force pilots and crews flew in airborne warning and control aircraft and in-flight refueling tankers within range of enemy aircraft, surface-to-air missiles and antiaircraft artillery.
- Air force women pilots flew and crewed strategic transport, tactical, tankers, reconnaissance (AWACS) and aeromedical airlift aircraft.
- Women who served in navy logistics ships resupplying aircraft

carrier battle groups in the Gulf and Red Sea were constantly at
risk from enemy mines, missiles and bombs.
• Army Major Dr. Rhonda Cornum was shot down and captured
on a helicopter rescue mission in Iraq. Tell her she was not in
combat.

The women who served and died in the Persian Gulf demonstrated to America that women possess courage, capability and experience—all key attributes for political leadership.

So had women who served and died before, especially in the
Vietnam War, where 7,500 women, most of whom were nurses,
served, says the Defense Department. Four hundred thousand
women, many volunteers, served in World War II.

**In Desert Storm, however, women were visible and in com-
bat, and there were a lot more of them; their sacrifice could not
be overlooked.**

Women remain a minority in the armed forces, but it is one huge
minority: in 1993 there were 1,773,996 personnel on active duty, including Army, Navy, Air Force and Marines. Of those, 206,908 were
women, about 11.7 percent, the highest percentage of women on
active duty in the world.

Gulf Duty

Women in the Gulf neither expected nor got any special treatment: "You're no longer a female here—you're a soldier, like everyone else," said Specialist Foy Harris of the Alabama National Guard.
Private First Class Meria Sanders says the men in her company were
"just as green as we are. . . . [They] have never seen war, either, except
for little stuff like Panama, Grenada."

But "Saudi," as the desert kingdom is called in military and
expatriate circles, was hardly the ideal theater for the first large-scale
deployment of women. The Saudi government rejected the notion of
female soldiers, calling them "males with female features." As if fighting Saddam weren't tough enough, women in the Gulf had to tackle
the prejudices of the Allies as well.

Of course, no women served in the armed forces of Saudi Arabia,
where women are not allowed to drive, let alone vote. Nine Kuwaiti
women underwent military training in the United States, but the war
ended before they made it home.

In wartime, with no experience except their training, and where an ally was permitted to infringe on what few rights a soldier has, U.S. women served their country and distinguished themselves magnificently.

Women in Combat

In August 1991 the U.S. Senate joined the House to get rid of a 1948 law that banned women pilots from flying combat missions. Until then most combat jobs were closed to women. It made for some very strange situations: women can *command* units in which they cannot serve and train men for missions they cannot carry out.

But combat jobs are the key paths to promotion. "Combat-exclusion laws do not protect women. They only protect women from promotions," wrote Representative Pat Schroeder (D-Colo.).

The new law, which Representative Schroeder called a "21-gun salute to women service members," applies to all four branches of the armed services, but combat jobs still remain off-limits to 99 percent of servicewomen, a source of frustration to many. "I volunteered for the Army, not the Girl Scouts," says Captain Leola Davis, commander of a heavy maintenance company. A *Newsweek* poll found an astonishing 79 percent of Americans think women should be allowed to volunteer for combat.

After the president signed the law, an 18-month commission was created to study the situation. The military was free to assign women to combat posts but did not move ahead. "They're kind of just sitting on it," said one source.

Then the commission issued its recommendations for a new rule banning women from air combat positions, the reverse of the law Congress had just repealed. The panel urged the exclusion of women from ground combat but did vote to allow women to serve on most warships.

Finally, in spring 1993, Secretary of Defense Les Aspin announced that the military must end most restrictions on women flying in combat. The Clinton administration asked Congress to allow women on many warships. The Army, Air Force and Navy were instructed to train women for air combat.

Much of Western Europe has opened combat jobs to women. In 1989 Canada abolished laws barring women from combat and opened *all* military jobs—except on submarines—to females. Norway allows women to be crew members on submarines, and fighter pilots. Denmark, the Netherlands and Belgium have opened some combat jobs to women.

Retired Brigadier General Evelyn "Pat" Foote concedes there are some U.S. military men who want to exclude women, "because they don't want them influencing the action."

"The people making these decisions are elderly males who don't understand young people," says Lawrence Korb, a defense analyst. "They didn't play soccer with women and go to school with them."

But most military men support women, says General Foote, "because they know how good they are." USAF Colonel Douglas Kennett at the Pentagon says his service "couldn't go to war without women and we couldn't win without them."

10. California and Texas

Women are gaining power in the nation's most populous, fastest-growing and economically powerful states—notably California and Texas, the states from which presidential leadership often emerges.

California, home state of Richard Nixon and Ronald Reagan, and Texas, the home of Lyndon Johnson and adopted home of George Bush, are hotbeds of women's political power. Ann Richards is governor. Dianne Feinstein and Barbara Boxer, representing the bellwether state of California, became the first all-female senatorial delegation in U.S. history in 1992. California's secretary of state is a woman, and state treasurer Kathleen Brown is widely expected to run for governor.

In both California and Texas—more than any other states— women have held the highly visible position of big-city mayor:

- Two of the three largest cities in California—San Diego and San Jose—have women mayors.
- There are women mayors in two of the eight largest cities in Texas—Corpus Christi and Fort Worth. In 1991 the four largest cities in Texas had women mayors—Houston, Dallas, San Antonio and El Paso.
- As cited earlier, the 1991 political power structure of Houston was female.

To many it is ironic that Texas, with its good ole boy image, has produced such a string of female leaders. It is a question Governor Ann Richards must often be asked. "The good ol' boys in Texas have a frontier mentality," she says. "They believe that anybody who works as hard as they do, who has a little grit, deserves promotion. And they don't care whether you're male or female, as long as you do the job."

Richards's chief advisers on education, commerce and the environment are women. As noted, Barbara Jordan serves as the governor's special counsel on ethics. Almost half of Richards's 973 gubernatorial appointments went to women and in her second week she walked into two state agencies and demanded, and got, resignations. She gets about 7,000 letters a week, almost four times what her predecessor received.

"She enjoys her job more than any governor I ever saw," says George Christian, White House press secretary under Lyndon Johnson and influential Austin lobbyist. He has seen 40 years' worth of Texas governors.

America's Megastate

The 1990 Census says one in eight Americans lives in California, whose population now exceeds Canada's. After redistricting, California sent seven new members to Congress, for a total of 52 in 1993. It will be the largest delegation in U.S. history, more than the other 16 western states combined.

In 1992 there were only three U.S. congresswomen from California. In 1992, nineteen California women won party nominations to run for the U.S. House of Representatives; seven won seats.

As noted, in 1993 California sent two women senators to Washington. Dianne Feinstein, who lost the governorship to Pete Wilson, defeated state controller Gray Davis in the Democratic primary, and ran for the Senate seat to which John Seymour was appointed.

Representative Barbara Boxer (D-Calif.) took the Senate seat Alan Cranston gave up in 1992. Boxer defeated Lieutenant Governor Leo McCarthy and U.S. congressman Mel Levine for the Democratic Senate nomination; she faced conservative Republican Bruce Herschensohn.

In 1991 Barbara Boxer raised over $2 million, more than any of her opponents, Democrat or Republican. As of February 1992 *Boxer had outraised every Democrat running for the U.S. Senate.* Feinstein had raised more than $3 million by 1992. She raised $19 million in her bid for governor.

The strength of women candidates in California is consistent with its role as a national trendsetter. Education, high income, high percentage of working women and relative youth of residents are all factors explaining California's tendency to elect women, reports Celinda Lake.

Women to Watch: Conventional Wisdom

"We believe 1992 proved that there is no office that women cannot attain in this country," says NWPC's Harriett Woods.

"The next time we have a conversation about who is going to be the Democratic nominee, we are going to hear a lot about women in the mix as candidate instead of vice president," says Ellen Malcolm of EMILY's List.

Who can resist speculating on who will become the first woman president? Will she be a Republican or a Democrat? Will she ascend to the presidency after serving as vice president? Is she visible today in national politics or a virtual unknown earning a brilliant record as a mayor somewhere or balancing a state budget?

In May 1991 *Time* speculated on women Bush might have considered as his vice-presidential nominee, in the unlikely event that, seeking women's votes (and for other reasons), he had dumped Dan Quayle. Mentioned were Senator Nancy Kassebaum, U.S. Trade Representative Carla Hills and Secretary of Labor Lynn Martin. (Secretary of Commerce Barbara Hackman Franklin joined Martin and Hills in 1992 as the third woman in the Bush cabinet.)

On the Democratic side,

- Geraldine Ferraro became the first woman to run as vice president on a major-party ticket.
- Former San Francisco mayor Dianne Feinstein was elected U.S. Senator from California.
- Many would welcome Governor Ann Richards's wit and outstanding speaking ability on the presidential campaign trail. In that department, she is certainly superior to every presidential candidate in recent memory.
- Colorado's Pat Schroeder, elected to Congress at age 32, is

known for expertise in defense matters. She has come up through the ranks and dealt with the male establishment on her own terms.

We believe that when it comes to predicting the first woman president, conventional wisdom is not to be trusted. The future first woman president of the United States is today, we would argue, a highly competent locally or regionally respected politician who is little known at the national level. She is toiling in a state legislature, holding the office of state treasurer or lieutenant governor or big-city mayor. She is already poised, however, to make her move to the governorship of a major state. Once governor, by the mid-1990's she will compensate for the lack of international experience with bold global moves in international trade, citizen diplomacy and new business development.

Capturing women voters, the public's desire for a new kind of political leader and profiting from the bonanza in political fundraising for women candidates in the wake of Clarence Thomas's ascent to the Supreme Court and the possible overturn of women's right to abortion, the first woman president will come on the national scene early in the 21st century. With the trends on her side, she will make her move, stun the pundits . . . and the rest, as they say, will be history.

2.
The Sporting Life

Women who are now in their 30's and 40's were told that their lack of athletic training, which is said to teach competition and teamwork, put them at a real disadvantage in business. Study football, women were told, if you want to master corporate strategy. Even though many women ignored that advice, they still became a critical mass in the workplace.

Today, business credentials established, millions of adult women, with little prior physical training, are flocking to the previously male-dominated arena of sports. Overcoming fear, imposing discipline, they are discovering strength, competence, endurance—and the self-confidence to achieve new levels of personal and career success.

The strength, endurance and confidence achieved in sports shatters the mythology of women as the "weaker" sex. That new "winning" psychology transfers into other areas, from business to politics to leadership.

The benefits of sports are well documented. People feel better, have greater self-esteem and are more creative when they exercise. A study at California State University found female athletes had more positive self-images than nonathletic women. Most mothers and fathers, 87 percent, believe sports are as important for girls as for boys.

But teamwork and competition are *not* the only benefits of sports. Mariah Burton Nelson, former college and pro basketball player and author of the landmark *Are We Winning Yet? How Women Are Changing Sports and Sports Are Changing Women* (Random House), says sports also develop "persistence, courage, desire, patience, humility, intelligence and self-confidence."

What contemporary woman would not want to learn—or have her daughter develop—life-affirming traits like those? Isn't a modern father going to support those characteristics in both his daughter and son?

Not that we would dismiss competition lightly. Women had to compete with men and other women to win the jobs they hold today—and will vie with others for better jobs again this decade. Furthermore, competition inspires all of us. When a champion like Susan Butcher competes with and defeats men in the Iditarod dogsled race, girls learn that boys are not *always* the best athletes. And all women relish her success.

Competition is one thing, aggression something else. Some value sports for teaching women that "killer instinct." Psychologist Michael G. Weiss, Ph.D., says women athletes must "engage in very aggressive, sometimes even hostile, behavior . . . and to be successful in the business world, most women have to make similar adjustments."

Perhaps. But it sounds as though Weiss is interpreting both sports and business according to macho standards many men have abandoned. Today, just as women are transforming the workplace, they are introducing female values into sports: caring about athletes and their physical well-being rather than the "winning is everything" mentality, for example. As the title of Nelson's book puts it, sports are changing women, but women are also changing sports.

Moreover, "competition and teamwork" *overemphasize* the functions of assembly-line industrial society. How important is teamwork for the supercreative independent individual? What if one aspires to compete, not with others, but with one's self?

Sports build confidence—no controversy there. Knowing she could defeat a strong opponent in tennis, survive three days in the wilderness or ski an expert run, can give a woman a psychological edge unavailable elsewhere. Sports develop leadership skills that make women stand out in middle management and catapult into the executive suite. What better way to prepare for leadership than to 1) confront fear, 2) challenge the body's resources and 3) master discipline and risk taking.

The Boom in Women's Sports

A 1991 *Sports Illustrated* poll showed 69 percent of American women participate in sports or fitness activities. Women are a majority in six of the seven most popular fitness activities: aerobics, exercise walking, exercising with equipment, calisthenics, swimming and bike riding. Women also make up 37.5 percent of the seventh fitness activity, running. Women make up the majority of cross-country skiers and hikers, and both of these sports are among the top 10.

Men are the undisputed champions of spectator sports, but women, it appears, are the more active athletes.

Women make up the **majority of new** participants in weight training, running, cycling and basketball. More than one third of *new golfers* are women—more than **1 million new players** each year.

Since Title IX, the 1972 law forbidding sex discrimination in schools that get federal funding, the number of girls and college women participating in sports has soared. There are now nearly 2 million high school girls in interscholastic sports, an increase of more than 500 percent. Many college women, about one third, play intercollegiate sports, up from about 15 percent before Title IX (see page 47).

Women's romance with sports spans all age groups:

- By age 6, Katie Zubricky had already climbed 6 of Colorado's 56 mountain peaks over 14,000 feet. Her goal is to climb a "fourteener" each birthday. "Katie Zubricky collects peaks, not dolls," says *Women's Sports & Fitness.*
- From 1989 to 1990 the number of girl golfers (age 12 to 17) increased almost 100 percent to 410,000.
- Kitty Porterfield of Virginia, who took up rowing in her early 40's, has several championships to her name.
- In 1992 Helen Klein, at age 69, became the oldest person ever to complete the Western States 100-Mile Endurance Run.
- Ruth Rothfarb didn't start running until she was 72, but ran the Boston Marathon in 1990. By age 89, she had completed 11 marathons.

For those who are skeptical about the power of role models, consider the case of Paula Petrucci of Randolph, Vermont.

"After reading about Ruth Rothfarb . . . I decided if she could run 26.2 miles, I could, too," Petrucci wrote to *Women's Sports &*

Fitness magazine. "Thanks to Ruth's spark, I went from running three miles a day to completing the 1991 New York City Marathon."

Older women are keeping up with men their age, though most of the women took up sports later in life. Active women age 50 and older exercise four times a week, compared with 4.5 times for active men their age. As youths, 41 percent of women had played sports versus 77 percent of men. Overall 19 percent of older women were active versus 25 percent of men. The October 1991 issue of *Women's Sports & Fitness,* devoted to older women who climb mountains, skydive and play ice hockey, was one of the most popular issues in its history.

Old Favorites and a Taste for the Nontraditional

Women are seeking out *nontraditional* sports:

- The first women's **ice hockey** world tournament was held in 1990.
- In 1991 Patty Wagstaff became the first woman to win an overall national **aerobatics** (that's aerobatics, not aerobics) title. "I've always been kind of an adventurer," Wagstaff says. "It's exciting, it's very difficult." Wagstaff won again in 1992.
- Karyn Marshall, a financial analyst, lifted 242.5 pounds to set a new world record at the 1989 Women's World **Weightlifting** Championships.

Rugby, a hard, physical, body-contact game, has long been considered a male sport. Twenty years ago, the United States had three women's rugby teams; today there are 162 clubs. French women formed a club in 1965. English women took up rugby in 1983. Today there are 115 women's clubs and 2,000 players. The UK's Sports Council calls women's rugby the fastest-growing sport. "I love tackling, getting muddy and enjoying the pleasure of a communal bath," says English rugby player Karen Almond.

A hot new sport for women is **boxing,** which builds strength and stamina and offers aerobic benefits. Some 150 of the 400 boxers at Brooklyn's Gleason's Gym are women, as are half the boxers at West Los Angeles's Bodies in Motion.

"You tone your arms, legs, stomach, chest and back while doing a great cardiovascular workout," says Stephanie LaMotta, daughter of former middleweight champ Jake "Raging Bull" LaMotta. "It also trains your hand-eye coordination, timing and reflexes," says Stephanie, who started boxing at age 12 and trains clients in Los Angeles. "If you think about anything else while hitting the speed bag, it will hit you in the head."

Think **fishing** and you probably think fisher*man*. Yet 14 million U.S. women fish in fresh waters, and 3.5 million head for the sea. There are two professional angling associations for women: Bass 'n Gal and Lady Bass.

While a new generation plays unusual sports, the old favorites are still popular. There are 2.5 million members in the Women's International Bowling Congress. More than 47,000 women attended the 1993 annual tournament in Baton Rouge, Lousiana. Their median age: 53.

About 17.5 million women play volleyball—America's second-favorite team sport for women. The National Collegiate Athletic Association (NCAA) boasts 722 volleyball programs for women versus only 52 for men.

Exercise walking surpassed swimming to become America's most popular activity among women 25 and older, says the National Sporting Goods Association (NSGA), which is also our source for the following numbers:

• Some 37.8 million women walk for exercise.
• 20 million women swim.
• 14.7 million women ride bicycles.
• 13.4 million women do aerobics.
• 12.6 million women exercise with weights.
• There are nearly 4.5 million female runners/joggers.
• 7.8 million women hike.

A comparison of the 1984 and 1990 NSGA studies of top women's sports showed declines in aerobics, racquetball, running, jogging and tennis and increases in backpacking, basketball, golf, downhill skiing and soccer.

Not everyone stays with vigorous sports after injuries start taking their toll. Some decide to walk to work, tend the garden or take up a sport like cycling or golf that is easier on the knees or ankles.

Marathon, Biathlon, Triathlon and Pentathlon

But the number of diehard always-looking-for-another-challenge women athletes is growing at very impressive rates—as is the demand for more events that test women's mettle, especially in the Olympics.

In 1966, when Roberta Gibb tried to enter the Boston Marathon, she was informed that women were not "physiologically able to run such distances." In 1967 Katherine Switzer became the first woman to run Boston wearing an official number. A race official tried to throw her out after the first few miles, but she finished the race. The Boston Marathon did not officially accept women until 1972. In 1993, 1,857 of the 8,925 entrants in the Boston Marathon were women—about 21 percent.

Women's participation in the New York Marathon soared from 36 (out of 303) in 1975 to 5,677 of 25,945 marathoners in 1992.

The first women's Olympic marathon was not held until 1984. When Joan Benoit Samuelson won it, her time would have beaten 13 of the last 20 men's Olympic marathon winners'.

The winter biathlon combines cross-country skiing and riflery. But in the summer biathlon, running replaces skiing. In 1991 there were almost 100 races in the United States.

Women of Iron—"The name refers to having an iron will, not doing the Ironman," says founder Andra-Nina Davis—is the first U.S. organization for women triathletes and duathletes. There are 1,000 members.

If marathons leave you with energy to spare, and triathlons are just, well, missing something, the five-sport pentathlon might be your event. Combining running, swimming, fencing, shooting and riding, the pentathlon was designed to test a messenger's ability to come through almost impossible situations. Lori Norwood is the first American woman and the second American to win the event at the Modern Pentathlon Championships. Norwood hopes the International Olympic Committee will make it a women's event in 1996.

Those Tennis Superstars

Much credit for the women's sports boom goes to professional tennis, which brought images of graceful, sweaty athletic women to a widespread television audience. Tennis is also establishing women as sports superstars.

• Billie Jean King, beloved for her 1973 defeat of Bobby Riggs in the "Battle of the Sexes" match, won 20 Wimbledon titles, six in singles, and founded Open Tennis, the women's pro tour, the

Women's Tennis Association and the Women's Sports Foundation.

• The wonderfully independent and outspoken Martina Navratilova set a record in 1990, winning her ninth Wimbledon singles title.

• Chris Evert led all players, male and female, with 157 professional singles titles until Navratilova passed her in 1992.

Tennis is one of the few sports where women can now earn more than men. In 1989 number-one-ranked Steffi Graf's prize money was $1,963,905, more than number-one-ranked Stefan Edberg's $1,661,491. Monica Seles earned a record $2.5 million in 1991. Meanwhile Jennifer Capriati, at age 16, had earned more than $8 million in endorsements and prize money.

Debunking Sports Stereotypes: Are Men Better?

To develop the basic level of competence required to enjoy a sport, many women must confront negative stereotypes and experiences from childhood. That requires risk taking. Not necessarily risking danger, but risking ridicule, failure, injury to one's self-esteem. The assumption that males come naturally to sports and that most females are klutzes begins early. But is it accurate? Are men better athletes than women?

As a rule, men are stronger and bigger than women. Anyone can tell you that. Men will succeed better than women in the sports that require those attributes, says Mariah Burton Nelson. Football and basketball, for example, "capitalize on men's natural assets," she points out. Strength is important in athletics, she concedes, but believes it is "overrated as the decisive factor in most sports."

Each sex has advantages and disadvantages, but, Nelson believes, physical traits are often used *against* women rather than in their favor: the fact that women are shorter and lighter has never yet excluded men from becoming jockeys.

The real "advantage" men possess is lifelong sports training. "Male athletic superiority is taken for granted . . . because men have been given lifelong physical training and indoctrination that they are the stronger sex," she states. "When trained men are compared with trained women, the male strength advantage shrinks," says Nelson.

Pat Harris, 43, couldn't play basketball at Oxon Hill High

School, in Maryland, in the late 1960's because she was a girl. Today she coaches boys' varsity basketball—the state's first female coach to do so. Harris, who coached girls for 16 years, says all her preconceived notions have gone out the window.

"I thought boys would grasp things faster," she admits. "They don't. I thought boys would have higher skill levels. They don't. I thought boys could play defense better, but I'm starting out with conventional man-to-man. The girls I coached before played more intricate defenses."

The Female Advantage

In an increasing number of sporting events, especially those requiring extraordinary endurance—distance swimming, dogsled racing, ultramarathoning—women and men are competing as equals. And women are winning.

The point is not to laud those triumphs over men. (There are not so many that women can afford to get arrogant, in the first place.) More important, it is graceless, unsportswomanlike and ignorant to put *anyone* down for losing. But after millennia of male dominance, don't women deserve to celebrate victories won with courage, endurance and hard work?

Closing the Gap

In long-distance events—ultramarathons, triathlons and cycling—women are closing the gap between the top women's and men's performances:

- In the 1989 Race Across America, cyclist Susan Notorangelo, the first female finisher, placed seventh overall with a time of nine days, nine hours, nine minutes. That time would have won overall **first place** in 1987.
- Triathlete Paula Newby-Fraser placed first among women, eleventh overall, in the 1988 Ironman Triathlon in Hawaii, a grueling mix of swimming, cycling and running. Her time of 9:01:01 would have **beaten all the men** in any Ironman triathlons before 1984. In 1992 she became the first woman to complete the Ironman in less than nine hours.
- Erin Baker finished eleventh overall in the 1988 Nice (France)

Triathlon. Baker's time in the running segment was **less than one minute slower** than the 1987 men's winner.

If the present trend continues, women will hold the long-distance records in events like triathlons.

"The implications of . . . these outstanding performances are fascinating, if not frightening, for many men," writes C. J. Olivares, Jr., editor of *Triathlete* magazine. "Is there the possibility that men and women will someday compete against each other in a new open division?"

Even in shorter events, where men hold an advantage in strength, the gap between men and women is narrowing. Florence Griffith-Joyner's 1988 100-meter world record of 10.49 seconds was only about **half a second slower** than Carl Lewis's 1991 record of 9.86 seconds.

Coming in 1998: Women Take the Marathon

Two researchers from the University of California at Los Angeles, Dr. Brian Whipp and Dr. Susan Ward, have analyzed 70 years of data on women's and men's performances and made a bold prediction: women will run marathons as fast or faster than men in 1998—and will match men's times in shorter track events like the 200-meter race by the middle of the 21st century. Their findings were published in the British journal *Nature*.

Whipp and Ward make that assertion because of statistics like this: women's marathon times have improved 61 percent since 1955, compared with 18 percent for men.

Men's times in track events have improved—and will keep improving. But "women's performance has been accelerating at **two to three times the rate of men's,**" said a *New York Times* piece by Natalie Angier about the new projections, "and in an unerringly linear fashion."

There are, of course, athletes, trainers and physiologists who dispute Whipp and Ward's findings (as well as those who support them). At least one marathon director is a little freaked out by the idea. "Women will never, ever catch up to the men," said Fred Lebow, president of the New York Road Runner's Club. "Women will never pass men. Never. Never."

Lighten up, Fred.

UCLA researcher Whipp is probably not surprised by the reaction, though: "If it weren't for the imperative of the data forcing me to this conclusion," he said, "I would have called this implausible and outlandish."

Breaking Through

As the sports world debates the issue, women are going out and winning events. Women have finished first overall in marathons, 50- and 100-mile runs and 24-hour runs.

In 1989 Oakland's Ann Trason, a microbiologist in her early 30's, ran 143 miles to defeat male and female competitors to win the Sri Chimnoy TAC/USA 24-Hour Race in New York, setting a world record for 100 miles and becoming the first woman to win a mixed-sex national championship. The fourth-place finisher was also a woman— Sue Ellen Trapp of Florida.

Placing ninth overall, Trason was the first-place woman (for the third time in a row) in the 1991 Western States 100-Mile Endurance Run, which crosses rivers, climbs 18,000 vertical feet and descends 23,000 feet. It "has been covered with snow for the first 25 miles with 15- to 20-foot drifts," says *City Sports* magazine. "Temperatures as high as 114 degrees . . . [and the course is] populated by bears, cougars and coyotes."

But in 1992 Trason smashed her own outstanding record, placing third overall—up from ninth—the first time a woman finished in the top three.

Swimming

Women have already won superiority in long-distance swimming. Californian Penny Dean has held the English Channel record since 1978. Diana Nyad's 1975 record 28.5-mile swim around Manhattan Island beat the record set by Bryon Somers some *50 years earlier*. Shelley Taylor-Smith won the swim around Manhattan in 1987, 1988 and 1989. Californian Lynne Cox, who in 1973 had set the world's English Channel record, holds the overall records for swimming the Bering Strait and the Strait of Magellan.

Janet Evans's 1988 record for the 400-meter freestyle beats Mark Spitz's 1968 world record by more than two seconds.

"Who knows what might have happened in the 1988 Olympics if Evans, a triple gold-medal winner, had been permitted to swim her best event, the 1,500-meter freestyle?" asks Mariah Nelson. "She would have beat everyone by 25 seconds," says her coach, Bud McAllister.

But it was not an Olympic event for women—only for men.

The Iditarod

"My goal was never to be the first woman or the best woman," says Iditarod champion Susan Butcher. "It was to be the best dogsled racer."

Butcher has won Alaska's grueling 1,150-mile trek between Anchorage and Nome four times and held the course record until 1992. She lives 100 miles south of the Arctic Circle in Eureka, Alaska (population 14), and has the only team composed entirely of dogs she has raised from birth. "Other mushers are constantly surprised by Butcher's gentleness with her dogs," says *Outdoor Life*, "and puzzled by why the dogs work their hearts out for her."

It is not that hard to understand. From the moment the dogs are born, Butcher cares for them, trains them and plays with them. "I want the dogs to see me doing everything for them," she says. "They have to trust me and know that I won't ask them to do something they aren't capable of."

Susan Butcher was not the first woman to win the Iditarod. That honor went to Libby Riddles in 1985, the year Butcher encountered a pregnant moose on the trail. It killed two dogs, injured 13 and even roughed up Butcher, who kept the animal at bay with an ax for 20 minutes until a competitor with a gun arrived and shot it. Butcher, who has run every race since 1978, dropped out of that one.

Going into the 1991 race, Butcher and rival Rick Swenson were tied with four wins each. Butcher had a one-hour lead but, when a brutal snowstorm hit 77 miles from the finish line, she decided to seek shelter, and Swenson went on to win.

Swenson, who often discounts Butcher's accomplishments, said, "Maybe she's gotten a little soft with four victories under her belt." When *Sports Illustrated* wrote about Butcher in 1991, Swenson refused to comment: "Every time I get interviewed about her, I wind up looking like a jerk."

Sailing

In 1990 Florence Arthaud became the first woman to break the world record for a transatlantic crossing, and the first woman to win the solo Route du Rhum race between St. Malo, France, and Pointe-à-Pitre, Guadeloupe.

Like women runners, she gained over men as the exhausting race dragged on. Just as she was poised to take the lead, her radio broke, her automatic pilot went out and she began hemorrhaging. Yet she pulled ahead and beat the record by eight hours, all the while wearing a surgical collar for a slipped disk.

"I think women project in me their desire for liberty," Arthaud says. "On the sea I am totally independent . . . I have realized my dream. . . . There are not a lot of people who get to do that."

Isabelle Autissier is the first woman to complete a solo round-the-world voyage. She came in sixth in the BOC Challenge; her time: 139 days, 4 hours, 48 minutes. "The bigger the boat, the longer the race, the easier it is for a woman," Autissier said, "because you need more of your brains."

In 1991 Texan Elizabeth Kratzig, 17, defeated nine male competitors to win the U.S. Yacht Racing Union Junior Championship in Mentor, Ohio.

Riflery

Riflery is the only NCAA sport in which men and women compete together. In 1989 women, for the first time, won both the individual smallbore and air-rifle competitions at the NCAAs. In the 1992 air-rifle event, women took first and fourth places.

Billiards

In 1991, for the first time, women competed with men in mixed doubles in the World Snooker Masters in Birmingham, England. It will take time, says former world snooker champion Steve Davis, but one day a woman will be world champ.

School Sports

It is impressive that women are competing with men in running, swimming and triathlons. But what if women had access to early sports training? The next generation of women will know that advantage.

Before Title IX in 1972, girls were 7 percent of interscholastic athletes, says the National Federation of State High School Associations. By 1991 they were 36 percent. Today nearly 2 million girls are playing interscholastic high school sports, up more than 500 percent since 1971. The number of boys playing sports has remained around 3.4 million since 1980.

Nearly 400,000 high school girls play basketball, the most popular sport. Track and field and volleyball attract more than 300,000 each. More than 200,000 girls play softball (fast pitch). Tennis, soccer and cross-country have more than 100,000 players.

"Everyone in this room has had a time when everything went perfectly in sports and he made the perfect catch or perfect pass," says Amateur Athletic Foundation president and International Olympic Committee (IOC) member Anita DeFrantz, when addressing male audiences. (DeFrantz was a 1976 Olympic medal–winning rower and one of only six women on the 92-member IOC.) "Now we have to make sure that every girl, every woman, has that moment as well. It's something everyone has the right to." In 1992 DeFrantz became a member of the IOC's 11-member executive board.

Little League

In 1974 the Little League was required to open its doors to girls. It responded by creating a softball league to channel girls away from baseball. In 1975 Nancy Winnard, one of the first girls to play Little League, was thrown out of a game—for not wearing the required protective cup on her groin. Incredibly, the Little League has no figures on how many girls now play baseball, though it does count how many play softball.

College Athletes

In 1972 the National Collegiate Athletic Association (which had opposed Title IX) was an all-male organization. Today women make up one third of NCAA athletes:

- The number of women in intercollegiate sports was 16,000 in 1962. By 1991 it had increased to 158,000.
- The most popular sports for college women are basketball, volleyball, tennis and cross-country.

Following are the top 10 women's college sports as determined by the percentage of colleges offering the sport for women:

1. basketball   96.2
2. volleyball   90.6
3. tennis   88.8
4. cross-country   82.1
5. softball   70.9
6. track   68.6
7. swimming/diving   53.6
8. soccer   41.3
9. field hockey   29.4
10. golf   25.8

Before Title IX only 2 percent of the athletics budgets were allocated to women's programs. Today it is about 30 percent. Before 1972 there were virtually no athletic scholarships for women. An estimated 10,000 women entered college on athletic scholarships in the fall of 1991.

That is not to say, however, that women are reaping the benefits Title IX had promised:

• Only 20 percent of the average athletic department's $1.3 million budget is spent on women's sports.
• Out of 646 NCAA colleges, only one—Washington State University in Pullman, Washington—has a roughly equal number of male and female athletes.
• No school has ever lost federal funding for Title IX violations.

Representative Cardiss Collins, an Illinois Democrat and chair of a House committee that held hearings on inequality in women's sports, says college presidents should go after discrimination in collegiate sports.

A February 1992 Supreme Court decision opened the way for female athletes to seek damages for discrimination in federally funded school sports programs.

Female athletes demonstrate a very healthy attitude toward sports—playing them as *part* of a holistic college experience including successful academics. College coaches say 90 to 95 percent of female athletes graduate, compared to about 50 percent for the typical freshman class. A *USA Today* survey of 257 Division I basketball programs found that women players graduate at a 60 percent rate—substantially better than that of either the student body (48 percent) or male athletes (46 percent).

In 1990 Sara Lee became the first corporation to make a major grant—$6 million—to the NCAA designated only for women's college athletics. (A smart move: 75 percent of Sara Lee products are purchased by women.)

Audiences for women's college basketball grew from 3 million in 1985 to 4 million in 1990. Starting in 1991, CBS covered the Big 10–SEC Challenge, the top women's tourney. Women's basketball should be more common on TV, says Mimi Griffin, CBS women's basketball analyst who owns a marketing agency.

"Everybody knows it's dollars that put programs on TV," says Griffin, who reports that women's basketball viewers have a $30,000 average income and are highly educated. "I don't think the people at the networks who are selling college basketball know the sports demographics."

Olympics to Pro

In 1988 almost 26 percent of the nearly 10,000 Olympic athletes worldwide were women—up from about 23 percent in 1984.

In both 1988 and in winter 1992, about 35 percent of the U.S. Olympic team was female. As noted in the introduction, women won the 5 gold medals awarded to U.S. athletes in the 1992 Winter games and took home 9 of the 11 medals Americans won. In summer 1992, women made up 37 percent of U.S. Olympians. Jackie Joyner-Kersee won her second consecutive gold medal in the heptathlon at the Barcelona Olympics. She's been called "the all-time greatest multisport athlete of either gender."

The 1992 Olympic Games introduced more new women's events—racewalking, judo, boardsailing, and canoe and kayak whitewater slalom. Yet one third of all Olympic sports remain "male only." The modern pentathlon, weight lifting, water polo, wrestling and soccer have world championships for women but are not Olympic sports. Women's softball will be added in 1996; ice hockey, in 1998.

Only synchronized swimming and rhythmic gymnastics are women-only events. And they are always the first sports the male-dominated International Olympic Committee talks about dropping, says IOC's Anita DeFrantz. "I maintain it's because they're the sports they know the least about or in which they would be less likely to be proficient."

Anita DeFrantz has been called "the most powerful woman—indeed person—in amateur sports in this country." She is the first American woman and the first American black on the IOC.

Sports: A Content Analysis

DeFrantz's Amateur Athletic Foundation (AAF) came into being as a result of a $93 million surplus after the 1984 Olympics. Under her guidance the AAF published two reports in 1991 and 1992 dealing with women athletes and media coverage—*Gender Stereotyping in Televised Sports* and *Coverage of Women's Sports in Four Daily Newspapers* (*USA Today, The Boston Globe, Orange County Register* and *The Dallas Morning News*). They found:

- Men's sports received **92** percent of airtime, women's sports, 5 percent. Gender-neutral topics had 3 percent.
- Men's sports stories in print outnumbered women's sports **23 to 1.**
- TV commentators called women tennis players by their first names **52.7** percent of the time, versus **7.8** percent for men players.
- Women athletes were often called "girls" on television, while men were never called "boys."
- **92.3** percent of sports photographs pictured men.

Among the newspapers, the report noted, *USA Today* ran significantly more women's stories and photographs than the others. Today there are many more women sportscasters and sportswriters, who can hopefully lobby for better coverage of women's sports.

Pro Ball (and Barbie)

The all-female U.S. Liberty Professional Basketball Association was scheduled to play its debut game in fall 1992. It didn't, but athletes and supporters have not given up hope yet. Some 300 U.S. women are competing in leagues abroad. American women who play pro basketball overseas can earn up to $70,000 in the seven-month season, says Bruce Levy, a women's basketball marketer and agent. "In Europe," says Levy, "the best-run and most publicized teams are run by women who own small businesses and put their money where their mouth is."

The National Fastpitch Association, a women's professional

softball league, is scheduled to start in 1994. There will be two six-team leagues, one in California, one in the Midwest.

If the idea of one sportswoman had been enacted when today's baby boom women were girls, both the softball and the basketball league might be realities today.

"Buy balls, bats and gloves for two-year-old girls," says Donna Lopiano, former All-American softball player and executive director of the Women's Sports Foundation. Lopiano, who as a youngster was picked first in her local Little League draft, was told she couldn't wear the uniform because she was a girl. "One of my personal goals," she says, "is to make sure Barbie has a line of sporting [uniforms]."

Breakthrough in the "Big Four"

In 1992 goalie Manon Rheaume, then age 20, became the first woman to play in one of the big four, all-male pro sports leagues—the National Hockey League. She debuted playing for the Tampa Bay Lightning in an exhibition game against the St. Louis Blues. Rheaume had been a leading member of the Canadian women's national team, which finished in first place in the 1992 world championship.

The Golf Boom

G. K. Chesterton called it "an expensive way of playing marbles." Mark Twain termed it "a good walk spoiled." But golf is one of the United States' fastest-growing sports: between 1988 and 1992 alone, there were 11.4 million new golfers. And women are America's newest golf nuts:

- More than one third of new golfers—37.3 percent in 1992—are women, says the National Golf Foundation (NGF). On average women have made up about 40 percent of new golfers since 1986.
- Between 1991 and 1992 alone, 1.7 million women took up golf for the first time.
- Nearly one quarter of the United States' 25 million golfers are women.
- Women golfers increased from 4.5 million in 1986 to 6.5 million in 1990.
- Although the number of golfers decreased substantially during

the economic downturn of 1991–92, there will be an estimated seven million women golfers by 1995.

Some women—about 10 percent—say they sometimes feel unwelcome by male golfers. If so, the men better get used to women on the green. All the trends show women golfers are here to stay.

Who are today's women golfers?

Older women, homemakers, businesswomen and teens are all taking up the game. Women golfers in their 20's increased 50 percent between 1986 and 1990. But the average woman golfer is 43 years old; 72 percent have attended college or earned a degree.

John Jacobs's Practical Golf Schools, based in Arizona, had 100,000 students in 1991 and is the country's largest golf school. The number of women students soared from 5 percent in 1984 to 40 percent in 1991.

One of golf's attractions is that you need not be a 26-year-old jock to have fun. It is easy on knees and ankles already torn up by skiing and jogging. "The baby boomers have played tennis and racquetball and done their marathons, but now their bodies are wearing out," says Shelby Futch, director and cofounder of the John Jacobs's Practical Golf Schools.

Business or Pleasure?

Only about 6 percent of women *started* golfing for business reasons. But the percentage is much higher among new young-adult golfers. Women in their 30's, for example, are twice as likely to play golf for business reasons. That proportion could grow even more after women read the following: 81 percent of Fortune 500 chief executives play golf; 70 percent conduct business at the golf course, according to a NGF survey.

Beverly Robsham, president of a Boston executive outplacement firm, took up golf after years of declining clients' invitations. Robsham, 52, is "crazy about the game," and installed a putting green in her office. Golf, she says, opened the doors at three companies where she sought business.

"It's not the business you do on the golf course that's most important," says Jan Thompson, marketing vice president at Mazda Motor of America. "It's the relationships you build . . . that become friendships later."

Some women take up golf to reach out to older male business

contacts. Says Ann Dean, a vice president at Boston's Shawmut Bank, golf "has really helped in crossing a boundary, especially with older male customers . . . it's kind of a bonding game, where you are able to go out and talk business."

But as the women's golf boom continues, it will be women-to-women deal-making on the green.

In May 1991 the first Golf Clinic for the Executive Woman was held in Bethesda, Maryland. Mazda hosted the one-day outing for 150 women seeking to improve their golf skills. Mazda held six clinics in 1992 and plans nine similar outings in other cities in 1993.

"I hope to use golf to do business in the future," said Cathleen Black, CEO of the American Newspaper Publishers Association. "You can be very productive with business, spending four hours on a golf course."

"Most of my friends are now taking up golf," says Mary Lou Bohn, a senior communications manager at Titleist and Foot-Joy Worldwide in New Bedford, Massachusetts. "They're finding that . . . a lot of different people have golf outings."

"I practice every day and play every weekend," says Joanne Beyer, a Bellevue, Washington, real estate agent who took up golf for business reasons and got hooked. "Golf is a fabulous hobby and it has definitely helped me in my business . . . when the opportunity presents itself, I pass around my business cards."

"As more and more women move up in the executive ranks . . . they're finding out that golf is a sport you can do business over," says Mary Jo Jacobi, an executive with New York's Marine Midland Bank and LPGA Tour chair. "That means more interest in our tour, and a demographic that corporate sponsors and television people can't afford to ignore."

Women's biggest problem is finding the time and patience to learn. It is a two-year commitment, says Jane Blalock, retired LPGA star. "Putting is 43 percent of your score," says pro Julie Ann Cole. "Women need to be better than men from within 100 yards of the hole because we can't hit the ball as far."

Every woman who has endured teasing from male golfers, take heart: in 1990 Juli Inkster of Los Altos, California, defeated 85 male pros to become the first female winner of the Spalding Invitational Pro-Am at Pebble Beach, the only pro golf tournament where men and women compete together.

Coaching

Since Title IX, opportunities for female athletes have expanded, but women coaches have lost ground. In 1972 more than 90 percent of women's teams were coached and run by women. But by 1991 women made up less than 50 percent of the 5,718 coaches of women's teams at NCAA schools and 15.9 percent of administrators. Of course, the number of women's teams has increased dramatically since 1972. Nevertheless, some women are angry that, as women's sports grew in money and prestige, more men got jobs coaching women. Did men get these jobs because they are more experienced? Not according to a 1990 study by Cynthia Hasbrook of the University of Wisconsin at Milwaukee, who found that women's qualifications, experience and training are as solid as men's.

There is another factor, however: so far, women athletes *like* male coaches. Mary Jo Kane, an associate professor of kinesiology and leisure at the University of Minnesota, says, "A few limited studies suggest some elite female athletes prefer to be coached by males rather than females."

Women "are used to seeing men as coaches, so they expect it," says Linda Delano, director of women's athletics at St. Paul's Hamline University. Researcher Hasbrook says until a lot more women become highly visible as coaches, "we're going to associate sports with men instead of women."

"Women deserve the best coach available, man or woman," says Ann Koger, head tennis and volleyball coach at Haverford (Pennsylvania) College.

"Gender, race or age shouldn't dictate a person's coaching ability," says Tara VanDerveer, head women's basketball coach at 1992 national champion Stanford University. "The issue should be qualifications."

But there *is* a case for women coaching women.

"If there's a woman who's qualified, I think she'd be preferable to an equally qualified man," concedes Coach Koger. "Women are more nurturing. . . . They also help women respect one another and enjoy the program.

"Post–Title IX, many women coaches have felt they have to imitate a man's coaching style—talking loudly, emphasizing win/loss and being a little more abrupt," says Koger. "Now, though, women are beginning to realize they don't have to imitate men to be successful."

Women Coaching Men

Very few women coach men.

As of January 1992, only 86 of 847 NCAA programs were headed by women: seven in Division 1, 21 in Division 2 and 58 in Division 3.

- Bernadette Locke-Mattox, assistant men's basketball coach at the University of Kentucky, is the only female assistant coach of a major men's team.
- In 1992 Amy Machin-Ward, former North Carolina All-American, became the first woman to coach men's soccer when she joined Denver's Regis University.
- Barbara Hedges, head of athletics at the University of Washington in Seattle, which had the United States' number one football team in the 1991–92 season, is the first woman to run a major university athletic department and the first woman to run a department with an NCAA Division 1-A football team. She hires coaches for men's and women's teams.

"A woman has been in space. Women are prime ministers. They're doing everything—but they can't coach? It boggles my mind," says Stanford coach Tara VanDerveer.

Glamour has urged a woman be named to coach a prominent men's basketball team and recommended several qualified candidates: Pat Summitt of the University of Tennessee, whose women's team won the NCAA championship three times; Debbie Ryan of the University of Virginia in Charlottesville; and Stanford's Tara VanDerveer.

Once a woman coaches a major men's team, says VanDerveer, it "would be like the four-minute mile. Once broken, it won't be that big a deal."

New Career Track: Sports Executive

Women may be losing out to men in coaching jobs, but a few have recently attained prominent positions in sports administration. In 1991 Judith Sweet, 44, athletic director at the University of California, San Diego, was elected the first woman president of the NCAA. There are hopes that her visible position and support will help women coaches get good jobs. "It's important to me that opportunities for women and minorities are a part of the agenda," she says.

- The Red Sox's Elaine Weddington, the first female assistant general manager in major league baseball, drafts player contracts and oversees compliance with the rules governing trades and minor-to-major league transfers.
- Susan O'Malley, named president of the Washington Bullets basketball team in 1991, is one of the highest-ranking women in professional sports.
- Georgia Frontiere owns the NFL's Los Angeles Rams. Marge Schott owns the major league baseball team the Cincinnati Reds.
- Linda Bogdan was the first female college scout in the National Football League.

Female Trainers

Women are moving into the field of athletic training, which delivers the first medical care athletes receive.

- In the past five years, more women than men have become certified trainers.
- Women make up nearly half, 44 percent, of the National Athletic Trainers Association (NATA).
- Between 1990 and September 30, 1992, 3,316 women joined the NATA, compared to 3,176 men.

Today there are only three female trainers in professional sports, but their ranks will increase as middle-aged male trainers retire.

"On the pro level, there are very few jobs to start with, and the middle-aged guys who have those jobs hold onto them," says Cal State-Northridge head trainer Rhonda Lowry, 32, who became California's first female trainer in 1983.

Sportswomen to Watch

Mountain Mistress

In 1975 Japanese Junko Tabei became the first woman to reach the top of Mount Everest. If a man had been leading the group, she says, she would not have made it. "A woman is unsentimental about another woman's endurance," she says. "A man could never drive a woman to her limits. It was the other women members of the team who drove me on."

After climbing Vinson Massif in Antarctica, she became the first woman to climb the highest mountains on six of the earth's seven continents. "When I die," she says, "I want to look back and know that my life was interesting. I want to leave behind a personal history."

Top Jockey

In 1993 about 11 percent of the licensed jockeys in the United States were women. The top female jockey is Julie Krone, whose lifetime earnings total about $50 million. She has won 2,660 races as of spring 1993.

"Krone rides with daring and verve that often seems to be reflected in the performances of the horses beneath her," wrote Paul Moran in *Newsday*. "They seem to respond, whatever the circumstances, to her daring, her willingness to take chances, and her determined, strong finishing style."

"She can ride with any jockey in the country," says all-time leading rider Willie Shoemaker, Krone's idol. He should know. In 1988 Krone beat him at Minnesota's Canterbury Downs. Shoemaker, a quadriplegic after a 1991 car accident, is said to drive his wheelchair "as if he were again riding two-time Horse of the Year John Henry."

Speed Server

Michelle Gilman ranks first in the Women's Pro Racquetball Association (1992). Her 165-mile-per-hour serve helped her win five national and world racquetball titles in 1989. Michelle in her early twenties is already eligible for the Racquetball Hall of Fame, but inductees must be at least 35 years old, so she must wait more than a decade!

Adventure

The American Women's Trans-Antarctic Expedition (AWE) was the first all-female trek across the Antarctic and the first without motor vehicles or dogsleds.

In fall 1992 AWE members Ann Bancroft of St. Paul, Sue Giller and Anne Dal Vera of Colorado and Sunniva Sorby of San Diego dragged 200-pound packs on sleds loaded with supplies for 660 miles, with constant headwinds of up to 50 miles per hour.

AWE raised $500,000 in grass-roots fund-raising and went $400,000 into debt. No corporations wanted to fund an all-female Antarctic expedition. Marlboro expressed interest, but the team didn't want support from a tobacco company. "What if you girls got hurt down there," one male executive said. It would look bad for his company's image.

The women stopped at the South Pole for weather and health reasons. Ann Bancroft became the first woman to reach both poles across the ice. (In 1986 she reached the North Pole by dogsled with the Steger International Polar Expedition.)

"We did it to challenge ourselves," says Sunniva Sorby, "and to encourage other women to challenge themselves."

Women's Adventure Travel

Today about 10 percent of travel falls in the adventure category, including more than 5,000 outfitters and travel agencies. Woman-only outdoor travel has become enormously popular.

Says Patricia Hubbard, editor of the magazine *Outdoor Woman,* "When women go on co-ed, heavy-duty trips, they often allow the men to be the leaders. With all-women trips, duties are totally shared. This gives the participating women a greater feeling of what adventure is all about."

"It's less intimidating to participate in a women-only trip," says Sally McCoy, vice president of equipment at The North Face, who has led trips for female employees. "A variety of women participate, from regular backpackers to women who have never slept in a tent before."

- Overseas Adventure Travel of Cambridge, Massachusetts, offers "Women's Cross-Cultural Adventures" to Tibet, Nepal, Bolivia and the Land of the Masai.
- Outdoor Vacations for Women Over 40 of Groton, Massachusetts, teaches women to sail in Key West, Florida, and raft in Costa Rica.
- Womantrek of Seattle began in 1983 when Bonnie Bordas led the first all-female bicycle tour of China. Now it offers trips to more than 30 countries.

People return from a Womantrek trip with a sense of accomplishment: "Back in civilization, the triumphant screams of running the rapids would echo in our ears," writes Hollis Giammatteo, a writing teacher at Seattle's Antioch University after a Woman-trek river trip. "We had experienced our strength, and pooled it and tested it."

Womanship of Annapolis, Maryland, which has schools in the Chesapeake Bay, Florida, the Northeast and the Pacific Northwest, has taught women to sail for just seven years, but was voted the second-best sailing school in the U.S. in 1991.

Since 1977 Minneapolis-based Woodswomen has taken women dogsledding, canoeing, hiking, rafting, skiing and biking in the Midwest, Nepal, Alaska, the Grand Canyon, the Alps and Mexico. Participants from various skill levels range in age from 20 to over 70.

"We're a cross between a spa and Outward Bound," says Debbie Sturgess of The Challenges in Glendale, Arizona, which offers biking, kayaking and hiking in Arizona and volcanoes in Maui. "You get luxury at night—gourmet vegetarian cuisine in a five-star resort—plus lots of outside activity during the day."

"Health-conscious people don't want to just sit," says Pat Halty, whose All Adventure Travel, in Boulder, Colorado, has grown from 150 clients four years ago to more than 1,000. "Baby boomers don't want to take a cruise and gain five pounds or veg out on a beach. Lots of older people walk every day and like the idea of hiking instead of getting bused from cathedral to cathedral."

Women's Week

"Women approach skiing differently than men do," says Elissa Slanger, who pioneered the idea of women's ski seminars in 1975. "They bring a different value system to skiing. Physical strength and style of movement also differ."

Almost every major ski resort now offers three-day to one-week seminars designed for and taught by women in an atmosphere where critiquing is positive and constructive. Small groups with the same skill levels ski five hours a day, learning through goal-setting, instruction and videotaping.

Squaw Valley USA in California hosts Slanger's Women's Way Ski Seminars, three- and five-day programs.

Janet Spangler, founder of Women's Ski Experience at Okemo Mountain in Ludlow, Vermont, says women avoid risking failure. "They tend to wait until they can perform a technique with finesse before moving on to the next challenge." She tries to get women to change the idea of "fear" to "thrill." Skiing is an opportunity to handle difficult or intimidating situations, she says, and to stop placing limits on one's self.

When 45-year-old Bonnie Jones enrolled in an Okemo women's ski seminar, she had not skied in 20 years, but the program gave her the confidence to head for the steeper slopes. "I found I could take up this activity at my age and do it well enough to satisfy myself," she says.

"Our original goal was to keep women interested in skiing, but we have achieved more than that. Women come back year after year to make new friends and move on to the next level," says Annie Vareille Savath, director of Telluride (Colorado) Ski School, which offers three- and five-day women's programs.

The goals of Telluride's Women's Week are 1) greater achievement in fun and skiing ability; 2) self-confidence through overcoming fear; 3) learning up-to-date techniques; 4) eliminating negative thoughts; 5) achieving body/mind integration; and 6) making new friends.

Equipment and Advertising

Women spent $21.2 billion on athletic footwear and apparel in 1991, versus $19.8 billion for men. That is an astounding statistic, considering we still think of men as the jocks.

It is a huge women's market, but evidence suggests it may not be serving its customers.

- Athletic shoes are one third of U.S. footwear purchases—400 million pairs a year, yet many manufacturers offer only one width.
- *Outdoor Woman*'s Patricia Hubbard asks "why a manufacturer of fishing clothes would think women want a fly-fishing vest with a floral inside."

"Women are starting to think of themselves as strong and capable," says Sally Edwards, founder of Fleet Feet stores, a $17 million athletic footwear and apparel chain. Women want ads to deliver that message. Often, they do not. "An ad featuring a model in Lycra was probably chosen by the male executives at the ad agency and the sporting goods company," says Kathy Button, Converse's director of marketing communications.

Charlotte Moore worked on the enormously successful "Just Do It" campaign for Nike at the Weiden and Kennedy Agency. Previously, she says, "the agency had a lot of male teams that were very successful at talking to men, but they weren't motivating woman to buy shoes."

About 30 percent of Nike footwear and athletic apparel is sold to women, but the company is after an even greater market share. Print ads aimed at women continue to connect self-esteem and exercise. "You're so emotional" and "This is a Goddess, you're not a Goddess," have evolved out of the initial "Just Do It" approach. Nike is fairly confident the campaign is reaching women and increasing market share: the company has received more than 45,000 favorable responses to the ads.

Some retailers are finally getting smart enough to begin understanding and catering to the women's sports market.

Missy Park, who previously worked for The North Face and Fisher Mountain Bike, founded Title 9 Sports, a mail-order catalog of products for women based in Berkeley, California. "For every 10 products we look at, we take maybe one," says Parks, whose firm tests products on women with five different body types. Revenues increased 25 percent in 1992.

"We feel that there's more long-term potential in the women's business," says Julie Whiteaker, product manager of InSport apparel. "All the statistics show that the women's market is where the growth is."

How Women Are Changing Sports

Sports enhance women's self-esteem, well-being and competence. But there is more. Just as women are creating a new leadership style in business (see page 97) and reintegrating the Sacred Feminine in religion (see Chapters 4 and 9), they are changing sports by introducing caring, cooperation and tolerance. Sportswomen are sensitive to people whose early attempts were frozen in ridicule. They want everyone from awkward middle-aged amateurs to the physically challenged to have fun.

Female coaches echo the words of the new female management gurus who "reject the star system." They seek to develop all team members.

Susan Schafer, a Colorado consultant, lectured the Women's

Basketball Association and drew on the early business advice advocating that women operate like men. But she ran into trouble. The coaches rejected the male model outright: "Don't you have another vision?" they asked.

Mariah Nelson says the female approach to sports

- rejects the battle, enemy mentality of the military sports model;
- rejects the notion that humiliating a player is how to "get the best out of her";
- emphasizes nonviolence, discourages play when athletes are injured;
- empowers, encourages and supports players;
- is inclusionary, adjusts the rules to include players of different skill levels.

This new breed of sportswoman particularly rejects Vince Lombardi's "Winning isn't everything; it's the only thing." So did the coach himself, who lived to retract the statement. "I wish to hell I'd never said that damn thing. . . . I sure as hell didn't mean for people to crush human values and morality."

"Winning is the only thing" is becoming "Playing is the only thing."

A fine example is Katie Donovan's American Coaching Effectiveness Program, whose philosophy is athletes first, winning second. More than 100,000 mostly male coaches have trained in the program. First they resist, she reports, but eventually she wins them over, and it is very emotional. Men come up and say, "I've been doing it all wrong. I've been harming my kids."

How Sports Are Changing Women

"Soccer has changed my whole personality," says Shari La France of the "World's Oldest Women's Soccer Team" in Minneapolis—which started when a group of women age 30 to 54 watched their daughters play soccer and decided they wanted to play, too. "Playing soccer has given me self-confidence and assertiveness that has carried over to other parts of my life."

Donna Coombs, 44, a health-marketing executive with Burbank Hospital in central Massachusetts, was a thirtysomething secretary to the hospital vice president when she took up racquetball—and became a good player. "I played with administrators and physicians, almost all men, and a fair amount of the time, I won," she says. "I could feel people's perceptions about me change." She was getting noticed and earning respect.

"My boss's sense of my capabilities was greatly enhanced," says Donna. "He saw how competitive and determined I could be." Shortly after, he recommended her for an in-house leadership/communication program, and her breakthrough from secretary to manager was well under way. "Sports showed *me* I was competitive enough to succeed," she says.

Race-car driver Lyn St. James says competitive driving changed her from a shy girl to a confident businesswoman. The first woman to win the International Motor Sports Association Camel GTO series, she holds many speed records. Her lap speed of 212.5 miles per hour was the women's record.

"Two hundred twelve! I can't believe a woman can drive that fast," exclaimed interviewer Mike Haffner. "Well, you see, the car doesn't know I'm a woman," St. James responded. She finished eleventh in the 1992 Indianapolis 500, her first time in the race; she was the top rookie finisher.

"Many women in law or business become devastated when they lose," says San Francisco lawyer Linda Stoick. "Their whole self-esteem is wrapped up in being competent and thorough. It's important to learn that winning and losing are all part of the system." Stoick says sports taught her it's okay to lose.

No Risk/No Reward

Miami attorney Sue Cobb was age 50, a wife and mother of two with about five years' climbing experience when she accepted a 1988 invitation from the Wyoming Centennial Everest Expedition to be part of their summit team. There was a chance she would be the first U.S. woman to reach the top. She anticipated and even savored the contrast between her comfortable life and loving family and the rigors of the expedition. Yet, she says, "there is no way I could have prepared myself emotionally for what I experienced. No way."

Her team faced avalanches, bitter early winter storms and lack of oxygen—more than seven weeks at altitudes above 17,000 feet, many days above 20,000 feet. They employed no Sherpas; everyone carried her or his own gear and supplies.

Sue battled three bouts of hypothermia, utter exhaustion and the creeping effects of lack of oxygen, which can cause fatal errors of judgment. As the group left base camp to begin the final assault, they received word that Portland's Stacy Allison had become the first U.S. woman to "summit."

Ultimately, 3,000 feet short of the almost 30,000-foot summit Sue Cobb was forced to retreat. Even returning 15 miles to base camp alone and weak, Cobb put her life at risk. After October snowstorms destroyed the group's high camps, the expedition sadly but officially began their retreat.

Totally restored today and ever upbeat, Sue Cobb is a dynamic, happy woman. "Never let the fear of failure put limits on you," she now tells audiences of young people. "The biggest cause of failure is the fear that others—including people you don't even know—will not hold you in high esteem. You just can't let someone else control *your* actions by what they *might* think."

Taking risks, she says, brings the exhilarating and awesome highs and the terribly disappointing lows—but both greatly enrich the middle ground of everyday life where we all live. What Sue took away from what in her case were life-threatening risks was great physical and emotional confidence, an unbelievable appreciation of her husband and sons and a palpable sense of how much friends and team members cared and supported her. Has she since faced a challenge remotely as fierce? "Not yet," she says with a smile.

New Route to Corporate Leadership

We believe in the "fits and starts" model of career development. Success does not follow a predictable continuum. After five unglamorous years of persistence and discipline comes a great breakthrough. Overwork too long and you crash and burn.

Contrary to conventional wisdom (and studies that supposedly prove it), we believe most women who take five years off to raise children damage their lifelong careers not one bit. Some careers will span 50 years, from age 22 to 72. **A women thriving on postmenopausal zest can accomplish three years of work in one.** Her colleague who has dutifully reported to work every day for 30 years may be totally stale.

Much is made of the scarcity of women in the top echelon of business. And of the competition too many baby-boom middle managers will face in achieving top executive positions. Wouldn't it be the supreme irony if the *fastest* way to the CEO's chair was to take time off—not to finish your MBA but to master a sport? To climb one of the world's highest mountains? Run a marathon? Learn to play a great game of golf?

What if the self-confidence and risk taking learned in the process was the "inexplicable" extra that made you stand out from the pack whether or not you actually practice your sport in a business setting?

American business has shifted the state-of-the-art from the management to the leadership model. Who you are as an individual, your courage and integrity, matter more today than ever before. Your company needs another predictable, uncreative workaholic like a hole in the head. Take a risk. Become the leader you were meant to be. Sports might be women's new route to corporate leadership.

3.
Women at Work: Opportunity, Leadership and Balance

Whenever we bullishly describe the "Decade of Women in Leadership" megatrend and predict that women will break through to top corporate posts this decade, our audiences, while enthusiastic, eventually raise this objection: why aren't there more women leading Fortune 500 companies *now*?

Scan the 1993 *Fortune* magazine list; there is but one woman CEO—the formidable Linda Wachner of Warnaco. That is proof, some would tell you, that women cannot make it in the top echelons of U.S. business, the implication being that they never will.

It gets worse. A report published in 1991 by the Feminist Majority Foundation showed that of the 6,502 corporate officers in the Fortune 500 at the level of vice president or above, only 175 were women.

The study went on to say it would take "475 years" before women reached corporate equality with men. Are the pessimists right? Is the glass ceiling intact? Will women forever be barred from the boardrooms of American business? We certainly do *not* think so.

The Feminist Majority is quoted frequently in this book, and we understand that it is their job to prod corporations to open top jobs to women. But that 475-year figure is just ridiculous. It is based on straight-line extrapolation at present rates, and no social scientists today think change happens in such a linear fashion. Change starts out slowly in fits and starts, sometimes even reversing itself, and then builds to an explosive critical mass. Look at Eastern Europe and the Soviet Union and apartheid.

But there is another issue at stake here: we believe it is high time to question the whole Fortune 500 mentality.

Here's why:

1. The Fortune 500 is an outdated, inappropriate standard by which to measure business success. It is *not* the most dynamic, or even the biggest, part of the U.S. economy. Small to mid-size firms make up a much, much greater percent of the U.S. GDP than the Fortune 500.
2. More than 6.5 million women today lead small-to-medium-size growth businesses that will *become* the top companies of the future.
3. Today's Fortune 500 will not resemble the 2002 list. Today's senior executives will retire in the 1990's. Just below them is a cadre of female talent age 35–45 that will break into CEO and senior executive positions by decade's end.

Remember "term limits" from Chapter 1? CEOs and other top executives are *compelled* to retire in most large companies by age 65, often earlier; that opens the way for younger people, many of whom are women.

"If you look at the ranks of any major corporation below the top 20 people," says Lester Korn of Korn/Ferry International, "you'll find that 50 percent of the next group of managers are women."

Today those women are ready to make their move. Korn predicts women will break through into top posts between 1995 and 2000. The cutting edge of the baby boom, the first generation of women to have lifelong full-time careers outside the home, will have 25 or 30 years of business experience around the year 2000. Harvard Business School professor Regina Herzlinger says women will become Fortune 500 CEOs in *large* numbers around 2010.

It is time women abandoned the Fortune 500 as the only criterion for business success. Bigger is not better. At best, the Fortune 500 is an outdated symbol. At worst, it represents a stagnant, bureaucratic sector of U.S. business.

Here is a smashing statistic to replace it with: **in 1992 women-owned businesses surpassed the Fortune 500 in numbers of people employed.** While the Fortune 500 has lost 4 million jobs since 1980, women-owned businesses have been generating new jobs every year. Furthermore, while the Fortune 500 figures partly reflect jobs outside the United States, most of the women's businesses generate jobs in the United States. That is the finding of a study by Cognetics, Inc., of Cambridge, Massachusetts, and the National Foundation for Women Business Owners.

There you have it, and you can quote them on it.

Where Women Are Succeeding—and How

This chapter, the longest in *Megatrends for Women,* is organized according to three themes: opportunity, leadership and balance.

First, we describe the great **opportunities** for women at work today. Whether you aspire to be a CEO, restaurateur or health-care executive, the trends we describe will instruct your plans. We also outline the new areas where entrepreneurial women will venture in the 1990's. Women are breaking into male-dominated fields from sportswriting to police work, yet the growing opportunity and financial reward in a traditional female job such as nursing may surprise you.

The great wave of female economic activity has generated a compelling new approach to **leadership**, extensively described in this chapter. It rejects military-style authoritarian management in favor of an approach that supports and empowers people, thereby increasing both productivity and profits. From Peter Drucker to Tom Peters, male management gurus applaud the Women's Leadership style.

But for some, success has not come without the costs of overwork, burnout and potential damage to health and relationships. The next great challenge for millions of women is maintaining success while restructuring their lifestyles for greater balance. We describe the trend data, role models and corporate policies that will help women integrate **balance** into work life.

The Megatrends List of Hot Career Areas for Women

What *are* the best careers for women? The best industries? What are the best businesses for women entrepreneurs? Following is our list of career areas, specific jobs and entrepreneurial opportunities.

1. Your dream job
2. CEO/Entrepreneur
3. Health Care

1. *Your Personal Dream Job*   Fulfillment

"Hot jobs" lists invariably analyze the demand side: how many accountants, surgeons or teachers the economy will need by, say, 2010. We shall cite projections like that, too, and place them in the larger context of the megatrends.

But first, a big caveat: don't get too carried away with society's needs. What about your needs, talents and desires for creative self-expression?

If your dream job is fashion designer, anchorwoman or U.S. senator, what do you care what the "high growth jobs" are? Many dream jobs offer no growth in the 1990's, and the competition to land them will be murder.

In the practical matter of choosing one's work, we believe the best advice is to follow your heart and be "impractical." People who love their work have a better chance at success. And if the projections of economists (or trend forecasters) are wrong, you have not wasted time on a job that is boring as hell.

Rule number one is follow your dream.

The title of an inspiring, well-written book by Marsha Sinetar says it all: *Do What You Love, the Money Will Follow* (Dell). It is a step-by-step guide to transforming a dream into economic reality.

2. *Chief Executive Officer/Entrepreneur*   Power

There are two ways to the CEO's chair: 1) the corporate route: draw up a 5- or 10-year plan to gather the skills for the top-executive job you hope to land in, say, 1998 or 2003, and 2) the entrepreneurial approach: start your own business now.

Both will continue to be major growth areas.

The job category "general managers and top executives" is a hot number six on the Bureau of Labor Statistics' list of the occupations that will create the *most new jobs.* Between 1990 and 2005 BLS projects the United States will need 600,000 *new* managers and top executives, swelling their ranks to 3.7 million.

Jill Eikann Barad, president and chief operating officer of Mattel, made her mark in girls' toys, primarily expanding the Barbie line. Mattel sales were $1.8 billion in 1992, a 14 percent increase over 1991.

"Would I like to be CEO one day?" asks Barad. "Absolutely. But do I fantasize of what it would be like? No. I'm very focused on what I have to do next—very focused."

Turi Josefen, executive vice president of U.S. Surgical, earned $23.6 million in 1991, more than her CEO made, and would have ranked number three on *Business Week's* 1992 listing of the highest paid CEOs if CEOs and non-CEOs were ranked together.

It is especially noteworthy because so many high-growth jobs are *not* prestigious or well paying—janitors and maids, waiters and waitresses and general clerical workers make the list, too.

The Entrepreneurial Woman

Women-owned business is one of the fastest-growing segments of the U.S. economy. The Small Business Administration (SBA) counts about 5 million women-owned businesses, and predicts women will own nearly 40 percent (others say half) of small businesses by 2000.

According to the National Foundation of Women Business Owners, however, the number of women-owned or controlled businesses grew 20 percent in 1992 to more than 6.5 million. Three women head companies with revenues of more than $1 billion a year. In 1992 women-owned businesses employed more than 12 million people and the Fortune 500, 11.7 million. The Fortune 500 is losing at least 200,000 to 300,000 jobs every year. **Women-owned businesses employ more people domestically than the Fortune 500 do worldwide.**

Entrepreneurial Woman says Arizona, California, Colorado, Florida, Illinois, Massachusetts, Minnesota, New York, Pennsylvania and Wisconsin are the best 10 states for women-owned businesses.

The track record of women in business is simply spectacular:

• In 1977, 2 million female-owned businesses had $25 billion in sales. By 1988 women owned 5 million businesses with revenues of $83 billion.

- From 1980 to 1988 the number of entrepreneurs increased 56 percent overall, but the number of female entrepreneurs grew 82 percent.
- In the same time frame entrepreneurial revenues grew 56 percent overall, but those of female entrepreneurs soared 129 percent.

(That litany will be even more impressive once SBA can supply more up-to-date figures.)

Why Women Win

Women are cautious, "strategic" risk takers, whose resourcefulness and resolve increase as circumstances become more difficult, said a study by Avon Corporation and New Work Decision, a research firm. Women business owners are *more likely to succeed,* says Janet Harris-Lange, president of the National Association of Women Business Owners, because women admit they need help and surround themselves with good people.

"A woman would no more let her business fail than she would let someone kill her child," says Beatrice Fitzpatrick, founder and president of the American Women's Economic Development Corporation in New York, which has assisted or trained 100,000 women in the past 15 years.

How Women's Businesses Will Grow

"Women's attitudes about team building and consensus are much more geared to leading through growth stages of businesses than men's are," says Edward Moldt of the University of Pennsylvania's Wharton School of Finance and Management. Professor Moldt says women will soon develop a lot more businesses in the $50 million-to-$100 million-a-year category.

"This thing is really a stair-step kind of a process," he says. "You get comfortable with running a business at a certain level and say, 'Gee, I can do more than that.' Then you step up to another size. That's the way men have done it . . . it just takes a period of time to get comfortable running a business."

The big growth industries—finance, health care, technology—and many smaller niches, from catering to carpentry to the arts, represent key areas for the entrepreneur who wants to be a CEO—now.

But advising an entrepreneur what business to start is usually not a great idea. Most know exactly what they want—to satisfy an unmet need by supplying a product they love or a service they perform spectacularly. Who has more unmet needs than working women? The whole range of products and services for working women have been underexploited. From child care to healthy dinners for the microwave, there are millions of profitable niches.

Businesses and Services for Working Women

Conservative estimates put the child-care industry well above the $15 billion-a-year mark. Today's mini–baby boom will soon double that figure.

There are 80,000 licensed day-care centers in the United States and another 118,000 regulated day-care providers, says the U.S. Department of Education. But the current supply of child-care services meets only half the demand, says Scholastic, Inc., publisher of *Pre-K Today*.

Clearly there are great opportunities in day care itself, but there is also a market for *information-based* companies in the day-care business.

Suzanne Schmidt started Monday Morning, Inc., in Bridgewater, New Jersey, to "add professionalism to what used to be a cottage industry." She matches career women with experienced day-care providers who take no more than five children per home. The firm has 150 day-care providers in New Jersey. In 1990 the company began to franchise. It now has operations in New York, Chicago and the Washington, D.C., area. Revenues in 1992 were $2.2 million, up 12 percent from 1991.

Monday Morning has an additional 102 providers in four franchises. The company was listed in the *Business Journal of New Jersey* as among the top 50 fastest-growing private companies in New Jersey. Schmidt was the highest-ranking woman on the list.

Special Care

The aging population and the need to cut health-care costs are creating a boom in home health care. Jean Griswold is founder and CEO of Special Care, a Philadelphia-based provider of home care to the elderly, handicapped and children, with 32 offices in seven states. Griswold, who is confined to a wheelchair because of multiple sclerosis, shows how a disabling disease is no match for a determined entrepreneur. "Being an entrepreneur is a state of mind, not body," she says. The wife of a minister, she saw firsthand how much elderly people need companions. Visiting nurses can stay only a few hours, but Special Care's more than 3,000 nurse's aides help with baths, shopping and companionship—and can serve around the clock.

3. Health Care   Growth and Caring

Any look at the boom industries of the 1990's must begin with health care—an $800 billion-a-year business that will soon reach *$1 trillion a year*. From technician to physician, from unskilled worker to Ph.D. researcher, from administrator and marketing whiz, there are lots of opportunities in health care.

There were 8.4 million health-care workers in 1990. In 1990 *alone* medical employment grew 7.7 percent—the largest for *any major job category*. All signs point to even more growth.

The Bureau of Labor Statistics says 6 of the 10 fastest-growing occupations from 1990 to 2005 will be in health care: home health aides, personal and home-care aides, physical therapists, medical assistants, radiologic technicians and medical secretaries.

These jobs are growing fastest in terms of *percentage*. The number of new jobs created is even more impressive. The medical-assistants category will increase 74 percent, which means about 122,000 new jobs.

That said, the need for nurses is awesome (see also pages 77–79). The United States needs 767,000 more nurses by 2005, not enough of a *percentage* increase to put nursing atop the "fastest growing" list, which, in this case, is a meaningless distinction.

Today there is a shortage of 17,000 pharmacists, but, says SRI International, that figure will double in the next 15 years. Average annual salaries exceed $40,000. If the shortage is that bad, look for salaries to grow.

Technology, the aging population and health-care investment all guarantee that health employment will climb. "Because of advances, patients are likely to undergo more tests and diagnostic procedures, take more drugs, see more specialists and be subjected to more aggressive treatments than before," says Valerie A. Personick, a BLS economist.

Technology usually displaces workers. Not in health care, where it only leads to *more* technicians. Says Connie R. Curran, a consultant and nurse, "The nurse is caring for a much sicker patient and is also caring for the machine."

"As long as the dollars spent on health care keep increasing, employment will continue to grow," says economist Eli Ginzberg of Columbia University.

The Health-Care Entrepreneur

In 1983, Karen Behnke, 26, armed with statistics on how much unhealthy employees cost employers, approached the human resources director at California's Pacific Gas & Electric and made him an offer he could not refuse: for the price of one executive physical exam, she would deliver an entire prevention program. Execu-Fit Health Programs, which designs, markets and delivers corporate health programs, was born.

"I convinced him that if we could prevent one heart attack, it would pay for the program for 10 years," she says. "I would go out and sell the program, then once I'd sold it, I'd create it," says Behnke. "Then I'd deliver it and I'd stay up all night typing each employee's health-risk-assessment report."

Three years later, after two male doctors from Los Angeles invested in the firm and became medical advisers, Execu-Fit became profitable. In August 1991 Behnke sold her firm to PacifiCare, one of California's largest HMOs. She is still president, and Execu-Fit has more than 100 corporate clients.

Karen Behnke's Execu-Fit is only one prototype of the millions of new businesses that will be created in health care in the 1990's.

4. Finance   Fast-Track/Results

Finance is one of the best places for women. Even an unreconstructed good ole boy is a sucker for sound financial results. More than half of U.S. accountants are women. Women make up 46 percent of financial managers in the United States. And one half of the nation's 14,000 credit unions are headed by women, says the Credit Union National Association. "Banking and financial services have been very good to women," says recruiter Lester Korn. Even so, women make up only 2 to 5 percent of commodities traders.

Working Woman listed international accountant as a hot career for 1991 and 1992. That fits with megatrends like the rise of the Pacific Rim and post-1992 Europe. Robert Half International reports the need for international accountants has grown 200 percent since 1980, and that growth will continue.

Finance is a fast track to top management, says John Challenger, vice president of the outplacement firm Challenger, Gray & Christmas. Judy C. Lewent, age 43, chief financial officer at Merck & Company, the world's largest drug firm, may be a prime example. She oversees $1 billion in pension funds and $2.5 billion in other investments.

Discount broker Muriel "Mickie" Siebert, the first woman to hold a seat on the New York Stock Exchange, celebrated her 25th anniversary there in 1992.

A *Business Week* survey of male and female MBAs from the top 20 business schools showed the narrowest wage gap was in finance— there women earned only 3.3 percent less than men.

One third of the 74 full-time professionals in the research department of Shearson Lehman Brothers are women. Shearson's high-profile market analyst, Elaine Garzarelli, who predicted Wall Street's October 1987 crash and 1991's bull market, earns a reported $1.5 million-a-year income.

Women succeed in fields where results are easily *measurable,* says business professor Judy B. Rosener, whose work on leadership is described later. One woman Rosener studied said her colleagues neither understood nor liked her leadership style, but, the woman said, "They love the profits I generate."

Finance is also a top choice for women who want to go it alone. "We are going to be a significant factor in the municipal-bond market in 1990 and beyond," says Phylis M. Esposito, who, with Robin L. Weissmann, Sandra Alworth and Aimee Brown, left established financial houses to start Artemis Capital Group. New clients, of course, will be a top priority. Appropriately, the new firm is named after the Greek goddess of hunting.

Women have made a few advances in the male-dominated field of venture capital. Patricia Cloherty runs New York's Patricof & Company and is the first woman on the board of the National Venture Capital Association.

About 70 women are stock-fund managers out of a total of some 800 fund managers, says a study by Morningstar, a fund-research service. That may not sound like a lot, but the number of women fund managers has increased rapidly since 1983, when only one of those women was on the job.

Beth Terrana, 35, runs the sixth-largest stock fund in the United States, the $4.5 billion Fidelity Equity Income Fund. Terrana's total return on the fund was 12.45 percent for the year ending September 30, 1992. For the five years ending October 1990, when she ran Fidelity Growth and Income Fund, total return was 98.04 percent, compared to an industry average of 43.36 percent.

Elizabeth Bramwell can boast the best long-term performance of a woman-run fund. Her fund, the $530 Gabelli Growth Fund, had a total return of 109 percent for the five years ending September 30, 1992, compared to 44.6 percent for similar funds. "The important thing is to be early and to make forecasts that take you beyond where other people are," says Bramwell.

Fiona Biggs, manager of the $25 million Dreyfus Strategic World Investing Fund, outpaced other "global flexible funds"—stocks, bonds and money-market securities, with at least 25 percent of the portfolio outside the United States. Her fund's annual returns have averaged 11.6 percent since 1988. Biggs is the youngest portfolio manager at Dreyfus, and in 1992 she was also given the $4 million Dreyfus Global Investing Fund to manage. Lipper Analytical Services ranks Biggs first among global funds. The price of success, however, does not include a good night's sleep: she gets one wake-up call at 1:55 A.M. from Japan, another at 4:30 A.M. from Europe.

Catherine Dudley's $310 million Phoenix Capital Appreciation Fund averaged an annual return over the past three years of 24.3 percent, almost twice the Standard and Poor's 500-stock index.

Ellen Harris, manager of the $151 million Paine Webber Growth Fund, Dorothea M. Dutton, manager of the $300 million Delaware Group U.S. Government Fund and Kathleen McClaskey, manager of the $54 million Pioneer Municipal Bond Fund, all experienced total returns over the past five years above the industry average.

"Wall Street has one equalizing force," says Nola Falcone, manager of the $1 billion Evergreen Total Return Fund, who has endured sexist insults from potential customers. "If you can deliver, you're rewarded."

5. *Traditional Jobs Revisited* Old Values/New Respect

Time was, a sharp career woman could choose to be a nurse, secretary or teacher. Period. But when millions of women broke into business and the professions, the demand for competent people in traditional female jobs increased. So did wages and status.

It is time to take a new look at "traditional" women's jobs, to reexamine the stigmas and prejudices attached to jobs that, in the past, were dead end "nonchoices." For some, being objective will not be easy: old labels die hard. But it is necessary, because this decade will bring unprecedented opportunity for nurses, teachers and secretaries—both as professionals and as entrepreneurs.

When *Working Woman* put nursing on its "worst jobs of 1988" list, nursing professor Ellen Baer of the University of Pennsylvania had had enough. "Feminism will have succeeded not only when women have equal access to all fields but when traditionally female professions like nursing gain the high value and solid social respect they deserve," she wrote in a *New York Times* piece.

"Professional nursing requires brains, education, judgment, fortitude, inventiveness, split-second decision making," she continued. "I consider myself a dedicated feminist," she added, "but I refuse to accept a sort of feminism that abandons feminine caring roles in order to achieve progress."

The same can be said for other "female fields." Besides schools, hospitals and corporations have restructured jobs to increase autonomy, responsibility and job satisfaction and to attract competent people.

- The master-teaching concept has raised salaries and spirits. Educational choice, described in Chapter 10, will create entrepreneurial opportunity for teachers.
- Nurses enjoy greater autonomy and authority.
- Many secretarial jobs are indistinguishable from administrative posts.

Nursing

By the year 2005, the number of registered nurses (RNs) will reach 2.5 million, up from 1.7 million in 1990, a 44 percent surge. Most newly licensed nurses—80 percent—describe themselves as "satisfied" with their jobs, reports the National League of Nurses.

The nursing shortage boosted average salaries for staff nurses to $34,500 in 1991. But "average" obscures the fact that many senior nurses, administrators and professors earn a whole lot more than that.

- *Top* RNs in major cities earn $50,000 to $65,000 a year, reports *The American Journal of Nursing.*
- A nurse-anesthetist can earn $100,000 a year, says *Working Woman,* which redeemed itself by placing that nursing specialty on its 1991 hot-jobs list.
- Nursing professors earn in the mid-$60,000's, says the American Association of Colleges of Nursing, but a nursing professor with a doctorate at a top private college can earn more than $100,000.
- Nursing directors *average* $62,300. Considering what top urban staff nurses and nurse-anesthetists earn, you have got to figure the best-paid nurses in this category command six figures.

With incomes like that, it is no wonder nursing would be ranked the eighth-best-paying profession for women, according to the Bureau of Labor Statistics list of 1991 median weekly earnings (BLS does not publish such a list; we simply arranged the jobs in order of salaries). What is shocking is the job at number nine: physician. The difference was not huge: the nurses earned only seven dollars a week more than the doctors. Furthermore, this particular BLS statistic **excludes** entrepreneurial doctors, who earn the biggest incomes, and counts only "wage and salary" workers, those who work for hospitals, HMOs or other health-care organizations. But that category covers 63 percent of female doctors. And it represents dramatic recent change: just five years before, in 1986, the women doctors in this category made $50 a week *more* than the women nurses. Not now.

In 1991 women nurses earned more money than nonentrepreneurial female physicians.

It is a startling metaphor of change in the health-care establishment—and a testament to how labor shortages boost salaries.

Nurses certainly ought to be making good money. Annette McBeth, vice president of Immanuel-St. Joseph's Hospital in Mankato, Minnesota, calculates nurses generate 50 to 60 percent of hospital revenue.

Job satisfaction among nurses has grown after hospitals restructured their tasks. Primary-care nurses are responsible for 24-hour planning for a patient, just as physicians are. They follow patients from admission to discharge, working with the physicians. At Boston's Beth Israel Hospital, nursing vice president and nurse in chief Joyce Clifford has equal rank with the hospital's chief of medicine.

Under "case management," in use as early as 1985 at New England Medical Center, a patient is admitted to an attending physician and a nursing group. "Politically, this puts nurses on a new footing within the health-care system," says Karen Zanders, who owns a case-management consulting firm.

Nurse practitioners, registered nurses with advanced education and clinical training in a specialty area, can be found in all 50 states. The American Academy of Nurse Practitioners in Washington, D.C., estimates there are about 30,000 of them in the United States. Nurse practitioner made *U.S. News and World Report*'s 1992 list of "hot tracks in 20 professions." The magazine went on to quote the American Academy of Nurse Practitioners: "For every graduate of a nurse practitioner program an estimated four jobs beckon." In 35 states, nurse practitioners can prescribe medication.

The need for more than 700,000 nurses this decade and beyond to 2005 means more prestigious jobs, too. More professors will be needed to teach the newcomers. Nursing supervisors and directors will have to manage them.

Only 6 percent of nurses have master's degrees and less than 1 percent hold doctorates. That concerns Ada Sue Hinshaw, head of NIH-based National Center for Nursing Research. "Without them (as faculty) we can't bring in adequate numbers," she says.

After more than 30 years in nursing, Dr. Margaret McClure, whose Ph.D. is in research and nursing-service administration, became chief operating officer at New York University's Medical Center. Her title is now executive director of nursing and vice president for hospital operations.

Nursing directors will increasingly break through into top hospital posts, successfully competing with finance directors and other executives for the chief operating officer job. But other executives will not match the depth of knowledge about hospital operations the chief nurses have. To win that competition, however, nurse/managers should start now to round out their administrative know-how with new skills in finance and marketing.

Teaching

As society faces up to the education crisis, teachers' wages and professional prestige have increased. The U.S. Department of Education's Vance Grant says the United States will need 200,000 new public-school teachers a year now and for the next several years. Other estimates put the figure higher: by 2000 the United States will need nearly 2 million new teachers. The United States will also need a lot more college teachers. One third of all tenured professors will retire by 2000.

In the Rochester, New York, Career in Teaching Program, mentor and lead teachers can earn close to $70,000. Teachers with master's degrees and several years of experience averaged $48,600 in 1992, while some are earning in the $60,000's and high $50,000's. In 1991 starting teachers earned $28,935, *a 50 percent increase* just since 1987—and as high as $30,000 in Alaska (see below).

Rochester's innovative mentoring program gets new teachers off to a good start. The mentor-teacher provides expertise to several new and inexperienced teachers, helps them develop goals and monitors their progress.

The average U.S. teacher's salary in the 1991–92 school year was $34,213. Starting salaries averaged $22,171, according to the American Federation of Teachers (AFT). If that does not sound too exciting, it is important to remember that some states pay a lot more.

The AFT says teachers earn the highest average salaries in Connecticut ($47,000 +), Alaska and New York ($43,000 +), New Jersey and Michigan ($40,000 +). In Alaska starting teachers average more than $30,000; in New York, Connecticut and New Jersey they start at more than $26,000.

In 1992, for the first time, U.S. high school principals averaged more than $60,000, averaging $61,768 a year.

Secretaries

The United States needs 250,000 new secretaries by 2005. In addition, we need 158,000 medical and 133,000 legal secretaries. For the young woman who does not want to attend college but is willing to go to a one- to two-year training course, being a secretary could have great appeal. But the job does not make any hot-careers list, because the women editing those lists fought so hard not to be stuck in a "dead end" secretarial job 20 or 25 years ago when it was the only job in the business world open to women.

In New York City a top secretary earns $75,000, according to a survey by the newsletter *Nine to Five,* published by the Dartnell Corporation in Chicago. An experienced "private" secretary in other major cities can earn $50,000 a year. The private secretary of a top CEO (there are 500 of them all over the United States on our not-so-favorite list, the Fortune 500) has power, prestige and plenty of perks—and can earn a salary approaching six figures.

Given that some middle managers in hot fields like computers often level off around $60,000, who's to say private secretary is not a hot job?

In drafting this section, we asked secretaries and former secretaries what they thought of our listing "secretary" as an opportunity area: they expressed real reservations. It's not the money, they said, or the work: both can indeed be satisfactory. The problem with being a secretary is the lack of respect and prestige. No wonder 62 percent of secretaries surveyed in 1991 wanted a different job title, and 52 percent preferred "administrative assistant," according to Professional Secretaries International.

It is high time that today's professional women remove the stigma *they* had against the field in 1968 or 1972. By now successful women know how important a great secretary is. They realize she should be paid well, called "administrative assistant" if she prefers that title and most of all, treated with respect.

6. *High Tech/Science*   Breaking Ground/Prestige

Superstars like Deborah A. Coleman, who made her name at Apple and is now with Tektronix (see page 111), IBM's Ellen Hancock, and ASK Computer's founder and CEO, Sandy Kurtzig, have captured media attention and serve as positive, successful role models for millions of high-tech women.

Ellen Hancock, senior vice president at IBM, started out as a programmer 26 years ago. The networking systems unit she heads had revenues of $5.2 billion in 1991—8 percent of IBM's total. The division, which develops and markets products that link computer hardware and operating networks, would hold the number 100 spot on the Fortune 500 list if it were a separate company. In 1993 *Business Week* listed Hancock as a contender for the number two job at IBM.

As CEO and Chairwoman of Autodesk, one of the world's largest computer-software manufacturers, Carol Bartz is the only woman to head a major computer company of which she wasn't a founder. *Working Woman* has listed her as one of its "10 Women to Watch."

Judy Sims is CEO of the Garland, Texas–based company Software Spectrum, whose 1992 net income increased 98 percent, to $3.8 million on sales of $158.9 million.

Monica Mehan, 45, is the first woman to head a major AT&T business unit. As CEO and president of AT&T American Transtech, she is responsible for more than 5,000 employees worldwide. In 1990 she streamlined internal operations and saved the company $70 million a year.

Mary L. Good, senior vice president of technology at Allied Signal, is one of the few female top scientists at a big U.S. firm. She served 25 years in academia before her business career.

Kathryn A. Braun, executive vice president of Western Digital Corporation, a computer-equipment maker in Irvine, California, is second in command and heir apparent.

That is not to say women automatically zoom to the top of high-tech firms. A survey of 29,000 high-tech firms found only 5 percent of executives at the vice president level or above were women. Only 3.3 percent of the CEOs and 1.9 percent of the chairpersons were women, about the same as for the Fortune 500.

Does high tech deserve the same dreadful reputation as the Fortune 500 when it comes to women? Not so fast. Bureau of Labor Statistics 1991 wage and salary figures show that two of the very best-paying job categories for women—computer scientist (and systems analyst) and engineer—are in science and technology. Women do not hold the top jobs, but they are earning a respectable income in high tech.

Furthermore, according to BLS stats, the wage gap for women computer scientists—at 89 percent of what male counterparts earn— was the narrowest of the top well-paying occupations.

The United States will need some 366,000 new systems analysts and computer scientists by 2005, about 79 percent more than in 1990. Of the fast-growing careers this is probably the best-paying. The United States will also need more than 300,000 computer programmers.

Barbara Jones, 42, a systems analyst with Keane, Inc., of Boston,

Massachusetts, "put herself through" Worcester Polytechnic Institute 12 years ago as a young divorced mother of two.

"Getting my B.S. degree in computer science is the best thing I've ever done for myself," she says. "Because the computer industry is so varied, it is easy to find a niche where you can develop a respected expertise. But it is also a challenge to keep up with constantly changing technology. I would advise any young woman with a mathematical bent to consider the computer field. She will be well rewarded."

Women with Ph.D.'s in science and engineering will find great opportunity in both academia and industry.

Math: The Great Equalizer

The teachers who said "Study your math" were right.

Women who took more than eight college credits of math earned more than other women, as much as men in some occupations and more than men in others, says a U.S. Department of Education (DOE) study. For nearly 20 years DOE tracked more than 12,000 college-bound graduates of the high school class of 1972. It found:

- Women accountants earned 2.6 percent less than males;
- Women engineers averaged 1.9 percent less than male counterparts;
- Women managers of financial institutions earned 4.5 percent more than male counterparts. **Women in manufacturing earned 7 percent more!**

Studying math did not eliminate the wage gap: women in 26 job categories still earned less than men. But when you consider that the wage gap overall is still about 25 percent, the DOE study is impressive indeed.

Each year, 3M Corporation sends women scientists into Minneapolis schools to encourage students, especially girls, to take an interest in science. The 12-year-old program called TECH (Technical Teams Encouraging Career Horizons) involves 150 scientists and 60 schools. Honeywell in Minneapolis has a similar program called "Women in Technology."

"Science has been seen as a nerd profession," says John Stangl, an eighth-grade science teacher at Maplewood Middle School in suburban St. Paul. "Then the kids see a normal-looking woman in a nice suit."

Stangl says enrollments in chemistry classes have doubled since the TECH program began.

In 1992, actuary made the hot careers lists in both *Working Woman* and *U.S. News and World Report*. Actuaries, who must major in math, determine the probability of accidents, illness and death, and estimate their costs so insurers can keep costs down while still making a profit. Women make up 14 percent of actuaries. The BLS estimates the need for actuaries will increase almost 40 percent by the year 2005.

Women are entering male-dominated fields in search of a fatter paycheck, says Christine Maitland, a higher-education specialist with the National Education Association. "If I had my education to do over again," she says, "I'd choose a math/science major."

7. *Food, Glorious Food*   Nurturing/Creativity

Millions of women put dinner on the table every night, but until recently the world's top chefs were male. Before 1970 the Culinary Institute of America, in Hyde Park, New York, did not admit women. Today women make up about 20 percent of students. At the up-and-coming New England Culinary Institute in Montpelier, Vermont, women, on average, make up one third of the students. Classes at the school are kept to a ratio of only seven students per teacher.

The San Francisco area boasts more women chefs and restaurant owners or partners than any American city. Women there head more than 20 top restaurants, a better record than in New York or Chicago. "I wouldn't be surprised if there were more restaurants here owned by women than by men," says Anthony Dias Blue, the author of several food and wine books.

Alice Waters, who opened Berkeley's Chez Panisse in 1971, is the inspiration for many. "Alice was responsible for giving me my break," says Joyce Goldstein, a baker who went on to open San Francisco's successful Square One restaurant.

Alice Waters took the top honors at the James Beard Awards in 1992. Waters not only received the chef of the year award, but her restaurant, Chez Panisse, was named restaurant of the year. Debra Ponzek, chef at New York's Montrachet, was named "rising star chef." Lydia Shire of Biba in Boston and Barbara Figueroa of the Hunt Club in Seattle were named the top chefs in their regions.

"People always warned me this was a male-dominated field," says Donna Nicoletti, who studied at the California Culinary Academy before opening Undici. "But here I found an incredible openness about women working in the kitchen side by side with men."

Restaurateurs say women and men adopt different styles of cooking and managing. "Women have an instinctive desire to feed," says Alice Waters. "Food that tastes good is what a restaurant is all about. Women are more concerned with whether people like their food than with making a statement."

Nora Pouillon of Nora's in Washington, D.C., and Boston's Michela Larsen of Michela's are also part of the new wave of women chefs delighting the palates of discriminating new customers.

Working Woman listed caterer in its 1991 top 25 jobs list, noting companies will turn to caterers to create on-site functions to cut the cost of restaurant entertaining and capture tax breaks.

Natural Groceries and the Microwave

"If it won't spoil, don't buy it, and if you can't pronounce an ingredient, don't eat it!" says Sandy Gooch of Mrs. Gooch's Natural Foods, one of the United States' largest natural-foods retailers with 1992 revenues of $90 million. She has seven stores in the Los Angeles area. *The Wall Street Journal* called the chain a "Company for the Future."

Like many entrepreneurs, Sandy Gooch got into the business in 1977 to fill a personal need: she could not tolerate the chemical additives in processed foods and figured others must be reacting the same way. Although her objective was never just to make money, she says, "It never occurred to me that it wouldn't be successful."

Mary Anne Jackson, founder of My Own Meals, Inc., in Deerfield, Illinois, says, "The idea was staring me in the face." Like all mothers, Jackson needed convenient, healthy food for her children, so she knew there was a market for all-natural microwave dinners designed for kids. Today she owns a multimillion-dollar business growing *several hundred percent* a year, with substantial sales to the military and government. Her product is sold in 1,000 supermarkets in 15 states.

Jackson, 40, who is the mother of three, says women entrepreneurs still have a lot of trouble with venture capitalists. One man who was considering investing in her business asked Jackson, "What happens to my money if you get knocked up?"

Nevertheless, through Mary Anne Jackson's personal efforts, the company *has* attracted 80 shareholders who have invested $2.5 million.

8. *The Professions*   Blue Chip

Law and medicine are not new areas for women, but they continue to be promising career choices. Women earn 40 percent of all law degrees and one third of M.D. degrees.

Women have moved up to 26.6 percent of physicians, says the Bureau of Labor Statistics. Furthermore, women make up 50 percent of new primary-care physicians, in specialties like family practice, with whom people have the most direct contact.

Women are demonstrating that doctors can be empathetic listeners, instead of distant, priestlike figures, and can encourage patients to participate in their own treatment decisions, unlike the authoritarian stereotypes of male doctors of the past. Finally, women physicians are putting more emphasis on women's medical issues. The American Medical Association, whose figures differ somewhat from the government's, counts 104,000 female physicians.

But there has been talk of a glut of physicians, and, in recent years, "doctor" is not making many hot-jobs lists (see p. 78).

Why include it in ours, then? Three reasons: 1) Earnings continue to be relatively high (especially when self-employed physicians are counted); 2) Health care is one of a handful of top growth areas (see number 3)—and that means more lucrative entrepreneurial opportunities for physicians—and 3) Growth specialties have emerged within medicine that will be particularly attractive to women—especially adult women's medicine (see Chapter 5: "The Menopause Megatrend").

As women physicians raise consciousness about women's medical issues, more women will demand a female internist, family doctor and ob/gyn. As young female doctors gain more experience and attract more women patients—and as the menopause megatrend unfolds—the incomes of women doctors will increase substantially.

Women attorneys are already bringing home the big bucks. Lawyer is the best-paying job for women (median weekly earnings), according to 1991 BLS statistics. Just when you thought the United

States could not need one more of them, comes the projection that the demand for lawyers and judges will increase 35 percent between 1990 and 2005.

San Francisco is rated most receptive to women attorneys, according to a survey of the *National Law Journal,* which found that 13.6 percent of partners and 40.2 percent of associates of city law firms were women, a higher percentage than in New York, where about 10 percent of partners were women. The number-two city in both partners and associates was Boston. Chicago and Dallas were three and four in partners. Los Angeles and Washington, D.C., tied for third, counting partners and associates. Cities with the lowest percentage of female partners were New York, Cleveland and Houston.

Working Woman's 1991 hot-jobs list included environmental attorney and bankruptcy lawyer. It was interesting to see how widely the incomes of the two jobs differed. Environmental lawyers at federal agencies could start out at $26,000, while at a corporation or law firm environmental specialists would earn between $45,000 and $50,000. As a senior partner in a major firm, an environmental attorney would earn between $200,000 and $400,000. A lot of money, at least until you look at the prospects for bankruptcy lawyers.

Bankruptcy lawyers earned more than any other job on the 1991 *Working Woman* list.

They start out at $60,000 to $90,000 a year, and senior partners in top firms rein in a cool million dollars in annual income. The theme for the 1991 list was great jobs "even in tough times." It seemed particularly appropriate in this case.

With the passage of the 1991 Civil Rights Act and the Americans With Disabilities Act, *Working Woman* magazine listed employment attorney on its 1992 25 hottest careers list. Salary estimates were right up there with bankruptcy lawyer. The EEOC estimates that the Americans With Disabilities Act will create more than 10,000 lawsuits a year.

9. *Breaking into Male-Dominated Occupations*   Challenge

A traditional male job is not every woman's cup of tea, but for the right person it can mean opportunity, a break from the office routine and a good paycheck. It is a kind of trade-off between two evils: sexual harassment is almost a given, but you probably don't have to wear panty hose.

Analyzing the percentages of women in male-dominated fields, however, is rarely an inspiring task. One percent. Five. *Maybe* 11 percent.

- Women make up 1.5 percent of the United States' 200,000 professional firefighters.
- Today women make up only 4 percent of airline pilots and navigators, says BLS; 436 of United Airlines' 8,400 pilots are women.
- Women made up 14 percent of U.S. law-enforcement officers in 1991, up from 9.5 percent in 1983. They are 11 percent of police department personnel and 18 percent of prison corrections officers.
- Five percent of sports reporters and broadcasters were women in 1990, says the Association for Women in Sports Media. But those 500 women were *twice* the 1988 number.
- The number of female postal carriers doubled since 1980.
- Just about 50 percent of all bus drivers and dispatchers are women.

The numbers may be daunting, but each percentage represents change at the roots of society. The policewoman whose life is on the line protecting a community, the sportswriter who confronts sexual harassment in the locker room, the carpenter apprentice who earns the respect of male construction workers—each is challenging individual perceptions about women on a daily basis. And that strengthens all women.

In 1990 Elizabeth Watson became Houston's police chief, the first woman to head a big U.S. force. Ten years earlier she was denied a supervisor's job because it was "too tough a job for a woman." When she made lieutenant, there was "a lot of booing and hissing," she says. "But it didn't take long for a couple of sergeants to notice I was working very hard, even if they didn't like me."

In 1992, when Bob Lanier replaced Kathy Whitmire as mayor, Chief Watson was relieved of her duties.

"Policing today requires considerable intelligence, communication, compassion and diplomacy," says Watson. "Women tend to rely more on intellectual than physical prowess. From that standpoint, policing is a natural match for them."

After the Rodney King beating, it was found that the 120 Los

Angeles police officers who were most cited for "use of force" were men.

"When you see a reference to a female," says Eileen Luna, former chief investigator for the San Francisco citizen review board, "it's often the positive effect she has had in taking control in a different way from male officers."

Women cops, says Joanne Belknap, professor of criminal justice at the University of Cincinnati, see themselves as peacekeepers and negotiators.

Construction

Women make up almost 3 percent of the U.S. construction industry. In Manhattan women hold 4 percent of the 100,000 construction jobs. California wants to see 20 percent women in construction-trade apprenticeships. In 1989 they reached 11 percent, up from 8 percent in 1983; women hold some 6,000 of California's 51,000 construction apprenticeships.

Amazingly, though, 13.2 percent of the managers/executives in construction were women in 1990, says the Labor Department. They—and the all-female crews that women homeowners would much prefer to hire—hold the key to employing more women in the trades.

Julia M. Stasch, 46, a former secretary, is now president of Stein & Company, one of Chicago's biggest real estate developers. In 1985, as vice president, Stasch wanted to see more women construction workers hired.

"You ask contractors to open jobs to women, and they say they'd love to, but that the unions don't have any women," says Stasch. "The unions say they'd love to, too, but that the contractors don't want any women."

Julia Stasch decided to take matters into her own hands. In 1989 she set up an all-female committee of women's advocacy groups to recruit, train and refer tradeswomen to construction projects. Normally, no more than five women would have worked on the development of a 27-story federal office building: Stein & Company had *82 tradeswomen* on the biggest construction site for women ever and now employs about three times as many women as the industry average. It requires contractors to meet strict affirmative-action goals. Because of Stasch, women worked 54,000 hours, about 7 percent of the total work hours, on the Metcalfe Federal Building in Chicago.

Ginger Evans, 37, is director of the new Denver International Airport and responsible for its December 1993 opening date. In charge of 6,000 workers and 200 construction and service contractors, Evans spends $35 million a week. "That's like opening two convention centers a month," she says.

10. *The Arts and Media*   Creativity/Glamour

Remember, rule number one is to follow your dream job. For an increasing number of women, that means working in the arts and media.

Marin Alsop had wanted to be a conductor since she was 11 years old. But her teachers told her, "Girls don't do that." Undeterred, she followed her dream. Today she conducts the Colorado symphony orchestra. She was the first woman to conduct the Boston Pops in its 105-year history.

A whole new generation of women are coming onto the conducting scene, says maestra (rather than maestro) Alsop, who adds: "Things can only get brighter for conductors who are also women."

The all-female Women's Philharmonic in the San Francisco Bay area is headed by Jo Ann Falletta.

Even if you are committed to following your heart, it is only natural to want to know the trends are on your side. The "Renaissance in the Arts" trend described in *Megatrends 2000* has served these women who pursued their dreams to the very heights of the arts world. In 1991 alone:

- Kathy Halbreich was appointed director of Minneapolis's progressive, internationally known Walker Art Center.
- Sian Edwards was named musical director and conductor of the English National Opera.
- Agnes Gund was elected president of the Museum of Modern Art.
- Deborah Borda became managing director of the New York Philharmonic.
- Composer Shulamit Ran won the Pulitzer Prize for her symphony.
- Lynne Cooke became curator of the Dia Center for the Arts in New York City, one of the country's wealthiest contemporary art institutions.

Anne D'Harnoncourt has been director of the Philadelphia Museum of Art since 1982. In 1992 she was considered as a replacement for J. Carter Brown at the National Gallery of Art in Washington, D.C.

Women in Television

In 1991 CNN's Catherine Crier started *Crier & Company,* a live half-hour show featuring three or four different female (and an occasional male) policy experts each day commenting on the issues facing American society. For years audiences have endured the sight of all-male panels (with an occasional token woman), but this was the first national network show with all-women panels every day—a signal for the 1990's. The show was renamed *CNN & Co.* after Crier moved to ABC to be a prime-time magazine correspondent.

CNN has the lead in putting women on camera, including the formidable Hannah Storm (now with NBC) on the sports beat. Who can forget Christiane Amanpour during the Gulf War or in Bosnia? In another CNN breakthrough, we are finally seeing women who do not look like models but are simply average, normal-looking, hardworking journalists. Of CNN's 151 anchors, including correspondents, 46 are women.

Cokie Roberts appears every other week on *This Week with David Brinkley* and fills in from time to time for Ted Koppel on *Nightline. Lear's* magazine even reported that she was briefly on Ross Perot's vice presidential list.

New York Times critic Walter Goodman said, "Anyone who watched the recent [January 1992] celebration of the 40th anniversary of NBC's *Today* show must have been struck by the contrast between Jane Pauley, Katie Couric and Faith Daniels on one team and Gene Shalit, Joe Garagiola and Willard Scott on the other." Goodman ended his column by saying that the "increasing use on all networks of ungorgeous women of a certain age to cover major beats bespeaks fairness and good sense."

Oprah Winfrey, Sally Jessy Raphael and Joan Rivers are at the top of a field once dominated by men.

Linda Bloodworth-Thomason and her husband created and produced *Designing Women*, which ended after a seven-year run, *Evening Shade* and *Hearts Afire*.

Lucie Salhany, chair of Twentieth-Television, earns an estimated $700,000 a year. *Working Woman* magazine listed her as the 13th "best-paid" woman in corporate America. She is one of the most powerful women in mass media, reported *Mirabella* magazine.

High-visibility women once feared to acknowledge that they were married. Now they are almost expected to publicize their pregnancies. Early on, it was seen that the pregnancy leaves and returns of Jane Pauley and Joan Lunden *helped* ratings. Now the networks see no reason to downplay a string of maternity leaves by Faith Daniels, Paula Zahn, Maria Shriver, Deborah Norville, Katie Couric and Mary Alice Williams. It gave new meaning to "the Mommy Track."

Film

"Lillian Gish once said that 'directing is no job for a lady,' " writes Larry Rohter in *The New York Times,* and "Hollywood has been only too happy to agree." In 1914 Lois Weber became the first woman to direct a feature film. But in the 1990's there has been an explosion of activity. Consider this list of women who have directed films in this new decade:

Martha Coolidge, *Rambling Rose*
Randa Haines, *The Doctor, Children of a Lesser God*
Penny Marshall, *Awakenings, Big, A League of Their Own* (*Big* and *A League of Their Own* each earned more than $100 million)
Nora Ephron, *This Is My Life, Sleepless in Seattle*
Amy Heckerling, *Look Who's Talking*
Barbra Streisand, *The Prince of Tides*
Jodie Foster, *Little Man Tate*
Jennie Livingston, *Paris Is Burning*
Joan Micklin Silver, *Stepkids*
Penelope Spheeris, *Wayne's World*
Euzhan Palcy, *A Dry White Season*
Mira Nair, *Salaam Bombay* and *Mississippi Masala*

Until the 1980's there were essentially no women directors. Of the 7,332 feature films made in Hollywood between 1939 and 1979, only 14 were directed by women. In 1990 there were 406 features made, of which 23 were directed by women. Still only about 5 percent, but accelerating.

"Five years ago there were three women directors," says Nora Ephron. "Now there are over 20. It's not enough, but it's a gigantic change."

Women are finally beginning to achieve more than token status as directors in Hollywood. Martha Coolidge says there are finally enough women directors that "everyone will see that not all women are the same, that we offer different points of view—different from men, but also different from each other."

Sherry Lansing, chair of Paramount Pictures, ranked number 32 on *Premiere*'s 1992 list of Hollywood's 100 most powerful people. Before taking over at Paramount, she produced *Indecent Proposal, The Accused, Black Rain* and *Fatal Attraction.*

The theme of the 1993 Oscar award ceremony was "Oscar Celebrates Women and the Movies," yet, as many critics noted, "no one would call this a good year for women on the screen."

"To celebrate the ludicrous nerve behind this," read a *New York Times* article, "imagine a parallel situation. What if Bill Clinton nominated no women for his cabinet and then declared that the inauguration theme would be 'Celebrating Women and Government.' "

Women Artists

Gains are also being made by women artists. In the '60's and '70's, a tour of New York City art galleries would only rarely turn up a show by a woman artist. That began to change in the '80's, and today there are almost as many women as men in new-artist shows.

"During the past decade women artists throughout the Western world have become more active, successful, and visible than ever before," says Nancy Heller in her book *Women Artists* (Abbeville Press).

In 1990 Jenny Holzer was chosen unanimously by seven critics and curators to represent the United States in the prestigious Venice Biennale. Not only was it the first time—in 93 years—that a woman's work was chosen to exclusively represent the United States, Holzer won the Biennale's grand prize. Other American cutting-edge women artists—Barbara Kruger, Rebecca Horn, Laurie Anderson and Cindy Sherman, among others emerged during the '80's to worldwide acclaim.

Publishing

Many of the key players in publishing are women, as are many top literary agents and authors. Putnam CEO Phyllis Grann, mother of three, is certainly one of the five most important people in publishing. Linda Grey is the president of Ballantine Books. Michelle Sidrane is the publisher of Crown. Caroline Reidy is president of Trade Books at Simon & Schuster. Our hardcover publisher, Villard, a division of Random House, has a woman publisher, Diane Reverand.

Women are also prominent in magazine publishing. Frances Lear created *Lear's* "for the woman who wasn't born yesterday." In 1991 Lisa Valk was named publisher of *Time* magazine.

Advertising

"More and more women are ascending to positions of power in advertising," reports *The New York Times.*

- In May 1991 Rochelle Lazarus became president of the New York office of Ogilvy & Mather Worldwide, one of the country's largest agencies, with billings of $700 million annually.

Also in 1991:

- Susan Gillette was named president of DDB Needham's Chicago office.
- Helayne Spivak became executive vice president and executive creative director of Young & Rubicam.
- Sue Reed was made director of creative services at Ayer in New York City.

Says Lori Spano, president of Advertising Women of New York and of Ackerley Airport Advertising, "We've bumped up against the glass ceiling and finally cracked it."

In April 1992 Charlotte Beers became chairperson and CEO of Ogilvy & Mather Worldwide, the world's fifth largest advertising agency.

Beers is in charge of more than 7,000 people in 273 offices worldwide. She is also the first female president of the American Association of Advertising Agencies.

Number Eleven?

One job that did not make our top 10 list is sexual-harassment consultant. Just as the Thomas affair galvanized women into political action, it also brought the sexual-harassment issue—always there simmering—to a vigorous boil:

- A *Newsweek* poll found 21 percent of women said they had endured sexual harassment; 42 percent said they knew someone who was harassed.
- Half the American Management Association's 500-plus members have had to deal with sexual harassment in the past five years.
- As early as 1988, *Working Woman* reported that 90 percent of Fortune 500 companies had received sexual-harassment complaints and that one third had faced lawsuits.
- The "most detailed" harassment study ever was conducted by the U.S. Merit Board, a federal agency. Its 1987 survey of 8,500 workers found 35 percent had experienced offensive remarks, 28 percent, suggestive looks and 26 percent, inappropriate touching.

Those percentages from a reliable large-scale survey tell us sexual harassment is a serious, nitty-gritty work issue—which you knew already, probably from personal experience or that of a friend.

What is new is that corporations, which have been well aware of the issue for a decade, now have to do something major about it. First, because the aftermath of the Thomas-Hill business brought more complaints forward: the number of sexual harassment claims filed is up almost 50 percent since the Thomas hearings, reports the Equal Employment Opportunity Commission. Consultants, employment lawyers and organizations like the NOW Legal Defense and Education Fund say they are receiving three times the number of calls they used to get for information on sexual harassment. Second, because of recent changes in the law, as of 1991, victims of sexual harassment can sue for damages of between $50,000 and $300,000, depending on the company's size.

Furthermore, the legal definition of sexual harassment broadened significantly after the landmark 1986 case *Meritor Savings Bank v. Vinson.* Previously, to prove sexual harassment, a case had to show "quid pro quo," that, for example, a woman employee would be fired or not promoted if she refused to have sex with her boss. But in 1986 the Supreme Court extended the definition of sexual harassment to "a hostile work environment" that made it difficult for someone to do her or his job.

Those two recent developments mean it is in a company's self-interest to stop sexual harassment before it starts.

How is a company supposed to do that? One way is through a lot of training, corporate "consciousness raising" that empowers victims and potential victims, distinguishes real harassment from harmless banter, clears the air—and eventually saves the company a bundle.

But there is a lot more than money involved. Susan Webb is president of Pacific Resource Development Group, Inc., a Seattle-based consulting firm specializing in sexual-harassment issues; she is also the author of *Step Forward, Sexual Harassment in the Workplace: What You Need to Know* (Mastermedia). Webb reports that companies that used to order 20 to 50 copies of training videos or manuals on sexual harassment now order 2,000 to 3,000 copies. Companies realize they need to educate *all* employees, not just senior management.

Webb says that, in addition to the financial burden, sexual harassment costs companies plenty in terms of lost productivity, morale, retraining and rehiring.

"Everything you can do to prevent sexual harassment before a lawsuit occurs is worth every penny," she says.

- Boston's First Seminar services, a corporate-seminar consultant, reports "a pronounced increase in harassment seminars."
- The American Management Association launched a course on sexual harassment just after the Thomas hearings and reports a positive response.
- James W. Wimberly, an Atlanta attorney specializing in employment law, reports more employer inquiries on harassment policies.
- Chicago's La Salle Street Management Theatre uses actors in a live performance to dramatize harassment incidents, followed by audience discussion.
- Eighty-one percent of Fortune 500 companies now have harassment awareness programs.

While the law sorts out "hostile environment" and "quid pro quo," Webb offers a simple definition of sexual harassment: **"deliberate and/or repeated sexual or sex-based behavior [including, of course, remarks] that is not welcome, not asked for or returned."**

But, she says, the whole issue is really about power: the harasser knows or thinks (consciously or not) that he or she has more power, Webb argues. Otherwise, the harassee could simply say "Stop"—and it would be all over.

From many corners comes high praise for Du Pont's four-hour sexual-harassment workshop, "A Matter of Respect." More than 300 employees have been trained to facilitate the workshop, and 70,000 of the company's 95,000 U.S. employees have been through it. In addition to describing company policies on the issue and procedures for reporting harassment, including a 24-hour hot line, the workshop presents videos that participants discuss at length.

"No employee has to wonder if the company will support them," says Dar Di Sabatino, a Du Pont diversity consultant. "You don't have to compromise your integrity for anybody."

So successful has Du Pont's approach been, the firm has started a new venture, Respect, Inc., to teach "A Matter of Respect" to other companies.

The New Female Leadership Style

"The pyramid structure," we wrote in *Megatrends,* "has been praised and blamed, but its detractors have never come up with a better, more successful framework for organizations." That was 1982. In the future, we concluded, "institutions will be organized according to . . . the networking model."

In *Reinventing the Corporation* (1985), we searched for examples of a new breed of manager still in the process of evolving—and found a few good men. In the future, we said, a manager's top responsibility will be "creating a nourishing environment for personal growth."

Meanwhile, in the 1980's, the United States shifted from an industrial to an information society and joined the global economy. In a time of change and crisis, women became leaders of small and midsize firms. With no backgrounds in sports or the military, the business metaphors of the industrial age, and few mentors to teach the masculine ways, women were thrown back on their instincts.

Some authors had advised women to imitate "male" strategies.

But the old ways didn't work for *anyone,* and no one knew how to manage under the new circumstances. That freed up the most creative people to start experimenting.

They asked themselves, "What would motivate *me?*" The answer was a supportive manager and a creative "think tank"–like atmosphere. Management innovators devised networks, lattices and webs to replace the time-honored pyramid.

Today that new approach is becoming known as Women's Leadership style.

Primitive descriptions of the "manager of the future" uncannily match those of female leadership. Consultants tried to teach male managers to relinquish the command-and-control mode. For women it was different: it just came naturally.

And it quickly won accolades from male management gurus. Peter Drucker vows that Frances Hesselbein, former director of the Girl Scouts and a foremost example of this new leadership, "could manage any company in America." Tom Peters, author of *In Search of Excellence* (HarperCollins), tells men "who wish to stay employed" to study women's ways of leadership.

"We have a different style of management than men," says Denver consultant Jean Yancey. "And we're seeing we get more productivity if we use it." Every item on the experts' lists of leadership qualities, she notes, "openness, trust, ongoing education, compassion and understanding," describe the female leadership style.

Let us be clear about one thing, though: this is not about being "nice" to people. Caring about people and supporting them *always* must be balanced with objectivity. In certain cases the way to empower someone may even be to fire them, express anger, impose strict discipline or have a knock-down drag-out fight—a verbal one, that is.

We sing in praise of the Women's Leadership style because it is a *better* way to increase productivity and profits. Anyone who thinks "supporting people" and being "nice" alone will cut it in the business world is in need of a serious reality check.

What Does It Look Like?

In behavior terms, what *is* Women's Leadership? Women leaders are said to reflect and express "women's *values.*" But how do those values get translated into leadership *behavior*? In particular, how does a woman leader translate behavior she was socialized to possess into valuable job *skills*?

For more than 10 years, we have worked on a chart (see page 100) contrasting traditional and new leadership, now recognized as Women's Leadership. Even though it is impressionistic rather than definitive (and a bit repetitive), it has been very popular with audiences. Recently, we tried to cluster the behaviors together to see whether any patterns emerged, to see whether there were three or seven (or however many) primary attributes of Women's Leadership under which the remaining behaviors could be organized. The second chart beginning on page 100 shows what we believe are the six central traits of the new leadership.

Crafting Your Personal Style

You will not succeed by imitating anyone's leadership style—male or female. Every woman must master her own approach. One way to begin, though, is to study the examples of successful women, as well as male mentors and teachers, who inspired you to do your best. Adopt the behaviors that work for you, reject the others.

It is critical to reject what does not work. The cheerful open-door policy lovingly called characteristic of women executives—"Women just don't seem to mind being interrupted by people. They see it as an opportunity to teach and interact"—is positively horrifying to the female member of the writing team for this book, who closes the door without guilt, then bolts it shut. Writing is one executive skill that is best performed in a most "unfeminine" way.

A New Generation of Women Leaders

Judy B. Rosener, a professor at the University of California's Graduate School of Management in Irvine, studied male and female executives with similar jobs, education and ages. Her conclusion, published in *Harvard Business Review,* is that women and men manage quite differently.

Men see job performance as a series of transactions—rewards for services rendered or punishment for inadequate performance, she concluded. They are what historian James McGregor Burns would call "transactional leaders."

Women leaders try to *transform* people's self-interest into orga-

Traditional Management vs. Leadership/Women's Leadership

Objective: control	Objective: change
Relies on order-giving	Facilitating/teaching
Rank	Connections
Knows all the answers	Asks the right questions
Limits and defines	Empowers
Issues orders	Acts as a role model
Imposes discipline	Values creativity
Hierarchy	Networking/web
Demands "respect"	Wants people to "speak up, act up"
Performance review	Mutual contract for specific results
Automatic annual raises	Pay for performance
Military archetype	Teaching archetype
Keeps people on their toes	Nourishing environment for growth
Punishment	Reward
Reach up/down	Reach out
Here's what we are going to do!	How can I serve you/bring out best in you?
Bottom line	Vision
Closed: information = power	Openness
Drill sergeant	Master motivator
Command and control	Empowerment
Little time for people	Infinite time for people
Rigid	Flexible
At the top	In the center
Mechanistic	Wholistic
Impersonal/objective	Personal

Characteristics of Women's Leadership

Empower

Management	Leadership
Punishment	Reward
Demands "respect"	Invites speaking out
Drill sergeant	Motivator
Limits and defines	Empowers
Imposes discipline	Values creativity

Here's what we are going to do!   How can I serve you?
Bottom line   Vision

Restructure

Control	Change
Rank	Connection
Hierarchy	Network
Rigid	Flexible
Automatic annual raises	Pay for performance
Performance review	Mutual contract for results
Mechanistic	Wholistic
Compartmental	Systemic

Teaching

Order-giving	Facilitating
Military archetype	Teaching archetype

Role Model

Issues orders	Acts as role model

Openness

Keeping people on their toes	Nourishing environment for growth
Reach up/down	Reach out
Information control	Information availability

Questioner

Knows all the answers	Asks the right questions

nizational goals. In Burns's terminology they are "transformational leaders" (though Rosener prefers the term "interactive leadership"). Women leaders:

- encourage participation;
- share power and information;
- enhance other people's self-worth;
- and get others excited about their work.

Women are likely to thrive in organizations changing or growing fast—"When change is rampant, everything is up for grabs," Rosener writes. Women also succeed in companies that employ educated young professionals who demand to be treated as individuals.

Another expert puts it more bluntly. Wharton's Edward M. Moldt says many men still "act like master sergeants. That's not working nearly as well as it used to." Women involve people in decision making, he says, so they are more successful with people who "don't want to be bossed around."

The E-Word

The word most used to describe women's leadership is "empowerment." But what is it? How do you foster it? How does it get from buzzword to behavior?

This is how we would define it: empowerment means feeling confident to act on your own authority. It means that your judgment is sufficiently respected by your leadership that they will support your decision. Should you make a mistake, that leadership will utilize it as an opportunity to teach a further point, not a chance to humiliate or berate you.

As that definition shows, empowerment is a two-way street. It engages the leadership every bit as much as the person to be "empowered."

Donna J. Goya is senior vice president of human resources at Levi Strauss, where empowerment is a stated corporate objective. Co-workers say she embodies the term. Perhaps it is because Goya has mastered an art that confounds most managers—delegating. Says former compensation director Gussie Stewart, Goya delegates "in a way that makes you feel *very responsible and yet very supported* at the same time." Goya helped establish Levi Strauss's AIDS-education program, one of the first in business.

Women's Managerial Advantage

Sally Helgesen's *The Female Advantage: Women's Ways of Leadership* (Doubleday) describes in detail the workdays of four executives—Dorothy Brunson, president, Brunson Communication; Frances Hesselbein, former head of the Girl Scouts; Nancy Badore, executive director of Ford Motor's Executive Development Center; and Barbara Grogan, CEO, Western Industrial Contractors.

Like Rosener, Helgesen describes women who *do not* adapt to the male business world ("Here I saw four successful women who had not gotten with the program at all"), but who succeed by expressing, not rejecting, "female" strengths such as supporting, encouraging and teaching, open communications, soliciting input and, in general, creating a positive, collegial work environment.

From Values and Socialization to Management Skills

Many of the attributes for which women's leadership is praised are rooted in women's socialized roles. The traditional female value of caring for others—balanced with sufficient objectivity—is the basis of the management skill of supporting and encouraging people and bringing out their best.

After the big split between John Sculley and Steve Jobs, Apple Computer was in turmoil. Debbie Biondolillo, then vice president of human resources, had to reorganize sales and marketing, a painful task, since many people had to be laid off. But she made sure everyone was placed in a job. "I've never seen anybody do what she did," said one co-worker. "There was a style and a humaneness to it."

Women have known enough arrogant male bosses to know how they do *not* want to come off. Humility, which most women hesitate to declare as a value, is the basis for *openness*. It says, "My ego is not so fragile that I have to act like I know it all. What are your ideas?"

Women have learned to more astutely read the nuances behind people's words, says gender expert Judith Hall, a psychology professor at Boston's Northeastern University. "Women are expected to be interpersonal experts; they facilitate, respond, empathize," she says.

The ability to tolerate ambiguity and juggle many things at once, often attributed to women, is a vital, but often underrated, management skill.

Men used to operating exclusively in the command-and-control mode are doomed to failure in the fast-moving, information-laden, constantly changing environment of modern business.

Author Sally Helgesen writes, "Increasingly, motherhood is being recognized as an excellent school for managers, demanding many of the same skills: organization, pacing, the balancing of conflicting claims, teaching, guiding, leading, monitoring, handling disturbances, imparting information."

The Hierarchy and the Web

One of the first things Helgesen discovered is how much women leaders disdain "that most traditional of business structures—the hierarchical ladder." Women leaders, she says, like being "in the center of things, rather than at the top, which they perceived as a lonely and disconnected position."

If empowerment is the first attribute of women's leadership, creating the organizational structure to foster it is the second.

No one has succeeded better than Frances Hesselbein, who described her weblike structure to author Helgesen at what must have been a memorable lunch.

"Here's me in the center," said Hesselbein, putting her iced-tea glass in the middle of the table. She then surrounded it with circular rows of cups and glasses—"and this is my first management team." Hesselbein built more concentric circles, linking them with knives and forks, Helgesen reports.

"The great thing about the circle is it does not box you in," the former Girl Scout executive concluded. "You can connect with any other point."

The web is especially desirable in a large organization, which can easily deteriorate into a lifeless bureaucracy just because it is so huge.

"If I had to put somebody in to take Roger Smith's place at GM," said Peter Drucker in 1990, "I would pick Frances." That is because, says Drucker, her strong point is turning around a huge bureaucracy. Hesselbein's track record illustrates the power of the web. When she took over in 1976, the Girl Scouts were in danger of becoming "irrelevant" to modern concerns. Membership was falling. Today the Girl Scouts of America is a successful, renewed organization.

Managers at IBM and Motorola watch Frances Hesselbein on video. Students at Harvard Business School study her techniques. Leadership expert Warren Bennis ranks Frances Hesselbein with the likes of Apple Computer's John Sculley. Said one Harvard professor,

"Frances displays a clarity of purpose and a management strategy and direction that very few for-profit CEO's traipsing through this campus have ever shown."

Networking

Web management, or networking, continues to be women's prime modus operandi in the work world. Susan Davis, founding organizer of the Committee of 200, brought together the nation's top women business owners in a network for the first time in 1982. Later, in a high-powered management job at Chicago's Harris Bank, she got managers who run $100 million portfolios to share information and operate collaboratively.

Today Davis brings her networking skills to the pioneering field of "social venture capital," which invests in, among other areas, energy, recycling and the environment. Davis's firm, Capital Missions Company, has launched "Investors' Circle," a network of socially responsible investors who meet to leverage their time, funds and experience.

The Teaching Archetype

Grace Pastiak is a director of manufacturing at Tellabs, Inc., a $213 million-a-year maker of sophisticated telephone equipment located outside Chicago. In the male-dominated manufacturing sector, a surprising 26.4 percent of executives and managers are women. Two days a month Pastiak teaches "Total Quality Commitment," a course for workers, the teaching of which, she believes, many male managers would delegate to a subordinate.

"I cannot think of anything more important that I should be doing than empowering people. . . . I have the bias that people do better when they are happy," says Pastiak, reiterating an old theme among women leaders. "The old style of beating on people to get things done does not work," she says.

But getting out on the shop floor and talking to people does. When an important order had to be filled just before Christmas, she called her people together. "I knew it was getting into holiday season, and many of the people would have family demands," she says. Instead of announcing compulsory overtime, she *asked* her people what they were willing to do. "They said, 'Go for it,' and that's what we did," she said.

Grace Pastiak meets production dates 98 percent of the time, compared to an industry average of 90 percent.

But What's the Downside?

Despite the overwhelming advantages of Women's Leadership style, it is critical to remember we are still in a time of transition. To lead in the new paradigm, women must understand how the new approach looks to those still locked in the old. For this is where women will appear most vulnerable. "Gushing with enthusiasm," as Judy Rosener puts it, is going to appear meaningless and naive.

It is important to remember that when you ask for people's suggestions and then do not use them, people can become frustrated. Remember, too: asking for people's ideas is a lot more time-consuming than making unilateral decisions.

Most important, you have to know what you are doing; it cannot be just style. Being open to and accepting of other people's ideas might make a leader vulnerable to criticism or to people seeking to challenge her authority. Worst of all, she might look as though she is asking because she really doesn't know what she is doing. When you know what you are doing, that sort of thing is not going to throw you off—especially if you anticipate it.

Still, one nagging question persists: how do you get the recognition you deserve while working in a culture that praises and rewards more traditional, male-dominated approaches?

Barbara Fittipaldi, a partner with Landmark Consulting, an international consulting firm based in Somerville, New Jersey, founded The Center for Women, Leadership and the Future to answer that question. In three-day seminars held throughout the world, she and her associates teach women to identify and operate with three different leadership paradigms:

- Adaptive—the traditional management paradigm, the way most companies operate day to day, "business as usual."
- Intervention—the operative paradigm in a company which *has* created a breakthrough in change or culture, but where leadership is incapable of replicating that success again and again.
- Generative—corporate leadership that has mastered the change

process, knows how to generate continuous change and keep reinventing itself by freeing people to think for themselves and change appropriately.

The emphasis is on how women fit into existing corporate cultures and how, even though they work in male-dominated cultures, women can be successful leaders.

"There is possibly no other aspect of our culture more influenced by myth than that of women leaders," reads the Center's materials. "Women in leadership roles must not only address issues of organizational culture but they must also address the organization's relationship to women and the attendant myths."

That is asking a lot, but, according to seminar graduates, the process creates results that are well worth the effort.

Denise Viola, commercial manager with Englehard Corporation, says she expanded productivity and confidence and learned to "bring more of 'me, the person' to my job."

Justina Ayers, division manager with AT&T, discovered herself as "a powerful leader," able to "take on big projects and stick with them, even when they seem the most difficult."

Publishing executive Ann McCracken learned how to lead by communicating her enthusiasm and vision to her employees; sales, she reports, are soaring.

Joyce Cofield, assistant to the president of Polaroid Corporation, says, "I see the design of how to cause culture change, and I have the tools to fulfill it."

The Only Way to Go

Judy Rosener identifies two generations of women. The older conformed to male standards. The second, younger group broke new ground "by drawing on the skills and attitudes they developed from their shared experience as women," she writes.

In fact most women *never* learned the military style of management—and would have been laughed out of the office if they had. "Co-workers are more hostile and negative toward women managers lacking human relation skills," concluded a study for the Center for Values Research in Dallas. That confirms the belief that aggressive women are rejected as bitchy.

There was really no alternative but for women to create their own way. It was completely in tune with the megatrends of the day and is now the dominant leadership model.

Balance

"In the 1980s, work was highly idealized and romanticized, much in the way family life was idealized in the 1950s," says Barbara Dafoe Whitehead, a senior research associate at New York's Institute for American Values. Now, she says, people realize that "work isn't everything; families are important."

People are not about to give up high-powered careers anytime soon, but a new word is entering business talk—"balance."

Most working women say they do not have enough time to be a CEO, mother, lover, exercise buff and gourmet chef plus put in a few hours a week at the local recycling center. Nevertheless, many do all that and more.

Almost one quarter of the United States' full-time workers spend 49 hours a week or more at work, compared with 17 percent in 1981. Dr. Arlie Hochschild, a sociologist at the University of California at Berkeley and author of *The Second Shift: Working Parents and the Revolution at Home* (Viking), says women work an average of 15 hours more per week, because of household chores, than men do. Some studies say Americans have cut leisure time substantially. That does not impress most working women, who report they have no leisure time whatsoever. What's to cut?

That is because working women often measure themselves against fiftysomething corporate men who enjoy the support of at-home wives. But now, 10 or 20 years into their careers, most women— and many like-minded men—find the rat race wearing pretty thin. They want successful careers and personal lives, too.

"Leisure time—not money—is becoming the status symbol of the 1990's," says John Robinson, director of the Americans' Use of Time Project at the University of Maryland. Robinson found 70 percent of the people earning $30,000 a year or more would trade a day's pay for a day of free time.

Baby boomers who want a break may have an ally in the new kids on the corporate block—those born in 1965 or after—the baby-bust generation. *Fortune* calls them Yiffies—young, individualistic, freedom-minded and few. They want job satisfaction, without sacrificing for the corporation.

Maybe this new group will help everyone actualize the growing ideal of a balanced life. Women in their 40's and 50's should understand the new generation—they raised it. Perhaps the young folks looked at Mom and said, "A successful career is one thing, but I'll never overwork myself like that."

Meanwhile Mom started changing, too, especially as she reached positions of greater corporate power:

- Lane Nemeth, CEO of Discovery Toys, a $93 million-a-year business with operations in Canada and Japan, says her daughter and husband are her top priorities. "I will not, if I can avoid it, work on weekends," she says. "I do not work till 9 or 10 o'clock at night." Sales grew 17 percent in 1992, and she plans to continue international expansion.
- Nancy Badore, a top executive at Ford and the mother of a young child, is cited as a model of female leadership. She arrives at the office at 8:30 and leaves by 6:00 P.M.
- Barbara Grogan, another top role model for up-and-coming women, is a divorced woman with two school-age children. She never goes to the office on weekends and discourages her employees from doing so. Grogan says point-blank: "I always put my children first," and "Having a baby gives you a sense of what's really important. You still work like hell, but it is all in perspective."

Women leaders are better at balancing than their male counterparts. The first reason is, obviously, intense family responsibility, but it does not stop there. Women do not identify exclusively with their careers, as most men traditionally have. Female leaders take time out for recreation—attending plays and movies, looking at and collecting art, reading inspiring literature, gardening.

For most women, a career is not a methodical rise to power, anyhow, but a zigzag course of ups, downs and plateaus. Years of caring for children contrast with years of make-it-or-break-it all-out dedication to work. In between, most of us seek balance: challenging job plus time for family, friends and recreation.

Is that too much to ask of ourselves, of our corporations?

The Mommy Track

One woman who must have considered herself a voice for balance met with backlash instead. Felice N. Schwartz, president of

Catalyst, which advises corporations on women's careers, wrote an article in *Harvard Business Review* suggesting corporations recognize two types of female managers—those who put careers first, and those who put family first—and need flexible schedules.

Her concept was dubbed "the Mommy Track" and it created a stir that hasn't died down yet. Feminists rightly bristled at the notion of corporate women being treated different from male colleagues (presumably fathers) and of women choosing between career and kids.

Fran Rogers of Work/Family Directions, a Boston research group, was disturbed that Schwartz "is devoted to fitting women into the existing culture instead of finding ways to change that culture . . . dividing women into two groups, but completely ignoring the diversity among men, is just horrifying."

"It's tragic," says Representative Pat Schroeder (D-Colo.), "because it reinforces the idea, which is so strong in our country, that you can either have a family or a career, but not both, if you're a woman."

Schwartz's critics made excellent points, but they also missed the valid part of her message—the need for greater flexibility.

Plenty of evidence (see also Chapter 8) shows families seek more time together. The executive recruitment firm Robert Half polled 1,000 career professionals; 82 percent of the women would choose a career path with flexible full-time hours and more family time but slower career advancement over a fast-track career with inflexible hours.

A recent Du Pont survey found 56 percent of *male* employees favored flexible schedules allowing more family time; 40 percent would consider working for another employer who offered more job flexibility.

As cited earlier, many people would trade a day's pay for a day off.

Ultimately, the Mommy Track was a case of well-intentioned people misunderstanding each other. Top leadership is not for everyone. Nor is it for everyone at every stage in life. Some need flexibility; others want to go full speed ahead in their careers. More flexibility and less grandstanding would have made the Mommy Track an enlightening discussion instead of an ideological debate.

The New Generation

There are two generations in the workplace today and "a real clash of values," says Margaret Regan, a Towers Perrin consultant who runs focus groups. "The older managers think that if the shoe doesn't fit, you should wear it and walk funny. The baby-busters say to throw it out and get a new shoe."

Roy Howard, Bell South's vice president for human resources, puts it this way: "The younger workers coming in now aren't as prone to mold their lives to fit our environment."

"There's a stronger sense of balance in their lives," says Glenn Blake, director of employment and management development at General Mills. "Quality of life is more important to them than it was 10 years ago."

"Maybe a career isn't all it's cracked up to be," says Linda Persico of Ford Motor Company. "It's still important to me, but it's not the number one thing in my life. I have outside interests. If it came down to career or relationship, I would have to think that the relationship comes first."

But, now married, Linda Persico Boren apparently did not have to choose. She and her husband, also a Ford employee, now work for the company in Europe.

"The idea of balance has been building," says one Silicon Valley psychotherapist. "Companies were first interested in stress management, then burnout and now balance."

A Tale of Two Women

In 1972 Sandra Kurtzig founded ASK Computer, becoming the most visible woman in the business. She worked 20-hour days, seven days a week. "Clearly, I didn't know how to balance family and career," she says. In 1985 she took time off to be with her children. In 1989 she asked her board for a permanent leave. Seven months later, Kurtzig's board persuaded her to return full time.

But in the meantime Kurtzig developed some strong ideas about balance. Women should not have to wait until age 40, when their careers are established, to have children, says Kurtzig. "If a company is not considerate enough to let you have a home life, then you shouldn't be there," she says.

In 1977 Deborah (Debi) Coleman became Apple Computer's chief financial officer. But the price of success included high blood pressure and extra weight. Coleman asked herself, "Do I want to be the best CFO in the business and have a heart attack by the time I'm 40?" She told fellow workers, "I decided that I could either wait until I'm burned out or deal with it proactively."

Coleman sold most of her stock, exercised, read magazines and attended conferences. "Before my sabbatical, I didn't have any time for friends or family or exercise," she says. "Now I've found time." A rejuvenated Coleman was back at Apple in 1990 as vice president of information systems and technology. She is now vice president of materials operations at Tektronix in Wilsonville, Oregon.

Jim R. Moberg, executive vice president of human resources at Pacific Telesis, which has a tradition of lifetime employment, puts it this way: "In the course of 32 years, an absence of two or three years is not the end of the world. These people are going to be with us for a long time."

In a move that put the CEO's imprimatur on balance, John Sculley took a nine-week leave of absence while at Apple to work on a barn in Maine.

Getting to Yes

Corporations can foster balance with policies that underscore flexibility: leaves of absence, part-time professional work, job sharing, flextime, reduced hours, sabbaticals. But you probably cannot wait for your company to take the first step. You must begin now to negotiate the lifestyle that works for you.

William Ury's *Getting Past No: How to Negotiate with Difficult People* (Bantam) (sound like your boss?) contains the kind of practical advice that will help you work out arrangements like the ones these women did.

• In 1984, when her children were young, Levi Strauss's Donna Goya, described on page 102, worked a three-day week and cut her responsibility from five to three divisions.

• Karen B. Appignani, a programming analyst at Johnson & Johnson, took six weeks' maternity leave when her daughter, Tara, was born in 1989. Then she worked at home on a personal computer for three months. Later, she worked at home two days a week and went into the office the other three days.

• Kathie McKirdy was "missing too much of my children's lives." She told her employer, DDB Needham Worldwide in Chicago, she planned to leave in 1989—"resigning seemed like the only solution." But DDB Needham didn't want to see her go. Now she spends 18 hours in the office over a three-day period and works one day at home. Carrying a cellular phone, she says, means she is easier to reach than "people who are in the office 12 hours a day."

Corporations that recognize the need for flexibility and how much it improves employee's work will attract the best people and increase productivity.

Juliet Schor, associate professor of economics at Harvard University and author of *The Overworked American* (Basic Books), is telling companies to cut people's hours but not their pay. Productivity would increase dramatically, she argues. During the Depression, the Kellogg Company cut the workday of production workers from eight to six hours. In one department that had been making 83 cases of cereal a day, production zoomed up to 96.

W. R. Kellogg himself concluded that employee efficiency and morale were so high and that accidents and *unit cost of production* so low, **"We can afford to pay as much for six hours as we formerly paid for eight."**

Schor says the workday could be cut to six or seven hours. She cites Medtronic Corporation of Minneapolis, which saw output increase when it cut work hours from 40 hours a week to 36—but paid people for 40 hours—and the Texas-based United Services Automobile Association insurance company, where sales increased when employees worked shorter hours.

Self-employed people—who have learned to be task-oriented, rather than bound by the Industrial Age's time-clock mentality—know this makes a lot of sense. They can do a full-time job in five or six hours by cutting out conversations with co-workers, scheduled and unscheduled breaks, formal lunches, unproductive meetings and other interruptions (not to mention commuting; see Chapter 8). Working shorter hours permits people to work in a more focused, more intense fashion. With the day's work accomplished, there is time left for family, recreation, fitness.

Self-employed people know this would work even better in today's offices than it did in a Depression-era cereal plant.

Is anyone else listening?

The Wage Gap

In an information society, brains are more important than brawn. Male-dominated unions have lost their power. Thirty percent of women hold managerial or professional jobs (versus 29 percent of men). There is no excuse for the "wage gap," whereby women earn consistently less than men. Yet from 1960 to 1980 women's wages stagnated at around 60 cents for every dollar men earned.

In the 1980's, however, something happened: women's wages increased from 60 to 72.4 cents to the dollar, according to the Bureau of Labor Statistics. By 1992, it was 75.4 cents. Not equality by any means, but not business as usual, either. What happened?

Men's earnings declined. That was one factor, but not the only one. In the 1980's market forces and demographics finally began to work in women's favor. Labor shortages in nursing boosted salaries. Older women who earned less retired. Baby-boom women moved into well-paying management jobs. Younger women with training in math and science won high-tech jobs.

Women age 24 to 34 earned 86.3 cents for every dollar their male counterparts earned in 1992, and 88.8 cents for every dollar in the first quarter of 1993.

Education, experience and labor shortages narrowed the wage gap in the 1980's and will continue to do so in the 1990's.

Discrimination

"We say the wage gap is due to discrimination," says Claudia Wayne, executive director of the National Committee on Pay Equity. Discrimination, of course, accounts for part of the wage gap, but that is not the whole story. The gap exists because of discrimination *and* market forces. Given the increase in women's wages in the 1980's, there is reason for optimism about closing the wage gap in the foreseeable future.

Most people are overly pessimistic about the wage gap—ourselves included. In *Reinventing the Corporation* (1985), we quoted the Rand Corporation's James Smith, who predicted the gap would narrow to 74 cents to the dollar by 2000. It was then 64 cents to the dollar. We figured we would catch heat for being too optimistic. But Smith's assessment was the most sensible we had heard, so we went with it. It turned out to be too pessimistic. By 1992, as noted, women were already earning 75.4 cents to the dollar. And in the first quarter of 1993, the overall gap had narrowed even further, to 77 cents to the dollar (younger women, as noted earned a lot more).

So much for being *too* optimistic.

The 85 Percent Factor

The wage gap will narrow in the 1990's (better salaries for nurses and teachers will be a big factor), but it will not be eliminated. There is growing evidence that among business and professional people of equal experience and education, a stubborn wage gap of about 15 percent persists:

- Baruch College researcher June O'Neill concluded that women without children earn 86 percent of the incomes of men without children.
- Some 87 percent of full-time women lawyers reported their salaries were equal to their male counterparts', says a study by the *National Law Journal.*
- Female MBAs from the top 20 schools averaged $54,749 one year after graduation, noted a 1990 *Business Week* survey, but their male counterparts earned $61,400, about 12 percent more.

Pinning It Down

Is it discrimination? Or too much flexibility on the part of women?

"As women get into a field, salaries go down because women are willing to work for less," charges Wendy Reed-Crisp, director of the National Association for Female Executives in New York.

Do women's wages inch back up as they gain experience, get angry and demand more money? Do men fight harder for each dollar because they interpret salary as a measure of their self-worth? In the previous section we noted that executive women do not identify with their jobs the way men do. How much does this cost women at salary-negotiation time?

"Women in some industries," says Lester Korn of Korn/Ferry, "are, well, managerial bargains." Some clients realize they save 25 to

30 percent by hiring women, he says. "We see it in executive searches all the time."

That ought to change. "Women managers need to develop a keener awareness of what their true value is, and then make it clear they expect to be paid accordingly," says Dee Soder, president of New York City's Endymion Company. Often women do not use their advantages and accomplishments to press for higher pay, she says.

Beyond Left and Right

Some women's groups want the government to equalize wages through a grand, top-down, across-the-board comparable-worth scheme. Every company employing a nurse would have to abide by certain standards, as would every corporation that hires a janitor. Does that sound like socialism? Most women do not support such a move; the rest of the country would reject it. And it would be bureaucratic hell to implement.

But comparable worth would work very effectively within the organic confines of a single employer. To enact a comparable-worth scheme, you have to analyze the "value" of a job's skills, its working conditions and other factors, including valuing a job's social contribution—here's where caring for children and doing society's dirty work have to get extra points. It is complicated, but compensation consultants know exactly how to do it. The best schemes factor in market forces, too. Obviously, it is good business to pay people what they are "worth."

Look at it this way: if men have been overpaid because they were the traditional breadwinners, it is in the self-interest of employers to correct that inequity.

The way to eliminate the wage gap is by drawing on women's economic **and** political power: 1) acknowledging the role market forces play; 2) isolating pure discrimination and going after it with the full force of women's growing political power; and 3) enacting comparable worth **within** each corporation.

Had a federal comparable-worth law been enacted a decade ago, conservatives and male chauvinists could say, "You didn't pull your own weight in the marketplace. You got the laws changed." Women would never have known their undeniable economic worth. Today they do. But now it is high time they were paid for it.

Opportunity, leadership and balance. This chapter's three themes say a lot about how women have fared in the marketplace. For most U.S. women, work was the ground floor of liberation—where they first encountered harassment and discrimination and pressed for "Equal Pay for Equal Work" laws.

It was also the theater for their first accomplishments, which increased self-esteem and delivered economic independence. Women are well grounded in the world of work; it is their turf. And, as the Megatrends Career List illustrates, there is plenty of opportunity out there for young women, midcareer shifts, new businesses and career advancement.

But for women who know their life's work and have established careers, it is time to move on, and there are three possible directions: balance, leadership or both.

After 10 to 20 years in the salt mine, the call of balance is important to heed. Is this the point where it makes sense to drop out and head for the health club, as Debi Coleman did? Take time off to train for the marathon? Or simply cut back hours to spend time with family, as many women described here have done? If you do not take command of your time now, then when?

The commitment to build leadership potential is as sizable as the one you made in seeking the right career and honing the skills to undertake it. Leadership might mean leaving the firm you have been with for 15 years to go it on your own or establishing a 10-year plan to become its CEO. As a leader, you will teach others what you have learned. It is a noble calling.

But answering it should not mean 10 or 15 more years of overwork. You have already done that. As Chapter 5 shows, when a woman hits 40, heart attack–preventing estrogen is already wearing thin. Stress and overwork and the heart-disease statistics are going to head upward for women in their 50's.

More important, look at the women leaders described in this chapter: they possess character, vision, autonomy, discipline, focus, clarity of purpose and communication skills. They are highly competent people, but they are not workaholics—and they have personal lives.

Having it all used to mean husband, career and baby. In a woman's prime the children are off to college or headed there soon, and the husband is someone you get to know all over again. Having it all can mean balance *and* leadership.

If that is what you want, you can make it happen.

4.
To Hell with Sexism: Women in Religion

Women of the late 20th century are revolutionizing the most sexist institution in history—organized religion. Overturning millennia of tradition, they are challenging authorities, reinterpreting the Bible, creating their own services, crowding into seminaries, winning the right to ordination, purging sexist language in liturgy, reintegrating female values and assuming positions of leadership.

Twenty years ago, there were almost no women in the seminary. Now women make up 30 percent of students in the almost 300-member Association of Theological Schools. At prestigious Yale Divinity School, nearly half the students are women, while at Harvard Divinity School women make up 60 percent of students.

- Thousands of Catholic and Protestant women worship in all-female groups.
- Contemporary non-Orthodox Jewish women are embracing the traditional Orthodox mikva (ritual bath) as a "spiritual and women's rights" ritual.
- The Episcopal Church has elected its second female bishop.

There are even some cracks at the heart of fundamentalism. TV evangelist Pat Robertson has teamed up with compassionate, articulate Shelia Walsh. Mormons no longer require women to obey their husbands; now they vow to obey God.

Central to women's spiritual quest is outright rejection of the notion that God is somehow male. While some women feel empowered by envisioning God as the Sacred Feminine, others insist Divinity is neither female nor male. But whether proper Bostonian nuns or radical California Goddess worshipers, women seek a rich new spirituality free from male-imposed limits, metaphors, language or interpretations. The Goddess movement is described in Chapter 9.

In November 1992 the General Synod of the Church of England voted to ordain women. The Church's 1,350 women deacons are now prime candidates for the priesthood.

"To insist upon maleness as an essential attribute of priesthood is, I believe, to commit the fundamental error of making the maleness of Christ more significant than his humanity," said Dr. George Carey, Archbishop of Canterbury. "God is calling us to ordain women to the priesthood."

The Vatican called the vote a "grave obstacle" to repairing the 16th-century split between Roman Catholics and Anglicans.

The ordaining of women is a measurable change in the mainstream. But it is by no means the whole story. The issue is no longer equality, says Margaret McManus of the Center for Women and Religion at the Graduate Theological Union, in Berkeley, California. "The issue is transformation of our religious institutions."

The first phase of change within Judaism is already complete, says Rabbi Ellen Dreyfus of Congregation Beth Sholom in suburban Chicago: women now serve as rabbis and cantors. "Phase two will be transforming Judaism to include women's perspectives and reflect women's lives in ritual, theology, language and imagery," she says.

Women-Church

Such total transformation will be a long time coming. Meanwhile some women pursue spirituality outside the mainstream. More than 150 groups of U.S. Catholics and Protestants worship in female-dominated clusters (some are open to men) in private homes and on college campuses. Collectively this network calls itself Women-Church.

The movement started with Catholics barred from the priesthood and then reached out to women of other faiths. A Women-Church international conference, held in Cincinnati in 1987, attracted 3,000 women. Twenty-five hundred women and a few men attended the "Women-Church: Weavers of Change" conference held in Albuquerque, New Mexico, in 1993. But ordaining women is no longer the major goal. It is rather to reinterpret the language, symbols and texts of Christianity to serve women's spirituality.

Says Mary Hunt, co-director of the Women's Alliance for Theology, Ethics and Ritual (WATER) and a member of Women-Church Convergence, "Women-Church is a statement of our humanity as women and our share in divinity as church."

"The desire to fight existing institutions like the Catholic Church is being replaced by the desire to *be* Church, to develop a separate and new understanding of Church, to resume worship," concludes an article in *Christian Century*.

What sort of woman is attracted to Women-Church? One reporter covering a conference was surprised there were so few radicals. "These women could have been my aunts, grandmother or next-door neighbor," she wrote.

Mary Hunt distinguishes her group from the Goddess movement, but, she observes, there is a great deal of indebtedness between the two movements. Whether they agree totally with each other or not, women on both sides seek a new brand of female spirituality.

A New Voice in Judaism

Jewish women's groups for prayer, study or healing "are everywhere," says Cherie Koller-Fox, rabbi of Congregation Eitz Chayim in Cambridge, Massachusetts. In study groups among all branches, including Orthodox, where women and men are separated during worship, women increasingly participate in Talmud study, asking their own questions of the Midrash, the rabbinical commentaries and stories people told about the Bible. They are raising issues no one had ever considered. "When Pharaoh let the Jews go," one woman asked, "what happened to the women who were in labor?"

"We've found a new voice," says Cherie Koller-Fox. "After being quiet for so long, it is a spiritual awakening."

Today, in all but Orthodox congregations, girls are called to the Torah for the bat mitzvah ceremony, the traditional coming-of-age ritual marking the beginning of religious responsibility. But in 1992 a very special one was held: a second bat mitzvah for the first girl ever to undergo the ritual, in 1922, Judith Kaplan Eisenstein, who was the daughter of Rabbi Mordecai Kaplan, the founder of Reconstructionist Judaism.

Judith Eisenstein, now in her eighties, thinks it is time to tone down the big party that traditionally follows the religious event. "Bat mitzvah began not just as a statement of feminism, but as a statement of dedication to something larger than oneself," she said. "To put it mildly, it's gotten less and less thoughtful."

Women rabbis trace the beginning of the religion's opening up to women, which led to women's full ordination, to Judith Kaplan Eisenstein's bat mitzvah.

"What appeared to be a rather simple act of a young Jewish woman in 1922 was in fact a gift that continues to be unwrapped to this day," said Rabbi Sandy Sasso, the first woman rabbi in the Reconstructionist branch.

Feminist Theology

Feminists reject traditional interpretations of the Bible, which, they argue, have been created and invoked by the male power structure to keep women submissive.

"Part of feminist biblical scholarship is to take a closer look at Scripture and ask, 'Is that really what the text says, or is it what men have told us the text says?' " says Sister Sandra Schneiders, professor of New Testament studies at the Jesuit School of Theology in Berkeley, California.

Some feminists insist the Bible is so sexist, it cannot speak to modern women. Elisabeth Schüssler Fiorenza, the author of *In Memory of Her* (Crossroad), disagrees. A former professor of New Testament theology at Notre Dame, now at Harvard Divinity School, she is devoted to developing a feminist reinterpretation of the New Testament.

While embracing the Bible, Schüssler Fiorenza does not let its patriarchal authors off easy: "Biblical revelation and truth are given only in those texts and interpretive models that transcend critically their patriarchal frameworks and allow for a vision of Christian women as historical and theological subjects and actors," she writes.

Schüssler Fiorenza believes, as did Elizabeth Cady Stanton (see page 125), that if women do not reclaim and reinterpret Scripture in their own way, it will continue to be used to oppress them.

To abandon Scripture because of its patriarchal culture and context, she argues, is a bit like throwing the baby out with the bathwater. It would mean losing the power and history of early Christian women, who, she says, "had the power and authority of the

Gospel. They were central and leading individuals in the early Christian movement."

Women were disciples during the ministry of Christ and highly active in the two or three centuries before male-dominant forces took control of the Church. "Paul's letters also mention nine women by name who were co-workers with him in the gospel ministry," writes the Reverend David Scholer, distinguished professor of New Testament studies at Chicago's North Park Seminary, in *A Biblical Basis for Equal Partnership: Women and Men in the Ministry of the Church.*

Schüssler Fiorenza tells the stories of these women, including the great missionary Priscilla and the prophetic leaders Mary, Elizabeth and Anna, in *In Memory of Her,* whose title comes from the New Testament story of the woman who, before Jesus' betrayal and death, anointed him with expensive perfume and washed his feet with her hair. Though the male disciples objected to the woman's action, Jesus approved and said, "And truly I say to you, whenever the Gospel is preached in the whole world, what she has done will be told in memory of her."

Feminist theologians are taking another look at how biblical authors portray women: Eve, Mary the Mother of Christ and Mary Magdalene. "The way the church has used Mary [the Mother of Christ] has been very harmful. She has been put on a pedestal as a symbol of passivity and receptivity," says Australian Erin White, former Catholic nun and now an ordination activist.

The outlines of a new Christian feminist theology are becoming visible: 1) God is not male; 2) Jesus did not intend for Christianity to evolve into a sexist institution (as far as his male followers go, that is a different story)—against the customs of the day, He was practically a feminist; and 3) the history of women has been edited out of the Bible.

"I call myself an Evangelical Christian feminist, which means I am a person who believes the Scriptures, when properly interpreted and applied, teach the full partnership of men and women in church, family, and society," says Roberta Hestenes, a Presbyterian minister and president of Eastern College, St. Davids, Pennsylvania. She is the first woman to head a college in the Christian College Coalition, an association of Christ-centered colleges and universities.

God Is Not a Male

Professor Mary Daly of Boston College, put it simply and well: "As long as God is male, the male is God." Female thinkers unanimously repudiate that traditional, absurd connection.

"To see God as male is idolatry . . . the worship of images in man's own shape," says Dr. Barbara Thiering, theologian at the University of Sydney. "God as male, as the father, is only a metaphor but . . . the church has taken it literally."

Some women insist the way to balance centuries of envisioning God as male is by worshiping the Sacred Feminine, the Mother. In so doing, they honor their femininity and empower themselves.

"Women are . . . talking about not only feminine names for God, but also feminine attributes as well," says Carol Ochs, professor of philosophy at Boston's Simmons College. "Moses talked about God as Mother, but this language has been deemphasized and forgotten in most traditions."

Nor Is He Two Men and a Bird

Many Christians worship God in the form of the Trinity: Father, Son and Spirit. "In many people's imagination . . . [this] comes down to an old man, a young man, and a bird," warns Sister Sandra Schneiders.

"First, God is not three people, much less three males," she argues. God, she says, is better described as "divine origin, source, ground of our being . . . divine communicator, divine communication, and redeemer . . . divine energy, mover, transforming power."

Although Sister Schneiders approves of invoking God as female, her words might still be construed as a warning to women who, in envisioning Divinity as female, might overplay the metaphor. The urge to turn God into three people is "the constant idolatrous tendency of humans," she charges. "We try to make God in our human image instead of the other way around. God is not a human being."

On the one hand, Divinity transcends human concepts of gender. On the other hand, envisioning God as Mother or the Sacred Feminine is a comforting metaphor, perhaps a justifiable antidote to millennia of envisioning God as male.

Jesus as Feminist; the Church as Sexist

When you consider that the institution that purports to follow Jesus Christ bans women from leadership, burned and tortured millions of women and continues today to deny hundreds of millions more the right to decide what size family they can support, you almost have to conclude that Jesus was one tough and macho man. But according to feminist scholars, he was not.

"Nowhere in the Gospels does Jesus put down women. Jesus defends women; he does for them what he does for men," declares Sister Schneiders. "He included women among his apostles and disciples. Jesus never takes the oppressive role other men took in relationship with women."

Dr. Elisabeth Schüssler Fiorenza says Jesus accepted women, prostitutes and the poor, quite a departure from the norms of that time.

The point has already been made that women were highly active in the early days of Christianity. When the apostle Paul says women absolutely must not preach in church, notes Dr. Schüssler Fiorenza, it could mean that Paul was threatened by the fact that women actually *were* preaching.

Early Church Fathers, like Augustine, Irenaeus and Tertullian, made sure women were not just kept from leadership, but branded as spiritually inferior to males. By the 13th century Thomas Aquinas called women defective by nature and "misbegotten males." The Inquisition used the 15th-century document *Malleus Maleficarum* (Hammer of Witches), which drew from Genesis its authority to persecute women as witches. Incredibly, men have invoked Genesis to justify the physical abuse of their wives.

"The tendency to sexualize, trivialize, and demonize women is part of the tradition of biblical interpretation," says Sister Schneiders.

Eve: Her story

The villain of the Garden of Eden story, tradition tells us, is Eve. Weak and sinful, she eats the forbidden fruit, and humanity is headed downhill from then on. This is supposed to symbolize the "evil in all women." Eve's portrayal has probably done more to destroy women's positive self-image than any other factor in tradition or mythology.

Elizabeth Cady Stanton's late-19th-century *Woman's Bible* tried to reinterpret the story of Eve in a feminist context. "It is amazing," she wrote, "that any set of men ever claimed that the dogma of the inferiority of woman is here set forth. The conduct of Eve from the beginning to the end is so superior to that of Adam."

Cady Stanton wanted to show that the Bible is a political weapon used against women. But she was a bit radical for the day. The project was rejected by the National American Women's Suffrage Association and received little notice. Women theologians in the 20th century are having another go at it.

The problem with the Eve story is not the text, says Phyllis Trible of Union Theological Seminary, but the sexist context given the text over the centuries: "Patriarchal interpreters claim that woman is inferior because she is created last (Genesis 2:22)," notes Trible, but they never argue that humans are inferior to animals because they were created later (Genesis 1:27).

"Why not speculate that the serpent questions her [Eve] because she is the more intelligent of the two?" asks Trible.

Rabbi Karen Soriah of Melbourne, Australia's Temple Beth Israel agrees. "It could . . . demonstrate woman's superior intellectual capacity. After all, Eve . . . had the first theological discussion."

Feminist Theology Is International

The Women's Commission of the Ecumenical Association of Third World Theologians is a network linking feminist theologians from Asia, Africa and Latin America. Third World women want in particular to explore the status of women in their countries before colonialism.

- Asian women started a monthly journal called *In God's Image*. It is published by the Asian Women's Resource Center in Hong Kong.
- Indian women focus on the thousands of women killed in dowry murders.
- Korean women examine national reunification, as well as the contrasts between North and South, male and female, communist and capitalist.

Young Kim, a Methodist minister ordained in the United States, was denied pastoral duties back home in Seoul because of her sex. Instead of responding with bitterness, she became the first pastor of Women Church of Korea, an ecumenical group that offers pastoral care and worship services and specifically seeks to serve oppressed women.

Women and Islam

Contemporary non-Muslim feminists might be surprised to hear that the Koran, Islam's holy scripture, does *not* brand women as unequal and inferior. Islamic experts say their religion is not to blame for women's narrow roles in many Islamic countries. It has to do with how a government *interprets* Islam, they say. During the prophet Muhammad's time women held active roles, but were later subjugated because of local customs. Today Islamic law *can* be implemented to prevent women's equality.

Benazir Bhutto became head of Islamic Pakistan. That could not happen in Saudi Arabia. "The Islamic religion is also our law," says Lolwah al-Ammari, a California-educated Saudi businesswoman.

Eunuchs: A European Best-seller

Eunuchs for the Kingdom of Heaven (Doubleday) by Dr. Uta Ranke-Heinemann, a feminist theologian and professor at the University of Essen in Germany, describes the Catholic Church's hostility to the body, sexuality and women. She carefully traces the antifemale writings of Ambrose, Augustine, Albertus Magnus and Aquinas— and that's just the A's.

When the book appeared in the United States in 1990, New York's cardinal, John O'Connor, blasted its publisher for "Catholic bashing." Cardinal O'Connor admitted to reading only the book jacket but nevertheless termed it "utterly preposterous." A number one nonfiction best-seller in Germany and Italy, the book had never been attacked by a prominent churchman until it hit the United States.

Seminary and Pulpit

"The Bible teaches the full equality of men and women in Creation and Redemption," states Christians for Biblical Equality, a 1,500-member group of Evangelicals and fundamentalists based in St. Paul, Minnesota. Both are "divinely gifted and empowered to minister

. . . women as well as men exercise the prophetic, priestly and royal functions" of the church.

- The number of women rabbis in all branches of Judaism is now approaching 300.
- The United Church of Christ, which has ordained women since the mid-19th century, counts more than 1,800 women ministers out of a total of 10,700.
- By 1992 the Presbyterian Church ordained 2,419 women.
- More than 1,000 of the 14,000 Episcopal ministers in the United States are women.
- The United Methodist Church counts more than 4,200 female clergy.
- The Evangelical Lutheran Church in America has 1,429 clergy-women.
- About 1,000 of the 14,000 ministers in the Disciples of Christ Church are women.

According to a *"USA Today* Snapshot" published March 29, 1993, women account for 12 percent of Episcopal priests, Presbyterian ministers and Reform Jewish rabbis, as well as 11 percent of Methodist ministers. Women are 9 percent of Baptist pastors and 2 percent of Conservative Jewish rabbis.

The ranks of fully ordained American women *doubled* between 1977 and 1986, to 21,000, says the National Council of Churches (incredibly, that is the last time anyone counted—and we have tried everyone).

The numbers of women ministers have grown rapidly since then. If 1,500 women were ordained each year since 1986, there are more than 30,000 women ministers today. The figure of 21,000 is well on its way to doubling again, to 42,000, sometime in the late 1990's.

The African Methodist Episcopal Church, a mostly black denomination, estimated that in 1990 women already made up one third of its 19,000 ministers.

Women make up a substantial part of "New Thought" ministries, perhaps the best known of which is Unity. These nondenominational groups focus on spiritual issues, especially faith and healing. More than half of the 600 or so Unity ministers are women.

Women Seminarians

In 1987 women represented less than 10 percent of the profession. But in the coming years that percentage will reach a critical mass of 25 to 30 percent. The reason: a huge increase in women seminarians.

One third of the 56,000 students in seminaries accredited by the Association of Theological Schools are women, compared with one eighth 10 years ago and almost none 20 years ago. Those are the findings of Joseph O'Neill, principal research scientist at the Educational Testing Service in Princeton, New Jersey.

Feminist theology is about to come out of the seminary and into the neighborhood church or synogogue.

At Columbia Presbyterian Seminary in Decatur, Georgia, 42 percent of the master of divinity students are women. "Women are taking the preaching prizes. Women are taking the academic prizes," reports admissions director the Reverend Rebecca Parker.

More than half the ordination candidates of the United Church of Christ are women. One third of Episcopalian, Methodist and Presbyterian seminarians are women.

Both women and men are entering seminaries later in life, often as a second career. Joseph O'Neill's findings show that seminarians on average are 10 years older than those of a generation ago, although this is now beginning to level off. Many women may have felt the call earlier but are only now free to enroll.

Bernice Kimel Weiss, the mother of two, was ordained a rabbi at age 47. "Even when I was young, I thought about the rabbinate . . . but knew it could never be a reality because of where women were in religious life," she says. Weiss commuted between Potomac, Maryland, and New York each week for four years to attend the Academy for Jewish Religion. "Never say it is too late to start something new in your life," she said during her ordination ceremony.

From Seminary to Ministry

Ordination, of course, does not mean an automatic ministry. Some women wait years for an assignment and say the reason is sexism in the religious hierarchy—"The laity is not the problem," says a female Anglican rector in Alberta, Canada. "The problem is the

church hierarchy." They may then tangle with male colleagues or a
congregation that is simply unsupportive—"I feel like I'm a missionary to my denomination," said the woman pastor of a Southern
Baptist congregation in Memphis.

Marie Wiebe, an ordained minister in the Evangelical Covenant
Church, tells how the daughter of the deacon who had most opposed
her told her father, "I'm going to be a minister—like Pastor Marie!"

Despite obstacles female clergy face, some fear the ministry may
become a "pink collar" profession—female-dominated and underpaid. "White men are withdrawing and looking for the prestige and
money that leads to the good life. In their place, women and minorities
are moving in," says Judith Berling, dean of the Graduate Theological
Union in Berkeley, California.

It is a risk many devoted women are willing to take. Most ministers are not exactly in it for the money. Love and service are certainly
what motivate today's women ministers and rabbis. The minimal
"prestige" would-be priests are after is the simple dignity of ordination.

Some women downplay the importance of ordination—insisting
they would reject it until church authorities are more participative and
power-sharing. Others declare that ordination is a prerequisite for
transforming the institution.

The Catholic Church's failure to ordain women is an exclusion
from decision-making power, says Sister Maria Riley, director of
women's studies at the Center of Concern, a Catholic research organization.

Carolyn Oehler, director of the Council on Ministries of Northern Illinois's United Methodist Church, says, "Ordination is the key
to empowerment in the church . . . the more hierarchical a system is,
the more key it is."

Women Rabbis

Helen Hadassah Lyons, the first U.S. woman to complete rabbinical studies, was not given the title "Rabbi." An advocate of
women's ordination, she lectured and preached widely. In 1988 Hebrew Union College–Jewish Institute of Religion honored her, saying,
"You are blessed, that in your lifetime, you are able to see others
travel the path that you cleared." She passed away in 1989.

Since 1972 women have served as cantors and rabbis in the
Reform branch of Judaism. Cincinnati's Hebrew Union College, of

the Reform branch, has graduated 171 women rabbis since then. Eight of the 16 members of the 1992 graduating class were women.

Conservative Jews ordained their first female rabbi in 1985. Ginger Greenspan, registrar of Jewish Theological Seminary, the only U.S. school that graduates Conservative rabbis, says they usually graduate two or three women each year. In 1991, five of the 21 graduates were women.

Julia Greenberg describes the year her rabbinical team consisted of three women. "There we were, draped in our ritual prayer shawls, one of us holding the Torah, one chanting the haunting High Holiday melodies and one holding the ram's horns. In front of us were the 30 children . . . beaming, expectant. And I knew they were not thinking 'lady rabbis.' To them this is Judaism," says Rabbi Greenberg. "The children are growing up with the changes we have struggled to create."

Bishop Barbara

In 1989 the Reverend Barbara C. Harris, a black woman, became the world's first female Episcopal bishop. In a ceremony before 8,500 people, she was consecrated in Massachusetts, the church's largest diocese. The Episcopal Church has about 50 black clergywomen. Episcopal clergywomen said the consecration filled them with a deep sense of belonging.

Bishop Harris's spiritual path is a study in the nontraditional. A former business executive and civil rights activist who marched with Martin Luther King, Jr., Barbara Harris is divorced and never graduated from college. In 1974 she led 11 women up the aisle of a Philadelphia church to be ordained in a ceremony later declared invalid. She left Sun Oil in 1980 to work as a priest and as a chaplain in the Pennsylvania State prison system. Four years later Barbara Harris ascended a bigger pulpit: she took over *Witness,* the Church's independent leftist newspaper. From that platform she spoke out against racism, political inequity and the "male-dominated, racist Church."

"I certainly don't want to be one of the boys," she has said. "I want to offer my peculiar gifts as a black woman . . . a sensitivity and an awareness that come out of more than a speaking acquaintance with oppression."

Bishop Harris brings a wonderful irreverence to the job. To those who move to kiss her signet ring, she has said, "Forget the ring, sweetie. Kiss the bishop."

Traditionalist backlash followed her election. The Episcopal

Synod of America, some 20,000 Episcopalians headed by Bishop Clarence Pope, Jr., of Fort Worth, Texas, was formed in 1989 to protest the ordination and consecration of women. They rebuked church acceptance of divorce and remarriage, cited a "loss of respect for the authority of Holy Scripture." The synod still remains active.

"My energy cannot be expended on worrying about the opposition," says Bishop Harris. "I didn't come here to win a popularity contest. I came here to do the best I can with the gifts God has given me."

Jane Hart Holmes Dixon became the second female bishop in the Episcopal Church, in November 1992. She is currently the assistant bishop of the diocese of Washington.

In 1992 German theologian Maria Jepson became the world's first Lutheran woman bishop.

Insert: Female Values

As women's power and presence grow within organized religion, they are freer to express female values and reject the outdated system.

The example of Women-Church shows how women prefer networks to hierarchy, which is associated with inflexibility and male dominance. "Church power is shaped in a pyramid structure, with domination from the top down," says Sister Donna Quinn, director of Chicago Catholic Women. "That is slanted, sexist and immoral."

Men see leadership as a chain of command running from top to bottom, all very hierarchical, says Dr. Rosemary Keller, professor at Garrett-Evangelical Theological Seminary in Evanston, Illinois, and coauthor with Rosemary Ruether of three volumes on women in religion. Women tend toward a collegial, interpersonal, shared kind of leadership style, says Keller. Women incorporate more people in decision making.

"What is holy? Who should lead? Women raise different questions in these areas," says Barbara Brown Zikmund, president of Hartford Seminary, Hartford, Connecticut.

Church women in leadership positions should be ready to challenge the status quo if necessary, says Bishop Barbara Harris. "Women might look to recapture some of the traits exhibited by biblical women . . . who were involved in substantive revolutionary activity," she says.

Women's supportive style of leadership suits the times. "The emphasis on reaching down and helping people has changed. Now . . . [it is] empowering people," says Sister Mary Hennessey, former director of ministerial studies at Harvard Divinity School, now with the Jesuit Urban Center in Boston. "The white male can't do that."

One member in her congregation told Presbyterian minister Shirley Wooden, "We've had supportive ministers we could talk to in the past here, but you're the first one who is really bothered by my pain."

Reverend Helen Smith of Wesley Grove United Methodist Church in Gaithersburg, Maryland, often takes one of her children on house calls. "When I walk into their houses with Elizabeth, they know I can easily identify with laundry spread out, having a homelike chaos around," she says.

Women's perspectives, once they attain greater power, will signal revolutionary changes in church policies: "The all-male hierarchy has resulted in an inconsistent set of ideals," says one Catholic grade-school teacher. "For example, contraceptives are wrong, but weapons of war are acceptable. The church needs the feminine influence."

Delete: Sexist Language

Change is in store on the linguistic front. The Lutheran Church in America's *Lectionary for the Christian People* is a collection of nonsexist readings for Episcopalians, Roman Catholics and Lutherans. It deletes masculine pronouns for God and substitutes "sovereign" for "king."

The United Methodists Hymnal Revision Committee has edited hymnist Charles Wesley:

- In his "Christ the Lord Is Risen Today," "Sons of men and angels" is out; "all on earth and angels say" is in.
- "Pleased as man with men to dwell" from "Hark the Herald Angels Sing" became "Pleased with us in flesh to dwell."
- "Good Christian Men, Rejoice" by John Mason Neale didn't have a prayer; it's now "Good Christian Friends, Rejoice."

With Vatican approval, U.S. Catholics now say Christ died "for all" rather than "all men."

Women in the Washington, D.C., area are rewriting the Haggadah, a prayer book that has many references to heroic male figures that is read during the ritual Passover meal. "We are trying to get women on an equal footing," says Susan Cohen, co-chair of the

Commission for Women's Equality of the American Jewish Congress. They have created a feminist Haggadah to be read at the seder.

"Every time we use sexist language, we're legitimating male domination, which is anti-Christian," says Sister Sandra Schneiders. "Sometimes we say, 'It's easier for practical purposes.' But what we're really saying is that it's okay for a male-dominated world to exist."

Catholics Push for Change

The ordination of women is being fought tooth and nail by the Roman Catholic Church. Nevertheless, when Pope John Paul II visited the United States in 1979, Sister Theresa Kane decided to go for it:

"Your Holiness, I urge you to be mindful of the intense suffering and pain which is part of the life of many women in these United States," she told the astonished pontiff. "The Church . . . must respond by providing the possibility of women . . . being included in all ministries of our church."

The Church's refusal to ordain women is important—it influences the lives of millions of women the world over. It concerns Protestant groups that still refuse to ordain women, because it dates back to 2,000 years of tradition.

Pope John Paul, of course, did not accept Sister Kane's petition. Jesus was male, the traditional argument goes, and selected only male apostles. Feminist theologians disagree.

"It's true that there was not a woman among the 12 disciples, but clearly Mary Magdalene had to be number 13, if not number one," says the Reverend Judith Stone-Horst, pastor of the Evangelical Lutheran Church of the King in Tucson, Arizona.

"Mary Magdalene is very clearly a female apostle," argues Sister Schneiders. "The risen Jesus appeared to her and personally commissioned her to preach (John 20:11–18). . . . Tradition, however, has turned her into a great sinner, whose sole claim to fame was that Jesus forgave her."

There was also the Samaritan woman, who, according to the Gospel of John, is the only person besides John the Baptist who preached the Gospel during Jesus' public life, says Sister Schneiders. "But tradition merely wrote this woman off as someone who had five husbands."

Women's Voices Rise

In the 1980's many Catholics hoped the Vatican would reverse its stand and ordain women. Protestants and Jews had already done so. But Pope John Paul dashed all hopes in his 1988 apostolic letter "The Dignity of Women," which reaffirmed the ban against women priests. Not surprisingly, many are appalled at the Church's stance.

"I am angry that a group of men, a 'good ol' boys' network if you will, can deny to half the world's population the possibility of serving God and others through the priesthood," Joan Garvey Hermes wrote in *U.S. Catholic.* "I find nothing in the concept of an all-male clergy worth supporting."

"There is something strangely perverse," said another Catholic woman, "about priests being required to have certain anatomical equipment and then being forbidden to use it."

In the 1980's U.S. bishops undertook an extensive study of women's issues, including ordination. They decried the "sin of sexism," but reaffirmed the church's ban against women priests. The bishops' first draft in 1988 encouraged women slightly—it suggested ordination might require "further study." But the 1990 draft restated the Church's traditional stand on the all-male priesthood, as did the third draft released in 1992.

Theologian Rosemary Radford Ruether of Garrett-Evangelical Theological Seminary in Evanston, Illinois, expressed her outrage in "an open letter" to all U.S. Catholic bishops.

> What you want, dear bishops, is to seduce us unto helping to rescue your patriarchal ecclesial system while conceding nothing. . . . You want us to throw our energies into . . . sweeping the floors, washing the linens, baking the cookies, serving the coffee, arranging the flowers . . . doing the pastoral counseling, organizing the catechetics, playing the music, even leading the prayers, above all, raising the money, for a celibate male, clerical, patriarchal church that is disintegrating at its center precisely because of the celibate male, clerical, patriarchal assumptions to which you cling so desperately.

The fourth draft, released later in 1992, called the male priesthood "willed by the Lord." To the delight of women activists, it was rejected by the National Conference of Catholic Bishops. While the bishops did not repudiate the Vatican's stand against women priests, they did reject the Pope's ban on even *discussing* the subject.

"It's an unprecedented vote and a new day for our church," said Sister Maureen Fiedler, co-director of Catholics Speak Out, a national coalition of activists. "This document was truly Neanderthal in many ways. It would have pushed us headlong back through the 19th century."

The Church's position is "untenable," said the Center of Concern, a Catholic research organization before draft four. "It tries to respond to the historical shift in human consciousness about women and simultaneously maintain its traditional patriarchal structures and processes."

"The male hierarchical, patriarchal institution is a dinosaur, and rigor mortis is setting in," says Ruth Fitzpatrick, director of the Women's Ordination Conference, which in 1990 had identified nearly 500 U.S. women qualified to serve as priests. The conference estimates thousands more may qualify.

They may have to subtract at least one name from that list.

"I was as Catholic as you can get," says Reverend Marianne Niesen, 41, a former nun who became a Methodist and entered the ministry. "Catholic family, Catholic grade school, Catholic high school—even before becoming a nun. And I loved being a nun. I wanted to stay a nun and be a minister at the same time. That was my dream." Instead she created a new dream and today is the pastor of two small Montana Methodist parishes.

Twenty thousand people from 25 countries voiced approval of women priests in an advertisement in *USA Today* on Ash Wednesday 1991 by Call to Action, a Chicago-based Catholic organization.

But it is not just the think-tank crowd: two thirds of American Catholics believe women should be priests, up 20 percent in seven years, says a May 1992 Gallup poll.

A Hideous Cover-up

Rosemary Radford Ruether's marvelous outburst quoted above twice uses the word "celibate." In the wake of the 1992–93 flood of child abuse allegations against priests, one wonders whether she would still choose to underscore that particular vow.

Psychoanalyst Richard Sipe, a former priest who has studied priest pedophilia for 25 years, estimates that the "average priest pedophile" has 20 to 50 victims. But what horrifies victims most, according to recent reports, is that once a family has gone through the emotionally draining process of exposing an abusive priest, he is often assigned elsewhere. The hierarchy's failure to act enables the perpetrator to abuse again.

More than polls, full-page ads and grass-roots protests, the issue of child abuse by priests calls into question the viability of an all-male celibate priesthood. Furthermore, it puts the Church's stand against natural adult sexuality into a particularly troubling light.

Celibacy is a powerful spiritual stand revered by many religious traditions. But one could argue this vow would be more meaningfully undertaken by a mature person acquainted with the nature of sexual energy and therefore aware of what she or he is vowing to sublimate, rather than by an 18-year-old being whisked off into the seminary or nunnery.

Should celibacy be required to serve? Couldn't celibacy exist as a particular devotion undertaken in response to a special spiritual calling?

The Growing Priest Shortage

Nancy DeRycke, 40, and a Sister of St. Joseph in Rochester, New York, for 19 years, wants to be a priest. She visits the sick in hospitals each week but is heartbroken that she cannot comfort them by hearing their confessions or anointing them.

What is shocking is how desperately the Church needs a new cadre of priests and how easy it would be to recruit them by ordaining women and permitting priests to marry. In 1989 there were 400,000 priests worldwide, 16,505 fewer than a decade before; meanwhile the world's Catholic population had grown more than 20 percent. The 53,000 U.S. priests will decrease to about 35,000 in the next 15 years. The average U.S. priest is 54 years old, not a promising demographic.

Frank Bonnike, a former priest who is now married, says that if the Church ordained women and married men, it "could triple the priesthood within 20 years."

The May 1992 Gallup poll mentioned above also found that 75 percent of American Catholics favor allowing priests to marry.

The Church of the Resurrection in Solon, Ohio, asked U.S. bishops to consider ordaining women and married men to solve the priest shortage, "so that the Eucharist may continue to be the center of spiritual life of all Catholics." Cleveland's bishop Anthony Pilla said it was not up to him to decide.

The pope says the shortage may be a divine test that will leave the priesthood strengthened and purified. It will not lead to ordaining women, he says, since the Church "bears witness to a divine wisdom not of this world."

Indeed.

Deputy Priests and Married Priests

The priest shortage is creating some strange church-approved situations. Women have been "deputized" to celebrate marriages and perform other duties once restricted to priests.

Patty Repikoff was appointed head of Seattle's St. Therese parish. The archdiocese took this "radical" step to avoid closing the parish, says John Reid, head of lay ministries for the archdiocese. Seattle has few churches and an increasing Catholic population.

Repikoff is expected to preach but is not permitted to administer the sacraments. "The Church has tied my hands because I cannot preside at Eucharist," she said. "If you bind my mouth, I cannot be a pastoral leader."

Ruth Wallace, a sociology professor at George Washington University, says lay people head about 300 of the United States' almost 20,000 Catholic parishes. Seventy-four percent of the lay ministers are women.

In remote areas of the Third World, where the shortage of priests is even greater, women often run parishes, says Sister of St. Joseph Crystal Burgmaier, a Catholic missionary in Brazil. They have the duties of a priest without the title.

So, the pope absolutely forbids women from becoming priests, but it is okay to head parishes, be "deputized," preach homilies, be a "parochial minister" and marry people.

"The pastoral needs are going to dictate our looking at the question [of women's ordination] faster than we realize," says Sister Theresa Kane, the nun who had that little talk with Pope John Paul back in 1979.

One male reader told us, "You might be able to predict 'trends,' but when it comes to the Church, trends don't matter. It is top-down, authoritarian. Plain and simple."

Ultimately, of course, he is right. But even if today's pope is no trend tracker, one of his successors will find it impossible to ignore the massive worldwide priest shortage, the refusal of U.S. bishops to parrot the Vatican line, the grass-roots support for women priests and married priests and the hideous specter of priestly child abuse.

The real breakthrough has already occurred; we just haven't noticed yet. Women can become "lay ministers," a second-class priesthood, to be sure, but also a back door into the hierarchy. The number of women ministers has grown slowly at first, but has already accelerated in the mid-1990's. In the first decade of the 21st century the distinctions between priests and ministers will begin to blur. Then the "Vatican Gorbachev" will emerge, a complete insider who nevertheless "sees the light" and grants women ministers all the rights and responsibilities of the priesthood.

Auxiliary Bishop Austin Vaughn of New York is widely quoted as saying, "Women priests are as impossible as me having a baby." Stay tuned, Bishop, and remember what business you're in—miracles happen.

Tradition Gets a Twist

The Catholic hierarchy argues that there is no precedent for women priests in Church history; male priests are a 2,000-year-old tradition. Once the research of Dr. Mary Ann Rossi, honorary research fellow at the Women's Studies Research Center at the University of Wisconsin in Madison, gets further attention, the Church may have to take 500 years off that "tradition."

Doing research in the Vatican Library, Dr. Rossi discovered the fascinating work of Italian scholar Giorgio Otranto, director of the Institute for Classical and Christian Studies at the University of Bari in southern Italy. Otranto's analyses of correspondence, art frescoes and other evidence document the existence of women priests and bishops in early Church history.

But until Mary Ann Rossi translated Otranto's work into English, their existence remained almost completely unknown. Rossi's work was published in the prestigious *Journal of Feminist Studies in Religion,* edited by Harvard Divinity School's Schüssler Fiorenza.

The Vatican Press Office was certainly not about to publicize findings such as the following:

• A fresco of women blessing the Eucharist in the Priscilla catacomb in Rome is associated with Priscilla, a female disciple of St. Paul.

- Inscriptions on monuments and gravestones identify women named Leta, Flavia, Maria and Marta as priests.
- A Roman mosaic pictures four bishops, one of whom, Theodora, is a woman.
- The correspondence of Atto, a ninth-century Italian bishop, affirms the existence of women priests and bishops in the early Church and indicates they were banned in the fourth century.

"Otranto's findings are important to all women—Evangelicals, Lutherans, Southern Baptists. It's not only Catholics who are hamstrung," said Catherine Kroeger, a Presbyterian theologian at Gordon-Conwell Seminary, a conservative divinity school near Boston.

In 1991 Giorgio Otranto did a six-city U.S. lecture tour sponsored by a group of U.S. seminaries and universities. "I am a historian and I am a believer and I will not take sides in the complicated issue of whether women today should be ordained," Otranto said. "But considerable evidence exists that women also filled this role."

When he presented that evidence and showed slides of the art described above, his audiences at Gordon-Conwell Theological Seminary reportedly gasped in awe. "Earthshaking," proclaimed Rosalyn Karaban, associate professor at St. Bernard's Institute in Rochester, New York.

Ordination activist Ruth Fitzpatrick said it all: "We have been waiting two thousand years for this."

5.
The Menopause Megatrend

Women baby boomers are members of the most health-conscious generation ever, known to transform every age through which it passes. Soon they will confront midlife, when the invincibility of youth gives way to the realism of mortality. It will be on a scale unmatched in history, as in the next two decades 40 to 50 million women undergo menopause.

"The boardrooms of America are going to light up with hot flashes," writes Gail Sheehy, author of *Passages*, in a personal account in *Vanity Fair*, which became the number one best-seller *The Silent Passage: Menopause* (Random House).

But the baby boomers will characteristically make the best of it, transforming the discomfort of menopause into an "in" passage, a trend.

Hell, a megatrend.

Women will write novels and produce films about the rite of passage that transformed them from childbearers to wisewomen. From *Roseanne* to *Murphy Brown*, sitcoms will reverberate with menopause humor.

Baby-boom women, dedicated to the memory of the youth culture their generation created, will break every stereotype of the postmenopausal woman, resurrecting and modernizing the great archetype of the wisewoman, freed up from family responsibili-

ties, revered for knowledge and experience and treasured as a great human resource.

Whether they proudly wear wrinkles and gray hair or endure face-lifts and tummy tucks, the wisewomen of the baby boom will embrace their power as mature adult women as no generation before them ever has.

In facing the truth about aging, they will confront its dark side more realistically than women of the past. For the badge of wisewomanhood does not come without anticipating and protecting one's self against the increased risk of serious, life-threatening disease that comes with aging. Without the protection that the female hormone estrogen once provided, the postmenopausal women is at increased risk for heart disease and breast cancer.

No matter how many step aerobics classes she has under her belt, or how many marathons she has run, no matter that she operates a multimillion-dollar company or has won a MacArthur grant for her work with migrant workers, the woman who's made the passage into menopause enters a whole new health-risk category. A new generation must rededicate itself to awareness, prevention and early detection.

But that is not all. It must also address a legacy of sexism in medicine that is only now coming to light, a tradition that until very recently has underfunded research into breast cancer and conducted a wealth of studies about heart disease—that focused only on men. Women must open their eyes to the new trend of health-care activism. Their very lives depend on it.

Granted, lifestyle changes in diet and fitness and today's high-tech medicine should give baby-boom women healthier and longer lives than their mothers. But in order to fulfill that potential:

Women must become personally responsible for the health risks they face and take the lead in their own care—demanding that the lump a physician dismisses as "harmless" be biopsied, calling a cardiologist when a fiftysomething woman's chest pains are "diagnosed" as indigestion.

That is the price to pay today in order to enjoy quality of life now and into old age.

The overall theme of this chapter is "new health issues" for women over 35 years old, including menopause. But it also examines the risks of breast cancer and heart disease that accompany that passage, as well as the outlook for hormone-replacement therapy in postmenopausal women. Without the baby boomers, the legacy of sexism in medical research and the women's health-care movement might be a trend. But the aging of that massive generation makes it a megatrend: breast cancer and heart disease are no longer abstract diseases that mostly hit older women: they are very real killers to face up to now.

This chapter will briefly discuss five other health issues of importance to women today: breast implants, Pap-smear inaccuracies, problems diagnosing ovarian cancer, AIDS in women, conception and contraception. Finally, it will describe one of the most positive changes in medicine today: the feminization of health care.

Menopause: The Health Issue of the '90's

So You Think You're Too Young?

Menopause is not a sudden event that happens when you turn 50 years old or 48. Many women become aware of the changes signaling approaching menopause in their mid- to late-30's. "We know now there are women who start experiencing change in their menstrual cycle in their late 30's," says Phyllis Kernoff Mansfield, a menstrual cycles researcher at Penn State.

Some women undergo menopause in their 40's. About one percent have a natural menopause before age 40. Furthermore, one third of U.S. women undergo hysterectomies. Most of them are between 25 and 44. If a woman's ovaries are removed along with her uterus, which many experts do *not* recommend, menopause will immediately result.

"The ovaries start producing less estrogen probably in the mid-thirties. . . . It's not unusual to see symptoms in the early forties as a sign of gradual estrogen withdrawal," says Dr. Trudy Bush, epidemiologist and associate professor of obstetrics and gynecology at Johns Hopkins School of Hygiene.

Many younger women experience the symptoms of menopause:

"I'm 42 and I don't think I'm going to be menopausal for 10 years," says Dr. Bush. "But in fact I've got maybe a 20 to 30 percent chance of developing some symptoms in the next two or three years. I know that because I work in the area."

The Menopause Transition

By the late 40's, the actual biological transition of menopause has begun. Once a woman has passed an entire year without a menstrual period, the initial transition is over, though changes continue for five to seven years, says Gail Sheehy, who adds that menopause marks the beginning of the "little-mapped" passage of postreproductive life. Until quite recently, it was rarely talked about—even among women.

Menopause affects some 300 different body functions, concluded a recent *Newsweek* story. "The ovary is an endocrine gland, and when you lose the function of that gland, problems develop," says gynecologist Wulf H. Utian, chairman of reproductive biology at Case Western Reserve University, a pioneer in menopause research. Dr. Utian founded the North American Menopause Society, which hosted more than 800 physicians from 20 countries at its 1992 meeting.

During this powerful time of transition, the body stops producing estrogen, and menstruation becomes irregular—from missed periods to unexpected gushing. Women report a whole range of symptoms, the most universal being "hot flashes." But there are many more: bloating, thinning and drying of the skin, urinary-tract infections, impaired touch, decreased sexual desire, vaginal dryness, mood swings and myriad others. Traditionally, women's menopause-related health concerns were dismissed by the male-dominated medical profession as "all in their heads." Symptoms of hormonal decline were treated with the suggestion that perhaps the medical attention required was psychiatric.

Fortunately, the baby boomers will be taken more seriously. There is strength in numbers. The Census Bureau predicts the number of women from 45 to 54 will increase 73 percent between 1990 and 2010. Because baby-boom women are so health-conscious, they will be highly aware of menopause symptoms and will demand relief—probably a lot more than their mothers did.

Besides, many of their physicians are women, going through the same damn thing.

Menopause will be the women's health issue of the '90's and beyond.

"There are going to be more women going through menopause in the next 10 years than at any time in history; it's almost an impending epidemic," says gynecologist Utian.

A lot of women will resent Utian's use of the word "epidemic." It is a throwback to the days when women's natural, sacred functions were perceived by the medical establishment as illness. But hear the doctor out:

The heart attacks and bone fractures postmenopausal women will endure could "overwhelm the health-care system in the next 15 years," warns Dr. Utian.

Osteoporosis: The Bone Thinning of America

The National Osteoporosis Foundation predicts one third to one half of postmenopausal women will be affected by osteoporosis, the dangerous thinning of the bones that comes with aging and is exacerbated by lack of estrogen. One third of women over 65 will suffer one or more spinal fractures, or complications from fractures—which are extremely serious and even life-threatening. The total annual cost of hip fractures will increase from approximately $7.2 billion currently to $16 billion by the year 2040, says the *Journal of Clinical Orthopedics and Related Research.* Estrogen-replacement therapy, discussed on pages 152–154, helps replace bone and greatly reduces the dangers of osteoporosis; unfortunately, it is not without its own risks.

A New Zealand study reconfirmed what researchers and medical experts had long asserted: taking calcium keeps bones strong after menopause. Just 1,000 added grams of calcium a day cut bone loss by one third, the study concluded.

The Upbeat Menopause

Menopause has long been thought to cause depression associated with the loss of the ability to bear children. AS IF women's sole function were to produce babies. Research shows most women are *not* depressed that they cannot become pregnant. Relieved is more like it. (Besides, researchers are testing methods to enable some postmenopausal women to conceive. One 52-year-old has already given birth. But it remains to be seen how many more will avail themselves of this breakthrough.) Women certainly experience mood swings, but the lows are more hormonal than emotional:

• A study by University of Pittsburgh psychologist Karen A. Matthews found women who had recently gone through menopause did not have higher levels of depression, anxiety or stress than women the same age who were still menstruating.

• Sonja and John McKinlay, epidemiologists at the New England Research Institute, conducted a five-year study of 2,500 women age 45 to 55; they concluded that three quarters felt "either relieved or neutral" about menopause. Only 3 percent considered menopause a negative. "For the majority of women," says John McKinlay, "it's no big deal."

Not mentally, perhaps, but a very big deal physically.

The Risks of Menopause

The decline in estrogen production that accompanies menopause robs women of their inherent protection against heart disease and the rapid bone loss that leads to osteoporosis and hip fractures. Post-menopausal women are at greater risk for breast and ovarian cancer. Women and the medical establishment have wrongly judged women as immune to heart disease, which kills twice as many women a year as all cancers put together. By the time a woman is in her mid-60's, she is as vulnerable to heart attack as a male, and more likely to die of it.

As women march toward menopause, many will act now to reverse the inconsistencies, lack of research, inadequate treatment and just plain sexism that can threaten the quality of life they experience in their 60's and 70's—and might even rob them of their highly productive 40's and 50's.

Reversing a Legacy of Sexism

For the past two decades, as most women focused on equal pay for equal work, the wage gap, abortion and child care, a dedicated cadre of female health-care activists have collected data that will make you mad and that might save your life. With the approach of menopause, women who are more vulnerable to disease are starting to pay attention to such shocking disclosures as:

• Women have been grossly underrepresented in clinical research trials for new drugs.
• Significantly fewer dollars are spent on diseases unique to women—until recently, especially breast cancer—than on diseases affecting other groups.
• Women are not treated as aggressively by physicians as men when presenting the same, or more serious, symptoms of heart disease.

Welcome to the change of life and the world of health-care activism.

Only Men Get Heart Attacks, Sure. But Breast Cancer?

What medicine knows about heart disease is the result of massive clinical studies conducted almost exclusively on men—even though, once into their 60's, postmenopausal women die of heart disease in virtually equal numbers.

Four years ago, a major research finding was splashed across the front pages of newspapers around the country: take one aspirin every other day and lower your risk of heart attack. A remarkable finding—for half the population, anyway. The research behind this headline-grabbing conclusion involved 22,000 physicians. There was *not one woman* among them.

"We don't know if aspirin works on women," says Cathy Bernau, project manager and former director of Rose Medical Center's Women's Center in Denver, Colorado.

Finally the answer may be on the way. In September 1992 Brigham and Women's Hospital in Boston began a five-year, $17 million study of 40,000 postmenopausal nurses to examine the influence of beta-carotene, vitamin E and low doses of aspirin on heart disease.

When the National Institutes of Health (NIH) launched its first study of the elderly in the United States, there was a tiny problem: for the first 20 years **no women** were included. (After all, women only make up two thirds of the elderly population, and as we all know, they age exactly like men—not.)

For skeptics of sexism in medical research theses: consider the Rockefeller University project on the impact of obesity on breast and uterine cancer: for the first three weeks, it studied only men.

Each year, there are hundreds of clinical trials for new drugs or treatments. Many exclude women. Between 1988 and 1991 women were "underrepresented in 60 percent of drug studies," noted a 1992 General Accounting Office report that looked at 53 drugs that won FDA approval. Scientists say women *complicate* research: changing hormones during menstruation or menopause can alter the way drugs work in the body (that does not seem like an explanation). They are

worried that exposure to experimental therapies might have dire reproductive consequences. (Fair enough, one supposes.)

**Ultimately both these excuses are meaningless, because
drugs approved after male-only clinical trials are prescribed for
women.**

That is particularly disturbing since women are *more* likely to
take over-the-counter medications and certain prescription drugs.
"The percentage is this: 70 percent of all psychoactive medications are
prescribed to women," says Susan J. Blumenthal, chief of the Behav-
ioral Medicine Program at the National Institute of Mental Health.

Women's Research Gap

NIH funds one third of all medical research in the United States.
As recently as 1987 only 13.5 percent of NIH's $6 billion research
budget was devoted to diseases unique to or more serious among
women. That is not to say 87 percent of the budget was spent on
diseases affecting only men. It does mean, however, that women are
underrepresented in medical research.

The Society for the Advancement of Women's Health Research
in Washington, D.C., says there are inequities in the study of breast
cancer, contraception and postpartum depression. Of more than 2,100
NIH researchers, the group notes, only seven are specialists in obstetrics and gynecology.

Women's rights advocates and some medical researchers now say
women's health issues have been consistently shortchanged through a
pattern of bias and discrimination that permeates the medical and
scientific community.

But that is not the half of it.

Less Aggressive Treatment: Does It Kill Women?

Evidence is mounting that women are treated less aggressively
for heart disease than men, even though it is the leading killer of both.

• *The New England Journal of Medicine* published a study of 2,231
men and women who had both been hospitalized with severe
heart attacks. The men were *twice* as likely to have had coronary
angiography, a diagnostic test to determine the extent of block-

age of the coronary arteries. The men were also twice as likely to undergo coronary bypass surgery, which reroutes blood flow around blocked arteries.

- Researchers at Boston's Brigham and Women's Hospital studied 82,782 heart patients in Massachusetts and Maryland. Massachusetts men were **28 percent more likely than women to have angiography and 45 percent more likely to have bypass surgery or angioplasty** (where a balloonlike device is used to unclog arteries). Maryland men were 15 percent more likely to have angiography and 27 percent more likely to have bypass surgery or balloon angioplasty.
- The Colorado Hospital Association reports 51 people had heart transplants over a two-year period; only seven were women. In 1989 and 1990 there were 3,430 coronary bypass operations; only 22 percent were performed on women.
- A Seattle study of 5,000 people found men were *twice* as likely to get "clot busters," which stop heart attacks in progress. The results, say researchers, "call into question whether women are being appropriately treated for heart attacks."

The data do not *prove* women would fare better if treated more aggressively. Incredibly, there is almost no data on the effectiveness of aggressive treatment on women. Says Dr. Nanette Wenger, a cardiologist at the Emory University School of Medicine, "Many of us have great concern about extrapolating data from middle-aged men to older women."

"The important question is whether the severity of heart disease in women is being underestimated," says Dr. John Ayanian, a heart-disease researcher at Brigham and Women's. "The studies certainly suggest the possibility that it is."

Gender bias is evident elsewhere: middle-aged women are half as likely to get a kidney transplant, and men are twice as likely to undergo a key diagnostic test for lung cancer, reports the American Medical Association's Council of Ethical and Judicial Affairs.

Sexism, misunderstanding, misdiagnosis, insufficient research—call it what you will, it keeps women from state-of-the-art treatment that saves lives.

"Being different from men meant being second-class and less than equal for most of recorded time and throughout most of the world," wrote Dr. Bernadine Healy, a cardiologist and the first female director of the National Institutes of Health, in *The New England*

Journal of Medicine. "It may therefore be sad, but not surprising, that women have all too often been treated less than equally in . . . health care."

NIH's "Women's Health Initiative," the massive, hopefully definitive study of women's health issues announced in late 1991 and begun under Healy's watch, will aim to correct that inequality. The study will cover 160,000 women age 50 to 79 and cost $625 million over the next 15 years. Twenty percent of the women involved will be minorities. The initiative, to be coordinated by Seattle's Fred Hutchinson Cancer Research Center, will include 16 university medical centers. It will study the causes of heart disease, cancer and osteoporosis, as well as the benefits of a low-fat diet.

"This initiative is a first step toward equity for women's health research," said Donna E. Shalala, secretary of health and human services, about the research program. "It needs to be followed up by insuring the place of women's health in the mainstream of biomedical research."

NIH, under cardiologist Healy, began requiring that women be included in *all* clinical trials funded by the federal government. That was not enough for health activist U.S. Representative Pat Schroeder (D-Colo.), who wanted the policy written into law and supported by funds set aside for women's health studies. Her proposal passed the House in 1991 by a 274 to 144 vote: the women's health movement has reached the halls of Congress.

Killer Disease Number One: Heart Disease

Women are terrified of cancer, especially breast cancer, and with good reason: this horrible disease strikes an emotionally sensitive part of the body and kills—about 46,000 women a year. But heart disease does not faze most women: it's mostly men who have heart attacks, right?
    Not exactly.

Cardiovascular disease—heart attacks and strokes—kills about 500,000 women a year, far more than breast cancer. In fact, cardiovascular disease kills twice as many women as all types of cancers that kill women put together.

The physiology that protects women during childbearing years plays catch-up at menopause. Before age 40, when most women are still producing estrogen, heart disease kills four men for every woman, according to the American Heart Association. But then the odds favoring women drop. By the time she is in her mid-60's, a woman's risk of a fatal heart attack or stroke is *equal to or greater than* that of her male counterpart, depending on other risk factors.

"The medical profession and women themselves have underestimated the importance of cardiovascular disease in females," says Dr. Antonio Gotto, chairman of the department of medicine at Baylor College in Houston and past president of the American Heart Association.

My Doctor Said, "Mylanta."

Ann Marino, now 60, would agree with that assessment.

Marino, a resident of Boulder, Colorado, had pains in her chest for five years. "My family doctor, who had treated us for more than 20 years, was actually annoyed at me for coming in," she says. "He treated me like a menopausal woman." Her problem, he said, was a "hiatal hernia."

Her "doctor" told her to take Mylanta every 20 minutes. Finally, when the pain became unbearable, she went to a hospital emergency room. A cardiologist was called in and discovered three vessels 75 percent clogged and one 100 percent clogged. There was evidence that she had had a heart attack. Marino was rushed into quadruple-bypass surgery, without which, her new doctor says, she would probably have died.

"I was a typical case," concludes Ann Marino. "My doctor wasn't even considering that it could have been my heart."

Is It More than Sexism?

In a thoughtful *New York Times* article, Lawrence K. Altman, M.D., argues that medicine's failure to recognize and treat heart disease in women is not sexism. One in five men will have a heart attack by age 60, versus one in 17 women, he notes. No excuse for prescribing Mylanta, but a possible explanation why physicians are conditioned to miss the signs of heart attack in women under 60, women like Ann Marino, described above, who was then 57.

There are other legitimate medical factors as well, he says. For one, treadmill stress tests are less reliable for women. Public education has not sufficiently emphasized chest pains in women. Women may be more stoic about angina pain than men.

Furthermore, the comprehensive Framingham heart-disease study, which began in 1948 and continues today, observed risk factors for heart disease in thousands. This study did include women, but most of them were premenopausal. So not much heart disease showed up. That gave women (and doctors) a false sense of security.

After the age of 60, a women is *more* likely than a man to *die* of heart disease or stroke. "If you get men through the 35 to 60 age period without their dying of heart disease, they are [in later decades] stronger and less frail than women," observes Ruth L. Kirschstein, former associate director for research on Women's Health at NIH, now director of NIH's National Institute of General Medical Sciences.

Hormone-Replacement Therapy: Curse or Cure?

Between 15 and 18 percent of postmenopausal women take estrogen (or estrogen in combination with progesterone) to relieve the symptoms of menopause. It prevents thinning of the bones, which leads to osteoporosis, makes skin look younger, enhances moods, stops or reduces hot flashes, restores vaginal moisture, restores sex drive and relieves many other symptoms.

Sounds like a wonder drug. But enthusiasm about synthetic estrogen has swung back and forth for almost 50 years. Today, because of the study discussed below, there is reason to think that more women than ever before will begin to take it; nevertheless, hormone-replacement therapy (HRT) is a controversial issue. In the 1940's, when it was discovered that Premarin, estrogen from the urine of a pregnant mare, could ease hot flashes, physicians prescribed it in relatively large doses to millions of women, especially after it was found to protect bone density.

As usage increased, however, so did the incidence of cancer of the uterus and the lining of the uterus. Many women who swore by their estrogen were not about to give it up. Furthermore, studies hinted estrogen reduced heart attacks, reinforcing its attractiveness. Overall, however, the cancer risk convinced many women to stop taking it—a real problem for women who welcomed the relief it brought.

After contradictory studies and confusing decisions, there is new information about estrogen.

A 10-year study involving 49,000 nurses was published in the *New England Journal of Medicine,* September 12, 1991; it concluded that women who take estrogen can cut their risk of heart attack in the first 10 years after menopause by almost 50 percent.

Dr. Lee Goldman, vice chairman of Boston's Brigham and Women's Hospital, and biostatistician Dr. Anna Tosteson, in an editorial accompanying the study's publication, write, "the benefits of estrogen outweigh the risks, substantially." The new study was larger than all previous studies put together.

It also concluded that taking estrogen *does* slightly increase the risk of breast cancer and increases the risk of cancer of the lining of the uterus six times. These risks, say Dr. Goldman and Dr. Tosteson, must be kept in perspective: "A twofold increase in the risk of a rare event," they write, "may not be nearly as important as a 10 percent decrease in the risk of a common event."

Overall, a white woman over 50 faces a 31 percent *absolute* risk of dying of heart disease versus a 2.8 percent risk of dying of breast cancer, a 2.8 percent risk of a hip fracture and only 0.7 percent risk of endometrial cancer. Their conclusion: "Even a small relative benefit for heart disease would dwarf all other effects."

At the same time, they insist, "a clinical trial of sufficient size is urgently needed to document that the epidemiologic evidence is not a function of bias or statistical legerdemain." Large trials should begin right away, they say, to study estrogen replacement after menopause.

That is exactly what the NIH study described on page 150 is supposed to do. Its results will not be available for 10 years, however, by which time millions of baby boomers will have to decide about estrogen on their own. To complicate matters a bit more, research published in the *New England Journal of Medicine* in 1993 found that adding progestin to estrogen decreases a woman's cancer risk (increased by the estrogen alone) and provides some added protection against heart disease.

Most authorities reject the idea of giving out hormones to everyone.

"I would not make a blanket recommendation. . . . It depends on how she feels, what she's concerned about . . . her own risks and benefits, her own particular anxieties," Elizabeth Barrett-Connor, professor and chair of the community and family medicine department at the University of California, San Diego, told an FDA advisory committee.

There is a lot of money at stake here. Sales of Premarin doubled from almost $200 million a year in 1987 to around $400 million in 1990. In 1991 Premarin was the second-most prescribed drug in the United States; 1991 sales of $569 million represented a 44 percent increase over 1990. Sales are expected to exceed $700 million by 1994, but projections were made before the *New England Journal of Medicine* study was published.

Gary L. Friedman of Kaiser Permanente in Los Angeles analyzed 30 studies under review by the FDA. Virtually all showed heart benefits for estrogen. Still, he said, "although the case for estrogen is strong, it is not open and shut."

The Natural Menopause

But suppose you have been "Ms. Natural" all your life, a devotee of alternative remedies, and are not going to take "synthetic" anything, even if it does, according to the medical establishment, prevent heart attacks. Can alternative approaches bring relief from the symptoms of menopause? That is the question we asked our favorite alternative healer, Dr. Valentina Lert, a chiropractor who draws on many new therapies in her practice in Telluride, Colorado.

"I would look to five areas to bring relief to the menopausal woman," she said. "Chiropractic and acupuncture—because they both deal with balance—and the body is going through a complete chemical rebalancing as complex as puberty."

She also suggests investigating a good nutritionist, homeopathy and Chinese herbs. "The Chinese have a depth of knowledge about female herbal formulas that goes back thousands of years," she says.

A good nutritionist is valuable for several reasons. Several symptoms of menopause can be coped with—to some extent—nutritionally:

- Vitamin E in the form of mixed tocopherals. It has been shown to help ease hot flashes.
- Vitamin B complex. Dr. Lert notes that some side effects of estrogen replacement are synonymous with B-complex deficiencies.
- Calcium. She recommends calcium oronate or calcium glutonate

in a 1,000-milligram supplement that comes in combination with magnesium.
• Vitamin C has been shown to reduce the intensity of hot sweats.

But Dr. Lert insists these nutritional supplements are important before menopause, too. "Don't wait until your first hot flash," she says. Furthermore, she adds, even if a woman is undergoing hormone-replacement therapy, nutritional supplements may prove important.

A quick browse in Dr. Lert's personal library uncovered several books of interest to menopausal women. *Homeopathic Medicine for Women* (Healing Arts Press) by Trevor Smith, M.D., has a chapter addressed to menopausal problems and suggests homeopathic remedies for hot flashes, vaginal thinning and heavy bleeding.

Acupressure's Potent Points: A Guide to Self-Care for Common Ailments (Bantam) by Michael Reed Gach, founder and director of the Acupressure Institute of America, suggests specific acupressure techniques for the relief of hot flashes that a woman can easily perform on her own.

Your local New Age bookstore will stock many similar books, including *Menopause, Naturally: Preparing for the Second Half of Life* (Volcano Press) by Sadja Greenwood, M.D., cited in a 1990 *Newsweek* story on menopause.

In the herb department, black cohosh root, known as cimicifuga in homeopathy, has been traditionally associated with menopause in Native American and herbalist circles. The vegetable molecule is so similar to estrogen, it has been nicknamed "the vegetable estrogen."

These represent a whole range of approaches within the new paradigm of alternative medicine, which can be systematically pursued under the care of a trained, professional chiropractor, homeopath, herbalist, acupressure (or acupuncture) expert or nutritionist. Self-care may work fine for minor ailments, but a systematic approach is a lot better for more serious problems.

Postmenopausal Zest

Menopause does not last forever. What follows, many women report, is better, a lot better.

Once a woman has passed 12 consecutive months without menstruating, she "enters a new state of equilibrium," writes Gail Sheehy.

"Her energy, moods, and overall sense of physical and mental well-being should be restored, but with a difference."

Women attain "a new plateau of contentment and self-acceptance," she writes, "a potent new burst of energy by their mid-50's"—what Margaret Mead called "postmenopausal zest."

"Do you know how you feel a week after your period ends—like you could climb mountains and slay dragons? That's how a post-menopausal woman feels all the time, if she's conscious of it," says Elizabeth Stevenson, a Jungian analyst in Cambridge, Massachusetts.

The Health Rights Revolution

A generation of women comfortable with their economic clout and schooled in the tactics of consumer pressure and political strategy will put women's health issues at the top of the nation's health-care agenda.

The new urgency women feel about health matters has much to do with the approach of menopause. Until now heart attacks and cancer were things old ladies had to worry about, or tragic, but thankfully rare, occurrences among younger women. Now these killer diseases are looking right at the baby-boom generation, the biggest, the most health-conscious in U.S. history.

A generation of activists is now approaching the age when medical sexism can threaten their lives. Legions of them will join with already established women's health groups and head for the front lines of medical politics. Fueled by menopausal baby boomers, the health rights movement will gain steam in the '90's, bloom in the year 2000 and beyond.

October is breast-cancer awareness month, and in 1991 activists tried to get 175,000 breast-cancer patients and their families and friends to write to the White House demanding more research funding and better treatment. To their surprise and delight, more than 527,000 letters arrived.

"There are many women who have come through the women's movement, but who have never made a call or written a letter before. Now breast cancer has profoundly affected their lives," says Ann Maguire of the Massachusetts Breast Cancer Coalition.

AIDS and Breast Cancer

Before AIDS, advocates for *specific* disease had little impact on health policy. But AIDS activists have forced policymakers to overhaul the way AIDS drugs are tested, released and financed, and successfully lobbied for billions of dollars in research, treatment and education.

"They have scored incredible coups," says Marguerite Donoghue, a lobbyist for the National Coalition of Cancer Research. "They've left all of us saying, 'Boy, let's learn from their techniques.' "

Though instructed by successful AIDS groups, women's health activists insist they are *not* competing with them for funding. They do, however, point out the disparity between government spending on AIDS and breast cancer:

In 1992 the National Institutes of Health (through which virtually all federal research funding flows) spent about $1 billion on AIDS research. AIDS killed about 29,000 people in 1992. NIH spent $145 million on breast cancer research in 1992—but breast cancer kills more than 46,000 women a year.

Federal health officials say the comparison is meaningless since AIDS is a contagious disease and is increasing so rapidly. Furthermore, officials claim, breast cancer gets more funding than any other cancer, including lung cancer, which claims 146,000 lives each year. (Reply: we know what causes lung cancer; we still do not know what causes breast cancer.)

Despite the protest, controversy and "explanations," the mathematical relationship between the figures on AIDS and breast cancer research is **not** going to change much over the next few years. In 1993, NIH expects to spend $873 million on AIDS research and $136 million on breast cancer research.

"Somewhere under a rock, millions of dollars have been found for AIDS research," says Amy Langer, executive director of the National Alliance of Breast Cancer Organizations. "We don't begrudge them that, but we would like to find that rock."

Maybe it's in the Defense Department: NIH expects to spend $196.6 million on breast-cancer research in 1993, but the U.S. army already received $200 million in 1993 breast-cancer funds.

So the Army got more money for breast-cancer research than the National Cancer Institute did!

Nevertheless, that is $400 million in total for breast cancer research, four times the funding of less than $100 million as recently as the 1991 funding year. Not what it could be, but a solid increase well worth acknowledging and celebrating. You can thank health-care activists for that one.

The Women's Health Movement

In cities like San Francisco, Dallas, Washington, D.C., Berkeley, and Cambridge, Massachusetts, breast cancer advocacy groups have demanded more action on the disease, which strikes one in eight American women and kills one quarter of its victims (but see page 161).

Borrowing tactics from AIDS activists, women are lobbying for research money, broader insurance coverage for mammograms and experimental treatments and more studies on the dietary or environmental causes of breast cancer.

Among groups pressing for change are the Women's Cancer Resource Center in Berkeley, the Komen Foundation for Breast Cancer in Dallas, described in the media as a "bastion of rich and socially prominent Republican women"; CAN ACT (Cancer Patient's Action Alliance) in New York; Breast Cancer Action in San Francisco and the National Alliance of Breast Cancer Organizations, an 800,000-member coalition of grass-roots groups.

Tactics range from dramatic to methodical.

• Thousands of women in Sacramento and Boston marched for more breast-cancer funding, carrying signs marked: THIRTY WOMEN DEAD FROM BREAST CANCER EVERY HOUR.
• In October 1991, 3,000 women marched to Boston's City Hall to hear speakers call for more research and better treatment for breast cancer. When *The Boston Globe* covered the rally with a photograph and no story, dozens of angry women called the paper's ombudsman. Said one woman, "If one man in nine lost a testicle, it would be on page one."
• In New York 50 breast-cancer advocates from CAN ACT demonstrated in front of the New York offices of Blue Cross/Blue Shield, demanding the insurer cover bone-marrow trans-

plants. CAN ACT claimed insurers blocked access to lifesaving treatments by declaring them experimental and therefore non-fundable.

What may be behind much of the militancy about breast cancer is the feeling almost of powerlessness in preventing it. "A lot of the political action reflects the frustration that the causes of breast cancer have not been elucidated, whereas the causes of heart disease and lung cancer have been," says epidemiologist Lynn Rosenberg of Boston University.

The Taste of Success

Women's health-care advocates, who know their task is far from complete, are nevertheless entitled to stop for a moment and savor a growing list of accomplishments:

- In 1991 Congress passed the Women's Health Equity Act, a 22-bill package ensuring federal funding for research on women's health issues.
- Medicare now pays for mammograms and offers partial payment for Pap smears.
- To date 40 states and the District of Columbia have passed laws requiring insurers to pay for or offer mammograms.
- In three of the eight states without such laws, pending bills call for at least some mammography coverage. In two states, coverage is optional for insurers.
- Thirty-three states require insurers to follow the American Cancer Society's guidelines on eligibility and frequency of mammography.
- California, Florida and Washington have mandated that, for insurers to pay for the tests, mammography machines must meet standards set by the American College of Radiology.
- Blue Cross/Blue Shield, target of protests by breast-cancer activists, reversed long-standing policy and agreed to pay an estimated $10 million for experimental breast-cancer treatment. One fifth of member plans will underwrite the cost of an experimental bone-marrow transplant for as many as 600 of the 1,200 women who will participate in an NIH study.
- In 1990 the NIH established the Office of Research on Women's Health, which will set goals and policies for women's health research and help get women their fair share of attention in

clinical research. In the words of director Dr. Vivian Pinn, its $10 million budget funds studies on women "that might not otherwise be done," such as a $1 million study of endometriosis and uterine fibroids.

With each success, the health rights movement grows stronger in its resolve to compel the medical establishment to change research protocols, increase research funding and guarantee women state-of-the-art treatment.

Killer Disease Number Two: Breast Cancer

Breast cancer is *no longer* the leading cause of cancer death in women. Lung cancer is. But breast cancer is the leading cause of death for women between 35 and 50. Today, as millions of women confront the statistic that one in nine will get this dreaded disease, the call for more comprehensive research and more effective treatments will grow increasingly militant. Women demand to know why thousands still die each year, when the technology exists to diagnose and treat breast cancer.

- In the United States a woman is diagnosed with breast cancer every three and one half minutes; every 12 minutes a women dies of breast cancer.
- In 1970 one in 13 women got the disease in the course of her lifetime. Today it is one in eight.
- Some 80,000 early-stage tumors were detected in 1990, up from 35,000 in 1975. That increase is certainly due at least in part to early detection.

Good News about Breast Cancer

What these depressing numbers do **not** say is that when detected early, the cure rate for breast cancer is extremely high. Physicians used to speak of 5- or 10-year survival rates, pretty demoralizing if you are a 35- or 40-year-old. But they are now willing to use the word **cure,** as in "treatment cures," that is, removes **all** traces of the disease for **20 years or more,** in more than 90 percent of patients with the earliest form of breast cancer.

Furthermore, intraductile breast cancer, an early form of the disease, is "100 percent curable with proper treatment."

"Many of us believe that we're now on the edge of totally curing breast cancer," says Dr. Larry Norton, an oncologist specializing in breast cancer at New York's Memorial Sloan-Kettering Cancer Center.

After years of confusion and controversy, clarity about the best way to treat early-state breast cancer has emerged: a consensus of specialists convened in 1990 by NIH says breast conservation is the treatment of choice. But in 42 states, 85 to 96 percent of patients get mastectomies, even though the American Cancer Society, the American College of Surgeons and the American College of Radiology estimate about one third of breast-cancer patients should be able to save their breasts. Dr. David Winchester of the American College of Surgeons says it could be as high as 50 percent. Breast conservation is not for everyone; for example, it is not effective if there are multiple tumors. But evidence like this should remove the pressure on women to decide for themselves whether to choose lumpectomy or mastectomy.

More good news: when chemotherapy is required, a new combination of chemotherapy drugs has reduced side effects: 85 to 90 percent of women on CMF (a chemo drug) never lose enough hair to require a wig.

A Case of "Bad Math"?

The other thing the frightening statistics on breast cancer—that one woman in eight will get it—*do not* emphasize is that those numbers describe the risk a woman bears *over the course of her lifetime.* In an article entitled "Faulty Math Heightens Fears of Breast Cancer," author Sandra Blakeslee concludes that the American Cancer Society publicizes "deliberately scary" and "misleading" statistics to "prod" women to examine their breasts and get regular mammograms. For example, when the National Cancer Institute announced one in eight women (rather than nine) would get breast cancer, most of us failed to note the fine print: the breast cancer rate had not increased; the new figure was based on expanding the pool of women to age 85.

The risk of getting breast cancer for women under age 50 is about one in 1,000, says Dr. Patricia Kelly, director of medical genetics and cancer-risk counseling at Salick Health Care in Berkeley, California. Even at age 60, a woman's chance of dying of breast cancer over the next year is one in 500.

The risk of breast cancer is real; it increases significantly after menopause, but there is no reason to be paralyzed with anxiety about this disease. Activism, early detection and state-of-the-art treatment will soon transform debilitating fear into healthy, sensible awareness and lifesaving action.

The Broken Record: Early Detection, Early Detection . . .

The entire platform on which the good news about breast cancer is built is early detection. Mammography can "see" tumors as tiny as 0.25 cm, or one tenth of an inch, usually well before metastasis has begun and before lumps can be felt. Experts say by the time a woman can feel a lump in her breast, it is already two to three years old. NIH estimates that deaths from breast cancer would drop by almost one third if women had mammograms as recommended. But less than one third of women over 40 have mammograms as regularly as they should.

The issue became more confusing when findings of 1993 studies showed there was no evidence that mammograms could reduce the breast-cancer death rate in women under 50, even though researchers reemphasized the clear benefit for women over 50.

In response to the controversy, the American Cancer Society continues to advocate that younger woman should have mammograms.

"We have found more than sufficient data to support the usefulness of mammography as a lifesaving procedure for women 40 to 50 years of age," said Dr. Walter Lawrence, former president of the American Cancer Society.

Mammograms, however, are no substitute for regular breast self-exam: 10 to 15 percent of tumors can "hide" inside normal structures and fail to show up in a breast X ray.

It is critical that a woman gets the most up-to-date advice, from the best sources. Only then will she know her options and be able to decide how to act on them. A story from a special report on breast cancer in the October 1991 issue of *Self* magazine illustrates the point.

Susan Fischer, then 41, was advised to get a mastectomy in 1988. She got a second opinion only because her insurance company required it. Fortunately she went to Memorial Sloan-Kettering, voted the best cancer center by doctors polled by *U.S. News and World Report*. She learned that she was an excellent candidate for lumpectomy and that her original doctor—who continued to argue against lumpectomy—had not kept up with medical developments. The cancer has not spread, and she has been fine ever since.

The best advice is critical in helping a woman to decide whether she needs additional radiation or chemotherapy. Women need state-of-the-art advice and treatment, not pressure when they can least deal with it.

"These decisions require the patient be very informed and sift through statistics at a time when her decision-making capabilities are not 100 percent," says Amy Langer, director of the National Association of Breast Cancer Organizations. "Without hard data, what a woman decides to do after getting advice is a very personal thing."

Why is breast cancer still the leading cause of death among women in the 35- to 50-year age group?

Tragically, part of the reason is money. Lifesaving mammograms now average around $100 but can exceed $300. Until recently they were not covered by insurers, Medicaid or Medicare. That has changed, thanks again to health-care activists. Many women who are not fully covered are unwilling or unable to pay for a test they consider not absolutely necessary. Besides, mammography is not available everywhere, and only one third of the United States' 11,189 facilities meet the stringent guidelines set by the American College of Radiology. That means they may fail to detect tumors, leading to a false sense of security.

As health rights activists rightly observe, a bad mammogram is worse than no mammogram.

In January 1991 Congress passed legislation permitting Medicare to pay for mammograms for women over 65. That is awfully late. Most laws at the state level do not cover women under 35. Women under 50 are usually eligible for screenings only every two years.

"How do you make the machines good, and how do you get the women to the good machines? How do you make them good at a cost that will allow the women to get to the machines?" asks Andrea Camp, an aide to Representative Pat Schroeder.

Says Dr. Susan Bates, a researcher at the National Cancer Institute, "For the medical community, the direction is clear—research. For women, the direction also is clear—take charge. Eat right, avoid a fat-filled diet and a lifestyle that might increase your risk of cancer. At the age of 40 begin to get mammograms and get them on schedule."

Breast Cancer and the Future

One objective of the massive NIH study will be to trace the link between nutrition and breast cancer, long considered an important factor.

Reducing the percentage of fat in one's diet is critical for all sorts of health reasons, including breast cancer prevention. One expert quoted in the *Self* story estimates that if we reduced fat from 40 percent to 20 percent of our diet, breast-cancer rates would drop 60 percent. If so, we should see rates *drop,* instead of increase around 2000, when baby boomers, who have already cut fat, hit age 50 or so. Vegetables from the crucifer family—broccoli, cabbage, bok choy, brussels sprouts, cauliflower—protect against breast cancer, as do foods rich in beta-carotene—carrots, squash, sweet potatoes, peaches, cantaloupes.

Tamoxifen, a synthetic hormone that blocks the action of estrogen in the breast and stops the growth of tumors, has successfully been used for years to treat advanced and even early-stage breast cancer: in 1992 the National Cancer Institute began a five- to eight-year study to see if it can *prevent* breast tumors. Some 16,000 women will participate. Researchers think it will also prevent heart disease and osteoporosis, like estrogen: paradoxically, while tamoxifen blocks the effects of estrogen in the breast, it mimics the effect of estrogen on the heart and bones.

Women whose close relatives have died of breast cancer and who live in fear of it welcome the study, but it has not been embraced throughout the women's health movement. Dr. Adriane Fugh-Beerman, an adviser to the National Women's Health Network, calls it "a perversion of women's health." Its side effects, risks and cost rule it out as a cure-all for healthy women, she believes. When some women's groups expressed concern about the potential side effects of tamoxifen, the National Cancer Institute responded in October 1992 by claiming that the benefits outweighed the risks.

Geneticists are honing in on the genetic markers that could indicate a propensity to the disease. Recent discoveries: in families with a history of breast cancer, a segment on chromosome 17 was inherited by all women who got the disease early. An oncogene or cancer-causing gene called Pradi 1 has been isolated by researchers at Massachusetts General Hospital. Geneticists say that one day they will be able to test women for the gene, catching the disease long before it might be life threatening or even show up on a breast X ray. "Something comparable to a Pap smear for breast cancer," says Mary-Claire King, of the University of California's School of Public Health.

Five Health Trends Concerning Women

Although this chapter focuses mainly on menopause and related health risks, we shall briefly discuss five additional health issues of vital importance to women, whatever their age. They are breast implants, the Pap-smear accuracy issue, detecting ovarian cancer, AIDS in women and fertility/contraception.

The Breast Implant Controversy

Implants made of silicone have been on the market for 30 years. Estimates of how many women have had the implants range from a low of 300,000 to 1 million to a much-quoted 2 million. The vast majority get implants for cosmetic reasons; but some 20 percent have used the implants in breast reconstruction after cancer surgery.

As early as the 1970's, however, Dow Corning, a leading silicone-implant maker, was aware of concerns about their safety. Women and their physicians became concerned about a whole host of problems and symptoms related to silicone leaking from the implants and affecting other parts of the body. The worst fears linked symptoms of scleroderma, a serious, even fatal, autoimmune disease, with the implants.

Less serious but still very troubling problems included scar tissue, deformities, rupturing and breast hardening. The scandal, of course, is that Dow Corning covered up these reports for nearly 20 years. In 1992 Dow made internal documents public, and many women with the implants were furious and felt betrayed after receiving assurances from the maker and their own doctor that implants were "safe." Now, it seems, they were not.

There is real disagreement about how many women have suffered problems with implants. Even so, they and everyone else had every right to know if problems existed. Most women report no trouble with implants. The issue is how big is the minority who have had problems—and what the chances are of very serious problems.

A survey of 600 implant recipients by the American Society of Plastic and Reconstructive Surgeons found 93 percent of them satisfied with results. Public Citizens Health Research Group, which was instrumental in bringing the issue to light, estimates that 155,500 women have endured ruptured implants or infections, that 123,300 more have had hardening of the breasts and that 250,000 women have experienced uncomfortable breasts. That is an awful lot of people, and it should be noted that these figures were extrapolated from the numbers of women they talked to and projected onto the implant population. They are not documented complaints.

But 8,000 women who belong to Command Trust Network, a support group, have experienced what they describe as "complications."

The FDA at first put a moratorium on the implants and then heard testimony from women, advocacy groups and the implant makers.

• Breast-cancer survivors were adamant about how important implants and reconstruction were to their healing process.
• Women who chose the implants for cosmetic purposes refused to be minimized for their personal decision. "The government can just keep its hands off my breast," one woman said.
• Women who had had serious health problems said, in effect, "The risk, however small, is not worth the hell I am going through." One woman said she sometimes wished she had simply died of cancer. "Then I would have only had six weeks of pain," she said.

The FDA finally decided to ban cosmetic implants (except for a few thousand women in clinical studies) but to permit implants for breast reconstruction. Saline implants and breast augmentation using the body's own tissue remain viable options.

Meanwhile women who have the implants live in fear that problems may develop and wonder if they should have them removed. Dow Corning has offered to pay $1,200 toward the cost of removal.

Furthermore, in March 1992 Dow Corning said it was out of the silicone-implant business. Whether because of bad publicity or the risk of even more lawsuits, Dow and several other silicone-implant makers have decided it is simply not worth it to keep making implants.

But for the women with these things in their bodies, it is not that simple. Every executive who participated in the cover-up and every FDA bureaucrat who looked the other way must be held personally accountable.

In March 1993 Dow admitted that studies on laboratory rats showed the silicone gel in implants was "a strong irritant of the immune system, at least in animals." Over the past 30 years, Dow supplied 75 percent of silicone implants.

In the final analysis, we believe every woman should be free to evaluate the risks of implants (many will disagree with us on this one)—*but only when all the data is out there and available.* At this point it is not—and you can blame Dow and the FDA for that.

Let's start a dialogue on why our society is so obsessed with, as Naomi Wolf (see Chapter 7) puts it, "anorexic bodies with huge breasts."

Soon enough the style will change (it always does): big breasts will be "out," and the flapper, Twiggy-type flat chest will be "in." Then what?

How about accepting ourselves as we are?

Pap Smears Save Lives,
But Can Their Accuracy Be Counted On?

Cervical-cancer deaths have dropped 70 percent, to 4,400 in 1993, since Dr. George Papanicolaou developed the Pap smear in 1943. Cervical cancer develops slowly, so it is very treatable when caught in its earliest stages.

"The overwhelming majority of women—if they have Pap smears taken on a regular basis—will have abnormalities detected in a stage when they can be readily treated and arc virtually treatable 100 percent of the time," says Ralph M. Richart, chief of gynecological pathology and cytology at Columbia-Presbyterian Medical Center in New York City.

Pap tests also detect cancers of the uterus or endometrium, its lining. In 1993 almost 45,000 American women will be diagnosed with either uterine or cervical cancer, 13,500 with cervical cancer and 32,000 with uterine cancer. Public-health officials estimate 90 percent of uterine-cancer deaths could be prevented with regular Pap smears. But a 1983 study concluded that only 57 percent of women ages 40 to 70 had a Pap smear at least once every three years. For younger women, the testing rate was higher—80 percent. Women over 18 should have regular tests.

But women who get Pap smears only every *three* years *quadruple* the risk of undetected cervical cancer, compared with women who have the test annually, says a University of Washington study.

The Problem Is . . .

It is pretty clear that an annual Pap smear is the way to go. How scandalous to read within the last few years that 10 to 40 percent of cervical cancers or the cell abnormalities that precede them may be missed because of sloppy laboratory work or poor tissue sampling.

Labor-intensive Pap tests depend on meticulous care, from cell collection and preparation to staining on the slide and interpreting each specimen. Improperly done, the value of the test is "seriously compromised," said the American Medical Association in a report on quality control in Pap testing.

Now medical organizations and the federal government want to investigate quality control in Pap testing and impose stricter standards to ensure more reliable results. It is about time.

- The Centers for Disease Control requires cytology labs engaged in interstate commerce to rescreen 10 percent of negative Pap smears for quality control.
- New York State licenses laboratories only after cytotechnologists undergo a mandatory exam.
- In California a cytotechnologist may not screen more than 75 slides a day.
- In 1988 Congress required quality standards for about 12,000 labs receiving Medicare and Medicaid funds or engaging in interstate commerce.

"We certainly could knock the incidence of invasive disease down to a greater degree," says Dr. William Creasman, professor and head of the Department of Obstetrics and Gynecology at the University of South Carolina in Charleston. "But we'll never get rid of it entirely because some women won't get Pap smears or won't get them done when they should."

Once again, the bottom line is women taking charge of their own health care.

Get regular Pap smears, and make sure your doctor uses a lab certified by a professional organization such as the College of American Pathologists.

Ovarian Cancer: The Silent Killer

Each year, 22,000 American women are diagnosed with ovarian cancer, the sixth-most-frequent cause of cancer in women; more than 13,000 die. The cause of ovarian cancer has not yet been established and it remains very difficult to detect early. While most cases are in women over age 50, a woman could be 35 years old and childless or 60 with five children.

"Ovarian cancer can happen at any time, including during pregnancy," says Michelle Dudzinski, a gynecologic oncologist at St. Luke's Hospital in Kansas City, Missouri.

Family history of the disease is the single greatest risk factor. At Roswell Park Memorial Institute in Buffalo, New York, M. Steven Piver has collected a national tumor registry of 200 ovarian-cancer families, where the disease reappears in each generation. He concludes that the risk of ovarian cancer is one in 70, or about 1.4 percent for the average American woman. "But if two or more first-degree relatives have it, you have a 50 percent chance of developing ovarian cancer," he says.

In December 1992 the FDA approved taxol, made from the bark of the yew tree, as a treatment for ovarian cancer. The drug won't cure women, but for some it shrinks the tumors, adding for a little longer life.

So far, no link has been found with smoking, fibroid tumors of the ovaries, diet, alcohol consumption, number of sexual partners or being overweight. But women ought to be familiar with the symptoms, because they mimic a number of gastrointestinal diseases—vague lower abdominal pain, bloating, gas and constipation—usually associated with other conditions.

Ovarian cancer goes undetected in 70 percent of women until it reaches an advanced stage when the cure rate is less than 25 percent. "The ovaries are in a very silent area of the body," says Maurie Markham, associate chairman of the department of medicine at Memorial Sloan-Kettering Cancer Center in New York. "One can have a fairly large mass that has plenty of time to grow and spread before any symptoms occur."

But new screening tests are moving in on the silent killer. A transvaginal ultrasound test, in use for about two years, has successfully detected small tumors. A blood test, called CA 125, registers elevated levels of a substance secreted by ovarian tumors.

Until such tests are widely available, pelvic exams are the main way to detect the disease. "We still depend on routine pelvic exams to detect ovarian cancer," says Robert C. Young, president of the Fox Chase Cancer Center in Philadelphia.

He also recommends that **women get an annual pelvic exam done by a gynecologist.** A family practitioner or internist may not be as trained—or as experienced—in performing the exam.

Dr. David Alberts, director of cancer prevention and control at the University of Arizona Cancer Center in Tucson, concurs. "Most physicians, except gynecologists, are not good at pelvic exams."

Several female doctors who aren't gynecologists were offended when that bit of advice appeared in this book's hardback edition. Perhaps Drs. Young and Alberts meant *male* physicians who aren't gynecologists . . . ?

Women, AIDS and Vulnerability

The public and even many physicians still see HIV and AIDS as a "gay male disease." So far, thank God and good public education, an epidemic of AIDS in heterosexuals has not materialized in the United States. So we can relax a little, right?

Wrong.

New evidence shows women are more vulnerable to the disease through heterosexual contact than men are, and that certain individuals, depending on the factors described below, are so infectious, they are even more likely than other infected parties to pass AIDS along through a single sexual act.

In 1991, 5,730 new cases of AIDS in women were reported, up from 4,888 in 1990—a 17 percent increase, compared with about a 5 percent increase overall from 1990 to 1991. But 1992 saw a huge increase when, in response to demands from female AIDS activists, the definition of AIDS in women was expanded to include the symptoms that most often appear in women; 1992 saw 9,858 new cases of AIDS in women, a 42 percent increase, compared with a 33 percent decrease in AIDS cases in the U.S. population overall. **Although more men have the disease than women, AIDS is spreading faster among women than among men.** Many more, of course, are HIV positive without symptoms, and still more do not yet know they are infected.

- AIDS is now the leading killer of young women in New York.
- Between 1,500 and 2,000 babies are born each year already infected with the disease.
- The majority of new cases in women (1990 and 1991) come from IV drug use (about half) and heterosexual contact (more than one third).
- Women are the nation's fastest-growing AIDS group. One in seven new AIDS cases in the United States is a woman.

"Increasingly, heterosexual transmission will become the predominant mode of HIV transmission throughout the world," says Dr. James Chin, an official with the World Health Organization.

New evidence shows women are much likelier to become infected with AIDS through heterosexual contact than men are. Reported cases seem to bear that out: in 1991 some 1,344 men got AIDS from women, while 2,119 women got it from men—of those, 1,251 got AIDS from contact with male IV drug users.

Experts now say women are between two and ten times more vulnerable during heterosexual intercourse than men.

New findings explain why, although experts say it is unlikely, it is entirely possible to become infected through a single heterosexual contact:

- An HIV-positive individual is more infectious in the *late and early stages* of the disease. Two or three months after a person is infected, the virus is strong because the body has not yet marshaled the resources to fight it. In the late stages of the disease, there is *more* virus in the body fluids, which makes infection likelier.
- People with other infections, like genital herpes, are more infectious.
- Women, as noted, are more vulnerable to the disease than men— and among women, teenagers, who have only one layer of cells covering the cervix (older women have several), are more likely to bleed during intercourse and therefore are likelier to get AIDS.

A study in the *New England Journal of Medicine* described a highly infectious male, a Belgian engineer, who infected 11 out of the

19 female sex partners health officials could locate (they were unable to track down dozens of others). *Of the 11 he infected, several of the contacts had been one-night stands.*

In late 1991 the *Washington Post* ran a story about a support group of six Montgomery County, Maryland, women—black, white and Hispanic, young and old, students and professionals—all HIV positive. One says she got the disease from her husband, who had a one-night fling, got AIDS and passed it on to her. Another says the man who infected her had deliberately lied about his drug use.

"Use a condom even if you are married," said one woman in the group, "because men lie."

Advances in Conception and Contraception

Birth Control

In 1990 the United States joined 16 European countries to approve Norplant, a contraceptive inserted under the skin that remains effective for about five years. Norplant prevents pregnancy with the hormone progestin, the active ingredient (with estrogen) in most contraceptive pills.

Six matchstick-size capsules are implanted under the skin of a woman's upper arm. It takes about 10 minutes. The hormone is released into the bloodstream. It was developed by the Population Council and Wyeth-Ayerst Laboratories. By 1992 about 100,000 U.S. women were Norplant users, less than one percent of those using oral contraceptives.

"I was very nervous, because I hate needles," says Eileen Kotecki, 28, of Baltimore. "But . . . it was fine." Kotecki was also concerned that the implant would be visible. "Check her out, she's got Norplant," she joked. But, she says, the implant is invisible unless she squeezes her arm.

If a woman wants to become pregnant, the implant is removed, and she is fertile again within 48 hours. Norplant's failure rate is extremely low: one tenth to one twentieth the rate of birth-control pills, which fail only 3 percent of the time.

Unfortunately, progestin is not perfect. It causes irregular bleeding in 75 percent of women. Some women report seven-week menstrual cycles—others, three-week cycles. Other women average eight days of bleeding or spotting instead of five days. Many women will find those side effects disturbing. The manufacturer says the effects diminish after two years. Too long for many.

A recent *New York Times* report downplayed the irregular bleeding and quoted several physicians who said their patients were happy, even "ecstatic" about the implant. It did note, however, that in clinical trials, 2 to 7 percent withdrew because of bleeding.

Some fear Norplant will be used to restrict the "reproductive freedom" of teenagers, drug users, convicted child abusers or the mentally ill (how people can get excited about the reproductive "rights" of convicted child abusers is beyond us).

Norplant is available at Baltimore's Paquin School, where students are either pregnant teens or new mothers. It is the first school to offer the implant. "Without it I'd probably have more children," says senior Consuelo Law, and "I want to complete my education."

In 1991 California judge Howard Broadman ordered a woman who had beaten her children to use Norplant during a three-year probation period. The woman initially agreed, but then objected and was not forced to accept Norplant. The Alan Guttmacher Institute reports that more than 20 bills in 13 states have introduced the use of Norplant as "an instrument of social policy." Governor William Schaefer of Maryland, in his 1993 State of the State address, discussed the controversial possibility of mandatory Norplant for welfare recipients with several children out of wedlock.

Drug firms are reluctant to devote a lot of money to contraceptive research, partly because of the painstakingly thorough FDA review process. In fall 1992, for example, the FDA finally allowed U.S. women access to Depo Provera, an injectable contraceptive effective for three months, even though 90 million women in 90 countries, including Britain, France, Germany and Sweden, have used it for a long time. Its developer, Upjohn Company, first sought FDA approval 26 years ago.

Also on the contraceptive front, the female condom, whose effectiveness in preventing pregnancy is mediocre at best, won FDA approval in 1993. Clinical trials on a new birth control pill composed of melatonin and progestin (and no estrogen) are scheduled to begin in 1993.

Given its effectiveness, it is no wonder some say Norplant —eight-day menstrual periods and all—is the best hope for a long-term contraceptive device for the near future.

The Fertility Revolution

The American Fertility Society reports almost 30,000 children are born each year as the result of donated sperm, a few hundred of donated eggs.

For women who are having trouble conceiving, the possibilities are mind-boggling:

- Fertility drugs such as Clomid, Serophene and Pergonal are frequently the first approach.
- Corrective surgery (for men and women) sometimes solves fertility problems.
- Artificial insemination helps a woman become pregnant.
- In vitro fertilization (IVF), which brings egg and sperm together in the laboratory, is a relatively new method that has worked for some couples.

The techniques listed below, described in the May 1991 issue of *FDA Consumer,* combine fertility drugs with medical intervention at ovulation.

- **Gamete Intrafallopian Transfer** (GIFT) is similar to IVF, except eggs and sperm are collected and immediately inserted into one or both fallopian tubes. GIFT requires the woman to have at least one healthy fallopian tube.
- In **Tubal Ovum Transfer** a woman's eggs are retrieved and put into the fallopian tube close to where it opens into the uterus. The couple then has intercourse or the woman is artificially inseminated. Since the eggs are placed beyond where the fallopian tube might be damaged, this method can be used when GIFT cannot.
- **Embryo Lavage** involves a fertile female donor providing the eggs artificially inseminated with the would-be father's sperm. If the donor conceives, the embryo is washed out of her reproductive tract and transferred to the uterus or a fallopian tube of the would-be mother, who is treated with fertility drugs to make her uterus receptive to the embryo.
- **Surrogate Motherhood.** Sensationalized by the Mary Beth Whitehead story, surrogate motherhood may work for women who do not respond to ovulation therapies, who have no ovaries or uterus, whose life would be endangered by pregnancy or who might risk passing on a genetic defect.

These techniques produce offspring genetically linked to at least one parent. But the UK's Cambridge and Hallam Medical Centre offers potential parents fertilized embryos from complete strangers to be implanted in the prospective mother's womb. "This is not adoption from the cot, but adoption from your womb," says Dr. Peter Brinsden, the clinic's director.

Americans spent $1 billion on fertility services in 1992, reported *Newsweek*.

A Question of Common Sense—and Love

The brave new world of baby-making requires choices and decisions. In the years ahead medical breakthroughs in both contraception and conception will present women with moral, ethical and personal dilemmas.

But the women involved, guided by common sense and love, are setting examples that show the ethicists may have blown some of these "agonizing decisions" out of proportion.

Arlette Schweitzer, the 43-year-old school librarian of Aberdeen, South Dakota, is the woman who bore her daughter and son-in-law's children. Her 23-year-old daughter, Christa Uchytil of Sioux City, Iowa, "one of those people who always wanted to be a mother," was born without a uterus. Their story, which appeared many times on national television, brought a tear to more than a few eyes.

A 1989 survey by the American Fertility Society counted 198 attempts to produce a child through gestational surrogacy the way the Schweitzer/Uchytil family did (though not with the same mother-daughter connection) and 33 deliveries. This sort of surrogacy is legal in all U.S. states. A similar case was that of Giants pitcher Dave Righetti and his wife, Kandice. Kandice's sister, who bore their offspring, may have delivered more than she bargained for—triplets.

In late 1992, two postmenopausal women, both age 53, gave birth to children after in vitro fertilization:

- Mary Sherling, mother of three by a previous marriage, was implanted with a donor egg fertilized in a test tube with the sperm of her husband, Don Sherling, 32. Twin girls were born in November.
- Geraldine Wesolowski was implanted with the fertilized eggs of

her son and daughter-in-law. Like Arlette Schweitzer, she gave birth to her own grandchild, a boy.

Age is not a factor, says Dr. William Cooper, who performed Mrs. Wesolowski's procedure. "All you need is a womb of any age."

Some experts think these procedures will encourage "thousands of families" to follow their example.

In an otherwise sensitive *New York Times* piece on Arlette Schweitzer, author Gina Kolata asked a series of male ethicists for their ideas. Sure enough, she found a few sourpusses:

Dr. Jay Katz, a Yale University professor, called it "a very, very bad idea." Dr. Albert Jonsen, a University of Washington in Seattle ethicist, asked, "Are there kinds of altruism that may be so troubling to important social and cultural traditions that we'd rather not have that altruism take place?"

Mrs. Schweitzer and her daughter obviously made the decision with care but not strain. "We discussed it continually over the years," she says. "You do what you do for your children because you love them."

That is apparently beyond the good doctors Katz and Jonsen.

The 21st Century Will Witness the Feminization of Health Care

Women's key allies in the struggle to put women's issues atop the national agenda are the growing numbers of women in medicine. Today 50 percent of the United States' new primary-care physicians, medicine's front line for diagnosis and treatment decisions, are women. Though a minority in some specialties, the number and influence of women physicians keep growing:

- Twenty percent of the 31,000 members of the American College of Obstetricians and Gynecologists are women, up from 7 percent in 1978.
- Fifty-four percent of doctors who began residencies in 1991 were women. And women will make up 30 percent of all practicing ob/gyns by 2000.
- Those numbers will increase even more: half the resident medical students in obstetrics and gynecology today are women.
- Women are 36 percent of U.S. medical students.

• Not only are there more women physicians, but more older women. In 1992 Jean Forman, 51, became the oldest person to graduate from the University of Southern California's medical school in its 107-year history.

There is little doubt about it. The growing number of women in medicine, the aging of the baby-boom women and the revelations by health-care activists that research into breast cancer and heart disease in women have been grossly underfunded, have combined to produce the critical mass to push women's health issues into the spotlight.

So far, however, women have been poorly represented in policy-making positions.

There are no women deans in U.S. medical schools, 98 percent of department chairs are men, as are 79 percent of medical school faculties. The American Medical Association has never had a woman as chief executive in its 144-year history. Even in the American College of Obstetricians and Gynecologists, whose sole mission is serving women, there have never been more than two women in its top 17 offices at any one time in 41 years. But eventually even those dismal numbers will improve.

Change is beginning to happen; consider these women in high-profile positions.

• Donna Shalala is the new secretary of health and human services.
• Antonia Novello, a pediatrician, past deputy director of the National Institute of Child Health and Human Development and professor of pediatrics at Georgetown University Medical School, was U.S. Surgeon General in the Bush administration and stayed until June 1993. President Clinton's nominee is Joycelyn Elders.
• Dr. Bernadine Healy, former chair of the Cleveland Clinic Foundation's Research Institute and past president of the American Heart Association and the American Federation of Clinical Research, directed NIH. No replacement had been announced before we went to press.
• Vivian Pinn, former chief of pathology at Howard University's College of Medicine and past president of the National Medical Association, a black physicians' group, and an expert in kidney disease, became the first director of NIH's Office of Research on Women's Health in 1991.
• Gail Wilensky ran the U.S. Health Care Financing Administration, which oversees the Medicare and Medicaid programs. (She

is now a senior fellow at Project Hope, a nonprofit organization that offers medical care and training around the globe.)

Women in decision-making health-care positions will change the health-care and medical profession's attitude toward women. In the coming decades health care will take on a decidedly feminine tone.

Nursing

The feminization of health care is also related to the growing status of women in the previously underpaid, overworked and underappreciated profession of nursing. As we said in Chapter 3, nurses may be responsible for 40 to 50 percent of hospital income.

- Dr. Barbara S. Heater, associate professor of nursing at the University of Missouri in St. Louis, analyzed 84 studies by nurse researchers covering 4,146 patients. She concluded that "research-based nursing interventions," that is, good nursing, produce 28 percent better outcomes for 72 percent of patients and save money by shortening hospital stays.
- Nurses at Ohio State University showed that several weeks of aerobic exercise before surgery and chemotherapy for breast cancer speeded the patient's recovery.
- Nurse researchers at the University of Wisconsin School of Nursing found that teaching the hospital staff to create a harmonious environment for premature babies improved their breathing, eating and neurological development, and also reduced complications and shortened hospital stays—saving about $12,250 per day.

There are about 6,000 nurse researchers today, up from only 600 fifteen years ago.

How well doctors and nurses communicate and cooperate is the most powerful determinant of hospital death rates.

That is the conclusion of a landmark 1986 study of 5,030 patients in 13 intensive-care units (ICUs) conducted by the George Washington University Medical Center. In the best-coordinated ICUs, there were *41 percent fewer* deaths than predicted. In the most poorly run ICUs, there were 58 percent more deaths than expected. Treating nurses as professionals with acknowledged expertise improves quality and cost of care as well as life expectancy.

When *U.S. News and World Report* polled 1,000 physicians in an effort to identify the country's best hospitals, they ranked quality of nursing care second only to the caliber of the medical staff.

Hospital CEOs went further: in a 1989 survey, 663 put nursing expertise above physician skill as the feature that marked excellent hospital care.

Dr. Kevin Morrissey, clinical associate professor of surgery at New York's Cornell University Medical College, says the growing number of women in medicine will help humanize the field, including surgery, the specialty where physicians maintain the greatest distance from patients.

Adult Women's Medicine

Women, and particularly postmenopausal women, demand to be treated holistically, not as an ovary that is past its prime. Medical professionals are beginning to recognize that. At the Comprehensive Menopause Program, at the University of California at San Diego, a woman's health is evaluated in terms of her history, current symptoms and psychological state. Some patients are premenopausal women seeking to prepare themselves for what's to come.

Premenopausal preparation can be *the* intervention that enhances postmenopausal health. In 1985 Dr. Morris Notelovitz, a gynecologist specializing in what he refers to as "adult women's medicine," founded one of the first menopause clinics that welcomed premenopausal women—the Women's Medical and Diagnostic Center in Gainesville, Florida. Notelovitz believes all women should have a thorough medical evaluation at 35, including screening for cardiovascular disease, instruction in breast self-examination and a baseline mammogram.

"Women's health is a field that's exploding right now," says Irma Groertzen, CEO of Magee Women's Hospital in Pittsburgh. If women's medicine were to become a formal specialty, medical schools and certification boards would have to set new standards to govern it.

Alice Dan, the organizer of a University of Illinois conference on the new women's health specialty, believes that "it's the culmination of the whole women's health movement."

One immediate benefit for women: seeing one physician instead of an internist *and* a gynecologist.

But Dr. Michelle Harrison takes a different position: instead of creating a new specialty, why not make medicine as a whole function better for women? Other feminists agree: *every* medical practitioner needs to know a lot more about women, not just specialists.

However you come out on the issue, one thing is certain: the medical establishment is finally becoming more aware of women—as patients and as consumers of family medical care. According to a report by the Boston-based consultantcy Marketing to Women, women make 75 percent (some put it at 80 to 90 percent) of consumer health-care decisions.

More than 1,000 of the United States' 6,000-plus hospitals have programs tailored specifically to women's care, says the American Hospital Association, or about 19 percent, up from 12 percent in 1987.

Most women's advocates believe this heightened consciousness will lead to better care, but acknowledge there's always the risk that some health-care organizations and practitioners will get carried away and exploit this "new trend" for all the wrong reasons. Sally Rynne, president of Women's Healthcare Consultants in Evanston, Illinois, tells hospitals that a "cheese and cracker basket" is not sufficient. "Women want substantial things like immediate results on mammography, pain-control options for childbirth, more women doctors and superior health-care information."

The primary focus of women's health centers has shifted from abortion to mainstream women's health care. Even though these centers do *not* focus exclusively on the concerns of menopausal women, they are poised to embrace that priority as the population ages. They include:

• Long Island's Penny Wise Budoff, M.D., Pavilion;
• Women's Health Associates at Boston's Massachusetts General Hospital;
• Mason City, Iowa's Women's Health Center.

Their approach is already holistic—from premenstrual syndrome, to cholesterol screening, to breast-cancer treatment, to psychological counseling.

"Mothers do a good job teaching little girls about menstruation," says Dr. Cynthia Stuenkel, medical director of San Diego's menopause program, "but they don't talk to their daughters about menopause."

Neither does anyone else. But the demographics behind the menopause megatrend are about to change how the medical community

deals with this rite of passage and the myriad health problems that can
follow.

The all-in-one breast-cancer center that opened in 1992 at Sloan-
Kettering is a prototype. "It's really important to gather everything all
in one place," says Dr. Larry Norton. "Otherwise it can be a nightmare for a patient to hunt down all the services she needs." Sloan-
Kettering offers psychological and nutritional counseling, an
education center to dispense the latest articles and a beauty program.
Boston's Dana Farber Cancer Center and the University of California
at Los Angeles have similar all-in-one centers.

Adult women's medicine is a growth industry, an area of specialization with a guaranteed clientele—perhaps a specialty all those obstetricians who have left the baby business due to astronomical
malpractice insurance might want to consider.

**As the baby boom ages, there will be a subtle shift away from
reproductive issues toward menopausal ones.**

Subtle is the key word. Women who have marched for or against
abortion rights will not give up their deeply held values. But if the
health crisis staring a woman in the face is breast cancer and she is
fired up about the lack of research on that killer disease, she will
express it by showing up at a health rights demonstration.

Many activists insist the medical community has a long way to
go before research protocols, treatment practices and attitudes toward
women's health issues are up to par. Women demand to be treated as
partners in their own care rather than passive receptacles for whatever
the medical community can throw at them. Finally, when time and
technology have run their course, women demand to make the final
decision about death with dignity.

Not long ago women's health issues were not discussed in polite
society. Today they are the subject of newspaper headlines, TV news
updates, magazine features and congressional hearings. The politics of
health care will heat up in the next two decades as women take control
of their destiny and rewrite the nation's health-care agenda.

6.
Collaborative Couples

In 1991 a research team won patent approval for a new method of growing human skin and other tissues in a laboratory. Science as usual. But in this case the team was a husband and wife—Gail K. Naughton, a cofounder of Marrow-Tech, Inc., in La Jolla, California, and Brian A. Naughton, an associate professor at the Hunter College School of Health Sciences in New York. Their new method may make it easier to replace the skin of badly burned people.

Claude and Donna Jeanloz bought a 200-year-old farmhouse in Millers Falls, Massachusetts, and started to renovate it themselves. It didn't take long to discover it was extremely difficult to find authentic replacement fixtures. The Renovator's Supply was born. It started out as a direct-mail venture distributed from their kitchen table. Now the company mails out 8 million catalogs a year, has spun off a quarterly magazine, *Victorian Homes,* and operates five retail outlets throughout the Northeast. Its diverse operation is Millers Falls's largest employer.

Judith Barnard and Michael Fain resigned their jobs to devote full time to writing a novel together. They gave themselves a year to get a publishing contract. The resulting *Deceptions* (Poseidon) by "Judith Michael" became a best-seller, and this collaborative couple has published three other best-selling novels during the last eight years.

The Collaborative White House

Hundreds of thousands of couples like these are making creative partnerships a new paradigm for the 21st century, but none are more visible than America's First Couple, Bill and Hillary Clinton. The two collaborate on politics, policy and personnel. To all appearances, it is an intellectually stimulating and emotionally comfortable union. Rooted in strong family ties, their relationship seems to move effortlessly into the dimension of public policy.

Hillary Rodham Clinton has twice been named one of the top 100 U.S. lawyers by the *National Law Journal* and the president, who met his wife at Yale Law School, apparently got used to having a strong, super-smart partner early on. If her accomplishments or popularity sometimes outshine his, Bill Clinton has been known to say, "It's law school all over again."

"She confirms something the public is ready to believe about women in politics—that they are as smart as men but likely to be more caring," says Democratic health-care consultant Greg Schneiders.

As the world knows, the president assigned his wife the monumental task of drafting legislation to reform the $1 trillion a year health-care industry, an awesome task by any measure, and the cornerstone of U.S. domestic policy. But Hillary Clinton seems to thrive on challenge, earning high marks even from much of the health care industry. The *Washington Post* described her as a "hard-working, glamour-shy, health-care reform grind."

Like most collaborative couples, their effectiveness seems to be enhanced by their different skills and approaches: he loves to press the flesh; she comes across as a passionate listener. He appears easy, open, approachable, sometimes even vulnerable; she, by all accounts, is strong, deep, efficient, not given to frivolity. He's emotional; she's more spiritual. When her father became ill, she dropped health care to spend two weeks at his bedside.

Is this the "workaholic nazifeminist" the "family values–loving" right wants to sell, or a spectacular role model of how the first generation of women with lifelong, full-time careers can exemplify the synthesis of worldly participation and personal values?

Summarizing Hillary Clinton's philosophical views, the *Washington Post* wrote: "Life has a transcendental meaning. To find it, you have to be involved with something bigger than yourself."

She is. Meanwhile, like many baby-boom women, she balances professional responsibilities with being a real mom to a young teenage daughter in a new city and moving her widowed mother into the White House.

From Nepotism to Collaboration

Couples have worked for the same company or institution for a long time, and the old-fashioned policies against hiring spouses have been on the decline for many years. A recent high point in couples working together occurred on January 14, 1990, when on Flight 419 from Denver to Phoenix, John Zimmerman and Leslie King became the first husband-and-wife team to fly a United Airlines passenger jet.

- Mark Lee and Jan Davis became the first married couple in space as part of the crew of one of the NASA space shuttles. NASA has two additional astronaut couples.
- Hallmark card alums Ginny and Stu Fraser run a thriving greeting card business from their home near San Diego, California.
- Tim and Nina Zagat publish the Zagat restaurant guide, which collates the opinions of frequent diners all over the United States. The guide represents more than 30 cities and generates $3 million in annual revenue.
- Michael and Marian Ilitch run the $2 billion Little Caesar empire, the nation's third-largest pizza chain. "He's marketing; she's finance" read the headline of a *New York Times* profile on the couple. She ranked second on *Working Woman*'s 50 top women business owners list.
- Ellen Gordon and her husband Melvin run the $245 million Tootsie Roll Industries, which she inherited from her father. Number 21 on the *Working Woman* list of the top 50 women-owned businesses, the magazine said, "Investors remain sweet on Tootsie Roll stock."

With collaborative couples we are witnessing a widespread new phenomenon: couples working together for themselves.

Collaborative couples bring the passion of their personal relationship into their work, which may provide the added energy for artistic and scientific breakthrough. The desire to be partners in both personal and public life leads some collaborative couples to go into business together. The 1980's was the decade of the entrepreneur— individuals committed to a new vision of business outside the corporate hierarchy. The 1990's will be the decade of entrepreneurial couples.

The Small Business Administration reports that husband-and-wife businesses represent the fastest-growing segment of the business population. From 1980 to 1989, there was an 83.9 percent increase in such teams. The National Family Business Council estimates that there are as many as 1.8 million husband-and-wife entrepreneurial couples.

Of course, some couples automatically think working together would destroy their marriage; others, though fearful, harbor a secret desire to go into business together. The examples this chapter describes can help you decide whether this new model might work for you.

Wherever opportunity exists, wherever creativity is expressed, collaborative couples can be found. There are high-profile collaborative couples like Bob Kersee, coach and husband to Olympic gold-medalist Jackie Joyner-Kersee; Debra J. and Randall K. Fields, of Mrs. Fields cookie fame; the famous designers Lella and Massimo Vignelli; and Genevieve and the late Bill Gore, who built W. L. Gore & Associates into a multinational company and gave the world Gore-Tex fabric. Also on the list are Patricia and Mel Ziegler, who created Banana Republic; Ian and Betty Ballantine, who founded Ballantine Books; and Reuben and Rose Mattus, who gave us Häagen-Dazs.

Legions of other couples who are not in the public eye are nonetheless part of an emerging trend that is reweaving America's cultural fabric to better fit the personal needs of the middle-aged baby boomers—many of whom have been to the top of the corporate ladder and didn't like what they saw when they got there.

Frank and Sharon Barnett, authors of *Working Together: Entrepreneurial Couples* (Ten Speed Press), say couples with a healthy relationship are in command of four factors that give them a winning edge in starting a business:

1. They are free of interpersonal competition and can use their energies to compete together against the outside world.
2. They have open communication.
3. They trust each other.
4. They share the same objectives.

Money isn't what drives collaborative couples, they say. "It's the independence they feel as a couple, the power of self-reliance, the total commitment and involvement in a service or a product over which

they have absolute control, and the gratification and bonding that
come from working together."

In her book *In Love and In Business: How Entrepreneurial Couples Are Changing the Rules of Business and Marriage* (Wiley), Sharon Nelton lists the "common threads" she found among successful couples:

• The relationship comes first. She quotes Randy Fields, one half
  of the Mrs. Fields cookies team, as saying, "Both of us concluded
  that the most important thing in the world to us was our relationship to each other. Without that, it wouldn't matter whether we
  had whatever is called business success." It is not that the business isn't a top priority or that you don't work like hell. It is that
  the business is *grounded* in a deeper spiritual principle.
• The spouses demonstrated enormous respect and support for
  each other.
• There is a high degree of close communication about both marriage and business.
• The partners complement each other's talents and attitudes, and
  they carve up turf accordingly.
• Spouses compete with the world outside, not with each other.
• They put their egos in check. Says Susan Harnett of Boston's
  Bread & Circus, "I respect Tony for what he is, and he respects
  me for what I am, and we don't ever try to hurt each other, step
  on each other's toes, call the shots or pull the carpet out from
  under each other."

As every two-career couple can attest, juggling children, home
and work can test the strongest of marriages; introduce a co-owned
business or creative partnership into the mix, and you have a recipe
for disaster—*or do you*?

Collaborative Couples: An Evolutionary Process, Not a Revolutionary Event

Webster's New World Dictionary defines "collaborate" in two
ways: 1) to work together, especially in some literary, artistic or scientific undertaking; 2) to cooperate with the enemy; to be a collabora-
tionist.

No wonder the very idea of a successful collaboration between
couples inspires skepticism.

"Popular culture gives much more credit to individual genius

than it does to collaborative genius," notes Michael Schrage, author
of *Shared Minds: The New Technologies of Collaboration* (Random
House). Europeans and Americans alike attribute heroic characteristics to the rugged individualist, the loner. Yet as Don Oldenberg
points out in a *Washington Post* review of Schrage's book:

**"Most of the paradigm-shifting breakthroughs of our
times—from the birth of quantum physics to the discoveries of
molecular biology—arose from collaboration."**

Where would Gilbert be without Sullivan, Tracy without Hep-
burn, Orville without Wilbur? Would the Curies have been as successful working as individuals?

Yet, observes Schrage, "Collaboration is not a word that gets
people enthusiastic. . . . They're fonder of words like cooperation."
What many fail to realize, claims Schrage, is "being a collaborator
doesn't mean giving up who you are. **It means using someone else
to amplify yourself at the same time that the other person is using
you to amplify himself."**

It's the stuff that successful partnerships—and marriages—are
made of. Every successful marriage is a result of the collaborative
efforts of two individuals with unique interests, abilities and expectations who are able to craft common values and goals to form a more
"perfect union." Yet, until recently, couples who expanded their life
partnership into a business partnership were thought to be begging for
trouble. Some did in fact get trouble, but many more got what they
went looking for—a business partner who shared their interests and
their values and in whom they could place their trust.

"In business you have to find people you can trust," says Norman Campbell, who with his wife, Eva, owns Newcorp Insulation,
Inc., a $5.2 million thermal-insulation and asbestos-abatement firm in
Houston. "I need to know that I can leave the office and that somebody will still be there who has the same goals, aspirations and sense
of integrity that I have."

Some couples collaborate later in life, perhaps in creating a
second career. After being trained as a speech therapist, Michelle
Rosenfeld decided to give herself a year to try dealing in art. Now, 20
years later, she employs five people full time, with offices in New
Jersey and Manhattan. Her husband, a retired head of a large sport-
ing-goods company, went back to college to get a master's degree in
art history and then joined his wife in the business. They are in Europe

often, attending auctions, visiting artists and checking out the galleries. "We haven't had so much fun since we were first married," says Michelle.

If "collaborative couples" makes you think of the folksy "mom-and-pop" enterprises of the past, think again. Couples today *do* own restaurants and shops, bakeries and bookstores, but they are just as likely to be proprietors of multimillion-dollar construction, health-care or electronics firms. For many, the meteoric rise to the heights of business success was rooted in the desire to create a new lifestyle rather than a desire to make a great deal of money.

Collaborative couples are found across a broad spectrum of society. Today more than 10,000 women sit behind the wheels of the huge rigs that roll down U.S. highways; the vast majority are half of a husband-wife driving team. In 1980 the big household mover Mayflower had fewer than two dozen couples on the road. Today 170 of their fleet of 1,215 teams are owner/operator couples.

Collaborative couples want more control over their financial and personal destinies. They are looking for independence, the power of self-reliance and the opportunity to be totally committed and involved in a service or product over which they have absolute control. They seek the gratification and bonding that comes from working together. "I don't see how much more romantic you can get than spending 24 hours a day together with the person you've chosen to be with," says Tom Dose, a veterinarian who with his wife, Sharon, also a veterinarian, owns and operates Kings Row Pet Hospital in Reno, Nevada.

Four Collaborative Couples

One of the most successful collaborative couples in America is Louise Erdrich and Michael Dorris. This literary couple has written nine novels. They coauthored *The Crown of Columbus,* published in the spring of 1991, for which they received an advance of $1.5 million.

They write books under their own names or as coauthors, but everything is a collaboration. As Michael Dorris wrote in his much-praised 1989 book *The Broken Cord,* "By the time any submission left our house . . . we had achieved—after many a heated literary argument—consensus on every word. As a result, both of us felt responsible for and protective of whatever book, article, poem, review, or story was published, regardless of who got the cover byline. We knew every paragraph by heart, so frequently had it been rewritten and revised."

Louise, 39, and Michael, 48, are of mixed American Indian descent. Michael was a single parent of three adopted American Indian children when they married in 1981. Their collaboration began that same year.

They live on a hill in a town near Hanover, New Hampshire, in a house built in 1772. Louise starts writing in longhand each day beginning at 9:30 A.M. in a little place across the road from the house. Michael is up and writing on a word processor by 5:00 A.M. For *The Crown of Columbus,* they worked out the plot together and did research together. Then they divided up the scenes and each wrote the first drafts alone. The first drafts and revisions were passed back and forth many times, sometimes read aloud at the kitchen table.

After the book's first draft was laid out end to end, each part was revised 20 times. The book as a whole then went through nine complete revisions before it was sent to the publisher.

"In fiction we certainly argue all the time, and it isn't easy to be the one to say, 'This piece of writing doesn't work,' or to be the one to hear it," says Michael. "Past experience indicates to us that the process works. We look back on books and stories and are very glad the other person was critical—but ultimately, not necessarily at the moment."

They see art and marriage as complementary processes. Of them, Vince Passaro, writing in *The New York Times Magazine,* said, "They are attempting as artists to make themselves, by mutual consent, into one voice, one vision, one language. Theirs is an art, as well as a life, directed toward synthesis and unity."

All this while raising six children. They say they take turns attending to their children's needs. But Louise also says that "when we married, Michael did absolutely everything. He was a single parent. So I slowly tried to take on some things, but I think Michael does more."

Michele and Will Beemer run Heartwood Owner-Builder School in Washington, Massachusetts. They teach people the skills needed to build their own homes from scratch. It is a three-week course with classroom instruction and a lot of hands-on work.

So far, more than 2,000 women and men (about equally divided) have completed Michele and Will's how-to-build-your-own-house program. Students ranging from 13 to 72 pay $800 each, or $1,400 for a couple. One of them, Jennifer Lee, a single mother with no experience in the building trades, built a house with the help of only her children, who at the time were 5, 8 and 11.

It is a very cost-effective proposition. The Beemers estimate that people who build homes almost entirely by themselves pay only about 40 percent of the cost of a commercially built house. Saving that much money is great, but Will says, "It's the experience that people want more than anything."

Both of the Beemers are master carpenters. Michele says she has "been doing carpentry since I was a kid." She initially learned a lot from Will, but "now we learn from each other." In addition to teaching with Will at the core school, Michele teaches a course called "Carpentry for Women," where women learn the tools and language of carpentry from a woman carpenter.

Will, 44, and Michele, 42, have been running the Heartwood School since 1985. The school runs from April until October. In the off-season they hire themselves out as general carpenters.

As with most collaborative couples, the Beemers emphasize "complementary talents" in the managing of their enterprise. Michele tends to take the lead in teaching the *hands-on* carpentry. Will says that Michele "cuts things better than I do." Both occasionally wear T-shirts with the master carpenter's motto inscribed MEASURE TWICE, CUT ONCE. He does the design work and is good at math, and she teaches most of the classroom work. Their secret is teamwork and open communication. "You can't work together without keeping communication open," says Will.

Both say their married and work lives are "totally intertwined." Michele says, "If I cook, he cleans. If I clean, he cooks." They like being together all the time. "When you commit yourself to a relationship, it's nice to enjoy that relationship all the time," says Michele. She says that working together at home is less stressful. "You don't have to work at making quality time."

She likes to emphasize, "What we do together would be impossible for each of us to do singly."

The Beemers report that there are a lot more couples attending their school these days.

Roger and Nana Sullivan own a specialty boutique on the North Side of Chicago just off Lake Michigan called Toshiro. The name is borrowed from the famous Japanese movie actor Toshiro Mifune. It is like calling a shop Bogart and selling pinstripes, or Marilyn and selling décolletage dresses. Nana's degree from the University of Chicago was in Japanese history, and she had lived in Japan before she and Roger were married.

Nana imported hand-dyed, hand-stitched Japanese cotton peasant clothing. The distinctive blue-and-white pattern looks like petite tie-dye and is achieved through an elaborate ancient dye process known as *kasuri,* or, more commonly, as *ikat.* The material is then fashioned into pants, jackets and kimonos. While in Japan, Nana initially bought *ikat* pieces for herself. Her friends loved the garments, and she and Roger thought there was a market for them. Nana started to make buying trips to Japan, her Japanese language serving her well in the farming communities where she bought some of the clothing and textiles for pennies. Back in Chicago, she washed and ironed and sold them, initially at yard sales and fairs, for high profit margins. Later she began having shows in galleries. People said she just had to open a store. Roger quit his job as a language teacher and they both threw themselves into the new enterprise, which opened in 1985. A year or so later, yen prices doubled overnight, forcing the Sullivans to buy from other markets and begin to create a new Toshiro look.

Having initially focused on traditional Japanese rural textiles, which actor Toshiro Mifune wore in *The Seven Samurai,* the store has diversified and expanded beyond its original intentions.

The boutique's first floor is modeled after a traditional Japanese kimono shop, and today sells comfortable, earthy, moderately priced clothing. The second floor, built three years later, has a turn-of-the-century Chicago architectural style. It specializes in more conventional clothing for the "creative professional," with an emphasis on comfortable cuts and high-quality fabrics at affordable prices.

Toshiro has a strong following and is on *Elle* magazine's international list as one of its "favorite shopping spots."

This entrepreneurial couple says the reasons for their success are 1) complementary skills, 2) a shared vision of what they want the store to be and 3) the ability to recognize their own limitations. Nana, 36, is the store spokesperson. She is also the buyer and has the "eye" for the clothing and the interior look of the store. Roger, 45, handles the promotions. He is the "idea" person and maintains the high service standards customers have grown to expect (helpfully, he speaks several languages).

From the beginning, Roger and Nana were deeply aware of the skills they lacked, notably financial skills. So they took in a partner, Marvin Brusman, Nana's stepfather, to handle all the financial considerations, business planning and the bookkeeping. "We would have failed miserably if we had not," says Nana. "We had to turn all of it entirely over to someone we could trust."

The Sullivans think it is important that collaborative couples share a similar vision. It "colors everything from employee relations to crisis management."

They also put a "willingness to compromise" high on the list of what makes collaborative couples successful. If one of them feels very strongly about something (and the other is neutral), then the one with the strong feelings prevails. In the first year their shop was open, this principle was fundamentally engaged.

From the beginning in 1985, they wanted the customers' *experience* of the store to be as important as what they acquired while shopping there. About one fourth of the first floor of Toshiro was devoted to a 12-mat tatami raised platform, a typical feature in a traditional Kyoto shop. Customers, in the Japanese manner, are not permitted to walk on the straw platform in their shoes. The Sullivans and their employees had to ask customers to take their shoes off before walking on the tatami platform. It was awkward. Some customers felt embarrassed and didn't come back. It certainly reduced the sales-per-square-foot ratio. A typical department store would see this as an enormous dead area. The Sullivans recognized that it hindered sales, but that it was also an interesting cross-cultural experience.

But Nana was concerned that customers were inconvenienced and wanted to remove the delicate straw tatami mats and replace them with trompe-l'oeil wooden tatami mats. Roger was adamant that the genuine Japanese mats remain: they provided a tranquillity to the store and were a unique feature that would pay off in the long run. They compromised by reducing the size of the platform to six mats and laying wooden flooring on half the area, giving customers access to shelving while still in their shoes.

The Sullivans say a couple must have a harmonious relationship to begin with. Working together can put extra strain on a marriage, they say, because the stress of doing business creeps into the home. The Sullivans have three children, ages nine, six and three, plus Roger's college-age son and daughter. Roger says they are constantly working together to respond to their children's needs, household needs and store needs. "For that you really have to harmonize." They become, Nana says, "masters of delegating." When Nana goes on a buying trip to New York or Los Angeles, Roger takes off work to be with the children.

Though it is tough to constantly juggle children, home and business, there are many pluses. First and foremost, says Nana, "our schedules are our own; we have control over our lives. If Rory [their eldest son] has a school play in the middle of the day, we can go see it." They take vacations or long weekends whenever they like.

Roger and Nana created a new lifestyle for themselves, and a successful enterprise. Between 1989 and 1990 their sales more than doubled. Sales during 1991, a flat year for most retailers, were up 41 percent over 1990's. In 1992, sales were up 24 percent. "We created the world in which we live and work. It feels good and allows us freedom," says Nana. "Our next goal is to live and do that work in the most beautiful place we can find."

In that sea of disaster, the Savings and Loan crisis, is what many analysts consider the nation's best-managed S & L, Golden West Financial Corporation in Oakland, California.

Golden West is run by a collaborative couple, Herb and Marion Sandler, who each carry the title "co-chief executive officer." Both in their early 60's, they have spent almost three decades shaping Golden West, the nation's sixth-largest savings-and-loan and among the most profitable. "Golden West is one of the best financial firms in the country, period," according to Peter Treadway, an analyst at Smith Barney, Harris Upham & Company.

The Sandlers run an extremely conservative operation. The company lends its money almost exclusively to finance residential housing. No shopping centers or office buildings. "We were damned by Wall Street," says Marion Sandler, for not being aggressive enough, for being old-fashioned.

Their conservative approach has paid off. Golden West has almost no bad loans (bad loans in 1991, for example, were an almost unbelievably low half of one percent), and the company's shares are worth 10 times what they were a decade ago.

"Perhaps we can best characterize Golden West's attitude toward lending by simply saying that your management likes to sleep undisturbed by worries and nightmares," the Sandlers wrote in a letter to shareholders.

"Over 20 years, running the institution in our fashion, through all the turmoil that's taken place, our compound annual rate of growth and earnings is 20 percent," says Herb Sandler. "To my knowledge, no other bank or thrift has done that."

They are going to keep their conservative ways. "We have a jewel of a company," Marion says, "and we're not about to do anything to jeopardize it."

The company has 230 branches in California and five other states (to accept savings deposits) and 65 loan offices in 16 states. Earnings in 1992 grew 20 percent. Although it is clear to everyone that they run the company from their adjacent offices, they rely a great deal on the team they have built. "This isn't the Herb and Marion show," says Herb Sandler.

Herb and Marion were well equipped when they took over Golden West. Herb graduated from the City College of New York and Columbia University Law School and had represented a number of savings institutions. Marion graduated from Harvard and New York University's business school before becoming a securities analyst following stocks of savings-and-loan companies. Neither was very impressed with the quality of the management running most savings institutions. They knew they could do better.

Married in 1961, they moved to the West Coast to look for a small savings company. In 1963 they made a deal to acquire Golden West for $4.1 million. The company's assets at the time were $34 million. Today Golden West has in excess of $25 billion in assets.

"You know that old saying about it being lonely at the top?" says Herb. "Well, it's not here."

Choosing a Business Venture
(Sometimes the Business Chooses You)

For some couples going into business together was always part of the plan. For others the business partnership evolved with the marriage. In either case, choosing the right business—one that suits the interests and talents of both partners—is the essential starting point.

For Sam and Libby Edelman, the footwear business came naturally. When they met, Libby was footwear fashion editor for *Seventeen,* and Sam worked in his father's business, Lighthouse Footwear. Later the couple joined Esprit in San Francisco, he as president of Esprit's shoe division, she as merchandise manager for Esprit Kids Wear. At Esprit they built a $55 million shoe business in four short years while discovering the benefits of working as a team.

In December 1987 the Edelmans launched Sam & Libby, California, a footwear line featuring fresh, innovative design at affordable prices. Within a year, the start-up company was shipping inventory to every major city in the country. Three years later, their 1991 revenues were $85 million, up 66 percent from 1990. Sam says, "What I've learned from our enterprise about our relationship is as enriching and as important as any financial gains we might get from it."

Nicola Pelly and Harry Parnass, owners and designers of the Montreal-based Parachute line of clothing, each were unhappy designing for someone else before they became business partners. Says Nicola, "We found that when we put our heads together, great things happened." Today they set fashion trends in Canada, the United States and Europe as designers of an extensive ready-to-wear line and as owners of a cross-continent chain of clothing stores. "If we had been rich and smart, we wouldn't have taken the risks that we did— and we wouldn't have the success we have," says Harry.

Making mistakes, yet realizing phenomenal success anyway, is a curious theme among collaborative couples. Today Anita Roddick is the fabulously wealthy, socially conscious owner of Body Shop, a chain of stores selling all-natural cosmetics, many manufactured in Third World operations financed and managed by Roddick's firm. Sales exceeded $200 million in 1991. There are now more than 400 Body Shops in 38 countries. Two shops were recently opened in Tokyo, and Japan is targeted to have 200 by 2001. Roddick's husband, Gordon, manages the financial end of the business.

The first Body Shop, in Brighton on England's south coast, was sandwiched between two funeral parlors. Its original bare decor was inspired by lack of funds rather than minimalism. The Roddicks knew enough about the cosmetics industry to realize that perfume was an essential commodity—but they couldn't afford to stock it, so they bought oils and displayed them in the compartments of a typesetters' drawer and invited people to sample and mix them with other products. They had 20 products—not much to offer customers used to thousands of choices. To make it look like more, they packaged the oils in five different-size bottles. The cheapest bottles they could find were those used for urine samples. **They went into business with none of the expertise everyone insists you need for success.**

An important though unwritten tenet at the Body Shop holds, "Whatever the cosmetics industry is doing, do something else." There are no photographs of women in any of the stores, and the word "beauty" is not written anywhere. Minimal packaging is the standard, and every piece of paper is recycled because Anita and Gordon Roddick's other passion is giving back—to the environment, to the community and to society at large.

If Liz and Nick Thomas hadn't found themselves stone broke, they might not be running Chalif, Inc., a million-dollar condiment business based in Wyndmoor, Pennsylvania.

For most of their married life Liz and Nick were very much the traditional couple. He was a successful pension expert in the insurance industry, she was a self-described "milk and cookies" mom. Then he made an ill-fated job change—the company went under just after he joined it. They looked at a stack of bills and made the decision to spend their last $200 on glass jars and ingredients for the "Hot and Sweet" mustard recipe that had been in Liz's family since the turn of the century.

It was strictly a family affair. Liz's brother designed the label; her mother paid their mortgage during their cash-poor start-up phase; their children worked at home (for free) and at outside jobs after school (for pay). A venture capitalist friend bought 30 percent of the business "and all the mustard he could eat." In June 1982 the company moved into an 8,400-square-foot processing plant. Today's inventory includes new mustard flavors and new product lines. The company has six full-time employees and many part-timers. It is still, however, a family affair. All four children work for the company; Liz and Nick's daughter—with two children of her own—is the company's accountant.

Financing a Start-up—
Where Does the Money Come From?

Tom and Gun Denhart abandoned two high-salaried Manhattan careers and sold a big house in fashionable Greenwich, Connecticut, to move to Portland, Oregon, and start their own business. Getting it off the ground took every bit of the $250,000 profit from their house sale (and then some) and a lot of lifestyle changes. But today they own a $34 million-a-year children's clothing mail-order business based on the pure cotton clothes Gun wore as a child in Sweden. She named the company "Hanna Andersson," after her grandmother. Its sales have doubled every year in its history. The company has long since moved out of the Denharts' house and now operates out of a 100,000-square-foot headquarters building. Says Gun, "If we first had come to a banker and said, 'We're going to start a mail-order company and we want to borrow $250,000,' they wouldn't have dreamed of it."

Entrepreneurial start-up companies almost never get capital from a bank or venture capitalist. Most get their initial money from savings, from borrowing from relatives or friends, or taking out a second mortgage on a home, or from selling something, like the Denharts' house in Connecticut.

Whatever the inspiration, a good idea without the capital to finance it remains just that, a good idea. Sam and Libby Edelman will tell you to forget relying on venture capital. Venture capitalists are notoriously unsupportive of collaborative couples. By and large, they get involved in a business with the intent of ultimately owning the major share. Few are willing to compete with the loyalty and personal bonds inherent in a collaborative enterprise.

"The story was the same with each of them," Sam recalls. "Because we were a couple, we were not considered a good risk." The Edelmans launched their business on their own, and so far, are proving the venture capitalists wrong.

Karl Friberg and his wife, interior designer Lyn Peterson, used $9,000 in savings from Lyn's family to lease and stock a tiny wallpaper store. Today their company, Motif Designs, Inc., is a $10 million operation, designing and manufacturing upscale wallpaper and home fabrics in New Rochelle, New York. Friberg held on to his job in the international-banking division at Citibank until Motif Designs, Inc., could support the family.

Passing on a legacy to future generations was one reason the Webbs of Pomona, California, decided to go into business together. Reggie Webb was well paid for his corporate position with McDonald's, but it occurred to him that his children—he and his wife, Rene, have three—couldn't inherit a parent's job. So, Reggie left the corporate side of McDonald's, and he and Rene spent $1.9 million to buy two McDonald's franchises. The couple put up 25 percent of the purchase price. The rest was financed through Metropolitan Life Capital Corporation.

Sharing the Load? Who's in Charge Here Anyway?

Starting a collaborative business requires confidence in one's own and one's partner's abilities, as well as the money or the imagination to finance it. But if couples can't agree on what role each plays in running the business, it isn't likely to succeed.

For many collaborative couples, sorting out who does what is simply not an issue. Tom and Sharon Dose, proprietors of the Kings Row Pet Hospital, are both veterinarians. They do not divide patients into "his" and "hers," nor do they divide any other business-related tasks into his and hers.

But for most people it is an issue. The key is dividing tasks according to the unique talents and expertise each brings to the partnership. It is critical to divide tasks according to temperament, abilities and instinct.

With four children and a $10 million home-furnishings business to mind, Karl Friberg and Lyn Peterson would certainly agree that achieving harmony is a desirable goal. But the term that best describes this couple is "synergy." "I remember meeting them over lunch at a sales convention," recalls Jerry Rosen, the owner of Wall-Pride, Inc., a wallpaper distributor in Van Nuys, California. "Lyn was on fire with this incredibly infectious enthusiasm about her patterns and her artistic vision. And Karl, although he was quieter, conveyed that he was in control of the financial end, that this was a real business."

For Lyn and Karl, the division of labor was fairly easy in the formative years. Lyn ran the design studio, planned and supervised annual collections and managed a few interior-decorating jobs that increased Motif's visibility. Karl managed the business end—negotiating with subcontractors, budgeting, warehouse, customer-service issues, selling, and managing the staff.

As the business grew, however, serious and complicated problems developed. They began losing money, and there was even a chance the company would go under. Fortunately, both were smart enough to recognize their limits and seek help. After the company began expanding very rapidly, Lyn's father, a retired IBM executive, joined them: the price of sanity was a somewhat authoritarian management style. While the couple did not entirely embrace Lyn's father's big-business approach, they did follow many of his recommendations, and the faltering company was set to rights.

For the first five years of their enterprise, Chalif, Inc., Liz and Nick Thomas were all but interchangeable. However, as the company grew, the need to divide responsibilities became apparent. Liz was responsible for public relations, advertising and recipe development. Nick controlled the finances and orchestrated marketing presentations.

The Jeanlozes of The Renovator's Supply have clearly defined areas of responsibility. Donna is responsible for the retail stores and handles legal matters—copyright infringements, patents and trademarks. She is the publisher of *Victorian Homes.* Claude runs the manufacturing end and oversees asset management.

"It's very rare, I think, that a business of any size is actually run by a couple," says Claude. "If it's run successfully, usually the two individuals have very specific and distinct areas of expertise or responsibility. That's the only way it can really work. Otherwise, it can end up in a divorce, with one taking the business and the other going off to do something else, or the company just closes down."

"In the case of our magazine, I'm the publisher," says Donna. "He hasn't got the foggiest notion what's going on, because it's really not necessary for him to know. It's profitable and it's under control and he leaves well enough alone—which I think is a terrific way to operate.

"Claude's not the president of the company, but he runs the business. Every one of our employees knows that," Donna explains. "He's the top of the organizational umbrella. But there are instances when I am more powerful—personnel matters, for example. He'll express his opinion, but then say, 'You take care of it.' And I do what I think is right."

Massimo and Lella Vignelli of Vignelli Associates are famous for the purity of design in their furniture and graphics, from Knoll stacking chairs to Bloomingdale's shopping bags. They have worked together for 30 years, the last 20 in New York City as Vignelli Associates for an international clientele.

Massimo is the dreamer and Lella the pragmatist. "Lella has a tremendous sense of practicality which I don't have," says Massimo. "Things that are ethereal or idealistic have to have a basis in practicality. However, if she goes too far, then I will come back and say, 'Hey, wait a moment, you are killing the idea.' "

"There was a time, years ago, when we were more partisan to our positions," admits Lella. "But we have learned to work together and appreciate what the other can bring."

Because both want to be deeply involved in all design projects, they have limited their staff to 30 employees. Lella sees smaller design studios becoming the trend in the '90's so that "quality can be maintained more easily."

Before starting Hanna Andersson, Tom, now 53, and Gun Denhart, 48, were, respectively, an art director at an advertising agency and an accountant. Today, as a collaborative couple, they are a mutual admiration society. Gun says that it has been "unbelievably nice to do it with my husband. I really respect and admire what he is doing. Tom has the creative talent, and I have the organizational talent. If you don't know where your money goes, you're in trouble. But you don't have to be an MBA. . . . It's common sense."

Tom thinks Gun is a management genius. "That women of her caliber can be passed over and underutilized for years . . . as far as I'm concerned, she's better than anybody I ever worked for, and I've worked with some fabulous people. I'm very happy to be in her shadow."

Gun makes liberal use of consultants to help navigate Hanna Andersson through business challenges for which there is no in-house expertise. "The computers are completely [programmed by] outside consultants," she says. "No one here can make program changes. Consultants also laid out the new warehouse. . . . And for the first time we're using a catalog consultant. We're mailing three and a half million catalogs—a million more than we've ever done before—and I want to make sure we do it the best way." In 1992 they mailed nearly 10 million catalogs, and 12 million catalogs in 1993.

In 1990, when the company tripled its staff from 50 to 150, Gun hired a training consultant "to train all those people consistently." But, she adds, "first you have to train the trainers." By 1993, the staff had grown to 280 and all the computers were being programmed in-house.

In March 1992 Gun Denhart was named a winner of the Business Enterprise Awards for her "marketing program that gives customers credit on future purchases for returning used Hanna clothing and then donates these tens of thousands of garments to abused women and children."

Walking the Tightrope—
Which Comes First, the Marriage or the Business?

Few collaborative couples will deny that the stress of maintaining both business and marriage can test even the most devoted. So how do couples weather storms? When does the marriage take priority over the business and vice versa?

The answers are as diverse as the couples involved.

When should the marriage come first? The business? Norman Campbell, of Newcorp Insulation, says, "That's hard to say because so much of our lives are interwoven in the business. But when push comes to shove, we won't let the company do [our marriage] in."

Friberg and Peterson, the wallpaper whizzes, make every effort to keep business problems outside their home. "We have always said that the most important thing to us was our family and that we would never, ever let anything happen that would put that in jeopardy," Peterson says. "Even if we lost the business and the house, all that mattered to us was that the family survive. . . . We could always go out and get other jobs. . . . But we know we couldn't replace the family."

For Friberg and Peterson, running their own business was also a way to build work life around their family life, not the other way around. Between them they work no more than a 70-hour week, leaving their evenings and weekends free to spend time with their children.

Some collaborative couples formally institute what they call "work blackout," certain evenings a month during which all shop talk is forbidden.

Nicola Pelly and husband, Harry Parnass, keep their life unencumbered in every way possible. They have few outside hobbies and don't keep up much of a social life. "We really enjoy our business; it has become our life. Everything else is done to support it. I really think you have to live design," says Nicola.

Frank and Sharon Barnett say collaborative couples experience remarkably complete relationships, without the fragmentation many couples endure. "These individuals appear to be building new layers of friendship, understanding, trust, acceptance, and maturity."

When the Bloom Is off the Rose—What Happens When the Marriage, and the Partnership, Fail?

Lest we imply that going into business together is the answer to every couple's prayers, a word of caution is in order. Marriages do unravel, and when couples are also in business together, the result can be a complicated mess. Many a warring entrepreneurial couple have made the movie *The War of the Roses* look like a day at the beach.

The most publicized breakup (unless you counted Ivana and Donald Trump as a collaborative couple—which we didn't) was that of Doug and Susie Tompkins, the cofounders of Esprit de Corps. As the couple's marriage faltered, so did the company. One might assume that an $800 million company would be immune to problems resulting from its owners' squabbles. But that was not the case. Meetings turned into face-offs, staffers felt pressured to take sides, the company's clothing lines underwent several abrupt design changes as the couple fought publicly for control of the company they had built together.

In 1989 the Tompkinses filed for divorce, and in December of that year Esprit was put up for auction. The company's very survival was in question until Doug agreed to sell his half to Susie and a group of investors. Today Susie is creative director. Doug retains an interest in the company's operations in southern Europe.

Less public but no less devastating for the people involved was the breakup of Christel and Jon DeHaan, who together had built their Indianapolis company, Resort Condominiums International (RCI), into a $100 million-a-year time-share empire. She returned from a three-week business trip to discover that her husband had moved out of their home, wanted a divorce and, as president and majority stock-holder, was firing her.

Jon claimed he owned 80 percent of the then-16-year-old company. Christel maintained the 80–20 division was set up for tax purposes. She sued. A superior-court judge in 1989 ruled that Christel could buy out Jon's half for $67.5 million before taxes. Jon appealed the decision. On February 14, 1992, Jon's appeal was refused by the court, and Christel now owns and runs the company. RCI's sales in 1991 were $180 million, and it is now the world's largest vacation-exchange company.

Kenneth and Jennifer Estridge were another golden couple. Joy of Movement, their Boston-based dance and fitness chain, grew out of the radical '60's to become a multimillion-dollar mainstream business.

Together, they had the Midas touch. He planned strategy for the business, she motivated the people. He wrote the music for pop tunes, she wrote the lyrics. They drove expensive cars and took exotic vacations. They had it all—until it started to fall apart and the name-calling began.

Kenneth maintains that a weak economy, some poor business decisions and growing competition threatened the company's stability. Jennifer insists that's only half the story. She says her husband closed the studios to shield company assets from her. She claims that once out of the marriage, her husband intends to open a new business with help from his family, who never approved of her.

"What does a successful businessman do when he wants to dump his wife? He dumps the assets," says Jennifer. "My wife is lying to the press, trying to hurt me," responds Kenneth.

This sort of public humiliation is enough to make any couple think twice about going into business together. That's understandable. But the bad experience of a few should not obscure the great track record of most. If everyone shied away from partnerships for fear that divorce is the natural conclusion, the world might never have Gore-Tex fabric, Hanna Andersson's all-cotton clothing for children or Liz Claiborne's popular clothing line for women. Debbi Fields might still be baking cookies only for her family.

What it does suggest is that couples should consider carefully whether their temperaments and their talents are genuinely suited for entrepreneurship and collaboration.

Marta Vago, Ph.D., a Los Angeles business consultant, suggests couples systematically ask themselves a series of questions to determine whether they are likely to be compatible in business. "I ask couples how they plan things and handle disagreements," she says. "Do they blame each other? Does each insist on having his or her own way? **People are painfully consistent: if a couple is unable to agree on what kind of wallpaper to put in the bathroom, chances are they're not going to have an easy time making decisions about where to locate the business or how much to spend on advertising or whom to hire."**

Dr. Vago, quoted in the April 1991 issue of *Glamour* magazine, suggests couples ask themselves these critical questions before entering into (any) partnership:

- Is your potential partner someone you respect, admire and trust? You can't afford to go into business with anyone who is secretive or possibly untrustworthy (and you certainly wouldn't want to be married to such a person).

• Do you share professional goals and values? Are you equally passionate about the venture? During the first year or two, getting a start-up business off the ground typically requires twelve-to-fourteen-hour workdays.
• Do your skills complement one another?
• Are you aware of the financial advantages and disadvantages of business partnership? Get a lawyer or accountant to spell them out in detail.

But perhaps Dr. Vago's best advice is to prepare in advance for the nightmare everyone prays will not happen—a sort of prenuptial agreement for couples who are also married to their business.

"Draw up a written business plan. With the advice of your lawyer and accountant, work out what percentage of the company each partner will own (be sure to find out whether your state has community property laws); define your individual roles in the business; provide for the worst-case scenarios (divorce, disability, death, bankruptcy or the dissolution of the partnership). Finally, couples should agree on a formula for determining the value of the company so that their lawyers can draw up a buy-sell agreement if the marriage goes sour."

Harmonizing Marriage and Business

Ideally, collaboration enhances a couple's close personal relationship. It intensifies the sharing and strengthens bonds. Joint business activities unify what would otherwise be a separate, individual experience.

Being part of a collaborative couple allows each partner to see and experience what the other deals with all day. That is very different from getting a "report" from a spouse and trying to imagine what the other went through "at work." When one or both work late or on weekends, both understand why.

Collaboration can also be the gateway to greater freedom. Once the business is stable, the couple is free to create a more enriching lifestyle—vacations, long weekends, going off to an agreeable spot to prepare a business plan—and to incorporate family into business travel.

It is easier to combine parenthood and a great career when you are dealing with a spouse-partner, as the lifestyles of Roger and Nana

Sullivan, Lyn Peterson and Karl Friberg, and Michael Dorris and Louise Erdrich illustrate.

There are advantages for business, too. Couples already know each other very well. Trust is established. They can often make judgments and decisions faster than ordinary business partners.

As Bill Criswell, who, with his wife, Sheri, created a real estate development company, says, "We know that our financial and personal interests are entirely compatible, which would *not* be true of partners—no matter how close they were—if they weren't financially tied to each other through marriage."

When business partners are married there is a greater and earlier commitment to the business. The late Bill Gore, one half of the great collaborative team that created Gore-Tex, once said, "A husband and wife are in it together. They win or lose together. Both of them are trying to make the business a success and whatever it takes to make it successful, that's what they'll do."

The checks and balances created when two people collaborate in an enterprise often produce better results than a single entrepreneur alone. Each member of this book's writing team has, from time to time, come up with an idea that was off the deep end. It was always clearly recognized as such by the other, who gently (or not so gently) steered it back to reality.

Why Now?

Collaborative couples have been working to make their dreams come true for a long time, but in the 1990's we are witnessing an explosion of this phenomenon. The reasons why this is happening now are fairly straightforward:

1. The computer. The computer magnifies the strength of an individual or a couple to compete with larger companies, who for a period of time had computers when individuals didn't. Computers help us keep track of things—our business—that we used to have to hire additional people to do. As Gun Denhart (of the kids' wear mail-order company) says, "As smaller computers have grown more powerful, we've been able to do things that only big companies could do before." Today millions of computers are doing the work of what it would have taken trillions of people to do.

2. New attitudes. The raising of consciousness for equality of opportunity for women is all in the direction of perceiving couples as equals, not only doing family things together, but pursuing business and professional goals together as a couple. One measure of this is that people today like to see couples succeed in the commercial world. Following several decades of sorting out what sexual equality meant, we are now seeking a new balance in the relationships between men and women—lasting relationships that allow for individual fulfillment.

3. *The revolution in telecommunications.* People can work together anywhere they want. During the industrial era, people were aggregated in towns and cities so that they could all come to the factory or office at the same time. Now we can do our work as individuals or couples *where* we want and *when* we want. When most of us were farmers, men and women were partners in making the farm succeed. During the industrial era that changed. We went our separate ways, to work or to take care of the house. As the Barnetts put it: "We have all too easily come to accept the isolation that most of us experience daily—traveling to work alone, working independently of our colleagues, and returning home to a partner from whom we are separated for most of our waking lives." In the new information era we are returning to the earlier, more natural male and female partnerships.

The Last Word on Hillary and Bill: It's Not Easy

Ultimately, how will the White House influence the collaborative couple trend? What does their relationship say about other partnerships in business, politics and elsewhere? Will those who favor a more traditional arrangement ever learn to embrace the new collaborative paradigm?

Some conservatives seek to paint the First Lady as an ultraliberal, while others ask why the president's wife, who was not elected, should function as a cabinet officer or, some whisper, "co-president." But we should like to raise a question that addresses the larger context:

What is the relevance and future of the title of First Lady as we approach the 21st century?

That ceremonial office looks to us like a throwback to earlier times, when full-time homemakers were compelled to "volunteer" their services to a higher purpose—their husband's career:

The parson's wife
The corporate wife
The political wife

Now many who might have filled that traditional mold in the past have actually joined the collaborative couples trend, sharing duties and rewards equally. As women make the megashift from liberation to leadership, how will the First Lady's role fare?

Not well, we would predict.

Suppose the next president is male. (That leaves the door open for the first woman president by 2000 or 2004.) What career will his wife hold? Suppose she's a cancer researcher at NIH, a concert pianist or CEO and founder of a thriving $50 million-a-year software firm.

Let's say she is 52 years old, just entering her prime career years. Is she supposed to give it all up for four years or more to become an unpaid volunteer in a ceremonial post?

And what about the First Gentleman? Will he leave a lucrative job on Wall Street to become America's answer to Dennis Thatcher?

By early in the 21st century, the role of First Lady could fade once again into a part-time, social position. The presidential spouse will appear at state dinners and the like, to be sure, but, during regular business hours, he or she will probably be working at his or her "regular" job.

Unless . . . unless the Clinton's political collaboration is so wildly successful that it becomes an attractive model for other couples, especially those just starting out in politics today. That would set the stage for the collaborative couples megatrend, so well established in business, as this chapter documents, to catch fire in politics, too.

Meanwhile, Hillary Rodham Clinton is making the very most out of a difficult, transitional situation. Elected or not, mainstream or liberal, the United States is privileged to have her brain power, dedication and unbilled hours harnessed to the pressing domestic issues of the day.

7.
Fashion:
Top Down to Bottom Up

Financial planners say women spend too much money on clothing. But for those who really love clothes, fashion is more about creativity than logic. Fashion for some women is a leisure-time activity, somewhat like spectator sports are for men. Like sports, it gets extensive media coverage. While he pores over the sports page, she might thumb through *Vogue, Mirabella, Elle*. Many a woman considers looking at fashion the ideal way to spend a Saturday with her best friend.

Fashion is a woman's ready muse in the quest for self-expression. It is her wardrobe mistress in the drama of corporate success. But if fashion is to support a woman's success and satisfaction, it *must* come from the inside out. When a woman's clothing accurately reflects her taste and style and flatters her body type, something clicks psychologically. She feels empowered to take on the world.

Fashion trends are a barometer of social change. In 1851 Amelia Bloomer introduced loose-fitting harem pants, or bloomers, but they did not become popular until bicycles became the rage in the Gay Nineties. Coco Chanel introduced "yachting pants" in the 1920's, but, says *The Encyclopaedia of Fashion* (Abrams), "The real pants revolution came in the 1960's." Notice how the twenties are associated with women's suffrage and the sixties with the women's movement.

Much as women insist they love pants for comfort, "Numerous studies have shown that the surge in pantswear corresponded to the more or less conscious desire on the part of most women to affirm their equality with men by dressing like them"—so says *Twenty Thousand Years of Fashion: The History of Costume and Personal Adornment* (Abrams).

Today's fashion, and the retail industry that sells it, reflect the shift from an industrial to an information society—which brought millions of women into the workplace. That megashift revved up the retail industry: millions of women needed new work clothes and had the income to buy them.

The "Dress for Success" look, that pseudomale costume of a dark suit and tie, made sense when women first entered the work force twenty years ago. Now that women are a critical mass in business and the professions, a new cadre of female designers, led by Donna Karan, are devoted to dressing customers comfortably, elegantly—and like women. "As a woman, my understanding of fit is unique," says Karan. Male designers once ruled Seventh Avenue. No longer.

Liz Claiborne generates almost four times the women's clothing sales of the top three male designers combined.

Today almost 54 million women need something to wear to work. Though affluent, they are in no position to afford clothing with a couture price tag. Top designers are following the lead of Anne Klein II, the first house to successfully launch a major "secondary line" of well-designed, moderately priced collections that bear the designer's name.

At odds with the financial advisers, who say, "Put the money you spend on clothes into tax-free bonds," are career experts, who say dress for the job you want, not the one you have. It is an interesting conflict. Can one justify spending more money on clothes as a career investment?

The movement of women over 40 into positions of corporate and political leadership will revolutionize fashion and retailing. As presidents of their own firms and corporate vice presidents, fortysomething women will be the first generation to define and perfect the female executive image of elegance and authority. A Donna Karan ad running in spring 1992 portrayed a beautiful woman running for and being elected to the U.S. presidency. Karan knew just how to dress her. (But, Donna, next time how about a gorgeous 50-year-old instead of a 30-year-old?)

The aging of the baby boom and the widening of its collective waistline is compelling designers to offer more options for women size

16 and up. Retailers, who are losing sales to catalogs, TV shopping and outlet malls, must find new ways to sell to time-conscious and price-conscious working women.

The New Woman

The multibillion-dollar fashion and beauty industry—and the fashion media that covers it—has a new customer. Its success in a postfeminist, postmaterialist 1990's is dependent on the ability to recognize and fulfill her changing needs. For centuries fashion and beauty set the trends top down. A generation of now-mature male designers honed their skills dressing the ladies who lunch and attend society benefits. Wealthy matrons loyally followed their every fashion dictums.

Today's new female consumer will have none of that. She is educated, experienced, confident, affluent yet cost-conscious. **The most basic megatrend in the fashion arena is the shift from top down to bottom up.**

The days when women followed fashion **blindly** are over; even the industry recognizes that. The new question is: will women "follow" fashion **at all**? Our answer is a resounding **no**. Fashion will have to start following women.

For the Industry: Good News and Bad

The fashion industry is in a classic good news/bad news situation. The bad news is that the booming 1980's are over. During that decade the industry benefited from consumer affluence **and** the need for women to build whole work wardrobes.

But there is good news, too: women will continue to work, get promotions and become more affluent. Despite economic ups and downs, women will keep buying fashion and beauty necessities, as well as a few extravagances.

- In 1986 (the latest year available) the Internal Revenue Service counted more than 400,000 female millionaires in the United States, up from about 150,000 in 1982.
- In 1991 about 11 million women had incomes of $30,000 or more.
- That year 2.3 million women had incomes of $50,000 or more.

Unfortunately, 1992 numbers were not available as we went to press, but both categories represented a substantial increase over the previous year. Between 1990 and 1991, for example, about 240,000 new women graduated into the $50,000-plus category, despite a recession. In that year, nearly one million additional women earned $30,000 or more.

The negative retail news of 1990 and 1991 was blown way out of proportion. You would think sales had dropped at least 10 percent. In the second half of 1991, for example, retail sales clustered around $152 billion a month, *matching* the best months of 1990 and *far ahead of the very best month* of prerecessionary 1989, when monthly sales hit only $148 billion.

"Retailers, to their vast relief, had a bang-up Christmas in 1992," reported *Business Week*. "Many chains reported 9 percent gains," the magazine said.

Cost-Conscious

Nevertheless, there is some disconcerting news for the fashion industry.

Many working women now spend less on clothes than in the early 1980's, when they purchased the bulk of their business wardrobes, said one *Wall Street Journal* story. Women with children have new spending priorities. They now head for outlets, discount stores and the mark-down rack, the story says. Three quarters of women say they buy most of their clothes on sale.

"There's a rush [for manufacturers] to open lower-priced lines and outlet stores, because that's where the consumer is," says Alan Millstein, publisher of *Fashion Network Report,* a monthly newsletter for manufacturers and retailers.

Women in their 40's can better afford higher-priced labels and designer clothes. If any industry has a stake in women breaking through the "glass ceiling," it is fashion. Promotions create the need to project a strong executive image of success and generate the disposable income to purchase a new wardrobe.

Older and Educated

As baby boomers age, so does the work force. Between 1970 and 1990 the number of working women age 35 to 44 increased two and a half times, to 14.6 million. Educated women spend the most time shopping, says John P. Robinson of the University of Maryland.

Older, educated working women can still afford a substantial fashion budget. But their clothing needs are not those of 20-year-old rail-thin models, who by the time they hit 30 are forced out of the runway business. Nor are they the society bunch. Women want to see what clothes will look like on them, not on someone half their age—or twice it.

But change is coming: New York's Ford Model Agency says advertisers who rejected models over 25 just a few years ago now feature 40-year-old female models—in national advertisements that are *not* addressed to older people. Much of the credit for this must go to *Lear's* magazine, which from its inception featured older models.

Ready to Be Feminine

"Most women of the baby-boom generation went from blue jeans to blue suits," says Laura Sinderbrand, a historian formerly with New York's Fashion Institute of Technology. "One uniform to another. They've spent years competing in a man's world, and now they're rediscovering their femininity. This is their first brush with dressing up."

Designer Donna Karan says today's woman is different from the working woman of the 1970's. "Women were still at entry-level positions in the workplace and worried about competing with men," recalls Karan. "At that time . . . women were basically wearing a blazer, a silk blouse and a pair of trouser pants or skirt. And that was sort of their uniform."

Once women won good jobs and began to feel secure at work, designers like Karan had a new challenge. "They [women] were saying: 'Okay, I'm bored now, I've done the executive routine. . . . Now I want to feel like a woman,' " says Karan. The '90's woman is more self-confident. Says Karan, "She doesn't have to constantly prove herself. She can wear what she wants."

The Beauty Myth

The Beauty Myth: How Images of Beauty Are Used Against Women (Morrow) by Naomi Wolf is the new focus of a long-standing debate about the proper feminist attitude toward beauty. For millennia of male domination, a woman's value was judged by male definitions of beauty. Has the women's movement changed any of that? Have women created their own standards of beauty? Are they still adapting to male standards? Is it somewhere in between?

Wolf, a Rhodes Scholar and Yale graduate, believes women are exploited and victimized by the perfect, youthful and impossible-to-live-up-to images put forth by the fashion/beauty industry. Many women think female sexuality is exploited by *Playboy*. Wolf takes the argument further: women-edited, women-read fashion magazines like *Vogue* exploit women, too.

Women in the workplace—be they plain or attractive—are overly judged by their looks instead of their competence, she charges. Women now have to work "three shifts"—taking care of a home, working full time at jobs and, finally, living up to the dreamworld of beauty and youth put forth by women's magazines.

Are men and the media and the workplace out to keep women down? Is it up to women to evaluate this nonsense and reject it? What standards of beauty do *women* believe in? If a woman wants to be attractive to a man, will she willingly adopt male standards? What if they conflict with her own?

"American feminism has gotten itself in a corner, because it is unable to explain the attraction of women to beauty and pleasure and sexuality," says Camille Paglia, a professor of humanities at the University of the Arts in Philadelphia, a self-described feminist, ultraconservative and author of *Sexual Personae* (Vintage Books). "Women enjoy color and fabric and fashion, and we should not have to apologize for that."

True enough, but sometimes the fashion media take pleasure and sexuality a bit far (see following section). Though one might disagree in part with Wolf's approach, she is raising all the right questions: whose standards of beauty are these, anyhow? Being slim and good-looking are an inadequate definition of real beauty, no matter what the magazines say.

Grandmother was right: beauty *is* only skin deep. Witness the miserable women with eating disorders, whose self-esteem is so low they cannot see themselves as attractive, even though they are strikingly handsome. Real beauty comes only from self-esteem, good health, knowing what looks great on you and a personal sense of style.

Wolf is right to criticize the fashion media's unrealistic standards. She represents a new generation of women who are smart enough and self-confident enough to start asking questions. That is the same thing readers are doing and, to their credit, the fashion press is printing their letters.

The Marvelous Media: Signs of Self-criticism?

The fashion media and the industry it covers fit like a manicured hand in a soft leather glove. A piece of clothing or accessory featured in a fashion spread is a "guaranteed sellout in the stores," says Wendy Banks, senior vice president of marketing at Liz Claiborne, Inc.

But readers are aware of this almost incestuous relationship and are increasingly skeptical of the editorial slant the fashion magazines are dishing out. The June 1991 issue of *Vogue* contained letters from readers criticizing the magazine for sexism and absurd standards of beauty.

"I read *Vogue* to . . . be surrounded by lovely images," wrote Meryl Shader of Beverly Hills, who criticized a particularly insulting reference to women in a story by David Mamet. "I certainly don't need to read *Vogue* to get yet another dose of careless misogyny."

Dawn De Gere of Mill Valley, California, was annoyed at both the substance and the bouncy tone of a feature entitled "Legs!" which had said, "Cottage-cheese knees . . . For that there's liposuction."

"I should hope that in the future you refrain from instilling such procrustean views in your readers," wrote De Gere. "After all, while striving for beauty is one thing, striving for perfection is quite another."

A 1988 *Glamour* magazine poll found skeptical readers, too. What they want, say the readers, is "fashion information to help them make choices." Instead, readers said, "the fashion industry tries to dictate style, assuming women will buy whatever is decreed as 'in.' "

Then there is the issue of *price*.

Fashion media that limit offerings to expensive designer clothes and "the sky's the limit" couture risk alienating most of their readers—especially fashion-conscious younger women.

Some have started showing affordable clothing: the January 1991 issues of *Mademoiselle* and *Glamour* displayed a $144 blazer by Evan Picone, and clothes by J. Crew and JCPenney retailing around $50. The January 1992 *Glamour* featured a $240 Liz Claiborne suit. Another *Glamour* issue showed an Esprit suit for under $140 and an Evan Picone suit for around $300.

"We want to reassure people that you can look as in vogue for $100 as you can for $10,000," says *Vogue* editor in chief Anna Wintour, who created the features "Dress for Less" and "*Vogue*'s Great Buys."

The April 1993 issue of *Vogue* bore this cover line: "Special Issue, Fashion's New Deal, 500 choices from $5 to $500."

"It's true that we're now committed to using more medium-priced resources," says former *Mademoiselle* editor in chief Amy Levin Cooper. "Readers aren't looking for fantasy anymore. They want to see something they can buy."

The fashion magazine *Mirabella* debuted June 1989 featuring successful, beautiful women from real life, as well as lesser-known models with figures more like the average American's. *Mirabella,* winner of the 1992 National Magazine Award for General Excellence, now sells 600,000 copies per month, a more modest circulation than that of the other top fashion magazines. Its circulation grew 21 percent in 1991, a much better growth rate than that of *Vogue, Elle* or *Bazaar.*

The new magazine *Allure* says it will take a critical look at beauty. Editor Linda Wells calls herself a skeptical person and recruited her staff from the ranks of investigative reporters, not standard beauty types. She told *Advertising Age* that *Allure* "won't hesitate to criticize products"—including those advertised in *Allure*—but says it will be done fairly.

Sometimes the fashion media make a good start, only to revert back to the good, old-fashioned, unrealistic, even sexist, images in the next issue. The December 1991 cover of *Allure* featured a seemingly naked woman posed in such a sexy way that it could easily have been mistaken for *Playboy.*

Letters to the editor and polemics like *The Beauty Myth* put the fashion media on notice that it is time to get real and:

- Feature models and real women who are older and/or normal in size—say a 10 instead of a 2—and to feature Roseanne- and Oprah-size women, too.
- Limit the pages of $3,000 de la Renta suits and the $5,000 Valentino ball gowns and feature affordable clothes from the collections most women really buy.
- Write *practical* articles, like "How to Find a Good Dry Cleaner and Sue a Bad One."
- Be critical about the absurd claims of many cosmetics firms.

The fashion media has not yet come to grips with the fact that readers are not 20-year-old models or ladies who shop on a $200,000-a-year clothes budget. They are fortysomething managers or thirtyish environmentalists. Either way today's reader lives in the real world. The fashion media will get to know her or lose her to increasingly successful magazines like *Lear's* and *Working Woman,* which feature practical stories and handsome but down-to-earth fashion.

The New Women Designers

Coco Chanel, possibly the most elegant designer ever, rose to prominence in the Paris of the 1920's and 1930's, traveling in circles with Picasso, Stravinsky and Jean Cocteau. After decades of corsets* and frills, she dressed women in simple, elegant, tailored clothes. The little black dress, the twinset over a plain straight skirt and the sweater with pearls were some of the looks she created. She closed her salon in 1939 and reopened it in 1954 at the age of 71. "By the 1960's, [Chanel] had become a symbol of traditional elegance," says the *Encyclopaedia of Fashion.* Chanel today is a $1 billion-plus empire.

Chanel used to look at a dress and ask, "Would I wear that myself? If the answer is 'No, I wouldn't,' I don't do it."

Only a female designer can bring that perspective, and a new generation of women including Adrienne Vittadini, Nicole Miller and Andrea Jovine are bringing it back to the design world. Adrienne Vittadini chalks up $165 million in annual sales, Nicole Miller, with about $36 million in annual sales, has profit margins at twice the industry standard and Andrea Jovine was expected to sell $50 million worth of clothes in 1992. In addition, the May 1993 edition of *Working Woman* put Carole Little sales at $205 million and Jessica McClintock sales at $125 million. Much of Esprit, with estimated sales of $550 million, is owned by Susie Tompkins, who bought out her ex-husband. Tompkins's new line is aimed at original Esprit customers now in their 40's.

Would Coco wear today's Chanel? Probably not (why is it so easy to picture Chanel in Donna Karan or Armani?).

"I never show anything I wouldn't wear myself," says Donna Karan. "I experiment on me . . . I'm not a perfect body, I'm a size 12. A garment has to work on me, not just on a gorgeous model."

Karan is like Chanel, says Polly Allen Mellen, former *Vogue*

*Chanel's innovation did not come too soon. When U.S. women donated their corsets to the World War I effort, the resulting 28,000 tons of steel was enough to build two battleships, says Lynn Schnurnberger in *Let There Be Clothes* (Workman, p. 336).

fashion editor, now creative director at *Allure*. "She has the same feeling for women. She always begins with a question: Why is it so hard for me to shop? What do I need? She always designs for herself first."

"I look in my closet, and if I need it, I design it. If it works for me, it's going to work for the customer, too," says Karan.

Women designers who know women's bodies are taking over from the men who dominated the industry with no such advantage.

"I have a great respect for male designers," says French designer Sonia Rykiel diplomatically, "because they do not have an image of themselves in the clothes. . . . They can do embroideries without stopping. But because I know that I have to wear that dress . . . I must stop. I respect the shape."

Liz Claiborne

Elisabeth Claiborne Ortenberg opened shop in 1976 after 25 years in the business. She was the first to see the mass-market potential of selling reasonably priced career and casual clothes to new women in the work force. Claiborne wanted "to dress the women who didn't have to wear suits—the teachers, the doctors, the women working in Southern California or Florida, the women in the fashion industry itself."

That vision made Liz Claiborne, Inc., a financial giant: the third-largest clothing manufacturer in the United States, and by far the largest maker of women's apparel. The label is carried by 3,500 retailers. It dominates one third of the better women's sportswear market. Liz Claiborne is sold in 26 stores in the UK and in six stores in Spain.

Liz Claiborne has been a public company since 1981 (whereas most of the other designers in this chapter are privately held). For that reason, we are able to describe Claiborne in more financial detail—of potential interest to women investors who want to put their money into an area about which they have intrinsic knowledge and an intuitive sense. After all, that is what the investment experts advise.

Forbes, Fortune and *Business Week* definitely think Liz Claiborne is one hot stock.

• In 1986 Liz Claiborne became one of only two companies founded by a woman to reach the Fortune 500 list of the largest U.S. companies.

- On the 1992 Fortune 500, Liz Claiborne ranked 207, up from 237 the previous year. (In 1993, *Fortune* transfered the company to its Service 500 list.)
- In 1990 the company topped the *Forbes* list of the most profitable U.S firms; in 1991 the company was number 39—still an excellent showing.
- In 1991 Liz Claiborne ranked 172 in *Business Week*'s top 1,000 U.S. companies ranked by stock-market value.
- Furthermore, in 1992 Liz Claiborne was rated the fourth most admired company in America by a *Fortune* survey of more than 8,000 businesspeople. Climbing up from number 10 a year earlier, it is now a leader within an elite including Merck, Johnson & Johnson and 3M.

For the five years ending in 1991 Claiborne's profits averaged 27.7 percent growth a year. Prudential Securities analyst Deborah Bronston thinks profits will grow 17 percent a year on average for the next five years. "Claiborne is the only company we follow where we haven't had to lower our earnings forecasts," says Bronston, who thinks 1992 return on shareholders' equity will exceed 27 percent.

While everyone else was bemoaning the weak retail sector, Claiborne was booming. Liz Claiborne, Inc., became a $2 billion company in 1991. Profits increased 12 percent in 1991, somewhat less than the 25 percent increase in 1990.

Claiborne and her husband-partner retired from active management in 1989. "I get much more of a kick out of seeing women on the street wearing my clothes . . . than on the cover of a fashion magazine," says Claiborne. Given her firm's success, it is an experience she must have almost daily.

Donna Karan

Alan Millstein, publisher of the *Fashion Network Report,* calls her "the only female world-class designer in the U.S." Karan fans would surely drop the "female."

"I guess I hit a nerve," says Donna Karan, designer and CEO, Donna Karan New York. "This isn't about fashion. It's just about being a woman and needing clothes."

Karan started out as an assistant to Anne Klein. When Klein died suddenly in 1974, Karan, age 26 and the mother of a newborn, became chief designer. She recruited her friend and former schoolmate

Louis Dell'Olio as her new partner. During her 10 years with Anne Klein annual sales increased from $10 million to more than $75 million.

In 1984 Tomio Taki, the Japanese owner of Anne Klein, backed Donna Karan in her own venture. Her first collection in 1985 was hailed as "a major breakthrough" in clothes for the executive woman. Karan's collections aim to dress women quickly and simply. Says Karan, "Women have much more to do in the morning than just get dressed. . . . You don't want to waste time worrying about what to wear."

Later, says Karan, "You can slip off your trousers after work, throw a sequin skirt over your body[suit], add gold accessories and a pair of high heels and you are ready to go again!"

"Donna's image is that of a healthy, aggressive, hardworking mother. Women identify with her," says Marjorie S. Deane, publisher of the *Tobe Report,* a leading industry newsletter.

Sales in 1991 were $215 million, up from $163 million in 1990. That is pretty heady growth, and it is not expected to slow down: annual sales were reported at $250 million in May 1992, by *Forbes* magazine. In 1993 *Working Woman* put estimated sales at $275 million. *Business Week* projects $400 million in sales by 1994; sales could reach $500 million by 1995, reports *Time.*

Her success is illustrated by this simple statistic: customers buy 70 percent of Donna Karan clothes at full price, says *Forbes,* compared to an industry average of 46 percent. When a Karan customer sees an item that fits and is the right color, there is no way she will wait to see if it is marked down. She scoops it up and heads for the cash register. Retailers, of course, love it: they make more money per square foot.

Joan Burstein of Browns in London was the first European retailer to buy Donna Karan. "She understands that women need to simplify their daily lives," she says. "The fabrics she uses are wonderful for women who travel, as they pack so well."

Karan plans to expand her fashion empire into Europe. European sales make up 15 percent of her turnover. Karan is planning to open an office in Milan by 1994.

Linda Allard

"Even though my name's on the label, too, a lot of people think there really is an Ellen Tracy designing all these clothes," says designer Linda Allard, who became executive designer at Ellen Tracy at age 24. "Ellen Tracy" was made up by the company's owner and chairman. (Anne Klein II, Adrienne Vittadini, Perry Ellis Portfolio and Tahari are among companies that compete with Ellen Tracy.) Linda Allard "is the Ellen Tracy customer," says Michael Scandiffio, former vice president at Esprit, now president of the Susie Tompkins Division. "She's a devoted, hardworking woman and really lives the life of the customer she is designing for."

Ellen Tracy sales reached $200 million in 1992, estimated *Forbes* magazine.

Sonia Rykiel

"I understand women. I am one of them," says French designer Sonia Rykiel. "I follow them in the world in a political way, in a social way, in an intellectual way. Then everything I do—in color, in shape, in costume—reflects the idea of a woman of today."

She started designing clothing for herself during her second pregnancy as an alternative to the restrictive clothing of the day. Her line is sold in 200 retail outlets. Thirty-five percent of sales are in the French market; 65 percent in exports. The U.S. market represents 20 percent of all sales.

Rei Kawakubo

Comme des Garcons designer Rei Kawakubo was the first Japanese recipient of France's Verve Cliquot 1991 award as business woman of the year. Unlike most in the fashion business, Kawakubo both designs and manages a $100 million global fashion empire. She has been called "the most revolutionary talent since Coco Chanel."

Margaretha Ley

The late Margaretha Ley's Escada label sells in 27 countries. In 1991, there were more than 100 Escada boutiques worldwide. Ley and her husband, Wolfgang (she designed, he oversees future growth), started the Munich-based firm in 1975. *Escada* is Spanish for "stairway," and sales continue to climb: they reached $900 million in 1992. During the first six months of 1991, sales increased 22 percent. But in 1992 Escada registered its first loss—$62 million. It closed unprofitable stores and, in general, is retrenching after losses on the personal and financial sides.

Paloma Picasso

Jewelry and accessories designer Paloma Picasso was born in Paris in 1949, the daughter of Pablo Picasso and Françoise Gilot. She studied jewelry design and worked for several companies before launching her signature collection for Tiffany & Co. in 1980.

The female influence is also strong in Italy's fabulous fashion families: Missioni, a collaborative couple, and the Fendi and Ferragamo families.

The Growth of Secondary Lines

Haute couture is for inspiration and promotion, rather than profit. Designers get great publicity lending creations to movie stars and first ladies. Wealthy "ladies who lunch" pictured at the big society balls may be able to pay $10,000 or more for a couture outfit or gown. Who else can imagine it?

"There is a change of mentality," says Pierre Bergé, president of Yves Saint Laurent. Orders for custom-made couture have dropped 50 percent. "Women no longer feel like flying to Paris for fittings and waiting three months for a dress."

Indeed.

Ready-to-wear from top designers is not for the faint of pocketbook, either. Donna Karan and Giorgio Armani jackets have crashed the $1,000 not-so-glass ceiling. Add a skirt, blouse and taxes, and your bill is over $2,000.

"In the late 1980's women were into designer labels. That's not where it's at now, and we may never get back there," says Frank Mori, president of Takiyho, which owns Anne Klein and 50 percent of Donna Karan. "Everyone is thinking about less expensive clothes," says Calvin Klein.

"Secondary," or "bridge," lines, which carry the designer name but also a smaller price tag, are the perfect solution. They are aimed at affluent career women who appreciate designer quality but want to put together an outfit for under $600—well under, if possible.

A *Working Woman* survey found most professional women, 62 percent, spend between $100 and $300 for a work outfit. Eleven percent spend between $300 and $500, and only four percent spend more than $500.

In 1983 Karan and Dell'Olio launched the enormously successful Anne Klein II, the first major designer secondary line. By 1989 Anne Klein II's annual sales hit $130 million. In 1991, though, they slipped to about $110 million. Ironically, DKNY, Karan's own secondary line, is blamed for cutting into Anne Klein II's market share.

Secondary lines have become a $1 billion market, doubling in dollar volume in just three years. Anne Klein II and DKNY are the industry giants. But other designers have followed their lead: Giorgio Armani, Michael Kors, Perry Ellis, as well as Ungaro, Givenchy and Saint Laurent have secondary lines. Calvin Klein and Ralph Lauren have already featured casual pieces under $100. Escada's Laurel and Crisca secondary lines—still pricey by most standards—are joined by the less expensive, sportier Apriori collection.

"Secondary lines are the only way to continue," says Aldo Pinto, chairman of the Italian house Krizia, which plans a secondary line.

For retailers and designers alike, secondary lines mean big bucks:

- Kal Ruttenstein, senior vice president of Bloomingdale's, says 1991 sales of secondary bridge lines were 28 percent ahead of 1990.
- Michael Kors's secondary line already makes more money than his expensive collection. "Just because a woman doesn't have a high income doesn't mean she doesn't have a great fashion sense," says Kors.
- DKNY sales, $100 million in 1990, reached $140 million in 1991. Who else recorded a 40 percent growth rate in a recession year? Sales hit $185 million in 1992.

Not surprisingly, Donna Karan's DKNY line emerged from personal experience. When her daughter started borrowing Mom's $900 jackets, Karan thought, What's wrong with this picture? Karan needed less expensive clothes, too. Finally, when Karan "could not find a pair of jeans made for a woman's body," she knew there was a niche for a new designer line for young women—and their mothers, too.

Fashion and Personal Finance

Emily Card, Ph.D., author of *The Ms. Money Book* (E. P. Dutton), writes, "Women annually spend five times as much on clothing as men. If your clothing expenses exceed 5 percent of your income, shift the remainder to savings." If you make $30,000 a year, that's $1,500 of pretax income—one spring and two fall outfits from a good secondary line at $300 each, a couple of pairs of shoes at around $75 and one good handbag at around $100. The remaining $350 has to cover hosiery, underwear, leisure wear, jewelry, belts and sales tax. Hopefully, you already have a coat.

Card is tough—even the U.S. Department of Commerce breakdown for U.S. Personal Consumption Expenditure budget allots a more generous 6 percent of income for clothing.

"Resist fashion pressure; shop discount stores and sales; pay cash," says Card. "Buy basics, borrow frills." It is sound financial advice. But if you love clothes, it is hard to follow. It gets easier as your career and income grow. The $100,000-a-year executive who presumably has already built a good wardrobe gets to shell out $5,000 a year to, as they say in the industry, "fill in." But women under 30, who need new work clothes most, have the least to spend.

For Emily Card the notion that fashion is a career "investment" does not hold water. Expensive clothing and accessories should be considered "a luxury indulgence." One can only imagine Emily Card's popularity within the fashion industry, whose financial advice is best expressed by Amanda Verdan, director of fashion buying for Harvey Nichols in London: "If a customer is emotionally drawn to a product and it enhances her lifestyle, then, yes, it represents good value for money."

The Image Makers

Even financial experts must concede that a person's looks play an important role in her or his professional life.

New York's Emily Cho of New Images/Emily Cho advises clients how to put forth a professional image. She believes 10 percent of salary is a reasonable amount to spend on one's clothing and image. "Whether you are vying for a promotion, competing for a new account or moving from a corporate job into a business of your own, how effectively you attain your goals can depend quite significantly on how well your image is projected," she says. In that case, she adds, it makes sense to splurge on a special outfit.

- Image Industry Council International counts 100 fashion consultants, designers and etiquette instructors worldwide, up from 37 in 1978.
- The 1991 *Directory of Personal Image Consultants* lists 364 image consultants, compared with 36 in 1978.
- 110 image consultants in the *Directory* sell voice and grooming lessons, and 161 firms offer color and wardrobe analysis.
- A national survey of 8,000 female executives found 17 percent had enlisted a wardrobe consultant.

Some management consultants and executive recruiters side with the image makers rather than the financial experts.

"There is much more competition out there now. Companies want a lot of reasons to hire you—and keep you—and how you look is one of them," says Susan Holland, president of Holland Rusk and Associates, a Chicago executive recruiting firm.

"We all get comfortable with a certain look," says Michael J. Pertschuk, M.D., a University of Pennsylvania psychiatry professor and director of the Image Section at the Center for Human Appearance. "We may subconsciously carry around a postdated image of ourselves."

It stands to reason that, after a promotion, the right executive look will boost a woman's morale and project a self-confident image. It's an externalization of the new role.

Many designers say their clothes are investments to be built on year after year. "The strength of a designer is continuity," says Donna Karan. "I don't think women want to change that much from season to season. Once they have a look they like, they keep with it."

The days when women were slaves to fashion are, thankfully, over. But some years, 5 percent of one's income is not enough to put together a wardrobe of sharp, well-tailored clothes that project the image that will get you hired or help you to look authoritative and professional after a promotion. According to a 1991 *Glamour* survey, most women spent less than 7 percent of their gross income on clothing—unless they earned $25,000 or less and were building wardrobes.

If adding a couple of new outfits makes you look as if you belong in the boardroom, it is probably worth it in the long run. Some years it makes sense to stretch your clothes budget to 7 or 8 percent, or even more. But when it exceeds 10 percent, watch out. Emily Card and other sensible people are watching.

The Next Generation

Women will continue to shape the industry. Consider the many young female designers in their 30's.

Sybilla Sorondo Myelzwinski is often hailed as Spain's most creative young designer. Born in the United States, she served an apprenticeship with Yves Saint Laurent in Paris, went into business for herself at age 20 and now resides in Spain.

Celia Tejada is founder and top designer of San Francisco's Celia Tejada, Inc. Her line, sold in more than 300 specialty stores, re-creates the distinctive look and feel of her native Spain. "In any field you're going to have challenges, but when you find something you love, you can rise above any mountain," she says. "Some days I work 15 hours and I'm dead, but then I go home and I smile."

Laura Marolakos who got her start designing Federal Express uniforms, has been called the female Geoffrey Beene because of her use of extravagant fabric mixes. She designs suits that evoke the '30's and '50's.

Pamela Dennis can't sew, doesn't sketch very well and has had no formal fashion training, yet *Vogue* called her "a master of the form: clean, crisp, sophisticated shapes." Her trademark is her special feel for fabrics.

"Women want sexy, feminine clothes that are still serious enough to function well in a work environment," says **Jennifer George,** who has had her own label since 1986. She aims to design "clothes that aren't fussy."

In 1988 **Emily Cinader Woods** was elected president of J. Crew, the company her father started in 1983. She oversees every aspect of the business—"every color, every fabric, every button," she says. Today it is a $300 million business with nine retail outlets. The company plans to expand to 23 stores by late 1993. In 1990 J. Crew mailed 50 million catalogs, up from 7 million in 1984.

The Widening of the Baby Boom

In the high-fashion world, life stops at size 12, or maybe 14. Size 16 certainly does not exist. Even Donna Karan, known for respecting the fuller figure, follows this unspoken fashion dictum. Most designers accept and promote the deeply held belief within the world of beauty and fashion—and in society in general—that weight is a terrible, terrible thing.

"They were always trying to give us these badly tailored clothes in black," says Kit Powell of northern Virginia, an account executive for United Airlines and a size 16. "I wanted vibrant colors, great fashion."

"Most clothing designers don't like fat women. . . . They just don't think large women fit the image they're trying to convey," says Nancye Radmin, a self-described connoisseur of couture, who grew from a size 4 to a size 16 during her second pregnancy.

Content with sales in the booming 1980's, designers were free to indulge in antifat prejudice at relatively little cost. But the frugal climate of the '90's has everyone looking for new ways to increase business.

It is an example of the dynamic confluence between changing values and economic necessity—the chief catalyst for social change. The new values are the growing recognition that society overvalues thinness, so much so—as the diseases of anorexia and bulimia demonstrate—that it is downright unhealthy. Economic necessity came with the retail doldrums of the early '90's.

It is also, of course, a matter of demographics. As baby boomers move into their 40's, many find their weight creeping up, despite exercise and good nutrition. Forty percent of women over age 40 wear a large size, usually 14, 16 or 18. Those who postponed pregnancies until over 35 must fight pounds from both age and postpregnancy.

The stage was set for the right entrepreneur to come along, and Nancye Radmin, the size-16 clothes lover quoted above, was it.

In 1978 Radmin started the Forgotten Woman, a boutique featuring clothes for large chic women. Customers came, all right. Today Forgotten Woman, with 19 stores, is a $30 million-a-year business. Radmin converted sizes 14 through 24 into sizes 1 through 6. "My customers love to come in and say they're a size 3," she says. "I also serve complimentary champagne and chocolates."

But at first Radmin could not get top designers to make the clothes she knew would sell. Radmin's eventual success sparked a fashion revolution that will be her greatest claim to fame. Forgotten Woman now carries Givenchy, Laura Biagiotti and Bob Mackie.

"As baby boomers get older, they're going to get heavier," she adds, "and many of them will want to continue wearing Bill Blass and Donna Karan designs." Radmin says, "It's just a matter of time," before she signs up those designers.

The average U.S. woman, says Radmin, is just under five feet four inches tall, weighs 146 pounds and wears a size 12 or 14. "There are as many women who wear size 18 as there are who wear size 8."

That is a lucrative market that other designers are finally beginning to acknowledge, too. Liz Claiborne started a plus-size Elisabeth line. Sales reached $100 million after just two years. There is Jones II by Jones New York and Adrienne Vittadini Woman. Victor Costa and Albert Nippon offer clothing in bigger sizes. Even designer Gianni Versace has come out with a large-sized line.

Saks Fifth Avenue's Salon Z stocks designer plus-size lines. About half of Nordstrom's 67 stores have Encore Shops stocking, among others, the Elisabeth line. Large-size retailers include Lane Bryant, with 800 stores nationwide, and August Max. Nationwide, 455 of T.J. Maxx's 470 stores feature plus-size departments. Spiegel, Inc., of catalog fame, owns the large-size chain For You, which had seven stores in 1991 and bullishly expanded to 10 by 1993.

"They are all realizing we are an ignored niche," says Debby Eden, corporate advertising director of *Big Beautiful Woman* (described below). "When this retail recession started, I think, everyone opened their eyes a little wider."

Plus-size women's apparel is a $10 billion business, up from under $6 billion in 1982, reports *Forbes*, which puts the designer segment alone at about $2 billion a year—and growing.

"These customers have had empty closets for a long time," says Bruce Nelson, manager of special sizes at Dayton Hudson. "Now they're making large multiple purchases while the rest of the world just needs to update their wardrobe."

Big Beautiful Woman—BBW

Big Beautiful Woman, with 200,000 subscribers nationwide, calls itself "a total concept magazine for large-size women." A recent issue of *BBW* showed clothes from JCPenney, Spiegel, Jessica McClintock, Creative Creations, Cristina Maxx, Harvé Bernard. *BBW*'s shopping directory tells customers where to find the fashions.

"We will deal in each issue with the latest and truly flattering fashions for our fully dimensional woman," writes Carole Shaw, editor in chief. "We are 30 percent of the population. . . . It's time we start respecting ourselves and demand respect from the smaller world around us."

Magazines like *BBW* have created a demand for models who eat more than celery and do not work out three hours a day. New York's Ford Model Agency says it handles 75 to 80 percent of the world's business on plus-size models. Ford believes it is one of five U.S. agencies that handle plus-size models.

"The '80's are over, and people are sick of trying to be thin and perfect," says Karen Fullem, general manager of the For You division. "The large-size customer is much happier and more confident and is demanding a great place to shop."

"They should all get on the bandwagon," says Phyllis Baylin, a shopper who traveled from Maryland to Virginia for the opening of a For You store, "because there's a fortune out there waiting to be spent."

New Directions in Fashion Marketing

Time was, a lady was delivered to the door of a big department store in Philadelphia or San Francisco or Detroit and, children cared for by servants, she would disembark to do her shopping: the "carriage trade."

Women in their 40's and 50's today remember taking the bus or taxi "downtown" with their mothers in the postwar 1950's and shopping in some of those same beautiful department stores.

But by the late 1960's, the direction had already shifted. Shopping meant a trip in the family car to a branch store in the suburbs or a residential part of town. With the arrival of shopping centers and strip malls in the 1970's, the decentralization of America—and fashion marketing—was well under way. Many of those old department stores, B. Altman, Bonwit Teller and Garfinckel's, closed their doors.

It may be sad, but it is not surprising. Times change, and it is up to retailers, like everyone else, to keep pace. Some stores survived by imitating the Bloomingdale's innovation of reinventing the department store into a kingdom of small boutiques.

But overall, the giant megamalls of the 1980's attract all the attention. They are state-of-the-art shopping. Or are they?

America's Megamalls

Walk through one at 11:00 A.M. or 3:00 P.M. on any weekday. Crowded they will not be. "Empty" is a better adjective. It is not just a fluke. A wealth of studies back that impression:

- The number of adults who *frequently* shop at malls dropped from 42 percent in 1987 to 36 percent in 1991.
- During that time, the percentage who *never* shop at malls rose from 12 to 18 percent.
- Between 1982 and 1990 the number of stores visited by the average mall shopper declined from 3.6 to 2.6.
- Over that time frame, the average time spent mall shopping dropped from 90 to 69 minutes.
- Monthly mall trips dropped from 3.1 in 1980 to 2 in 1990.

"Shopping at the Galleria used to be fun," says a White Plains, New York, woman. "I went there all the time just to wander around." Now with three children, however, she shops for "something specific." She is not the only one; the percentage of shoppers seeking a specific purchase rose from 20 in 1982 to 33 percent in 1990.

Other trends conspire against the mall business.

Mall attendance declines with age, and America is not getting any younger. Young adults (18–29) are the best mall customers: 43 percent visit malls "very often" or "fairly often." But, says the Census Bureau, Americans under age 30 will drop 10 percent in the 1990's. Only 27 percent of people 60 and older visit malls "very" or "fairly" often—but that group will grow 8 percent this decade.

The Mall: What Went Wrong?

The number of shopping centers and malls grew from 3,680 in 1960 to 36,650 in 1990. But by 2000, some 20 percent of regional centers will close, predicts an *American Demographics* story, and declines will continue into the 21st century.

In late 1992 the *Wall Street Journal* described the failure of "downtown shopping centers in Minneapolis, Atlanta and San Jose." The United States is "overstored and overmalled," concludes *The Future of Retailing: An Agenda for the 21st Century* (Quorum Books), edited by University of Texas professor Robert A. Petersen. Developers are finally "getting it." The numbers of centers under construction nationwide declined to 552 in 1991, down from about 1,000 in 1990 and 1,642 in 1988, according to the New York–based International Council of Shopping Centers.

In 1992 retail analyst Steven C. Clayton, president of Chicago-based MAS Marketing and author of *Demographic Trends Shaping Retail and Allied Industries for 1992*, told the *Rocky Mountain News* that 42 percent of Denver area malls would likely fail.

"The industry is run by older, chauvinistic retailers who haven't come to grips with the changing demographic population," says Clayton. "For example, women and minorities are the fastest-growing and largest segment of the retail business, yet only a small percentage of companies research the buying trends and habits of those populations."

(Mr. Clayton wins the 1993 *Megatrends for Women* "Men we love to quote award" hands down.)

Retailers hire all sorts of analysts to figure out where they went wrong. Theodore Levitt, in a *Harvard Business Review* article that has since become a classic, blamed problems like the retailers have today on "marketing myopia"—executives who focus too narrowly on the financial side: rates of return, operating efficiencies and profit margins.

Levitt's analysis makes many good points but omits one the author could not have possibly anticipated in 1960, when the article first appeared—women. How could malls *not* be empty in 1992? Virtually all their potential customers—women age 25 to 50—are at work. The argument could be made that malls should be open from 4:00 P.M. to midnight and stay open Friday night straight through until Monday, as so many grocery stores are.

Either change is accelerating even faster than any of us imagined, or megamall developers never heard of working women. Probably the latter.

Retailers failed to study them, cater to them, anticipate their changing needs. Had they done so, all the financial expertise Levitt describes would be working in the retailers' favor, not against it. Just ask the finance whizzes minutely calculating rates of return and profit margins for the catalog business.

Retailers also missed the boat on basic demographics. People age 50 and older possess at least half of the United States' discretionary income.

"Mall owners today haven't caught on to changes in demographics and psychographics," says Harris Gordon, a partner in Deloitte & Touche's TRADE Retail & Distribution Group. "Stores are being created as if the entire population is between 14 and 35 years old."

Older shoppers want security, quality, comfort and convenience, socialization, and recognition, says Donnelley Marketing's 1989 study of the mature shopping market. Guess what most malls lack? You can't find the rest rooms, can't read the tiny print in the directories and cannot sit down anywhere.

Retailers—who invested billions in flashy malls that are now empty, except for teenagers and mall walkers (more about them later), who ignored women and seniors—now whine about weak sales.

Meanwhile someone else is cashing in big: the people who figured out how to save working women **time** and sell to seniors in the **comfort** of their own homes and appeal to everyone's instinct to **save** a buck. Those are the people running the outlet malls, the TV shopping channels and the shop-by-mail (or, better yet, fax and Federal Express) catalogs.

Factory Outlets

Factory outlet malls are the fastest-growing segment in retail. There are about 330 malls, up from 32 in 1982, and they house more than 9,000 stores. In 1990 and 1991, more than 100 opened or were near completion. Thirty outlet malls opened in 1992 alone.

There will probably be another 100 by 1996, for a projected total of 450 outlet malls, says Dawn Frankfort of *Value Retail News* and the author of *The Joy of Outlet Shopping*, which alerts customers to the best malls and has sold 75,000 copies.

Outlet sales in 1991 reached $9 billion, just a fraction of retail sales, but outlet revenues enjoy double-digit growth; not many retailers are talking double-digit.

Who is the outlet customer?

- The factory outlet customer is a person "enamored with brands and saving money," says John Morton of Total Research Corporation, a Princeton market-research firm. That describes a lot of people.
- The trade journal *Value Retail News* reports nearly 40 percent of U.S. outlet shoppers earn at least $50,000 a year.
- A nationwide survey of 2,100 people in 13 outlet malls found shoppers averaged five outlet visits in the past six months and *planned at least that many in the next six months.*

"Outlet stores save consumers about $4 billion a year," says *Value Retail News* publisher Terry Dunham. Another reason for the attraction: outlets just get better. Some get merchandise soon after it hits top retailers; more outlets now permit exchanges. Nordstrom, Woodward & Lothrop and Bloomingdale's are opening their own outlets. So are manufacturers. Since 1987, Harvé Bernard has 70 outlet stores, Gitano around 100 and Van Heusen 200.

Says Terry Dunham, "The factory outlet malls have learned to prosper in all kinds of climates, but . . . the recession has helped them win over people from higher-priced department stores."

Reading, Pennsylvania, the birthplace of outlet shopping, drew 10 million shoppers in 1991. Freeport, Maine, once known only as the home of L. L. Bean, now boasts dozens of outlets. There are outlets in Rockford, Michigan; Lake Havasu City, Arizona; and Boaz, Alabama.

Says Robert Carson, general manager of Harmon Cove Outlet Center, a four-mall complex in Secaucus, New Jersey, "There has been an absolute tidal wave of people. . . . Our mall alone gets 40,000 or 50,000 people a week."

Shopping Channels

"At the same time retailers were wondering where their customers were, our phones were jammed," says Joseph Segel, founder of QVC (Quality, Value, Convenience) cable channel. Segel was one of the first to recognize that shopping could be part of the entertainment industry. In January 1993 Barry Diller joined QVC as chairman and chief executive officer. QVC operates 24 hours a day and is seen in more than 47 million homes. Sales for the year ending January 31, 1993, were more than $1 billion.

TV shopping is a $2 billion-a-year business. Once there were some 20 channels, but an industry shakeout left just two: the QVC Network and the Home Shopping Network, each with about half the total market.

"Fashion and beauty are our fastest growing areas at QVC," says Kathleen Holliday, QVC's senior vice president of marketing. "And about 70 percent of the purchases are made by women—busy active women who seem to like the convenience of televised shopping."

In private executives note that much of their apparel sales are in large-size women's clothing and speculate that customers are more comfortable trying clothes on at home in private.

TV and computers provide instantaneous feedback: when the

QVC network premiered Diane Von Furstenberg's silk fashions, sales totaled $1.2 million in two hours. No one had to wait days, or weeks, or months, as most retailers must, for sales data.

"It's a logical progression," says one TV shopping executive. "First came Main Street, then came the malls, then the catalogs, and now it's television. We think electronically is the way consumers in the next decade will choose to shop—and in very large numbers."

Catalog Shopping

From museum-shop reproductions to blue jeans, from compact discs and computer equipment to designer clothes, you can buy almost anything from a catalog. Merchandise from Neiman-Marcus, Eddie Bauer and Williams Sonoma is available by catalog.

The catalog boom has a lot to do with the electronic heartland trend we described in *Megatrends 2000.* Elizabeth Sherwood left mall-filled Los Angeles to settle in Santa Fe, New Mexico, better known for Native American artifacts than for designer clothes. Sherwood, a Ph.D. and Rhodes Scholar, is associate director of a U.S.-Soviet project at Harvard University (no need to live where you work anymore) and must travel to Moscow almost every month.

"With catalogs, I can shop at home in Santa Fe, in a hotel in Cambridge or at midnight on a plane to Moscow," says Sherwood, who takes dozens of catalogs.

- In 1991 catalog sales reached $48.8 billion, says the Direct Marketing Association.
- Some 102 million Americans made shop-at-home purchases in 1992, compared to 57 million in 1983.
- More than half (55.2 percent) of the adult population shopped by mail or phone in 1992, up from about 25 percent in 1983.
- Catalog firms sent nearly 14 billion pieces of mail in 1992, up from 6 billion in 1980.

"Mail order is part of the larger cultural trend," says Jay Walker of Catalog Media Corporation, a catalog marketer. "People don't have any time and they need more control."

Mail order accounts for about 7 percent of the women's apparel market, up from 5 percent in 1990.

Beyond "Mail Order"

But for a growing number of customers mail order is hardly the point. They don't order by mail and they don't get the products that way either. They simply fax in their order and have it sent Federal Express.

With Prodigy and a personal computer, you can purchase more than 100,000 items, including clothes from Spiegel and JCPenney (as well as buy and sell stocks, make travel reservations or check airline fares, pay bills, check your bank balance and transfer funds).

Givenchy and Round the Clock offer a toll-free number for ordering panty hose, delivered to your office the next day.

Bringing Customers Back to the Mall

Malls have to fight outlets, mail order and TV shopping—and now toll-free panty hose. It is not that they are not trying. Malls are embracing the bottom-up mall-walking craze and opening up for walkers long before shopkeepers arrive. At least people can window-shop on the run, and, retailers pray, come back to shop.

"I like watching the people, and where I live I'm afraid to walk in the streets alone," says Ruth Dixon, a Brentwood, New York, resident who walks four miles a day at the South Shore Mall in Bay Shore on Long Island.

The National Organization of Mall Walkers says that in the last decade 80 percent of enclosed shopping centers in the United States have opened to free morning strolls.

Doing the Mall Stroll

Early-morning walking clubs—dominated by the senior citizens—have started at most malls in the last several years. "I think you could find organized walking in the vast majority of malls in this country," says Don Pendley, public relations director of the International Council of Shopping Centers. Maryland's Wheaton Plaza has 2,000 registered walkers. At most malls, between 30 and 150 mall walkers show up each day.

• Avia Athletic Footwear has introduced a walking shoe designed "to give extra traction for smoother, slicker mall floors" and "to propel the body's momentum forward."

- Boulder, Colorado's Crossroads Mall has exercise stations for walkers to flex and stretch.
- "The mall eliminates just about every excuse not to walk," says Ben Beres, director of physicians at Quincy (Massachusetts) City Hospital.

"No hills, no dogs, no curbs," says Carmen Campagnoli, 74, of McLean, Virginia. He walks three miles at Ballston Commons mall twice a week. "There's always someone to talk to," he adds. Representatives from nearby Arlington Hospital drop by the mall once a month to check the mall walkers' blood pressure.

Says 59-year-old Molulela Monyake, "You feel safe here. You hear so much about crime on the streets and in wooded areas. And here, there's no traffic."

Jean Addison, 59, says she rarely shopped at Columbia Mall, in Columbia, Maryland—until she started mall-walking five days a week. "Now I shop here a lot because I'm here so often. I look for sales."

Reinventing the Mall for the 1990's

That retailing and consumer patterns would change from the 1920's to the 1960's is hardly shocking. What is shocking is that megamalls, born of the 1980's, are practically empty during business hours in the '90's. Given the size of these malls and the resources that went into creating them, the numbers of people free to shop between 10:00 A.M. and 5:00 P.M. weekdays hardly justify the kind of investment developers and retailers have sunk into these potential dinosaurs.

For the malls to succeed in the 1990's they will have to reinvent their expensive showcase developments into user-friendly, high-on-service, high-traffic gathering places. They are on the right track staging special events, inviting celebrities, hosting antique shows.

Long term, megamalls must position themselves as modern versions of the marketplace of ancient Greece or the Grand Palaces of guilds and merchants of the Middle Ages. That means making the mall a more multipurpose gathering place. Setting restaurants up like cafés for people-watching. Cinemas, Weight Watchers, health clinics. The dentist. Aerobics. Free valet parking for seniors.

A key goal has to be making shopping more convenient for parents by offering services for school-age children, from orthodontia to music lessons. Some already have child-care services. American Cartoon Theaters has opened Kids Only Cartoon Theaters in shopping malls—that should give Mom enough time to check out a new suit.

How well have the fashion establishment, the media that cover it and the retail industry kept pace with the lifestyle changes in the women customers they purport to serve?

During the last two revolutionary decades, women have become as important a part of the U.S. work force as men. That megashift in women's lives—the implications of which society has yet to fully absorb—has altered women's values, economic status, family life and leisure-time patterns.

Fashion and retailing complained about weak sales in the early 1990's. The problem, as they saw it, could be explained in one word—recession. How many designers or retailers asked themselves whether *they* were the problem?

Clearly women who are out of work or terrified about losing a job are not out on shopping sprees. But that is not the whole story.

If it were, how do you explain the thriving market in catalog sales, plus-size clothing, designer secondary lines?

How is it that Donna Karan is doing so well, she plans a Milan operation? How come TV shopping, which retailers initially scoffed at, is expected to double by 1995? Why did sales at the Gap, the second-largest label in the United States, soar 21.7 percent the last three quarters of 1991?

There is a lot of good news for the fashion/retailing establishment: the vast majority of women *have* jobs and are making more money than ever in history. As fortysomething women aim for top executive positions in the 1990's, they possess every incentive to look healthy and stylish. But they are not about to follow the top-down dictates of male designers who have been dressing socialites for decades. Neither are women in their 20's and 30's.

This book documents how dramatically women have changed in two decades. All most women ask is that designers and retailers keep pace. The smart ones are.

8.
The Family Revival

There is no doubt about it: the march of women into the workplace disrupted the family unit. With no support from companies or government, parents faced a simple but overwhelming question: who is going to care for the kids? Then, as women's power grew, some escaped marriages in which they had been economically imprisoned. Divorce increased for other reasons, too, but the net result was the same: more disruption.

Working mothers. Divorce. Inadequate child care. Kids living in poverty because absent dads don't pay child support. Stepfamilies. Two-career couples. Overwork. For the past two decades doomsayers and thoughtful observers alike could make a pretty good case that the family was disintegrating and that society was the worse for it.

When the family is in trouble, the children suffer most—robbed of love, emotional security, values, role models. Some observers have offered their "ideas." The political right argues: the only hope is putting women back in the home (where they belong). The left says: it is government's responsibility to provide free day care.

Marijean Hall, president of Parent Action, has it quite right: "We have to be able to blend the growth of women and the women's movement into a new family movement, rather than moving backward in time."

We believe parents need options, not ideology.

There is no dominant family model, so how can one monolithic answer restore the family unit?

The traditional family—homemaker, husband as breadwinner and children—now makes up only 10 percent of families. **The multiple-option family** comes in all shapes and sizes: married couples with children, stepfamilies, single parents, lesbian couples, adopted kids, househusbands, you name it.

There is no "moral" or politically correct way for the woman in each family to juggle home and family responsibilities. Some are giving up successful careers to care for children. Others start home-based businesses. Most schedule child care and work full time. Yet examples like these do not even begin to describe the diverse courses families take.

Yet one thing is certain. Women are a critical mass in the work force. By 2000 almost half of the work force will be female, and more than 80 percent of women age 25 to 54 will work. Most women with infants, 53 percent, now work, up from 38 percent in 1980. Educated women are more likely to work: 68 percent of college grads work, versus 32 percent without a high school degree.

Yet despite these overwhelming numbers, the environment in which an explosion of social change could be expected to occur— American business—has been very slow to adapt and change, to acknowledge that employees are attached to a family.

Millions of parents have acted independently to secure family time: arranging part-time work, creating home-based businesses, telecommuting. But to restore the family to the core of our lives, parents need help—business and the government must do their part, if they believe it is in *society's best interest* to strengthen the family.

Despite the need for even more options and support, the 1990's mark a new phase in family history, a turning point: **people are finally beginning to revalue and again appreciate the importance of the family.**

A wealth of studies, surveys, polls, only a few of which we will have the space to cite, show a family revival is getting established. Many parents who may have overworked in recent years now want to change: time off work to spend time with family is emerging as the status symbol of the 1990's.

There is good news about the family: parents want time off to be with families; women who can afford it and who choose to are now confident enough about careers to take a few years off; some corporations big and small have been very creative and responsive about family issues. Dads are getting more involved. **An overwhelming amount of evidence shows children of working women fare as well or better than those of homemakers.** Families actually eat dinner together.

We believe that after decades of disruption the family is moving into a new era of stability. The family is more important than ever: we realize how much we need each other.

The Multiple-Option Families

"There's been a change in the typical American family," says University of Maryland sociologist Norman Epstein. "Our society is much more varied."

First, **families are smaller.** Back in 1950, the average family had 3.5 people. In 1991 it was 2.6.

Second, **more families are headed by single parents.** In 1970, 40 percent of households were composed of married couples with children under 18. By 1991 that percentage fell to 26 percent, because so many new single-parent households were formed.

Single-Mother Families

"The increase in households has taken place outside of traditional families," says Linda Waite, a sociologist with the RAND Corporation.

In 1991 there were 10 million single parents, up more than 40 percent since 1980. Most, about 8.7 million, were single mothers. Women now head 29 percent of U.S. households.

But the increase in single-mother households is now slowing. In the 1980's single-mother households grew 35 percent, compared with 82 percent in the 1970's. The number of divorced mothers grew 1.6 percent a year in the 1980's, compared to a huge *9 percent annual increase* in the 1970's.

One child in four, including 60 percent of black children, is now raised by a single parent—about 16 million kids. By 2000, demographers say, most kids under 18 will spend part of their childhood in single-parent families.

Poor Women and Deadbeat Dads

One of every five children lives in poverty. More than one third of female-headed households are poor. In 1990 there were 3 million women who had never married and were raising children under 21. Less than 15 percent of these women were receiving child support.

Should the fathers' Social Security numbers be recorded on birth certificates, so the government could collect support from them? Either they pay, or you—the taxpayers—do.

Stepfamilies and Blended Families

"We will all have to work toward changing our internal maps of what a family should be," says Baltimore therapist Mala Burt, former president of the Stepfamily Association of America, a 14-year-old group with 72 chapters in 28 states.

- In 1990, 7.3 million children lived with stepfamilies, up from 6 million in 1980.
- Stepchildren make up 16 percent of the children in married-couple families.
- By 2010 one third of married couples will have a stepchild or an adopted child.

Single Mothers by Choice and Middle-Aged Moms

A growing number of unmarried adult single women adopt or give birth to children. In 1990, about 118,000 children were born to unwed mothers age 30 to 34—more than *three* times the 1980 number. In both years 30 percent had some college education.

Jane Mattes, a 49-year-old psychotherapist in New York City, says she felt like a "pioneer" when she decided to become a single parent in 1980. "I decided I couldn't go through life without a child," says Mattes, who started Single Mothers by Choice, a support group with 1,500 professional, unmarried members nationwide. It is not an advocacy group; half the women who join decide not to go ahead with single parenthood.

Between 1980 and 1990 the number of women 40 and over giving birth to their *first* child more than quadrupled, reports the National Center for Health Statistics.

Marrying Later, Remarriage, Not Marrying At All

In 1992 the median age for first marriage was 26.5 for men and 24.4 for women—*the highest since 1890,* when the Census started keeping track—and much later than in 1970, when women married at 20.6 and men at 22.5.

If you are a parent, "married with children" can now mean adult children: the percentage of adult children (18- to 24-year-olds) living at home increased from 43 percent in 1960 to 54 percent in 1992. That leaves some parents longing for the good old days when kids married at 22.

Nearly *half* the 2.4 million weddings in 1990 involved at least one person who had already been married, up from 31 percent in 1970.

The percentage who *never marry* has doubled, from 5 percent in the 1950's to 10 percent today. In 1991 the marriage rate fell to its lowest level in 10 years. Twenty-four million people live alone.

Living Together

There were 3 million unmarried-couple households in 1990, up *80* percent since 1980. Half of them eventually marry. As of 1988 nearly half of women age 25 to 29 had lived with someone without marriage, as had one third of women 44 and younger. Experts say the increase in couples living together is because of higher education, working women and less pressure to marry.

"It's tremendously different for this generation," says Barbara Foley Wilson, a NCHS demographer. "Women are not as reliant on men. These are profound changes."

The Grandparent Family

The U.S. Census Bureau says about 3 million children live with grandparents, an almost 40 percent increase during the 1980's. *U.S. News and World Report* says the figure could be three to four times higher. Four percent of white children live with grandparents, as do 12 percent of black children.

Grandparents as Parents meets monthly to share coping strategies. Nationally there are more than 150 such support groups, including Second Time Around Parents in Pennsylvania. Says one grandmother, "As long as there's the drug problem, grandparents are going to have to be taking on the responsibility."

"All of them felt they were the only person raising their grand-children with all these problems and these feelings," says Tearalla Lee, of Case Western Reserve University, who adds, grandparents deserve a lot of compassion. "They are not asked to be placed in this position. They are just there because of some unfortunate mishap."

Divorce

Divorce rates doubled in recent decades but dropped slightly in 1988, 1989 and 1990. The divorce rate is now holding steady at 4.7 per 1,000 people.

There were about 400,000 divorces a year in 1960; by 1976 there were 1.1 million. But divorce did not increase substantially after that: in 1992, 1.2 million couples were divorced, and about 1 million chil-dren were involved.

The number of children affected by divorce has fallen 12 percent since its 1981 peak. Since the 1970's, there have been more than 1 million children of divorce per year.

Today's young adults are the first generation to emerge from the period when U.S. divorces rose sharply. Said one *Newsweek* story, "Some experts believe that these young people, knowing the pain of their parents' divorces, will fight harder for their own marriages."

The Good News about Families

Good News about Families: We Want to Change

"If we are serious about preserving 'family values,' we are going to have to abandon our consumerism vision of the good life. It is consumerism that drives the 80-hour work week," says critic Christo-pher Lasch, author of *Haven in a Heartless World: The Family Be-sieged* (Basic Books).

We are not at all certain that consumerism is the driving force, as Lasch suggests. Paying the mortgage may be more like it. But one theme comes through all the studies loud and clear: people want and realize they need more *time, not money.* Workaholic baby boomers, as noted in Chapter 3, finally realize work is not the be-all and end-all of existence.

"There's a stirring in the hearts of many baby boomers reassess-ing priorities, questioning the sacrifices that are often required in terms of family life by unbridled careerism," says William R. Mattox, Jr., of the Family Research Council in Washington, D.C.

A Robert Half International survey found 78 percent of adults said they would prefer to work flexible hours, even if it meant slower career advancement, so they could spend more time with their families.

"There's a shift from being achievement-oriented to finding your sense of identity and fulfillment in the family," says researcher Barbara Dafoe Whitehead at the Institute for American Values in New York.

"Leisure time—not money—is becoming the status symbol of the 1990's."

We are repeating that quote from Chapter 3 by John P. Robinson, who directs the Americans' Use of Time Project at the University of Maryland, because it is so fine a capsulization of changing values.

Robinson's study for Hilton Hotels Corporation found 50 percent of people from various income levels would sacrifice a day's pay for an extra day off each week. As we said in Chapter 3, the percentage is higher—70 percent—among people who earn $30,000 or more.

Many Americans now value time as highly as money. It means employers can use flexible hours, job sharing and longer vacations as rewards instead of big raises. That will cuts costs and increase profits and productivity: rested people get more work done.

The market research firm Yankelovich Clancy Shulman found 28 percent of working women in 1990 wanted to quit their jobs to put more energy into being mothers and homemakers—nearly double the 1981 number.

These are astonishing numbers, yet they are corroborated by other studies.

Some 43 percent of employed women (age 26 to 45) expect to reduce job commitments during the next five years, as do 33 percent of men, says a recent Gallup poll.

An *American Demographics* story reports 23 percent of female and 11 percent of male baby boomers plan to quit work altogether within the next five years. These numbers are "startling," the story noted, since these people are supposed to be at the peak of their careers.

Is everyone getting ready to drop out? Or are we all just so burned out we cannot envision any creative ways to enjoy satisfying work and family life?

Corporations large and small must realize that the overwhelming majority of their employees are parents who desperately need options and flexibility. Those that stop resisting change will retain the best people and increase both profits and productivity.

More Good News: Children of Working Moms Do Not Suffer

Psychologist Rosalind C. Barnett, a senior research associate at Wellesley College's Center for Research on Women, and journalism professor Caryl Rivers of Boston University extensively surveyed research on women and work. It clearly shows, they concluded, that work is a positive factor for children and mothers alike. "The public is being engulfed by a tidal wave of disinformation that has serious consequences for the life and health of every American woman," they say.

To recap the positive research the media and others keep ignoring:

University of Michigan psychologist Lois Hoffman reviewed *50 years* of research and concluded that, whether mothers work or not, children did not differ in terms of child development. But children of working mothers have a "less sex-stereotyped view of the world," Hoffman found.

A 1982 study by psychologists Cynthia Longfellow and Deborah Belle of Harvard University's School of Education found children of working moms had *fewer* behavior problems and that homemakers showed more depression than working women.

"The recognition that a quality child-care arrangement can actually be educational for children represents an entirely new perspective," reports Barbara Reisman, executive director of New York's Child Care Action Campaign. "As recently as 15 years ago, child care was seen as just an unavoidable necessity for working families." Reisman co-authored a survey for *Working Mother*, which found that 75 percent of mothers thought their child learned more in day care than by staying at home with Mom.

Paid work is good for mothers, too: a 1990 University of California at Berkeley study followed 140 women for 22 years. At age 43 homemakers had more "chronic conditions" than the working women and seemed more "disillusioned and frustrated." The working mothers were healthy and "seemed to be juggling their roles with success."

Barnett and Rivers's own research shows that married women in high-prestige jobs have the highest level of mental well-being.

"I don't think my children lost out because I worked," says U.S. Supreme Court justice Sandra Day O'Connor. "Of course, I had to cut corners on some things. I never worried about what they wore, for instance. I think the only clothes I ever bought were for the oldest of the three boys. The other two wore hand-me-downs."

The Daddy Trackers

In 1990, 36 percent of working men—24 million—were fathers of children under 18. Half, 12 million, had children under six years old.

Not too many women brag that their husbands assume 50 percent of parental responsibility, but there is mounting evidence that today's dads are *a lot* more involved with their young than their own fathers were.

Some psychologists call it "father hunger." James Levine, director of New York's Fatherhood Project at Bank Street College of Education, says "many baby-boom men missed out on a relationship with their own fathers and are determined to be real fathers."

Seventy-four percent of men would rather have a "Daddy Track" job than a "fast track" job, says a 1989 survey for Robert Half International. Nearly half, 45 percent, would like to put off advancement for more family time.

Those are huge numbers, way beyond critical mass, but change is not happening rapidly because of the overwhelming need to make a living and, as we argue in greater detail in the conclusion of this chapter, because the environment—American business—has until now been so resistant.

Some companies offer family leave, but old behaviors die hard: a Catalyst survey found 114 companies offered new fathers unpaid leave. When companies were asked how much time fathers should take off, 41 percent said *none*.

Nevertheless, human resource experts say the number of men taking "family leave," though still quite modest, has increased noticeably.

"We have a guy in Boulder, Colorado, who took a six-month leave to be with his newborn," says James E. Smith, IBM senior information representative. "As a result of what he's done, he tells me other men out there have taken it. He's a crusader."

At AT&T, the ratio of women to men who took family leave went from 400-to-1 in 1980 to 50-to-1 in 1990.

Eastman Kodak launched a family-leave program in 1987. By 1990, 52 of the 849 employees who took time off were men.

Lotus Development offers up to four weeks' paid leave, plus an added four weeks of unpaid leave; 25 men took leave in 1991.

A 1991 survey by Du Pont, which offers a year of family leave, showed men's interest in family issues has increased dramatically in just five years. Nearly two thirds of men favored leave to care for sick children, up from 40 percent in a 1986 survey. More than one third favored leave to care for newborns, up from 15 percent.

Les Sotsky was the first man, and the first partner, at Washington, D.C.'s Arnold & Porter law firm to go part time. Sotsky worked Tuesday through Friday. Every Monday, "It's just me and her," he said about time with daughter Sophie. After two years, he is back full time.

"It's generally known not to try and schedule lunch with me," said Don Reynolds, a Washington, D.C., tax attorney. Four days a week Reynolds would "do" lunch with his two- and four-year-old at their day-care center near his office.

In Sweden only 2 percent of new fathers initially took parental leave after the law was passed in 1975. Now it is more than 27 percent. That is a lot more than U.S. dads, but, as the surveys cited so far indicate, men are becoming much more family-oriented.

Good News About Families: They Eat Dinner Together

"The symbolic meaning of dinner has not changed very much," says Thomas S. Weisner, an anthropology professor at the University of California at Los Angeles. Weisner studied the role of dinner in the lives of 20 families. "Even though it may not be enacted every day, the family dinner is still there as a cultural ideal."

A whole assortment of recent studies, surveys and polls say 70 to 80 percent of families eat dinner together:

- Eighty percent of Americans with children say most of the family eats dinner together on a typical weeknight, says a *New York Times*/CBS News poll.
- Eighty-six percent of people polled in a *Los Angeles Times* survey called eating dinner with their families "very important."
- A mail survey by New York advertiser DDB Needham attracted 4,000 responses: 75 percent of Americans said they "usually" eat dinner with their families.

In a recent poll, most families (56 percent) said they engage in conversation at the dinner table, with the television off.

"Despite all the pressures, the priority of the family in people's lives is clear," says sociologist John R. Kelly with the University of Illinois (Champaign-Urbana) Department of Leisure Studies. "Dinner together is one of the absolute, critical symbols in the cohesion of the family."

The New Baby Boom

If you question the revival of family concerns, look at another indicator, birthrates. In 1989 the Census Bureau published a prediction: there would be 3.7 million U.S. births in 1990. Wrong—there were 4.2 million, the most since the late baby-boom year of 1961, when 4.3 million children were born.

And most of these are not births to unwed teens.

Births to married women began to rise in 1988 after declining for 20 years. *Parenting* magazine reports that 57 percent of 1990 readers (average age: 30) planned to have *more* children, up from 44 percent in 1987.

The fertility rate will dramatically increase in the 1990s, says Richard Easterlin, a University of Southern California demographer. While births fell in 1991 (and 1992) to 4.1 million, that is still more than the Census had predicted—3.7 million for 1991. Easterlin attributed the fall to recession. As we pull into recovery, the "pent-up demand" for a new little one will mean a higher birthrate in 1993.

Even the Law Is Changing: Mothers-in-Law

"When I got pregnant with Chelsea, 13 years ago," says First Lady Hillary Rodham Clinton, "no one in my office knew what to make of it. It was as if there had never been a pregnant lawyer before. In those days there wasn't any real discussion of maternity leave or part-time work, and I didn't talk about it either." Fortunately, she had made partner that year and was able to work out a suitable arrangement.

Alice Burkin of Wayland, Massachusetts, a trial lawyer with a small Boston firm, made partner in 1990. She has a small child, a supportive husband and a nanny, but still found life very stressful.

"I'm personally maxed out," she says. "I can't do one more thing than I am doing now. . . . I have a very supportive and helpful husband, [but] this 50–50 stuff in a marriage is a myth." Burkin started Mothers-in-Law, a support group to help deal with the stress of being a full-time lawyer and mother.

"I only remember one bad incident," she says. "I was very, very pregnant and a not-nice judge wanted to start a trial the following week. I said I couldn't do that. He asked why. I said I was going to have a baby. He just looked at me. Fortunately, the lawyer on the other side spoke up and agreed to a delay. Right then I started having labor pains, and delivered [daughter] Liz that night."

The Boston Bar Association recommends parental leave for men and women, part-time and flexible work schedules, child-care services and, if possible, on-site centers and child-care tuition assistance.

"Things are changing," says Margaret Marshall, a partner at Choate, Hall and Stewart and 1992 president of the Boston Bar Association. "Men with young children are regretting that they can't spend more time with their families. Older partners in law firms are regretting that they didn't spend more time with their own children and are watching their daughters and sons struggle with the work/homelife balancing act. And, of course, there are the sheer numbers of women entering the law profession."

To recruit and keep the best lawyers, law firms must allow people to work part time. That normally relegated lawyers to the "Mommy Track," with no hope of partnership. Now it may merely delay partnership.

"Ten years ago large firms did not have part-time options available to their lawyers generally," says Lisa Hill Fenning, a federal bankruptcy court judge in Los Angeles. "Five years ago, they did have the options, but they were . . . usually off partnership track. Today . . . being part time does not make you less a lawyer. It is becoming more acceptable to stay on partnership track."

Both the *Washington Post* and the *Wall Street Journal* have run stories about female lawyers working part time and still making partner. San Francisco law firm Pillsbury Madison & Sutro, the seventh largest in the United States, has a written policy that partnership consideration will not be delayed for part-time lawyers unless they request it.

"We're in for a long-haul relationship with our attorneys and this is a very positive tool to use," says partner Mary Craston.

Parents Need Options

Option 1: I'm Out of Here

"I'm going to need a job that fits around my family rather than the other way around," said Margaret Larson when she left the news anchor job on NBC's *Today* show. "[My work is] very important to me. . . . It's just that in the battle of priorities, the family needed to win at this point." Larson moved to Seattle with her eight-month-old son and husband.

"Women who are leaving jobs are making a very strong decision as to the quality of life," says Kathleen Christensen, associate professor of the graduate school of The City University of New York. "They are making the decision to have much less discretionary spending and even basic staples."

Dina Weiser Brodman, of Tenafly, New Jersey, gave up a six-figure income when she sold her executive-search firm during the mid-'80's to work part time and have kids. "The clock was ticking," she says.

The overwhelming number of women still work, of course, but in 1990 for the first time since 1948, when the Labor Department began keeping statistics, the percentage of women in the work force dropped. During 1990, 74 percent of women age 20 to 44 were in the labor force, down from 74.5 percent in the first half of the year. Admittedly, it was a tiny drop, but for the first time the direction has changed. (It held at 74 percent during 1991, but hit an all-time high of 74.7 in 1992, then dropped again to 74.2 percent in the first quarter of 1993.)

"It's the first time in the post–World War II period that we've had a change like that," says John Bregger, assistant commissioner at the Bureau of Labor Statistics.

Supreme Court justice Sandra Day O'Connor took five years off from paid employment to raise her sons but remained active in the community. Asked if she thinks it is still hard for a woman to do that, she responded, "I am sure they have exactly the same worries that I had. Looking back, however, I can see that I shouldn't have been as concerned as I was. Women live much longer these days than they used to. We have ample time for two, maybe three, careers in our long lives."

Option 2: Nannies

The International Nanny Association (INA), a nonprofit organization based in Austin, Texas, estimates there are 75,000 experienced nannies nationwide.

"This is becoming a real middle-class phenomenon," says Janet Shannon, INA executive director. Nannies are not just for the rich: families who have room and can give up some privacy find nannies convenient and economical.

At Sacramento's California Nanny College, students take six months of classes in child development, infant and toddler health and safety, nutrition and CPR certification, among other courses. The students must also complete a supervised internship. The college graduates about 200 each year. The American Council of Nanny Schools in University Center, Michigan, is in the process of accrediting programs. Fourteen schools had been accredited by mid-1993. San Francisco–based Here's Help and Boston's Beacon Hill Nannies reported booming business in 1992.

Option 3: Home Business

The number of Americans who do income-producing or job-related work at home *full* or *part time* increased to 39 million in 1992, up 9 percent per year from 1988, says LINK Resources, a New York research firm. Of these, 12 million were self-employed home workers. Another 10.5 million were moonlighters or people who had several part-time jobs done at home.

Five million women earn their primary income from home-based self-employment, according to LINK's 1992 annual survey. The number of self-employed women working at home full time (35 hours or more) tripled between 1985 and 1992, from 378,000 to 1.1. million, says LINK Resources.

"Baby-boom women with children want the work-at-home lifestyle," says LINK Resources's Tom Miller, who says the trend extends to women in corporations. "There is an increase in telecommuting and bringing work home from the office."

LINK predicts there will be 49 million home workers by 1996.

How do parents who work at home get anything done if kids are there? Many work at night after kids are asleep.

When you figure the cost of gas and expensive lunches, a $40,000-a-year job is worth only $20,000. Plus you spend plenty of time commuting each day, says Bernadette Grey, executive editor of *Home Office Computing* magazine.

"Working at home is the dream of the '90's," she says.

Linda and Edward Risse of Fairfax, Virginia, run SYNERGY/ Planning, Inc., out of their home. Their objective is helping employers and employees save money through working at home. The Risses' study on telecommuting, conducted with William Howell, a Virginia House delegate, found "home-based workers accomplish 10 percent to 20 percent more by working at home."

Traffic, pollution and quality of life considerations have compelled government agencies and businesses from coast-to-coast to study telecommuting and home-based businesses.

Working at Home:
The Architecture of the Electronic Age

Home builders are well aware of the working-at-home trend.

"More than 50 percent of my clients want an office designed in their home," says Andrew Ades of Ades Design in Evergreen, Colorado, "with beefed-up electrical lines, dedicated phone lines, built-ins and special lighting. They're saying, 'I want control over my life. My father was gone so much. I don't want that to happen to me.' "

What Happens When Your Business Grows?

Dian Felton, president of Micro Support Services in Colorado Springs, a home-based desktop-publishing company, found business doubling each year—and beginning to compete with family life. "I had two choices—keep my business at a standstill or move my office to another location," she says.

She asked herself whether to move to a conventional office or find another, bigger house. A commercial location would make it easier to expand in the future and help draw the line between personal and business time. Felton finally chose a house with more office space. Being there when her children came home from school was why she started a home business in the first place.

"Where else can I bake bread, go barefoot, do my laundry and work at the same time?" asks Felton. "I can still go on field trips with the children without worrying who is going to mind the shop."

Franchising Moms

Ten years ago Betty Russotti quit her job as a United Parcel Service manager: too many long days and too much travel away from her baby daughter. Russotti and her husband started Shipping Connection, Inc., a packaging-materials retailer, in Denver, Colorado. They have now sold 20 franchises—10 went to mothers seeking flexibility. Says Russotti, "If they want to bring the baby and have him sleep . . . that's fine."

Mr. Build Handi-Man Services, Inc., a Connecticut home-repair franchise, and Decorating Den Systems, Inc., of Maryland, seek out moms as franchise operators. "You'll find franchise companies beating a path to their door because these women offer past business experience, stability and motivation," says John Reynolds, a spokesman for the International Franchise Association, a trade group in Washington, D.C.

Joanne Lewis bought a franchise from Mr. Miniblind, Inc., of Santa Ana Heights, California. Lewis and her husband sell, install and service miniblinds from 9:00 A.M. to 3:00 P.M. each day. She picks up her daughter, Jamie, after school and spends the rest of the day with her. After Jamie is in bed, she completes her work.

Option 4: Telecommuting

LINK Resources defines a telecommuter as a company-employed person who works part or full time at home during normal business hours. By their count, telecommuters grew 16 percent, to 6.6 million between 1991 and 1992.

LINK predicts 8 million telecommuters by the end of 1993, most of whom telecommute only part of the time.

There is a new willingness on the part of corporate America to bend the iron rule of nine to five. Many work tasks must be performed on a computer, but it really doesn't matter where it is. Thirteen percent of small businesses have formal arrangements to let employees work at home some of the time, says LINK.

Companies from Sears Roebuck to Pacific Bell, New York Life, John Hancock Insurance Company, JCPenney and IBM employ telecommuters who work two or more days at home.

- Almost 100 AT&T employees work out of their homes in Los Angeles, more than 1,500 nationwide, and the number is growing.
- The University of Maryland put personal computers in the homes of 40 administrative employees, allowing them to telecommute if necessary.
- Pacific Bell has 590 people in a formal telecommuter pilot. Another 400 are in an informal pilot—they have informal arrangements with their managers to work at home at least some of the time.

Gil Gordon of *Telecommuting Review* defines a telecommuter as a regular salaried employee who normally would go to the office to work but now spends two to three days working at home or off-site from the company.

Los Angeles, San Diego and other California city governments are putting telecommuting into practice. Employees of state and city governments from Florida and Washington to Virginia and Arizona also telecommute. There is more telecommuting internationally than in the United States, says Gil Gordon.

Even former President Bush caught the telecommuting bug. He told the California Chamber of Commerce that if 5 percent of Los Angeles County commuters telecommuted one day a week, it would keep 47,000 *tons* of pollutants out of the atmosphere. "Telecommuting means saving energy, improving our air quality and quality of life," he said.

"Sometimes the best transportation policy means not moving people, but moving their work," Bush told a National Transportation Policy Meeting. "Millions have found their productivity actually increases when they work nearer people they're really working for—their families at home."

Along with flex-time and job sharing, telecommuting will become another benefit enabling companies to get and keep talented people. Businesses find they can save office space and expenses and increase worker productivity by as much as 25 percent with telecommuting.

The Corporate Contribution: Who Is Creating the Real Innovations?

The signs are clear: in the 1990's Americans are putting less emphasis on money and more on meaning. Businesses can gain their loyalty by integrating family issues into corporate life.

Social critic Christopher Lasch views "the most important element of a 'family agenda' as *policies* that make it possible for both men and women to work more flexible hours, shorter hours and when possible—through technological advances like personal computers and fax machines—to work at home."

That is the issue all right—options. And it is in the interest of companies to create them. Remember the conclusion from John Robinson's time study cited on page 108—people want time. Companies that pioneer the new ways to satisfy the burning need for time can cut costs and grow profits as well as a loyal, happy work force.

"Large numbers of women still seek alternative work patterns or schedules they can't find in the conventional workplace," says Kathleen Christensen, author of a recent Conference Board survey on flexible staffing and scheduling in U.S. corporations. "The majority of jobs still don't have that flexibility built into them."

Furthermore, when companies calculate the real cost of family programs, it is clear that benefits make good business sense.

• Xerox manager Thelma Spriggs introduced flexible schedules in her 10-person department and watched productivity grow 10 percent; absenteeism plunged.

• Gerri Tyler, a systems software manager at U.S. West, gave her 12-person department the option to do some work at home. Morale and productivity increased, as did client satisfaction. Again, absenteeism dropped.
• For every dollar we spend on family care and fatherhood programs, we get back $2.50 in reduced absenteeism and turnover," says Beverly King, human resources director at the Los Angeles Department of Water and Power.

Family-Friendly Index

New York's Families and Work Institute analyzed work schedules, leaves, financial assistance, corporate giving, community service and dependent care in 188 corporations. The result was the **Family-Friendly Index.** The four most family-friendly companies recognized for "enduring commitment to the subject of work and family life" were **IBM, Johnson & Johnson, Aetna Life & Casualty Company** and **Corning, Inc.**

"Each of these companies . . . packaged an innovative array of strategies to address child care, elder care, health and wellness and time off for their employees," said Dana Friedman, copresident of the Institute and coauthor of *The Corporate Reference Guide to Work-Family Programs.*

Other high-scoring companies tended to be *profitable, nonunionized,* in the *service* sector, with a high percentage of *female* employees. Companies instituted programs with "the full intention that they will yield a return on investment," says coauthor Ellen Galinsky.

A handful of companies have made "a fundamental cultural and institutional change in the way they do business," says Friedman. But, she adds, the vast majority have not done much, if anything.

True enough, but a decade ago family-friendly programs did not exist. Now all large employers offer some benefits, such as maternity leave, yet nearly half still view work-family concerns as *women's issues.*

A Look at the Top Four Family-Friendly Firms

IBM will spend $22 million by the mid-1990's on child care and another $3 million on elder care. IBM offers up to three years' parental leave, approved on a case-by-case basis. Personnel vice-president

Bill Colucci calls it "a wise business decision, not done out of altruism."

In 1989 **Johnson & Johnson**'s then CEO James E. Burke introduced 12 new family-work policies. He changed the company credo—only the third time since 1943—adding, "We must be mindful of ways to help our employees fulfill their family responsibilities."

In 1985 **Corning** found women and minorities were leaving the company at twice the rate of white men—which cost $3.5 million a year. The solution: a new coaching program that provides mentors for women and minorities and sets goals for their advancement. Turnover has decreased by 50 percent. Corning includes family issues in evaluating managers.

Sherry Herchenroether, manager of family services at **Aetna Life & Casualty,** found most women who did *not* return after giving birth were "higher performers." She asserted, "The company simply couldn't afford to keep losing this type of employee." After Aetna extended maternity leave, 91 percent of mothers returned from leave. "Women who take maternity leave want to return to work," says Herchenroether, "and they'll be much more productive and loyal if their company is understanding about their personal lives."

Aetna employees can work as few as 15 hours a week without losing benefits. But it isn't just employees who win: family-friendly policies saved Aetna $2 million in 1991.

Working Mom List

Working Mother publishes an annual list of the 100 best companies for working moms. In addition to the four companies described above, its 1992 top 10 list, published in the October issue, included Boston's Beth Israel Hospital, Fel-pro, Merck, Morrison & Foerster, St. Paul Cos. and SAS Institute. The list, which began in 1985 with 30 companies, emphasized companies in the geographic areas of Silicon Valley, northern New Jersey and Research Triangle Park, North Carolina, in 1992.

"Once you get a big employer in a certain area [to take the lead in family benefits]," says Betty Holcomb, an editor with *Working Mother*, "the others also have to begin."

"Parents at Work"

At San Francisco's Genentech, Inc., employees meet twice weekly for "Parents at Work," a company-sponsored discussion. "We need to nurture parents so they can then nurture children," says Patty Wipfler, director of Palo Alto's Parents Leadership Institute, who led a recent session. "Many parents feel all alone—there is nobody to talk to." She adds, "Parents are a group of people aching for change."

But national leadership has not yet emerged, she says. "We haven't had a Rosa Parks refusing to give up her seat on the bus."

Corporate Child Care

In 1965 three quarters of the care for preschoolers with working mothers came from relatives, reports University of Maryland demographer Harriet Presser. By 1985 it had dropped by one half, as the baby-sitters got jobs, too. It doesn't take a demographer to figure out that the percentage has dropped even more since.

The rate of childbirth among women 30 to 44 in professional and managerial positions soared 41 percent between 1983 and 1990.

The number of employers in the United States offering child-care assistance rose from 110 in 1978 to 7,000 in 1990, says research analyst Daniel Dreyer of Work Force Program of the Conference Board. The increase from 1989 to 1990 was remarkable: from 4,200 to 7,000.

That is the kind of dramatic growth that looks like critical mass.

"Our people tell me that having their children on site is one of the best benefits we could offer," says Linda J. Vann, director of children's services at **American Bankers Insurance** in Dade County, Florida, where turnover among parents is low, "lateness is near zero and morale is at an all-time high."

Corporate Consortia

Corporate child-care centers and accompanying liability costs are expensive, so companies are working together to create corporate day-care consortiums.

The American Business Collaboration for Quality Dependent Care, a coalition of 137 organizations, committed $25 million for child and elder care programs. Spearheaded by IBM, AT&T and nine other major companies, the effort will fund 300 projects in 44 communities in 25 states and the District of Columbia.

An important earlier collaboration was a a $2 million, 194-child center in Charlotte, North Carolina, financed by IBM, American Express, Allstate, Duke Power and University Research Park. The center, which is open to the public, hires a lot of teachers and pays them well. "That drives up costs," says Ted Childs, director of IBM's work-force diversity programs. "But as long as it supports an increase in the quality of care, we're willing to support it."

In Dallas–Fort Worth, IBM teamed up with Travelers on a $375,000 program to recruit and train day-care providers, and to fund efforts for day-care centers to gain accreditation.

Other large corporations, from Travelers and Burroughs Wellcome to Pepsi, have teamed up with IBM and others to cooperate on day-care issues in cities like Dallas, Rochester and the Research Triangle, North Carolina. For example, Honeywell, First Bank System, 3M and 12 other Minneapolis companies provide "referral and subsidized in-home care for sick children."

Indeed, the number one problem for working mothers is the lack of emergency child care, reports *Working Mother*. Barbara Reisman, of New York's Child Care Action Campaign, says child-care emergencies cost companies $3 billion a year.

Detroit employees of Chrysler, United American Health and Detroit Edison can send their sick children to one of four area hospitals.

Time Warner, Colgate-Palmolive and 12 other New York City and suburban firms employ the services of Child Care, Inc., one of the city's nonprofit private resource-and-referral agencies. It provides care for sick children and emergency child care. Employees appreciate the service and don't abuse it, says Joyce Rittenburg, program manager for Emergency Child Care Services.

"We wanted to look at work and family issues together with other New York City companies, because none of us could address them individually," says Karol Rose, manager of work and family programs at Time Warner.

Sick children are one problem; holidays and vacations, another. Parents still have to work, so who's minding the kids? In the Washington, D.C., area, AT&T, IBM, Allstate and Mobil pledged $60,000 for child care on school holiday and vacation days. Similar programs exist in Boston, Atlanta, Chicago, Denver, Dallas and Tampa.

Small firms do not have the resources of big corporations; what they lack in dollars, they make up for in creativity.

Child Care Action Campaign, a nonprofit advocacy group based in New York City, shows how companies employing fewer than *250* people still create centers, subsidies, referral services, flexible benefits and dependent-care plans. The small companies say it is great for business and employee morale.

- Portland, Oregon's Pro Tem Professional Temporary Services, Inc., subsidizes child care by simply paying parents an extra 50 cents an hour. In 1991 the company earned a $50,000 profit on the work of 216 parents alone.
- Stackpole Ltd. U.S.A., a metal bearings maker in Brownsville, Tennessee, employs 100 people but has its own on-site center.
- Broward Business Services, Inc., a 110-person answering-service company in Fort Lauderdale, Florida, subsidizes employees' child care costs.
- Bowles Corporation, a *12-person* engineering firm in North Ferrisburg, Vermont, has an on-site child-care center, as does Byrne Electrical Specialists, Inc., in Rockford, Michigan, which employs 110, and Chalet Dental Clinic, with *45 employees,* in Yakima, Washington.

The Innovation Honor Roll

A handful of companies have started innovations so clever and, for the most part inexpensive, every company—big or small—can learn from them.

When **Hewitt Associates** of Lincolnshire, Illinois, sends a consultant away from home overnight, it recommends someone to stay with the children and pays for it. "We help them deal with guilt and finances," says human resources director David J. Wille. Hewitt Associates' "Mothers' Rooms" are equipped with refrigerators and electric breast pumps.

"We need people to work weekends during tax season, but we don't want to keep them from their kids," says Leslie A. Murphy, a partner at **Plante & Moran,** an accounting firm in Southfield, Michigan. So January through April, the company uses a conference room for day care on Saturdays.

During holidays and school breaks, **John Hancock Mutual Life** sponsors field trips for employees' children. "It solves a tough day-care problem for clerks and vice presidents alike," says Katherine B. Hazzard, coordinator of work-family programs.

Stride Rite Corporation converted part of its Cambridge, Massachusetts, headquarters into an intergenerational day-care center for both children and elderly parents. Stride Rite's Karen Leibold says the firm sends out about 60 packets of information about the center a month.

Du Pont headquarters in Wilmington, Delaware, paid the Girl Scouts to extend its summer program four weeks, and provide transportation for children to and from camp. DuPont's Brevard, North Carolina, plant has its own on-site camp.

Ohio Bell's TeenLine "offers counseling to parents on how to handle everything from homework conflicts to eating disorders."

Older Day-Care Workers

Low morale and education are shared among child-care workers. Add to that a high turnover—about 40 percent a year. For some centers the solution is hiring older workers. Center managers like their reliability, patience and tendency to stick with the job longer.

"Older people fit the bill for the kind of people you want in child care," says Cathy Ventura-Merkel, of the American Association of Retired Persons. "It's a win-win situation for everybody."

The number of Americans age 65 and older working in child care increased 28 percent, from 35,000 to 45,000, just from 1989 to 1991, says the Bureau of Labor Statistics. Many older adults, of course, have considerable child-care experience—having raised their own children.

Mervyn O'Connor, a widow in her early 70's, works at the Bel Pre Child Development Center in Silver Spring, Maryland. "I give love to them, and they return it," says O'Connor, who works five hours a day every workday.

Bronwyn Chisholm, director of the DoorKey Day-Care Center in Washington, D.C., says the children love Cleo Warren, a 67-year-old grandmother of 19: "When she comes in, they go right to her," she says. "She's very nurturing."

KinderCare Learning Centers, Inc., the nation's largest child-care chain, makes a concerted effort to recruit older people, who make up 9 percent of employees, says executive director Jeff Jones.

"I see it as a way to supplement and enhance programs, but I don't see it as a solution to the staffing crisis," says Marcy Whitebook, executive director of the Oakland, California-based Child Care Employee Project. The problem, of course, is that child-care workers are not well paid.

Elder Care: From Family Issue to Employee Benefit?

There are well over 2,000 adult day-care centers in the United States.

There are nearly 32 million Americans over 65, says the National Council on the Aging.

More than one in five working adults provides some care for an elderly relative, usually a parent or parent-in-law, and loses an average of one week's work a year, according to social-welfare researcher Andrew Scharlach at the University of California, Berkeley. The average age of caregivers is 50 years old.

Three quarters of caregivers are women, says the Older Women's League (OWL). According to OWL, **nearly 2 million women care for kids and parents at the same time.** "Many do so willingly," says executive director Joan Kuriansky, "but at a tremendous cost. We are asking them to balance the unbalanceable."

More than half the women caring for elderly relatives have paying jobs; nearly 40 percent are still raising their own children, reports *Newsweek.*

Says Kuriansky, "We get letters from women who are taking care of their children and their parents and possibly their parents. How do we expect them to do that and stay employed?"

The American Association of Retired Persons says 12 percent of caregivers have had to quit their jobs and 14 percent work part time so they can tend the aged. In addition, some adults help their elders financially: 69 percent of adults provide up to $250 a month to parents, says a report in *USA Today.*

"The need for elder care is really going to reach crisis proportions in the next few years," says Karen Leibold of Stride Rite.

"This [elder care] is one of the hottest new benefits issues because employees are desperate for practical help," says Dr. Daniel Thursz, of the National Council on the Aging.

At IBM, "32 percent of our population had some responsibility for an elder relative," says spokesman John Boudreaux. IBM's Elder Care Referral Service offers "flexibility in dealing with home and family."

In 1987 IBM looked to Work/Family Directions in Boston, Massachusetts, which had previously helped IBM with child care, to help create their Elder Care Consultation and Referral Service. Work/Family Directions has developed programs for 90 U.S. firms, linking more than 2 million employees with agencies.

Work/Family Directions has grown into a $35 million business, with offices in San Francisco, Chicago and New York. It helped coordinate the American Business Collaboration for Quality Dependent Care mentioned on page 258.

Corporations Accept Gay Families

In San Francisco members of Levi Strauss's Lesbian and Gay Employees Association talk about their lives in a 20-minute video, shown as part of Levi Strauss's mandatory diversity-training seminars. "If our colleagues get to know us more as individuals, we all become part of the same company team," says Cynthia Bologna, corporate communications assistant and cofounder of the association.

In companies all across America, gay and lesbian employees are gaining acceptance and in some cases winning corporate family benefits.

Gays at Apple, Digital Equipment, AT&T, Boeing, Coors, Du Pont, Hewlett-Packard, Lockheed, Sun Microsystems and US West, among others, get together to share problems and solutions and present issues to top management.

Benefits/Health Insurance

In April 1991 New York's Montefiore Medical Center became the first large private employer to offer health and life insurance to the long-term partners of homosexual employees. Unmarried heterosexual couples are not eligible.

"We were concerned about the cost of [insuring] every couple who lives together," says Barry Stickler, associate vice president of compensation and benefits for the 9,000-employee center. But when a lesbian employee asked for the benefit, Montefiore tried "to deal with it."

In September 1991 Lotus Development extended to long-term partners of homosexual employees the same benefits as to heterosexual spouses. With 3,100 employees, Lotus became the largest for-profit company to do so. Live-in heterosexual partners are not covered, says human resources vice president Russ Campanello, because they can get married. To qualify, gay couples must sign an affidavit stating that they live together, intend to stay together and are responsible for one another. During the first three months of the plan more than 100 companies asked Lotus for information about its plan.

In 1993 Microsoft became the largest company to offer health benefits to partners and dependents of gay employees. Digital Equipment and Du Pont are reportedly studying the issue.

Other companies that extend benefits to gay couples include Ben & Jerry's, the Vermont ice-cream maker, New York's *Village Voice* weekly and the municipal governments of Seattle and of several California cities.

The United States is experiencing the greatest revival of family values since the 1950's. It is a great homecoming. And we enter it, not with the naïveté of the 1950's when women had no options for economic independence or meaningful work outside the home. This time, in choosing family values, we do so with our eyes wide open—fully conscious that we are making a free choice. Both mothers and fathers want more family time—and that represents important change. Women may have temporarily abandoned exclusive nurturing roles to develop their careers—or for simple economic necessity. But the net result is that both parents are reembracing the nurturing role.

Now it is time to take that positive value and transform society. Millions of individuals have restructured their schedules to juggle evening work hours so they can be home when their children return from school. Others work part time or telecommute. But individuals are bucking a system that is still largely based on "Dad the Breadwinner" and "Mom the Homemaker."

Business and government represent the larger social context in which families exist. Both are eager to pay lip service to "family values." They are certainly not shy about invoking that old dictum that the family is the basic building block of society, but what about creating policies that support it?

What Role Should the Government Play?

We all read with envy the great things Scandinavian countries do for families. Many Americans, however, would not necessarily like to pay the tax bills Swedes do. The United States is not about to institute universally free day care (and readers who know our work know *we* are not about to advocate big, top-down government programs), but in 1992, when the majority of the work force consists of parents, it is not exactly socialism to expect family leave, tax credits and deductions, starting with the $2,000 federal income-tax deduction per child.

Says David Popenoe, a sociology professor at Rutgers University, "If that amount were the equivalent of what President Truman instituted in the 1940s, it would be worth $6,000 or $7,000." Now, that would give parents options.

Family Leave

Even before President Clinton signed the Family Leave bill, which became law in 1993, quite a few states had already taken action:

- In California companies employing 50 or more people must allow leaves of as many as 16 weeks without pay over a two-year period to care for a newborn or newly adopted or sick child, an ill spouse or parent.
- In Oregon workers can take up to 12 weeks without pay every two years to care for ailing relatives.
- Hawaii's family-leave law covered state and county workers in 1992. By 1994 it will apply to private companies with at least 100 workers.

All told, 11 states and the District of Columbia guarantee some sort of family leave for private-sector employment. The federal law does not override state laws, but it requires employers to abide by whichever law provides the best benefits to families.

The federal law requires businesses with 50 people or more to grant up to 12 weeks of unpaid leave per year for birth, adoption or foster care, or to care for a child, spouse or parent with a serious illness. It will cover about 5 percent of businesses and about 40 percent of the work force. Employees can also take leave for their own health reasons. Employers must provide preexisting health benefits and guarantee a comparable job when the employee returns. To qualify, workers must have 12 months' experience and have worked 1,250 hours.

Former president George Bush had vetoed the bill and many business groups opposed it, but, according to Families and Work Institute, "the average cost of leave is 32 percent of an employee's annual salary, compared with 75 to 150 percent to replace the employee permanently."

The Corporate Contribution

State and federal governments help, but most of the responsibility is going to fall to corporations. What is the critical mass needed for companies to realize that children and families exist and to integrate them into corporate policy?

It is shockingly high.

Almost half the work force consists of women, most of whom are mothers, and the other half are their husbands.

We are way beyond the numbers needed for critical mass here. We are talking overwhelming majority—and still change is sluggish. The reason is environment, one of the key factors in building critical mass for social change. The speed with which critical mass is achieved also depends on quality of input (more about that soon) and the nature of the environment. Both factors, until very recently, were working against speed.

Until a few years ago, American business was a bastion of male domination. Corporate policy toward working women was, "*You have kids? That's your problem.* Do your job, without letting them interfere, and we'll get along just fine." Same goes for single fathers. (And gays: pretend you are straight, and there will be no problem.) To succeed within the business culture, you go along—or get out, as millions of entrepreneurs did. After all, corporations saw no reason to change: they had always hired men whose wives handled child care.

But over time those men retired, and in their places were women with children and men more involved with their families than their dads or older brothers ever dreamed of being. In *Reinventing the Corporation* (1985), the employer-sponsored day-care programs we counted were in the hundreds; in *Megatrends 2000* (1990), we cited 3,500. The latest count is 7,000. Now, instead of just focusing on day care or "women's issues," corporations are judged on how "family friendly" they are.

The other factor in achieving critical mass for real change is the "quality of input." Even though millions of parents with child-care concerns were flooding the labor market in the 1970's and 1980's, they lacked the power and experience to enact corporate policy changes. Highly placed male executives with homemaker wives could not empathize with their problems. But as those parents gained status and experience and started their own businesses—look at what the tiny companies cited on page 259 are doing in child care—they began to rewrite the rules of the work-family relationship.

Women are a critical mass in the work force, and baby boomers of both sexes are finally in policy-making positions—but there is one more unexpected factor, another catalyst tipping the balance for change, one that many a 45- to 55-year-old female executive has been around long enough to notice:

Male CEOs and senior executives around 60 years old are becoming sensitized to family issues through the work-family struggles of their successful daughters in their thirties. "Corporate leaders who would not listen to the word 'day care' five years ago now worry about how family-friendly the company is," say experienced women. "And the reason is their daughters."

9.
The Goddess Reawakening

As bishops and businesswomen, prime ministers and mayors, CEOs and entrepreneurs, activists and ambassadors, women are more powerful, more visible, than ever before. A great metaphor for this new energy is the archetype of the Great Goddess: the Divinity expressed as the Sacred Feminine.

- Inspired by archeology as well as mythology, academic and popular books about Goddess worship have become a publishing phenomenon.
- Mainstream denominations—like Methodists—sponsor a course on the Goddess called the "Queen of Heaven."
- Goddess theology is debated in the ivy-covered divinity schools of Cambridge, Massachusetts.
- In Germany there is renewed interest in the Nordic deity Freya.
- North American women are reembracing the wisdom of the feminine spiritual tradition of Native American Indians.
- On Earth Day in 1991 four women and two men stood on a hill near Mount Horeb, Wisconsin, praying to Mother Earth. From Boston to Berkeley, similar rituals were enacted.

Perhaps it is the spiritual side of feminism.

"Women first wanted to apply feminism to political and economic realms, then to their families," says Judith Auerbach of the

University of Southern California's Institute for the Study of Men and
Women. "Now they want it in their spiritual lives."

The reason is empowerment. So long as people visualize God as
male, women are diminished and inferior. For millennia women have
internalized this often unconscious self-deprecation. As women grow
better educated and more economically self-sufficient, and as they
reach for leadership, they are discarding the absurd notion of a male
God. Says Michelle Beasley, 29, an attorney in Washington, D.C., "I
have no conception of God as a male figure. When I think of a caring,
life-giving presence, it has got to have a maternal aspect."

The collective memory of the Goddess is reawakening as millions
of women acknowledge their power, experience freedom from male
domination, and channel sweat and creativity into transforming the
world.

Whether a woman espouses traditional religion, New Age
spirituality or atheism, her sense of personal power is enhanced by the
mythology of the Goddess, which awakens confidence, belonging and
self-esteem.

The Goddess is associated with reverence of the earth and its
environment. Her image is reemerging as humanity seeks to make
warfare obsolete and heal planet Earth. Even the male establishment
must concede that the Goddess's life-affirming values of cooperation
and creativity are key to human survival. The Goddess influences all
humanity.

The Goddess Movement

The Goddess movement is a rich, unstructured, multidisciplinary
wave of artistic, intellectual and spiritual activity. It defies theology,
reinterprets archeology, and transforms *his* story into *hers.* Although
many scholars trace the Goddess revival to the field of "women's
studies," it now spans art history, mythology, folklore, literature,
sociology and modern art. *Time* magazine terms Goddess worship
"the effort to create a female-centered focus for spiritual expression."

New academic scholarship has generated a sea tide of publishing
activity. Any New Age bookstore worth its salt devotes a large section
to Goddess books. Though it began in academia, the strength of the
Goddess trend now lies in how rapidly it has spread at the grass-roots
level.

The active U.S. Goddess movement is estimated at from 100,000 to half a million. One group alone—the Circle Network—claims 100,000 people. "We're smaller than the Unitarians but larger than the Quakers," says priestess Selena Fox of the Network. Many more are quietly integrating Goddess theology into their lives through reading and personal worship.

Across the United States women gather to learn about the Goddess in churches or at local bookshops. They create celebrations and invoke her in poetry, song and meditation.

- Circle of Aradis in San Francisco and Women Spirit Rising in Los Angeles hold large public rituals.
- The Los Angeles area has a cable television show called *The Goddess in Art* hosted by Starr Goode.
- A Goddess magazine, *Sage Women,* has some 3,000 subscribers.

"Goddess worship has been around for a long time," concluded *The Wall Street Journal.* "But a recent spate of academic books on Goddess religions and growing debate in traditional faiths about male bias in theology, have brought a new wave of believers."

Wicca

The Goddess movement might be termed a mixture of Wicca, the New Age, feminism and mythology. Some Goddess worshipers are part of the ancient tradition of Wicca, or witchcraft. Present-day witches insist that their tradition, long vilified by organized religion, is actually life-affirming and based on the power of the female and the earth.

The author Starhawk, who calls herself a witch, is deeply involved with the Goddess movement. She serves on the editorial board of *The Journal of Feminist Studies in Religion,* a "Who's Who" of mainstream theologians, and was recently appointed to the staff of the California Theological Institute headed by maverick Catholic priest Matthew Fox.

"Cakes" and Burning Sage

Suburban Boston's Unitarian Universalist Church sponsors a Goddess course called "Cakes for the Queen of Heaven," which attracts young mothers and older women, careerists and homemakers alike. Graduates create a service for the whole congregation. "It was the most powerful spiritual experience I've ever had," says Claudia Luck.

Written by Unitarian scholar Shirley Rank, the course has been adopted by Methodist, Congregational and Episcopal groups and a Catholic order of nuns. More than 800 of the Unitarians' 1,000 congregations have signed up for "Cakes," as the course is affectionately known.

In Sudbury, Massachusetts, Apara Borrowes-Toabe, a longtime student of Goddess religion, teaches a workshop at Native Spirit, a bookshop and center specializing in Goddess worship and American Indian experience. Students chant, burn sage and meditate. Says Janice Drake, "This is still very much feminism, but it's not so angry. It's power without the anger."

One woman who graduated from both Boston area courses has really "got religion" now. When the congregation at her Episcopal church says, "Our Father," she reports, "I say as loudly as I can 'Our Mother.' "

How God Became Man

If the metaphor of the Goddess is now being "remembered," how did such a powerful principle become lost or forgotten? Since the female brings forth life from her body, wouldn't it be natural to associate her with divinity? The way the new Goddess-centered view of history, described more fully on pages 276–282, sees it, an advanced peaceful society of Goddess worshipers existed before recorded history, but was destroyed by a violent, male-dominated culture. That patriarchy wiped out the notion of the Goddess and compelled people to envision God as male.

Elinor Gadon, author of *The Once and Future Goddess* (Harper & Row) and an art historian who taught a course in the Goddess at Harvard Divinity School, puts it this way. A three-part heresy removed the Goddess from her throne: 1) a male God created the world, 2) humans have the right to dominate nature and 3) Men have the right to dominate women. So deep and unconscious are these assumptions, they have been rarely challenged until the recent past.

The new female-endorsed three-part view of history, Gadon says, is: 1) in the beginning was the Goddess, 2) the patriarchy suppressed her power and 3) the Goddess is reemerging now.

Reenvisioning the Divine as female reconnects women with personal power. Whether she seeks to heal the earth or start a business, run for political office or raise a child, when she invokes the Goddess, she draws on her legitimate divinity and asserts that it is in every way equal to that of the male.

Why the Goddess is Reemerging Now

How is today's Goddess revival related to feminism? U.S. feminism since the 1960's has not been considered particularly spiritual and rarely reached for mythology to craft its social or political arguments.

"Many women find themselves drawn to this movement," says Christina Robb, a reporter for *The Boston Globe*, "because it takes them beyond the political anger of Feminism . . . to a deeper place."

The roots of Goddess culture may lie millennia ago, but the Goddess commands recognition today because of several other trends not *directly* related to 20th-century feminism: 1) revaluing the nonrational and 2) the information megatrend that increased women's economic self-sufficiency.

In the late 19th century, rationalism and empiricism—worshiped virtually since the Enlightenment—were weakening ideologies. After the findings of Freud and Jung gained popular acceptance, Western thought conceded there was more to life than we could see or measure. By the 1960's, when a new generation of women called themselves feminist, there was a growing sense that, female or male, we had lost a most precious aspect of our humanity—the richness of the emotional, the deep nonrational knowledge of the intuitive.

The rise of U.S. feminism coincided with the revaluing of the intuitive.

It took a while before people saw the connection. But through the efforts of pioneers like Merlin Stone, author of *When God Was a Woman* (Harcourt Brace Jovanovich), the first new sprouts of Goddess-wisdom emerged in the 1970's, at a time when Joseph Campbell was gaining initial recognition for his important work in mythology. The ground for the Great Goddess was indeed being prepared.

The Goddess and the Arms Race

By the 1980's the insanity of the arms race and the threat of nuclear war had propelled the activism of millions. For many women the arms race was the logical conclusion of a destructive drama based on "masculine" values whose final act would wipe out the planet. Women raised their voices in protest, knowing that although their shrieks seemed "irrational" to the male elite, disruptive protest was the only rational position.

Those were cries for the wisdom of the feminine to be reborn, and they were heard. The trickle of writing about the Goddess became a great wave: new books by Starhawk, Susan Griffin, Charlene Spretnak and others were published.

In 1987 California scholar and activist Riane Eisler published the landmark work *The Chalice and the Blade,* a reappraisal of history. She theorizes there are two possible societies: a dominator model, which imposes power by force (or the threat of force), symbolized by the blade, and a partnership model, based on egalitarian relationships, where the art and spirituality symbolized by the chalice are paramount.

A new theme permeated the writings of the 1980's—the relationship between women and the earth. Now environmentalism is frequently associated with the female, the Earth Mother and the ancient goddess Gaia.

The Goddess and the Information Megatrend

The Goddess revival was accelerated by the shift from an industrial to an information society, the most important economic megatrend of the 1970's and early '80's.

An industrial society values physical strength and puts women at a distinct disadvantage. After World War II, male workers, most without much education, massed together in the factories of the centralized industrial economy and formed male-dominated institutions like unions. The women who "manned" the factories during the war were no longer welcome. Physically segregated in residential areas, many women may have welcomed a domestic role as they turned to more creative pursuits—bearing the children of the postwar baby boom.

Industrial society broke the bonds between work and home, between men and women. Monetarily, it valued only *men's* industrial work. A far cry from the agricultural era when men and women generated economic value working side by side at or near home.

In an information society, however, brains matter more than brawn; work is decentralized and can be conducted almost anywhere. That changes everything for women. By the 1970's, when the information shift was well under way, women were again welcome at work. Initially, they toiled in low-wage clerical jobs. (Of course, many women who are today over age 45 had good jobs, lifelong careers and are currently leaders. But in their generation, they were the exceptions. Behind them looms the massive baby-boom group, where almost *everyone* has been working since graduation.)

The first wave of baby-boom daughters, college degrees in hand, landed jobs around 1970 in banking, retail, management, computers, insurance, finance and health care. Twenty years later they and the women who followed had revolutionized the workplace. Those women are now a critical mass in business and the professions and will attain leadership positions this decade.

The attributes of the Goddess—freedom and self-determination—were born mythologically and on that most mundane, deterministic level, economically.

Whether women freely sought challenge or were compelled by the Great Mother of necessity, they pushed the boundaries of their evolution to embrace economic and social tasks that once belonged primarily to males. Considering the social, political and economic power women wield today, the emergence of Goddess worship might be construed as a form of spiritual catch-up reflecting new sociological realities that have unfolded over the past 25 years.

The Pantheon of the Goddess

When Chinese students in Beijing's Tiananmen Square raised a wax statue of the Goddess of Democracy, a contemporary aspect of the Great Goddess became visible. With peaceful students at her side, she was mowed down by a cruel male elite. But like other forbidden goddesses, she lives on in people's hearts.

The Great Goddess (or Great Mother) manifests as many different goddesses across history, continents and cultures: Inanna, Isis, Athena, Venus, Kali, Shakti, the Hopi Spider Woman. The Goddess has many names and attributes. She assumes different identities to enact the stories and dramas of humanity.

The Book of Goddesses and Heroines (Llewellyn) by Patricia Monaghan lists more than 1,000 goddesses. An elaborate indexing system helps readers look up African, Baltic, Chinese or North American goddesses, for example, and determine which areas, such as beauty, scholarship or birth, they rule.

In Asia alone, where the Goddess is still worshiped in many villages, there are many, many manifestations of the Great Goddess:

Kuan-yin, the Buddhist bodhisattva of compassion, is the most popular Chinese deity. Like the Virgin Mary, she is known for bestowing mercy.

The Hindu manifestation of the Great Goddess is Shakti, the active life force and mate of Shiva; a popular Indian folk saying is, "Without Shakti, Shiva is a corpse."

The Tibetan Tara is a full Buddha who incarnates only in female form. She chooses to delay entering nirvana until all humanity is saved. She protects Buddhists from the eight traditional dangers: pride, delusion, anger, envy, wrong views, avarice, attachment and doubt.

The Goddess is also portrayed in the Hindu goddess Kali, dark-skinned and holding a sword and a severed head. The sword of wisdom cuts through to release the ego and the rational mind. She knows the realm of Death and symbolizes the knowledge that transformation comes only by facing the dark side.

The Hindu queen Maya, mother of the historical Buddha, Prince Siddartha, is portrayed with sensuality and eroticism.

Virgin Goddesses

The patriarchy sought to usurp the Goddess, but was only partly successful. The Greek oracle at Delphi, once sacred to the Goddess, fell to the male god Apollo, but a priestess still delivered the oracle's messages. The Goddess survived, if occasionally in distorted form. The Greek Athena is said to have sprung fully grown from the head of Zeus. Goddess of warfare, she is often depicted with shield and armor. Athena so lacks female characteristics, she sometimes looks like a football player in drag. But Athena knows how to stand up to the male gods. She is accomplished in many areas and a famous patroness of the arts.

Artemis, the goddess of the hunt, is athletic and loves nature and animals. She is often depicted with a deer, whose antlers represent her power. She is a goddess of sport, recreation and the great outdoors.

Artemis and Athena, who both take lovers, are called "virgin" goddesses, because their identity is self-contained. Their myths do not focus on family members, the way the myths of Isis and Demeter, described below, do. For this reason psychologist Jean Shinoda Bolen, author of *Goddesses in Every Woman* (Perennial), suggests women think of Athena and Artemis as animus figures, the Jungian term for the male aspect within a woman.

Mother Goddess

The Egyptian goddess Isis is associated with fertility, crops, healing and transformation. After her husband, Osiris, was murdered, Isis miraculously brought him back to life long enough to conceive their son, Horus. She was worshiped as far away as France and England and is considered the patron of mothers and women in health care.

The Greek Demeter, goddess of the grain, is the central character of the Eleusinian Mysteries of Ancient Greece, said to depict the triumph of immortality. When Demeter's daughter, Persephone, is abducted by Hades, lord of the Underworld, Demeter stops the earth from producing grain. Finally mother and daughter are reunited and crops again grow.

The symbol of their dramatic reunion, kept secret for 2,000 years, is a single sheaf of grain. It was held up to the initiates, who had fasted and kept silence in preparation for the Mysteries. The returned Persephone, however, is no longer an innocent maiden, but queen of the Underworld and mistress of her own dark side.

The Goddess in North America

These myths only hint at the multiplicity of the Great Goddess. In the traditions of Native Americans, the **Hopi Spider Woman,** associated with weaving, personifies all creativity. She possesses unlimited wisdom, knows all languages and has the gift of prophecy.

White Buffalo Calf Woman, revered as a messenger from Wakan Tanka, the Great Spirit, gave the sacred pipe to the Sioux Indians of the plains and prairies.

New Mexico's Keresan people venerate **Thought Woman,** said to have conceived the entire creation plan and to contain within herself both male and female *and* all of life's possibilities.

Lady of the Beasts (Harper San Francisco) by Buffie Johnson organizes Goddess lore according to animals that represent her, including the butterfly and the serpent, symbols of transformation long associated with the Goddess.

When the Goddess Ruled

Activists who seek equality, disarmament, a balanced environment, eventually come face-to-face with the same cynical argument: "It has always been this way. It's just human nature." In the late 20th century, a new generation of feminists offer a counterargument: "No it hasn't."

Archeological discoveries after World War II present evidence of a peaceful, remarkably advanced, prehistoric agricultural society where the Goddess was worshiped extensively and where women and men lived in harmony, neither dominating the other. This civilization extended across Turkey and into the Middle East, as far west as France, as far north as southern Poland.

This stunning new view is most frequently associated with Marija Gimbutas, a Lithuanian-born professor at UCLA, though it is also accepted by many scholars, including British archeologist James Mellart. Now in her 70's, Gimbutas has devoted most of her career to collecting evidence of Goddess culture. Gimbutas knows mythology and folklore, reads more than 20 European languages, is a veteran of five European excavations and has written 20 books and 200 articles, including *Goddesses and Gods of Old Europe* (University of California Press) and *The Language of the Goddess* (Harper San Francisco). The description of the Neolithic period in what she calls "old Europe" that emerges from her work has fascinated people everywhere.

The vast majority of European Neolithic sculpture portrayed the female body. Thousands of figurines of women, some from as far back as 30,000 B.C., were initially considered erotic art. Gimbutas disputed that conclusion, arguing they were Goddess figures intended for worship.

Furthermore, she asserts, Goddess worshipers lived in a peaceful society:

There were no archeological findings of weapons, ramparts or defensive structures from 7000 to 3000 B.C. in southeast Europe or from 4500 B.C. to 2500 B.C. in western Europe.

"The absence of fortifications and weapons attests to the peaceful coexistence of this egalitarian civilization," writes Gimbutas. In villages chosen for their beautiful settings, rather than for defensive purposes, the Old Europeans built comfortable homes and temples.

Gimbutas's research shatters the Neolithic stereotype of uncivilized primitives. Old Europe had already discovered agriculture, domesticated animals and invented weaving, tools and pottery, she says. Sophisticated painting representing nature and honoring the Goddess covers the pottery that has survived. There was even a rudimentary form of script.

The controversial Gimbutas is not without critics. Some academics are skeptical. While admiring her knowledge and the extensive evidence she musters, they question both her assumptions and conclusions.

Gimbutas's response is that most archeologists want to focus very narrowly on their material. Terrified to draw conclusions, she says, they become passionless and unintuitive. What really bothers her critics, she concludes, is that her analysis incorporates a spiritual perspective, a major taboo in archeology.

Two distinguished men have come to her defense. Anthropologist Ashley Montagu called her recent work "a benchmark in the history of civilization and knowledge." The late Joseph Campbell, a friend in his latter years, compared her work to the deciphering of the Rosetta stone.

One of Gimbutas's most revolutionary assertions is that Old Europe, rather than ancient Greece and Rome, which came thousands of years later, is the genuine root of Western culture. "We are only beginning to discover our long alienation from our authentic European heritage—a nonviolent, earth-centered culture," she says.

The Patriarchy Revolution

By 4200 or 4300 B.C., the Goddess-worshiping society fell victim to massive aggression from the East. A mighty wave of warriors—Gimbutas calls them "Kurgans"—swept out of the grasslands of the Russian steppes and across Europe. On horseback and armed with swords, they had military superiority over the defenseless Old Europeans, whose homes, temples and civilization they destroyed. The last

Kurgan invasion, a holocaust of rape, pillage and destruction, occurred around 3000 B.C.

With the destruction of Old Europe, "Millennial traditions were truncated," writes Gimbutas, "towns and villages disintegrated, magnificent painted pottery vanished; as did shrines, frescoes, sculptures, symbols and script."

The contrast between Kurgan and European is aptly expressed in the title of Riane Eisler's *The Chalice and the Blade*. The Old European chalice, a feminine symbol, was usurped by the "lethal power of the blade," worshiped by the invaders.

"The power to take rather than give life," writes Eisler, "is the ultimate power to establish and enforce domination."

"The Kurgan ideology . . . exalted virile, heroic warrior gods of the shining and thunderous sky," writes Gimbutas. ". . . The dagger and battle-axe are dominant symbols of the Kurgans who . . . glorified the lethal power of the sharp blade."

The Kurgans reduced the Great Goddess, the Giver of all Life, to consort, love object or subjugated wife. In her place was a new pantheon of male war gods, often represented by their weapons. Warrior lords who rose to the top of this violent society were buried with their weapons.

"Weapons, weapons, weapons," says Marija Gimbutas. "It's just incredible how many thousands of pounds of these daggers and swords were found from the Bronze Age. This was a cruel period."

Weakened remnants of Old Europe were integrated into the new patriarchy, but eventually died out entirely.

"The fall of the Roman Empire, the Dark Ages, the Plague, World Wars I and II—all other times of seeming chaos . . . are dwarfed in comparison to what happened," writes Riane Eisler. After millennia of cultural and spiritual regression, there was a spark of humanism in ancient Greece. But, say Gimbutas and Eisler, that spark, from which the West traces its heritage, originated in Goddess-worshiping Old Europe.

Theology and the Goddess

Male domination was mightily reinforced by the Judeo-Christian heritage. When the ancient Hebrews reached the Middle East, they found a Goddess-worshiping culture in Canaan. As the Old Testament shows, they sought to replace her with their male God Yahweh (contradictory evidence shows the Hebrews also worshiped the female goddess Asherah, a form of the Great Goddess).

Riane Eisler suggests the battle between Yahweh and the Goddess is dramatized in the Garden of Eden. The Tree of Knowledge is a metaphor for the Goddess, as is the serpent, which sheds its skin to become an age-old symbol of rebirth and transformation. The aim of the Bible's writers is to subjugate the Goddess cults of Canaan to the new Hebrew God Yahweh. In so doing, they vilify women and the Great Goddess symbol—the serpent.

For millennia, the subjugation of women has been justified because Adam was supposedly created first. But, feminist scholars point out, there are two versions of the story in Genesis. In the first chapter (verses 26–31) Eve is created simultaneously with Adam. The second version, where Eve is created second, falls in Chapter 2 (verses 4–23).

Christianity fully matched the male dominance of Judaism. In retrospect, that is ironic, since feminists find little fault with Jesus Christ and since women played a key though often ignored role in the early Church (see Chapter 4). Early Christian literature offers many examples of women as activists, preachers and teachers. By the fourth century, however, the forces of male dominance had won out. The Church Fathers banned the Gnostic tradition, which had honored the feminine, deleted references to the female aspect of Divinity and barred women from leadership. Only men could be priests; only priests could mediate between humanity and God and deliver salvation. Goddess religion was branded as pagan, portrayed as evil and associated with the Devil. Feminine power was seen as threatening to the social order.

Virgins and Witches

A recent issue of *Time* magazine called Mary the Mother of Christ the most celebrated woman in history. Author Elinor Gadon goes a step further: "The Virgin Mary is the most venerated image in Western culture," she says. Yet it is a miracle her memory survived and a tribute to the age-old need to worship the Sacred Feminine.

When the fourth-century "Church Fathers" put together the "official" (canonical) version of the Christian Bible, it included few references to Mary the Mother of Jesus in the Gospels. Stories about Mary appear in the popular literature, the Apocrypha.

But Mary's revival centuries later in the Middle Ages gratified the long-suppressed need for the Goddess, her earth wisdom and healing powers. Around the 12th century, pilgrims and crusaders returning from Byzantium brought back the custom of venerating her. Tales about Mary were gathered together by the 12th century in the highly popularized *Golden Legend* by Jacobus de Varagine.

The zenith of the Virgin's power was in the 12th and 13th centuries. Between 1170 and 1270 in France alone, 80 cathedrals, including Chartres Cathedral, were built to Our Lady, *Notre Dame*.

"The Virgin gradually took on much of the Power of the Goddess," says Gadon. "Shrines and temples of the Goddess were rededicated to the Virgin." The great Gothic cathedrals were built on sites sacred to the Goddess, she adds. It made little difference to the average woman whether she prayed to the Goddess or the Virgin Mother. She offered "cakes and wine" to Mary just as she had to the Goddess.

But the Virgin posed a real problem for theologians. What were they supposed to do with her very physical womb and breasts, which, to complicate matters, were symbols of the Goddess whose memory they were still trying to eradicate? The only way around it was to acknowledge her motherhood while denying her any human sexuality whatsoever. Hence the Virgin Mother.

Many goddesses, including Venus, Ishtar, Astarte (who enjoyed many sexual encounters), were called "virgin," meaning whole unto herself, not under a male's control. Christianity, with its new emphasis on a spirituality devoid of the physical or sexual, totally reversed the accepted meaning by adding the notion of sexual virginity, thereby divorcing humanity—especially women—from sexuality.

"Her asexuality and virgin motherhood make it impossible for any woman to be virtuous, powerful and sexual at the same time," writes Gadon. The contrast between Mary the Virgin and Mary Magdalene, still vilified as a prostitute, her important role as a disciple ignored, sets up the false polarization between virgin and whore that inhibits women from experiencing their natural sexuality.

The cult of the Virgin was greatly influenced by the goddesses of antiquity: the Egyptian goddess **Isis,** who is portrayed nursing her son, Horus, was well known in pre-Christian Europe and may have been the precursor of the cult of the Black Virgin in France. The Greek goddess **Demeter** brings forth a child, Persephone. That daughter undergoes death, descent into the Underworld and resurrection. Mary is also associated with **Artemis**: she is said to have spent her last years at Artemis' shrine at Ephesus (in present-day Turkey), where she supposedly was assumed into heaven. At the Council of Ephesus in 431 she was proclaimed "Mother of God."

The Goddess was not denied in Christianity, or at least in Catholicism, but given a new name and stripped of her sexuality.

In *The Chalice and the Blade* Riane Eisler puts forth the disturbing notion that the veneration of Mary at its height in the 13th century was followed by a cyclical backlash against women, culminating in the holocaust of witchcraft trials, persecutions and executions that reached their apex in the 16th and 17th centuries. "Men's fear of their own attraction to women and carnality [was] projected onto the opposite sex," writes Gadon.

In the late 15th century Pope Innocent VIII declared witchcraft a heresy. In 1486 two Dominican friars published *Malleus Maleficarum*, or "Hammer of Witches," a handbook used for the next two and a half centuries. An estimated 9 million people, mostly women, were tortured and put to death for what Gadon calls the "constellation of beliefs and practices we have come to recognize as the way of the Goddess."

"The terror was indescribable," writes Starhawk. "Once denounced . . . a suspected Witch was arrested suddenly, without warning, and not allowed to return home again . . . every imaginable atrocity was practiced—the rack, the thumbscrew, 'boots' that broke bones in the legs, vicious beatings. . . . Witch hunters and informers were paid for convictions and many found it a profitable career."

It was open season on midwives, herbalists, old wisewomen, widows and spinsters. Starhawk adds to this list village beauties who rejected the advances of powerful men. A climate of absolute terror prevailed. Anyone slightly odd could be accused of being a witch. Once accused, she could be tortured, hanged or burned alive (strangled first, if lucky).

"In the Bishopric of Trier in Germany, two villages were left with only a single female inhabitant apiece after the Trials of 1585," writes Starhawk. In some villages, there were no women left alive.

The witchcraft trials in Salem, Massachusetts, in 1692 are generally believed to be the last gasp of the persecution.

The Virgin's Revival

By the 19th and 20th centuries, the witch burning that came before was nearly forgotten, and the veneration of the Virgin reached new theological heights. In 1854 Pope Pius IX proclaimed the "Immaculate Conception," meaning that the Virgin was herself "the only human creature preserved from taint of original sin," and had been "chosen for her role from the beginning of time."

In 1950 Pope Pius XII proclaimed that Mary had been taken up body and soul into heaven, which was then celebrated in the feast of the Assumption. A good artist is ahead of the times: back in 1518 Titian had painted the Virgin ascending bodily into heaven.

Before the Second Vatican Council, popes had proclaimed Mary Co-Redeemer with Christ, but at Vatican II (1962 to 1965), the Church stopped short of according Mary this almost coequal status with Jesus. "The great terror is that she will be worshiped above her son," says Marina Warner, author of *Alone of All Her Sex: The Myth and Cult of the Virgin Mary* (Random House).

Vatican II wanted to be sure Mary was seen as "subordinate to her Son" in Church teachings.

In 1992, however, the veneration of Mary is again on the rise:

• Millions of people, especially young ones, worship at her shrines.
• Sightings of the Virgin—from Denver, Colorado; Santa Ana, California; the Ukraine; Cuapa, Nicaragua; and Medjugorje, Yugoslavia—are on the rise.
• Pope John Paul II is said to believe the Virgin was responsible for the fall of communism and the upswing in religious belief in the former Soviet Union.

Concludes Sandra Schneiders, a professor at the Graduate Theological Union in Berkeley, "There has been a stupendous upsurge in goddess research and the feminine divinity as an antecedent to the male god. It's not unrelated that the Virgin Mary's popularity has also increased."

The Wisewoman

In the third millennium B.C. at Avebury in Great Britain, the Great Goddess was celebrated in a holiday for every season: Candlemas in early February; Beltane, a sort of May Day feast, in spring. The November festival of Samhain marked the beginning of winter, when the Goddess went underground. The Celts worshiped the Goddess in three aspects: Maiden, Mother, Crone.

The Crone is often represented as a witch, traditionally associated with a knowledge of herbs and health. But perhaps this third manifestation of the Goddess can speak to modern women better as the powerful archetype of the wisewoman. Past childbearing years, she possesses the experience and spiritual depth younger women lack.

The leadership to which women now aspire—in politics, the arts, business—*requires* the age, experience and maturity of the wisewoman.

A new generation of baby-boom women, 40 to 50 million of whom will enter menopause in the next two decades, will revitalize the image of the wisewoman, according to her the honor she has long deserved.

Women over 45 come face-to-face with stereotypes about age. What identity does a woman possess once youth and motherhood have passed? How does her sexuality change? How can she feel powerful when her 50-year-old husband has run off with a woman of 30?

The women who came of age during the past two decades survived these issues, redefined their identities and set an impressive precedent for future generations. But, except for the fortunate few, change has not come without the painful growth after divorce or the death of a spouse, job loss or illness. Survivors have intuitively called forth a great power from within that of the wisewoman.

Once invoked, the wisewoman initiates revolutionary change. Women—whose ex-husbands put them down for incompetence—run multimillion-dollar businesses. Women break taboos as if they were going out of style. To the shock of their adult children, they move in with old high school boyfriends or take lovers 10 years their junior.

These women, in some cases the mothers of baby boomers, prepared the ground psychologically for their daughters, who, with two-decade-long careers behind them, stand to capitalize on their dynamic maturity. This is the great gift from one generation of women to the next.

Better health care and physical fitness will also help women over 45 enjoy 25 more years of business and political leadership, grandparenthood, travel, second (and third) careers and meaningful contributions to society. A new generation of active women will be freer than ever to heartily embrace their middle and later years.

As the baby boomers enter maturity, an updated, more youthful wisewoman will become the most powerful archetype of the 1990's. **Television commercials already feature attractive silver-haired women riding motorcycles.** Busy with career and community, less

fearful of menopause, women will embrace the stage beyond motherhood with great enthusiasm. Out of the empty nest, where women of
earlier generations clung to an old, familiar role, an exuberant young
crone will fly, eager for the next adventurous stage of life.

The Test of the Wisewoman

Becoming the wisewoman is not an automatic proposition. It is
a life test, whose meaning is hinted at in mythology. The Eleusinian
Mysteries focus on Persephone's transformation from maiden to
queen of the Underworld. But in the same drama Demeter the mother
becomes a crone. **As mature writers and artists validate their own
journey to wisewomanhood, this** *rite de passage* **will be increasingly celebrated in film, literature and the arts.**

Demeter is of an age where her daughter is attractive to men.
Persephone will not be her "baby" much longer, the first nonphysical
hint of menopause. The myth says Persephone is "abducted" to the
Underworld. But in another version, she willingly leaves to explore
her sexuality. Either way, Demeter's days in the comfortable, loving
role of mother are numbered.

She roams the world over in search of Persephone.

"The mother seeks the maiden as her own earlier state, her
original being, her source," writes philosopher Beatrice Bruteau. "We
are all seeking our original virginal, i.e., . . . unitary or wholeself and
are saved when reunited with it."

But whom is she *really* seeking? Not her daughter, but herself.
She must get back in touch with her individuality, previously surren-
dered in part to become a mother. Self-knowledge, beyond the mother
role, is the prerequisite for the wisewoman.

Part of proving herself is defying the powerful male figure Zeus,
standing up to the patriarchy. There is no wisewoman who lives in fear
of father, husband, male god or authority figure. Women sometimes
charge that a male-dominated society keeps powerful older women in
their place by valuing only youthful beauty.

**If so, the status of the wisewoman can come only through
validating one's self and/or from other women.**

Female leadership today requires the archetype of the wisewoman, who grows beyond motherhood, who reintegrates with her

source of being, who has the courage of her convictions. The mature woman who judges herself powerful, competent, loving and beautiful is prepared to meet men on her own terms, as colleagues, competitors or lovers.

"Time and trouble will tame an advanced young woman," wrote Dorothy L. Sayers. "But an advanced old woman is uncontrollable by any earthly force."

A Question of Values

Since the 1960's, men and women have questioned and often rejected stereotypes based on gender. What is a "real" man? Do successful women sacrifice "feminine" values? Extrapolating from the individual to society, women ask: are "masculine" characteristics *overemphasized* in a male-dominated society? What would a society built on feminine values look like? Merlin Stone, author of *When God Was a Woman,* asks if there is a universal feminine principle. She remarks that, for many women, "feminine" suggests a *masculine* notion, incorporating submissiveness, of what a women should be: helpless, fragile, soft, selfless, delicate, etc. As Stone puts it, "almost the antithesis of the images we [women] strive toward."

Stone is, nevertheless, prepared to offer a list of "masculine" and "feminine" traits. In an age of growing respect for individuals, we should all approach such lists with skepticism. That said, Stone's lists are a useful point of departure, even if we agree that "masculine" and "feminine" traits are cultural stereotypes and that most people are a mix of both.

"Masculine" traits are said to be aggression, competitiveness, rational thought and behavior, wisdom, practicality, objectivity, protectiveness, heroism, goal orientation, courage, risk taking, linear thinking, creativity at the highest levels and the ability to plan and organize on a grand scale.

Women are said to be: passive, compassionate, nurturing, intuitive, cooperative, emotional, subjective, impractical, conciliatory, dependent, relationship oriented, sympathetic, empathetic, creative on the "lower" levels, that is, crafts and home decorating, capable of sensing natural cycles and flows.

Many women would reject passive, impractical and "lower level creativity" as negative, illustrative of a male concept of femininity or simply inaccurate. On the masculine list, few people find aggression, one of the male traits, very attractive. And many of us think competitiveness, especially in an interpersonal environment, is unhealthy.

In sum, there are positive traits on both lists. On the feminine list are the most important traits for human interaction. And although the masculine list appears outer-directed and success-oriented, many of the characteristics required at the very *top* levels of leadership appear on the female list. What leader can afford to sacrifice cooperation, fail at nurturing and supporting or ignore the flash of intuition where every piece of data comes together? An elite male leader named General Norman Schwarzkopf certainly did not.

The point is: *successful human beings possess a combination of masculine and feminine traits.* The most creative are a hybrid of supposedly conflicting characteristics: competitive and compassionate; goal-oriented and nurturing; intuitive and risk taking. Cardboard, one-dimensional females and males alike are doomed to failure.

Attributes and Evolution

Which sex best expresses the positive attributes of both sexes?

Women, we would argue, have absorbed positive masculine traits far more successfully than most men have integrated desirable female characteristics.

In defense of men, perhaps it is easier for women, who put their minds to it, to master outer-oriented male traits. Maybe the vulnerability men must sustain in order to experience healthy relationships is actually more difficult than, say, starting a successful business.

Furthermore, "feminine" characteristics have been devalued for so long, many men have had little incentive to integrate them until recently. For millennia, they have feared to be perceived as "effeminate."

Women, in developing their so-called masculine traits, are bringing out characteristics a male-dominated society validates. That makes it easier.

Even so, it is women who have evolved into a more complex state of wholeness.

How did that happen?

Did women first have to possess the *power* to declare "feminine" attributes worthy of emulation? Did women have to develop their "masculine" sides in order to see for themselves the value and importance of the feminine? Did women have to demonstrate strength of character, independence from the opposite sex, the ability to earn money, before anyone would listen to their praise for ecology, nonviolence or supportiveness?

Perhaps answers to questions like those will emerge in the 1990's.

Another interesting question is: now that many women have, to a great extent, achieved independence, economic sufficiency, more political power—that is, a range of traditional male benefits—will women now reject them? That might seem a stupid question to which the answer is an automatic "No!"

Not so fast. Sometimes the Goddess movement is so intent on advocating "feminine values," it appears to reject the ideal of a complete, balanced human being.

The constant litany of *strictly* "feminine" traits espoused in some Goddess books is enough to nauseate many thinking women. Most women would have a real problem with the "compassionate, emotional, nurturing mother" who begs for mercy for her son who has been arrested for dealing drugs now for the sixth time. Compassion, as valuable a trait as it is, is best exercised with a dose of objectivity.

It is reassuring to see that one contemporary painting of the Japanese Goddess Kannon, a version of the Mercy Goddess Kuan-yin, by contemporary Japanese-American artist Mayumi Oda, bears a sword—to "cut through the bullshit of compassion." Says the artist, "Sometimes we have to be ruthless in order to be compassionate, to have the wisdom to know what is right action."

Says Beatrice Bruteau, author of "The Unknown Goddess," an article in Shirley Nicholson's *The Goddess Re-awakening* (Quest Books), "If today's female archetype is to carry all of society forward," it must come laden with the richness of the male, "the fruits of rationality, intelligence and literacy."

Goddess mythology is reemerging in the late 20th century as the spiritual reflection of social change that has rapidly unfolded over the past 20 or 25 years. Millions of women all across the globe have expanded the bounds of their own evolution by growing into new roles previously occupied only by males. The result ought to be a reaffirmation of their feminine nature without a rejection of valuable skills once considered masculine.

Two Vancouver women, therapist Jean Napoli and screenwriter Donaleen Saul, have written a provocative critical piece about the Goddess movement, which they term "a nostalgic longing for a golden age."

"Let us be blunt," say the authors. "What the proponents of this interpretation of human history are really saying is that men are responsible for the horrific state of our planet and that if women had continued their rule, life would go on in peace and harmony."

The authors characterize the overly supportive atmosphere of Goddess gatherings as "let's never, never, never really challenge each other" women's groups. The Goddess the movement describes, they charge, possesses only positive qualities—"strength, beauty, fertility, love, harmony, peace."

"What about the dark side of the Goddess?" they ask. "Mother Earth isn't simply a huge saintly tit. . . . She is also terrifying and destructive . . . as awe-inspiring and chaotic as an erupting volcano."

The women in the Goddess movement, say the authors, deny or abstract these forces *within themselves* and "project them onto men," which may be simply a convenient way for women to avoid taking responsibility.

"To hide behind the skirts of the Goddess and take shots at our male-dominated culture, however cleverly cloaked in scholarly erudition, is childish in the extreme," they conclude. Male or female, we are part of the same collective unconscious. To reach maturity, we must contact both the creative and destructive forces within each of us.

"We need to acknowledge and liberate the energies of the witch-hunter, the murderer, the coward, the broken child, the starving lover, who reside *in us,* not simply whine and point the finger at the bastions of neurotic male authority. Such transformation demands everything of us—our bodies, hearts, spirits, our softness and our hardness. The Goddess will not do it for us."

They are right. There is no going back to the Neolithic Goddess Age. Until we make war and weapons obsolete, we cannot recapture the innocent time before they were created. We must push our evolution forward by *healing* the relationships between women and men, conservatives and leftists, abuser and abused, pro-choice and pro-life.

The task before us is to *create* a new culture where feminine values are celebrated alongside positive masculine traits. Old Europe had one dramatic and fatal flaw: the inability to defend its civilization. The right balance of masculine and feminine values brings the creativity to create and the courage to defend.

10.
Save the World:
Women as Social Activists

When humanity reaches out to those in need, the feminine values of caring and compassion are at work. As women embrace the goddess within, we are witnessing a renewed valuing of the environment, a rededication to the needy. Women are highly visible in the quest for justice and the search for solutions.

This chapter will highlight women activists, the goddesses and heroines of modern mythology. It will discuss many issues concerning women today, from world population to violence, from housing to grass-roots economic development.

When it comes to "saving the world," or a part of it, street by street, neighborhood by neighborhood, women are the catalysts through whom the critical mass for social change will be achieved.

At the grass roots of society, from the inner city to villages in the Third World, women are reasserting their power to change the world. In the United States they are the tenant managers and neighborhood-watch organizers. In the developing world they are taking control of their lives with family planning and creating economic independence through small businesses. Third World women hold the key to stabilizing population and fostering economic development. In the United States it will be women who break the chain of pregnancy, poverty, poor education and welfare that cripples the spirit of millions and threatens to disrupt the U.S. economy.

Though they *are* victims of domestic violence, rape, poverty, poor housing—or none at all—women are rejecting the victim role in favor of a more powerful assertion of activism. Indeed, the first to reach out to those who suffer child abuse, battering or rape are its former victims. Women like Brenda Muhammad, described on page 293, whose child was murdered on the inner city's mean streets, are transforming their outrage into organization—to prevent the horror from happening to others.

American women making charitable contributions increasingly insist they be earmarked to serve women—in shelters for battered women or programs to help pregnant teens finish high school. Social entrepreneurs like Mary Houghton, described on page 299, attract the investments of socially conscious people in the United States and abroad to invest in an inner-city Chicago neighborhood.

Women are trading in their old roles as underappreciated volunteers to serve as activists in African-American, Hispanic and Asian communities. They are also reinventing volunteering by compelling charitable organizations to offer people meaningful work and time schedules working people can handle.

This chapter will be far from comprehensive. Our focus is women, and we do not even begin to address the critical needs of children and teenagers, in large part because our scope is already wide enough to generate too many pages and chapters as it is. There are so many successful activists, it is impossible to describe more than a few, let alone record their good works.

What we will do, however, is attempt to introduce a new element to the discussion of issues by advocating a shift from discussing problems to emphasizing solutions. After describing the efforts of a host of women activists, we will approach the issue of "what works" in projects and programs aimed at social change. We shall propose six principles of effective change and then describe projects initiated by and for women with a view toward illustrating those principles. Finally we address volunteering.

From Defeatism to Action

The list of what is wrong assaults us each day: violence against the most vulnerable; human lives eked out in poverty; drug wars; incurable disease; the destruction of the earth's precious resources. If we are to solve these problems, we must of course hear about them. And the media is doing its job by telling us.

But constantly headlining what is wrong can also bring a demoralizing sense of helplessness and then numbing resignation. Most of us empathize with the suffering of others. But, since we are not sure *what* to do, and even less certain our efforts would bear fruit, we eventually block out that suffering; we forget. Life must go on, we tell ourselves.

Amartya Sen, a Harvard University professor who teaches economics and philosophy and is also involved in hunger issues, decries the "pessimism and defeatism" that characterize the discussion of poverty and hunger. "While pictures of misery and starvation arouse sympathy and pity across the world," he says, "it is often taken for granted that nothing much can be done to remedy these desperate situations."

Carolyn Long is vice president of InterAction, an association of 132 private voluntary organizations whose members range from the well-known Save the Children to the small, innovative Trickle Up program described on pages 314–315. "Our community can analyze problems and say what is needed," she says. "But underneath, there is often a feeling that the problems are too big to be solved."

What if we heard more about the successful efforts to transform our planet and the inspiring individuals, so many of them women, whose mission is to "save" one particular corner of the world—and the people in it? What if the emphasis were on role models, successful projects and principles of social transformation?

The result, we believe, would inspire people to act.

Women as Social Activists

When George Bush talked about "a thousand points of light—the people and institutions working together to solve problems in their own backyard," did he realize how many of them are women?

In 1985 **Oprah Winfrey** revealed on her TV show that she had been abused as a child. In 1991 she proposed the National Child Protection Act, which requires states to report convicted child abusers to a national registry, thereby preventing known abusers from moving from state to state to gain access to children. Child-care providers could check the backgrounds of prospective employees in the national registry.

Oprah's child abuse documentary *Scared Silent* ran on all three major networks and PBS simultaneously in September 1992, generating an unprecedented number of calls to the National Child Abuse hotline.

Washington, D.C., makeup artist **Kim Foley** decided to teach the tricks of her trade to children with disfiguring scars, burns and birth defects. Her first patient, Terrence Taylor, age six, had his entire face rebuilt with skin grafts. Half his body was covered with burns. But with makeup, he looked in the mirror and said he "looked normal for the first time." Working with both children and adults, Foley has touched up port-wine stains, cleft-palate defects and large scars. For the children who cannot afford makeup, she organized a benefit at a Georgetown restaurant and raised $7,000.

Dr. Cynthia James, a volunteer minister at an inner-city church in Oakland, mortgaged her home to purchase a local crack house, which the community renovated for emergency housing. James organized late-night marches to force drug dealers off the streets. Eighteen months later, four crack houses were closed, and drug activity dropped significantly.

The night **Pauline Hopkinson** was raped in her home, she vowed, "I will do something about this." She volunteered at the Fairfax Victim Assistance Network in Virginia. When she moved to Gaithersburg, Maryland, she went through a 40-hour volunteer training program at Sexual Assault Service (SAS). When a 1:30 A.M. call tells her a woman has been raped, Hopkinson is at the hospital to comfort, counsel, advise and provide clean clothing. Hopkinson received SAS's annual Outstanding Service Award in 1991. "I only have to read articles in the paper, and it gets me so angry that it's going on every day, still," she says. "I'd like to think I've helped one person, at least . . . that's what volunteering is all about."

Home in Saigon, **Theresa Do** taught kindergarten and French, but in the United States she found little demand for her skills. Experience taught her the obstacles Indochinese refugees faced in the United States. She knew that women often suffer even more than men. In 1983 she invited 100 women to the first Refugee Women's Association meeting; 99 showed up. Today Theresa Do's Refugee Women's Association in San Diego, with 400 members and a mailing list of 5,000, advocates human rights, self-sufficiency and mutual assistance among Indochinese women.

Says Margaret Iwanaga-Penrose, executive director of the Union of Pan Asian Communities, Do's association provides "recognition and visibility to refugee women, who then serve as models for other refugee women."

Winnie Kelly of Washington, Missouri, has taken in more than 200 foster children in 20 years. "The best thing to do is ask them what they like to eat," says Kelly. The kids arrive by way of the Division of Family Services, churches, the police and other foster parents. "When a kid comes here . . . [t]he first thing she does is hug them," says social worker Tamee Bruenderman. "Mrs. Kelly is the only one in the county we can call any day, any night. She doesn't say no."

Brenda Muhammad's son was shot in a dispute over his expensive jacket. In October 1990 she turned her grief into determination, founding Mothers of Murdered Sons (MOMS) in Atlanta. It has more than 600 members in Georgia and 3,000 nationwide. MOMS operates in Detroit, Boston and New York and is planning an L.A. chapter. "We need to bring attention to the problem of young blacks killing young blacks," she says. Before her son's murder, Muhammad was already involved in her community, as a business owner for 12 years. She watched the increase in violence with dismay. "I felt it could happen to anyone, including me. It did."

MOMS offers crisis intervention, support groups, counseling, tutoring, legal assistance and surrogate fathers. It refers people to mental-health centers where black psychologists volunteer.

Black-on-black violence is an epidemic as life-threatening as cancer or AIDS, MOMS declares, and the government should fund it accordingly, Muhammad says. "God has given me this mission," she adds. "The more people know, the more they will care. In your heart, you know you're making a difference."

Concerned about children with no place to go, **Elizabeth Flood** began an after-school program in her Newark 540-unit apartment building in 1978. In a space the building donated, she organized games, craft work and music. Flood's center now takes care of more than 250 children, ages 4 to 18. Older kids return to tutor youngsters. Flood organizes Easter egg hunts and Halloween parties.

After a lifetime of working with the poor, **Maria Varela** received a $305,000 grant from the MacArthur Foundation. Twenty years ago she came to northern New Mexico's Chama Valley and began working with sheepherders, weavers and housewives to create profitable businesses turning wool into yarn, clothes and rugs. "It is not enough to pray over an injustice or protest it or research it to death, you have to take concrete action to solve it," she says. "You have to stick with it for two generations at least to really change a culture," says Varela. "That's why we have a children's program to start training our future work force and leaders."

The money, which is intended for personal use, will come in handy, since her line of work does not provide retirement benefits. Some of the grant went to pay bills. Varela, her husband and their daughter live in a trailer—without running water. "I am going to be a community organizer for as long as I can," she says. "Then I am going to go retire, preferably somewhere warm by the sea."

"The police can't do it all," says **Tonda Brown,** manager of the 810-unit Kent Village Apartments in Prince Georges County, Maryland, once filled with open-air drug markets. Brown organized 70 residents to walk the complex with two-way radios and report drug activity. "We, the management and the residents, decided that we were going to start fighting the battle ourselves," she says. Now pedestrians and schoolchildren can safely walk the streets. A banner reads: "We, the residents of Kent Village Apartments, are taking back our community from drugs."

Dr. Mimi Silbert founded San Francisco–based Delancey Street, the world-acclaimed, and arguably the most effective, rehabilitation and training center for hard-core criminals. Silbert, a criminologist who interned as a prison psychologist, says, "It was clear to me that this system of punishment doesn't work."

Beginning with four drug addicts in 1971, she and John Maher, her colleague and partner who is now deceased, began what has become a $3 million-a-year self-supporting enterprise with 500 residents at the San Francisco center and another 500 in three cities with Delancey Street centers. Ten thousand have been through the two-year program, learning at least three marketable skills and earning a high school equivalency certificate.

The average resident is from "four or five generations of poverty and two or three generations of prison." These people have both committed and been themselves the victims of violent crimes. But at Delancey Street, where behavior rules are obviously extremely strict, they gradually learn to take responsibility, to be self-reliant and to care about themselves and fellow residents.

Silbert's next project: a training institute to teach others to replicate the Delancey Street model.

"Sister, Can You Spare a Dime?" Asks a *Business Week* Headline

Hell, yes, and more. Women increasingly want their contributions to help other women—battered wives, unwed teens, displaced homemakers. The National Network of Women's Funds counts 48 funds that focus giving programs on women and girls. Together they raised $15.4 million in 1992 (not counting contributions from private foundations and wealthy individuals or families). Most of these women's funds simply did not exist 10 years ago (many were created in the mid-1980's), but by 1991 their combined endowments totaled nearly $35.6 million. In 1992 women's funds awarded $8.5 million to programs for women and girls. The network expects women's funds to grow substantially in the next decade.

"Historically, men always gave to organizations controlled by men," says Terry Person, executive director of the Boston Women's Fund. "Women are starting to do the same."

Philadelphia's Women's Way recently gave $62,000 to a local rape-crisis center. Part of the funds were collected through the city's payroll-deduction program, an innovation women's funds in other cities should investigate.

In 1986 Swanee Hunt, who gives some $1 million a year to women's causes, helped start the Women's Foundation of Colorado, which funds many programs that help women. The foundation's *first-year* goal was $1 million in pledges: it raised $2 million. By 1992 it had raised half of its long-term goal of $10 million.

Some fund-raisers complain that while many professional women give generously, others still leave it up to their husbands. "We have to educate women to see themselves as philanthropists," says Jane B. Ransom, president of Women & Foundations.

Women's Funds, available from Washington, D.C.'s National Committee for Responsive Philanthropy, describes 60 funds dedicated to raising money for women's and girls' organizations and projects.

Women as Environmentalists

In 1990 legislators from 42 countries called for a "global Marshall Plan," in which industrial countries would help developing countries grow without destroying the environment. Vice President Al Gore, then a senator, organized the three-day meeting. Attiya Inayatullah, then a member of Pakistan's Parliament, said she left with a new global vision: "In the 20th century, the issues are democracy and security; in the 21st century, they are going to be the environment and sustainable development."

That vision is already being actualized. In November 1991 the Global Assembly of Women and the Environment brought together women from all over the world to hear 218 success stories from women at the grass-roots level throughout the developing world about what they had done in their local communities to clean up the environment. Most of these women had never before been outside their countries. Said one participant, "These are ordinary women with extraordinary perceptions of problems."

Good News About the Environment

"More things are going right than people realize," writes Linda Starke in *Signs of Hope* (Oxford University Press), a catalog of *positive* environmental actions between 1987 and 1990. Starke's good news headlines include:

- Southern California's comprehensive proposal to clean up the air.
- The Montreal accord to halve production of chemicals that harm the ozone layer.
- Suspension of commercial logging permits by Brazil and Thailand.
- Danish subsidies to farmers who convert to organic farming.
- The international treaty controlling the movement of hazardous wastes.
- The world's first "carbon tax" on fossil fuels in the Netherlands.

"I have tried to pull together as much as I could of the scattered good news, to give people a feeling of movement," says Starke, who says 1989 was the year things turned around. She previously edited the World Watch Institute's "State of the World" reports.

The Green Belt Movement

The world's most prominent environmentalist is arguably Dr. Wangari Maathai, the Kenyan woman who got people hooked on planting trees. Fifteen years ago, Dr. Maathai, a biologist who studied in the United States, started the Green Belt Movement, which plants "belts" of trees in open spaces, near schools and along the roadside. Its long-term objective is to stop soil erosion, protect water systems and replenish firewood and building supplies.

Green Belt projects are 99 percent women-run. The most important thing, says Maathai, is for women to be independent, to acquire knowledge and techniques and to become empowered. The movement's 50,000 women and children have planted 10 million trees, created 1,500 nurseries and provided seedlings to 38,000 households.

Wangari Maathai's international support is profound: when the Kenyan government tried to crush her protest over plans to build a high-rise party headquarters in Nairobi's Uhuru Park, a beautiful recreational area, an international uproar resulted, and the World Bank withdrew funding.

In 1991 Dr. Maathai was the joint recipient of the 1991 Africa Prize for Leadership, a $50,000 award by the Hunger Project, a nonprofit organization with more than 6.2 million members in 152 countries. It is dedicated to creating a "wave of commitment" to end hunger and is headed by a woman, global executive director Joan Holmes.

From Problems to Principles

The female cry of compassion also demands concrete results. Successful programs share common approaches or principles, which, when integrated into other projects, increase the chances of, though do not guarantee, a better outcome. What, then, are the *guiding principles* of successful social change?

No one really knows, because, for the most part, those principles are unelucidated. They are so hidden and so invisibly welded to successful case studies that no one has yet identified and extricated them, let alone shared such valuable information with the world at large.

Author Tom Peters did it for business in the best-selling *In Search of Excellence* (HarperCollins). When he told people that successful companies "Stick to the Knitting," he was putting forth a useful, though not infallible, guideline: the companies that stuck to their basic business instead of diversifying into a far-flung list of wild new ideas usually won.

We do not have the answers (and are hardly experts in economic and social development), but as researchers/generalists, we should like to propose several possible principles of success, expressed in the "From/To" format of *Megatrends:*

From win/lose to win/win
From top-down to grass-roots
From "politically correct" to what works
From educational bureaucracy to choice
From victims to advocates
From government to government aid to investing in entrepreneurs

We are not attempting to impose these notions on activists who are in the trenches doing the job every day. What we are trying to say is, "Here is another way of looking at it: what ideas does that give you?" If you, as an activist, have discovered more effective principles, splendid; we should certainly like to hear about them.

From Win/Lose to Win/Win

In classic capitalistic terms, money is supposed to make more money. In a "zero sum" theory of economics, if you win, someone else has to lose. Gaming houses and state lotteries operate on this principle.

Financial capital plays a key role in social transformation, but notions of win-lose and "making money is the name of the game" are giving way to "win-win" ideas like social investing and social entrepreneurship.

The Social Entrepreneur

There is "a new breed of entrepreneur," says Peter Drucker, "whose goal is to identify a social cause, cultivate an opportunity, and turn it into a profit." It is a radical notion for hair-shirt types: one can create social change and make money, too. But these examples illustrate that by turning a need into a profitable opportunity, one can very effectively serve people.

Carol Bateson converted her concern about asbestos in schools into Dec-Tam Corp., an Andover, Massachusetts, asbestos-removal business. Says CEO Bateson, "When we walk away from a school knowing that we have cleaned out all the asbestos and that the children are safe, I just plain feel good about what we do."

Dec-Tam employs 100 people and 1991 annual sales were $19 million. Bateson creates an environment that rewards people for doing "a tough job right." Known as a pioneer in an industry that offers few perks, Dec-Tam puts more than 35 percent of revenue in protective employee gear. The company operates in the Northeast and is licensed to work all down the Eastern Seaboard.

Yvonne Scruggs-Leftwich, a former investment banker, created the United States' first nondepository bank, designed for low-income people who usually do not use banks. "I decided to create a business to serve the people," she says. Customers cash checks, wire money, buy money orders and pay bills in cash. "Instead of a social problem," she says, "I saw an opportunity for me to make money." After her first center in Buffalo turned a profit, she opened two more in New York State.

Mary Houghton, president of Chicago's Shorebank Corporation, says banks can be "socially responsible and financially sound." In 1973 Houghton and three colleagues raised capital from "socially conscious" investors to buy the failing South Shore Bank and make it the first U.S. commercial bank devoted to community revival.

Today the bank operates in five neighborhoods, boasts $213 million in assets and a 10 percent annual growth rate. Half its assets come from about 16,000 local depositors. The rest is from some 2,500 individuals from all 50 states and 16 foreign countries. How do they attract these "social investors"? By being able to tell them exactly what their money is *doing*—for example, buying a building to fix up and rent to low-income families.

"Rather than siphon deposits out of a poor neighborhood and invest them in more prosperous areas for a better return," says Houghton, the bank generates deposits "for reinvestment right here in the community."

South Shore is a prototype for other social entrepreneurs: Brooklyn's Community Capital, modeled on South Shore, opened in 1990. South Shore also inspired Vermont's Socially Responsible Banking Fund, part of the Vermont National Bank in Brattleboro. Elk Horn Bank in Arkadelphia, Arkansas, was developed by a management team from South Shore.

President Clinton "considers South Shore Bank a model for his proposed nationwide network of 100 community-development banks," reported *USA Today*. As governor of Arkansas, he was influential in setting up the Elk Horn Bank.

Social investing is great for the heart; but how does it affect the pocketbook? South Shore's repayment rate is a stunning 98 percent on $190 million in loans—most of which were considered risky.

Lisa Conte, a woman in her 30's, raised more than $10 million from traditional venture-capital firms to launch Shaman Pharmaceuticals in California, a "socially responsible" environmentally based drug company. She works with the world's leading botanists to find rain-forest plants that tribal shamans have used for healing. Conte buys the plants—which provides income to the people of the rain forest—imports them, extracts the medicine and introduces new drugs to the marketplace. One reason investors have supported her company: she has a track record for getting fast approvals from the usually slow-moving FDA.

From Top-Down to Grass-Roots

Local initiatives, independent of top-down government assistance or even outside philanthropy, develop strong, secure roots. Self-sufficient programs will not wither if a state budget is slashed, or if a funding source shifts priorities.

Gleaners

TOUCH IT. TAKE IT. NO LIMIT, reads the sign at Gleaners supermarket for the needy in Las Vegas. Shocked by how much good food markets threw away, Celeste Tate persuaded a store manager to donate expired items. She and David McKinley set up shop in a garage in 1982.

The Las Vegas store is now in a warehouse, and 20,000 people a month pay about two dollars for a cart of groceries. It is set up exactly like a grocery store. Shoppers take carts down the aisles of fresh, frozen and canned food or into the bakery section.

Las Vegas Gleaners gets most of its food from casinos, but the Youngstown store really gleans from Ohio fields. Most food comes from wholesalers, grocery stores, caterers and military commissaries. Most shoppers are elderly people on fixed incomes and single moms.

Today there are 194 stores based on the Gleaners model in the United States, Great Britain, Australia, Holland and China.

If you want to start a store, you can learn how in a two-week program in Las Vegas. The Department of Health and Human Services recently called Gleaners the most outstanding food program in the United States.

From Free Speech to Free Vouchers

In Berkeley, California, some 30 stores sell vouchers for food, bus fare or laundry that can be given to homeless people and redeemed at 15 outlets, such as the Berkeley Emergency Food Project, which sells dinners for 25 cents. Wendy Georges, who has run the Food Project for eight years, says it has definitely increased the number of diners. The plan, called Berkeley Cares, is staffed in part by student volunteers.

SHARE

The Self-Help Association for a Regional Economy (SHARE) in Great Barrington, Massachusetts, persuades local people to put their savings to work helping entrepreneurs. SHARE collects passbooks from local banks and offers them as collateral for loans of up to $3,000. Sue Sellew expanded her organic goat-cheese business, and knitter Bonnie Nordoff was able to lower costs by purchasing wool yarn in bulk. In addition to repaying the loan, entrepreneurs must create a business that provides jobs or fosters regional self-sufficiency.

From "Politically Correct" to What Works

Effective solutions come from community groups, churches, even (believe it or not) the U.S. government. What matters is whether they work. The programs described below are in the critical area of tenant management and affordable housing and all receive federal funds.

Grass-Roots Housing

Women's Development Corporation (WDC), a nonprofit Rhode Island group, began in 1979 when women architects from New York and Boston decided to use their talents to help low-income mothers get housing. Founders Alma Felix Green and Susan Aitcheson chose Providence because it was a midsize city without a low-income developer.

When Cheryl Leary moved her six children into a WDC apartment in Providence's Indian Village, she celebrated windows that close properly and not paying 80 percent of her income for a place where the ceiling was caving in.

WDC develops, designs, finances, builds and manages housing for low-income mothers. They combine funding from federal, state, local and private sources. By 1992 WDC had $13 million in real estate, including 200 new or renovated units, and was building 100 more.

Beyond Welfare

"It is our experience that most women don't want to be on welfare, that they want to work," says Mary Nelson, president of Chicago's Bethal New Life, a community group that builds housing as part of a welfare-to-work project.

Tenant Nora Bryant, mother of three, has been on and off welfare for 15 years. She always wanted to work, she says, but didn't have day care or transportation. Now she will operate a day-care business out of her home in West Garfield Park, where the group plans 50 more homes, half of which will be used for day care. Her day-care income will finance payments on the town house and support her children.

Nora was "paying $375 a month for a basement, a dank, dark hovel, where there's raw sewage coming out of the walls," says Mary Nelson. "Can you imagine emerging from there every day . . . what that does to her own self-esteem? Moving into a brand-new beautiful home changes her whole image and her own sense of confidence and her kids' future."

Washington, D.C., Showcase Is Model Project

Kimi Gray and fellow tenants at Washington, D.C.'s Kenilworth-Parkside housing project won national acclaim for getting rid of drug dealers, sending 600 kids to college and revitalizing an area where 85 percent of families were once on welfare.

Twenty years ago, when Gray took over the residents' council, the project was often without heat and hot water. Crime rates were among the highest in D.C. Gray figured she and the residents could run the project better than the housing authority. "We couldn't do any worse," she says. Ten years ago, after nine months of training, Gray and her staff took over the 464-unit property. Kenilworth-Parkside is *the* prime example of tenant management. "There's a Kimi Gray in every neighborhood," says Gray. "They just haven't been brought out."

The resident-management movement is exploding. More than 1,300 groups attended the 1991 conference of the National Association of Resident Management Corporations; 17 U.S. public-housing projects are managed by tenants. Some 200 tenant groups are involved in dual management or training to run projects.

From Educational Bureaucracy to Choice

Polly Williams, a black Democratic state representative in Wisconsin, is on the cutting edge of revolutionary reform in American education—and education is Everywoman's *cause célèbre*. Beyond nurturing a child's basic needs, what is more important to a mother than seeing that her child is well educated?

In 1990 Williams pushed through legislation creating the nation's first experiment introducing market mechanisms to education through vouchers. That September 385 low-income students in Milwaukee used vouchers worth $2,446, paid for by the public-school budget, to transfer to private, nonsectarian schools. The education establishment challenged the legality of the Milwaukee school-choice system in the courts. "All of this is happening because 385 students left the system and threatened their cozy setup," said Polly Williams.

"If public schools want to keep students, that's fine," she says. "Just educate them. If the schools can't do that—and in my hometown of Milwaukee that seems to be the case—then let's get as many hostages out of there as we can. Let them choose better schools."

The Milwaukee program involved just one percent of students. Families of four had to earn less than $23,000 to qualify. Ten of the city's 20 private schools agreed to participate and to accept any student who applied, regardless of academic or disciplinary records.

Choice is a bipartisan issue, says Michelle Easton, former director of the Center for Choice in the U.S. Department of Education. "The best example is the Milwaukee parental-choice program, where conservative Governor Tommy Thompson joined with Jesse Jackson Democrat Polly Williams," she said.

Indianapolis

In the fall of 1991 Indianapolis's Golden Rule Insurance Company committed $1.2 million to provide private education for 500 low-income students in inner-city schools. Golden Rule pays half of private-school tuition, parents the other half.

The 500 slots were immediately filled. Golden Rule increased its support to 764 students, and the waiting list grows. Other firms, including Eli Lilly Company, and individuals are contributing to the fund, too. The Michigan-based Vandenburg Foundation is planning similar programs in Grand Rapids and Detroit.

J. Patrick Rooney, chairman of Golden Rule Insurance, says it is not abandoning the public schools but challenging them. "If inner-city students do better when they are empowered to choose their own schools, then public education funds should be redirected to parents," he told the *Wall Street Journal.* "When all families, no matter how poor, have the freedom to walk away from bad schools, competition will force the public schools to improve."

Sylvester Turner, a black state legislator from Houston, says poor and minority parents favor choice more than anyone else, since they see competition as "the only way to secure a quality education for their children."

"I see choice emerging as a major civil rights issue in the 1990's," says Clint Bolick, director of the Landmark Center for Civil Rights of the Landmark Legal Foundation. "There's tremendous pent-up re-sentment among low-income people in the inner city who recognize that education is the only means to escape poverty, and see absolutely no hope of achieving educational opportunities in the current struc-ture."

Polly Williams, who supports the Indianapolis Golden Rule pro-gram, says choice in education is "coming no matter how much the bureaucracy tries to stop it," adding, "if legislatures won't allow choice, then maybe corporate America can support it and shame the politicians into letting my people go."

Schools Don't Work Because They Are Monopolies

The idea that monopolies are inefficient is widely understood. Why have we not seen more clearly that public schools are monopo-lies, too? By definition, they are inefficient, destined to remain so until we allow competition. Monopolies are essentially socialist institu-tions—centrally directed and managed systems with no competition or market incentives. Much like factories in the former Soviet Union.

Some individual public schools compete with individual private schools, but the public-school system has no competition. You buy the product—public education—or you don't. You don't get to buy it in 10 different varieties.

In the '90's a revolution is getting under way that will challenge those monopolies, creating more change than at any time in the history of U.S. education. And that revolution can be summarized in one word: "choice." Every student should have the freedom to choose whatever school she or he wants to attend. The schools, for their part, compete to get students to choose their school.

Choice is even beginning to win over the education establishment. New Milford, Connecticut, superintendent Stephen C. Tracy says he has "opposed ideas like this for most of my 20 years in public education." Now he wants to give choice a chance. "I am convinced that the absence of choice . . . explains the incredible resistance that public education has exhibited toward reform," he says. "As long as parents and taxpayers have no alternative, the system will prefer the status quo to the rigors of improvement. It is no longer a question of better teachers, new programs or more money. It is a question of the system itself."

The choice movement mushrooming in the United States *is* nothing short of a revolution. Not the well-meaning measures of merit pay, team teaching and magnet schools, but turning the system upside down: shifting from schools run by school boards and administrators to schools run by the demands of the marketplace.

"Choice is not a system-preserving reform," say John Chubb and Terry Moe, two of its best-known advocates. "It is a revolutionary reform that introduces a new system of public education."

Choice would stop giving money to school systems and start compelling schools to *earn* money by attracting students with "scholarships"—vouchers, certificates or entitlements, roughly equal to what is now spent on each student.

Under broad guidelines, organizations or educational entrepreneurs could set up and run schools. Entrepreneurial teachers who know their field best could create schools, instituting change from the bottom up. It would open up education to for-profit corporations—*if* they can do a better job educating young people.

Schools would compete primarily on the basis of quality, but subject emphasis would play a key role, too. Come to our school: we emphasize science. Our school specializes in computers. We emphasize the arts and literature. Come to our school; we focus on learning how to learn.

There is strong public support for choice. In the 1991 Gallup–Phi Delta Kappa Poll 63 percent of Americans supported allowing parents and students to choose which public schools students should

attend. Extending choice to private schools has strong support, too—
50 percent favored the government paying for each student and allowing parents to send the student to any public, private or parochial
school; 39 percent opposed. Support rose by 6 percentage points over
the result in the same poll in 1987.

Choice is not completely unknown territory. As a result of ex-
periments across the nation, we are amassing a database about how
it works. Furthermore, the most successful education experiment in
U.S. history was a choice system: the post–World War II G.I. Bill,
which catapulted a whole generation into the world of higher education, laying the groundwork for the booming postwar period.

**In March 1992 Polly Williams and the students and parents
won against the education establishment when the Wisconsin
Supreme Court declared that the nation's first education-choice
program that includes private schools was constitutional.**

From Victims to Advocates: Violence Against Women

The reality of violence against women is horrifying: 25 percent of U.S.
women will be victims of domestic violence at some time in their lives.
Half of female murder victims are killed by boyfriends, husbands or
ex-husbands, says the Federal Bureau of Investigation. Every state in
the United States requires doctors to report cases of child abuse, yet
not one requires domestic violence cases to be reported.

"There is an epidemic of violence against women," says Kathy
Spillar, national coordinator of the Fund for the Feminist Majority.
"Well over half of all 911 calls are calls of violence against women."
A 1992 study by the Crime Victims Research and Treatment Center
(described more fully below) concludes that most rape victims—61
percent—were attacked before age 17.

Violence against women is our primary focus here, but we must
acknowledge the intrinsic violence in the sexual abuse of children.
Experts in child abuse estimate one third of children are sexually
abused by the age of 18. The National Committee for the Prevention
of Child Abuse says more than 2.7 million children are abused each
year, though it does not know how many are raped.

Heidi Vanderbilt, the author of an exhaustive, graphic landmark
report on incest published in the February 1992 issue of *Lear's,* defines
incest as "any sexual abuse of a child by a relative or other person in
a position of trust and authority over the child."

Incest is about the betrayal of trust, says Vanderbilt, who quotes psychiatrist Judith Lewis Herman, author of *Father-Daughter Incest* (Harvard University Press), as asserting that it is "always inevitably destructive to the child."

Women fortunate enough to be untouched by this violence and abuse may be naive enough to think (or hope) it has been overstated. Its victims know better.

Is the pain, betrayal, violation and injustice of this violence a "fact of life" that women and their daughters must live with? Or is it possible that women and supportive men can act purposefully to raise consciousness and *isolate from future victims* those sick enough to use physical strength or perverse threats to violate women? So women will be safe. So these men can learn to comprehend their actions and maybe even learn to heal themselves.

Former NOW president Eleanor Smeal, founder and president of the Fund for the Feminist Majority, told *USA Today*, "Everybody keeps talking about the problem; let's start talking about the solution." We shall do that. But first we must cite some horrible statistics. Doing so cannot help the suffering victims have known, but it can raise consciousness about the extent of violence, and that is the first step toward addressing solutions.

Domestic Violence

Domestic violence is a woman's number one health risk, according to the office of the Surgeon General. A woman experiences domestic violence every 13 seconds. In addition, domestic violence is more common than automobile accidents, muggings and rapes combined.

More than 2 million women *report* assaults by their male partners every year, according to the American Medical Association. But, says a 1992 report in the *Journal of the American Medical Association*, more than 4 million U.S. women are severely assaulted each year. Every day four women are beaten to death. Battering inflicts more injuries on women than auto accidents, muggings and rapes combined.

"One of the most common things that physicians have done when patients have reported domestic violence has been to offer them Valium," says Nancy K. Sugg, a clinical assistant professor of medicine at the University of Washington, co-author of the 1992 report. "That is not an appropriate response."

Says M. Roy Schwartz, senior vice president for medical education and science at the AMA, one third of women entering an emergency room have been abused, and almost one-quarter of pregnant women seeking prenatal care have experienced domestic violence. The AMA now advises doctors to ask female patients about domestic violence.

"For too long, wife battering has been thought of as a private matter," says Sally Goldfarb of the National Organization for Women's Legal Defense Fund. "In fact, it's a public health problem of epidemic proportions."

Rape

In April 1992 the U.S. Department of Justice announced that 207,610 women were raped in 1991. Just days later, the Crime Victims Research and Treatment Center released its own report: 683,000 women forcibly raped per year, three times the Justice Department figures. As noted, the Crime Victims Center study said more than half of rape victims are children and girls.

The study's coauthor, Dean Kilpatrick, a nationally known expert on rape, says the study is the only one to "look at rape over a lifetime." Conducted over a three-year period, the study involved 4,008 adult women and 370 rape-crisis agencies.

The Justice Department's widely circulated, chilling and often quoted statistic—that a woman is raped every six minutes—is completely out of date. According to these latest figures, at least one woman is raped every minute. The Justice Department estimates that just 14 percent of rapes are reported to the police.

The Structure of Aggression

Experts and activists alike have attempted to figure out the root cause of violence against women. Theories range from a violent society to anger at mothers to unemployment to a backlash against women's increased freedom. Eventually one realizes there are as many "reasons" for violence as there are violent acts.

But one simple explanation cannot be ignored: rape and domestic violence are the direct result of male aggression. Any solution to the brutal reality of violence against women must begin with an analysis of how society deals with aggression.

Society is structured to safeguard its members from the aggression of other, "less social," harmful beings. You walk down the street, and someone takes your wallet and punches you in the face. If you can find the criminal and have witnesses, the justice system will probably rule in your favor.

But if a woman is beaten up by her husband or raped by a fellow college student, the batterer and rapist will probably get off. Domestic violence and acquaintance rape happen within the confines of the private spheres of the home or a personal relationship. Most rapes (between 60 and 85 percent) are "acquaintance" rapes. So far society has been ambivalent about "getting involved." The legacy of sexism is such that property rights are stronger than a woman's right to safety as a private individual. (Even when a woman is raped by a violent stranger, the evidence that he brutally raped five other victims may not be allowed.)

But for the aggressive individual the private domain of relationship offers an easy, available target for the killer instinct he is unwilling or unable to subdue. That is the ultimate reason why the tendency to "blame the victim" is sexist and unjust. It violates both human rights and the basic social contract.

So long as society fails to punish aggression and to protect its victims, it colludes with the perpetrator and "enables" women to be victimized.

Empowering the Survivor

Following are five areas for the development of solutions to what has rightly been called the epidemic of violence against women. They share one underlying theme—their objective is to empower the victim/survivor.

1. New Laws and Tougher Enforcement

Assaulters must be treated severely. Studies show that if society treats domestic violence as a serious matter, the perpetrator is a lot likelier to get the message. As Eleanor Smeal said in *USA Today,* there should be "mandatory arrests—first time." She adds, "It would be more likely that it's the only time, if he is arrested right then."

A shockingly low *one* percent of rapists are convicted. Women must utilize their political power to change the laws that let rapists go free, including introducing evidence of past offenses. Senator Joseph Biden (D-Del.) has introduced legislation to double the federal penalties for rape, making it a hate crime that would permit victims to sue and authorize $300 million for local law-enforcement officials to combat sex crimes. Known as the Violence Against Women Act, it was reintroduced into both houses of Congress. Thirteen states have already passed laws providing victims with a bill of rights.

2. Self-Defense

Women are confronting both fear and the physical superiority of their attackers when they learn effective ways to defend themselves; in so doing, they are refusing to follow the old, victimizing advice of many law enforcement officials—that fighting back can endanger a woman's life. Not if you know how.

Washington, D.C.'s extraordinarily successful three-year-old IMPACT/Model Mugging program ought to be replicated in every major U.S. city. Its strength is creating realistic, physically threatening situations and instructing women in the most effective and reliable strategies for surviving them.

Founded by karate expert Matt Thomas, who studied police reports to learn how rapists and muggers attack women, the course has male instructors, wearing 40 pounds of heavily padded gear, "attack" the women—and the women, instructed that their legs are five times stronger than their arms, learn to kick the assailants' most vulnerable spots—eyes, chin, groin, knees and feet. The padding is to protect *the male teachers* as the women get in touch with their anger and really fight back with full force.

After some 20 or 40 years of being socialized not to be aggressive—even in order to defend themselves—graduates have learned a lesson and accessed a new power that they can draw on to survive.

As of winter 1991, 50 graduates of the course were subsequently attacked—37 of them knocked out their attackers within five seconds. Eleven escaped without knocking out the assailant and two chose not to fight because their assailants had weapons.

The program operates in California, Boston, New York and Kansas City under the national names IMPACT Self-Defense or Model Mugging. A London chapter is planned.

The self-defense trend is related to women's learning to use the energies of the physical body in sports. Chapter 2 describes trainer Stephanie LaMotta, who teaches private clients boxing. When

LaMotta herself was attacked by a mugger, she punched his solar plexus and knocked him out cold with a jab to the jaw.

After Shelley Reecher was attacked by four men, she gave up running—which she really loved—out of a paralyzing fear. That is, until she got Jake, a Doberman pinscher trained as a personal-protection dog. Today she operates Project Safe Run, which lends trained dogs to women to run or walk with.

"They are not attack dogs," says Reecher, who owns 39 dogs in the Northwest and took her project nationwide in 1992. "They just match aggression with aggression."

3. The Feminization of Law Enforcement

A campaign led by Brazil's Council for Women's Rights convinced the government to establish 30 all-female police stations, "to provide a sympathetic atmosphere for victims of rape, battering and incest," writes Lori Heise in "Crimes of Gender," an article in *World Watch,* a publication of the World Watch Institute.

It is something "developed" countries like the United States should consider. Women make up about 10 percent of police officers. That means the law enforcement is still 90 percent male. There should be a lot more women in the justice system, says Eleanor Smeal, who makes the case for affirmative action in hiring more women as police officers, district attorneys and judges.

There are about 2,000 shelters for battered women, says the National Coalition Against Domestic Violence. Shockingly, that is not enough. Women activists uniformly demand that shelter space increase.

4. Learning from the Arts

Do the arts have a role in social activism? Wasn't it playwright Moss Hart who cynically said, "Got a message? Call Western Union." Too much message makes for neither good art nor social change. But why shouldn't artists and activists collaborate to educate while entertaining? Ultimately, Hart was wrong. Great art raises social issues while inducing emotional catharsis.

Performing *Please Listen to Me* is a therapeutic experience for the cast of formerly battered women who have started new lives. Written by Angela M. Lockhart, a drug-program coordinator with a theater degree, it draws on the women's actual experiences. Audiences include social workers and probation officers. One scene reenacts the denial of a woman who lied about her injuries until she went blind in one eye. After one performance two women asked where they could get help.

Minneapolis's award-winning *Illusion Theatre* is a collaboration between actors and human-service professionals. The theater's repertoire includes "Touch" for elementary-school children, aimed at preventing sexual abuse, "No Easy Answers," about sexual abuse prevention for teenagers, addressing rape and incest, and "Family," about preventing interpersonal violence. "Both Sides Now" examines sexual harassment. One million people in 50 states have attended.

5. Attract More Men to the Antiviolence Movement

More men must be recruited to the movement to end violence against women. Look at the service male instructors in IMPACT render female self-defense students. More than one has been knocked out cold for the sake of teaching women to survive. Good men understand how to harness aggression positively in business, sports or even in battle. It is the duty of healthy, well-balanced men to make abusers pariahs in male society. Men can use peer pressure on other men who never learned the schoolyard admonition to "pick on someone your own size."

The participation of healthy men may even shed light on the shocking relationship between spectator sports and violence. Shelters for battered women report the days after the Super Bowl are some of the busiest of the year. "Men get psyched up and macho," says Margaret Caven, executive director of the St. Louis Abused Women's Support Project. "This creates an atmosphere where there's less inhibition against expressing aggression against women."

Take the strange case of the 27-bed battered-women center near Philadelphia. In 12 years, it has been empty for only one month—the one after the Phillies won the World Series.

Violence in the Third World

The next section describes the crucial role of Third World women in economic and social development. Yet few would deny that they confront violence even more brutal than American women endure. To cite only some of the outrages: thousands of Bosnian women have been raped by Serbs; brides have been murdered in India for their dowries; China is notorious for the infanticide of baby girls; in parts of Asia and the Middle East, raped women have been murdered by family members, writes Lori Heise, "to cleanse the family honor."

African women have vowed to stop the most widespread, systematic and horrifying violence women face, the unspeakable atrocity of genital mutilation, which is practiced in much of Africa, including Egypt and in part of the Arabian Peninsula. Euphemistically called "female circumcision," it is pure butchery—cutting and removing all or part of the clitoris and sometimes the labia. This is the price a girl must pay to be considered suitable for marriage.

Women in 20 African countries are affiliated with the Addis Ababa– and Geneva-based Inter African Committee, whose objective is the prevention and eradication of all female genital mutilation. The group's education campaigns and seminars alert the general public, midwives and practitioners of traditional medicine to the excessively damaging medical impact and sheer inhumanity of mutilation. African women have demanded that all governments outlaw the practice. Women the world over stand ready to support them in every way possible.

From Government to Government Aid to Investing in Entrepreneurs: Women in the Third World

Big, top-down government programs, from the Great Society to some overseas development projects, do not have a great track record. Too often they showcase flashy projects or encourage corruption. By fostering dependency on outside assistance, they destroy initiative, instead of empowering people to achieve self-reliance. United States aid programs look a lot like socialism: for 40 years American aid has supported central economic planning for developing countries, the approach that brought the collapse of the Soviet Union.

If the U.S. believes in capitalism, why does it not devote more resources to entrepreneurs in poor communities at home and abroad?

Instead it is increasingly small private agencies such as the Trickle Up Program, profiled below, that foster economic development based on entrepreneurship. Why not funnel more government money to small groups with track records of success instead of into big bureaucratic projects?

Real prosperity comes from the organic growth of community-based entrepreneurs—farmers, craftswomen, small businesspeople. This decentralized, micro approach is smaller in scale and takes time to reach large numbers of people, but it is economically realistic, and for those it reaches, it starts bearing fruit relatively quickly.

Women and Global Economic Development

The critical role women play in Third World economic development cannot be underestimated:

- Worldwide, women are the sole breadwinners in one in three households.
- Seventy percent of small businesses are run by women.
- Women produce 80 percent of the food in Africa, 60 percent in Asia and 40 percent in Latin America.

India's Self-Employed Women's Association (SEWA) Bank offers credit to poor, self-employed women working as weavers, garment workers, embroiderers and domestics. Loans to women who would be considered "questionable credit risks" resulted in an extraordinary 96 percent repayment rate. The SEWA Bank has about $1 million in working capital and 25,000 savings accounts. The bank provides legal aid, productivity training, social security and child care to its members.

Bangladesh's 15-year-old **Grameen Bank,** one of the most successful projects in global economic development, loans $6 million a month and serves 700,000 villagers with loans averaging about $67. It boasts a startling 98 percent repayment rate. What few know about this "success story" is that **90 percent of borrowers are women.**

The Foundation for International Community Assistance (FINCA), a nonprofit private voluntary organization, creates revolving loan funds—village banks—in poor communities. As individuals repay loans and build enterprises, they build self-help, self-sufficiency and self-worth. FINCA has made loans to more than 35,000 families.

The most dependable, productive and creative members of impoverished societies are women, FINCA has found. Women's entrepreneurial potential is one of the least-utilized resources in development programs today, the group believes. For that reason it is increasingly directing loans and training toward women.

The Trickle Up Program specializes in making grants to the world's poorest people. Its aim: to make them small-time entrepreneurs. By 1991 Trickle Up had made grants to 120,000 people in 90 countries and helped start some 19,000 businesses. **Women make up nearly two thirds of entrepreneurs.**

Glen and Mildred Robbins Leet, a collaborative couple, founded Trickle Up and ran it out of their New York apartment for the first 10 years. They believe the major cause of poverty is unemployment. That might initially sound obvious, but how many overseas development programs focus on the job-creation principle?

Trickle Up tries to create jobs and economic growth by encouraging unemployed people to invest skills, ingenuity and "sweat equity" into small businesses. When five or more people agree to invest at least 1,000 hours of their time, they can apply for a Trickle Up grant of U.S. $100, paid in two $50 installments. They agree to save or reinvest at least 20 percent of its initial profit.

Grace Mbakwa of Tugi, Cameroon, is the proprietor of Aniyen Fashions, which creates clothing from traditional village textiles. She used her $100 grant to lease a sewing machine, rent a market stall, advertise, collect orders and purchase materials.

If all the world's underemployed people could start a business, Trickle Up calculates, the value of the time they invest (at 40 cents per hour) would exceed the total official development aid within one decade. So low are its costs, so practical its approach, Trickle Up asserts, that were its methods adopted on a grand scale, it would be possible to end poverty worldwide by the year 2000.

Agricultural training in Africa is directed at men, even though women grow 80 percent of Africa's food. **Dr. Esther Afua Ocloo,** managing director of Nkulenu Industries, Ghana's first indigenous food processor and exporter, is devoted to changing that. Entrepreneur, industrialist and philanthropist, Dr. Ocloo trains thousands of women in food preservation and creates opportunities for women through credit.

"I can assure you that if the right environment and incentives were created for *women farmers,* and the problems facing them now were addressed, the sustainable end of hunger would be a reality," she said, accepting the Hunger Project's 1990 Africa Prize for Leadership, which annually honors a distinguished African who has exhibited exceptional leadership in bringing about the sustainable end of hunger.

A 15-year veteran of the World Bank, **Nancy Barry** now heads Women's World Banking, (WWB), which backs commercial bank loans averaging $200 to women entrepreneurs. Founded in 1980 by a worldwide group of 20 women, including Dr. Ocloo, its first chairwoman, and Michaela Walsh, its founding president, WWB now has 50 affiliates in 40 countries. In eight months Barry won promises of $12 million in new capital and project support, as much as was raised during WWB's first 10 years. Barry's latest project: linking women in six Latin American countries with Italian clothing and leather makers.

Women: The Key to Stabilizing World Populations

That women are the key to stabilizing population growth is axiomatic. Yet few focus on that critical aspect. Indeed, most have a sense of helplessness about confronting the issue of world population. We have come to accept the Doomsday scenario on world population, which goes something like this: the 1990 population of 5.3 billion will double in 39 years, then *more* than double again to reach 27 billion by the end of the 21st century. Many accept that projection.

Not Dr. Sharon L. Camp, senior vice president of Population Action International, formerly Population Crisis Committee, a nonprofit group in Washington, D.C.

She says population *can* stabilize at 9 or 10 billion in the 21st century, if birth control is universally available by the year 2000. "We have what it would take, the financial resources and the know-how to solve the problem . . . in our children's lifetime," she says.

The key is contraception. As soon as 70 percent of sexually active women use birth control, average family size will drop to about two children early next century. To achieve that end, annual family-planning expenditures mostly funded by the developed world must reach $11 billion by the year 2000. Funds would go to education and contraceptives. It might sound expensive, but it would cost on average only $16 per couple per year—very cost-effective.

Says Dr. Malcolm Potts, president of Family Health International, a nonprofit organization, "This . . . gives people a businesslike plan to work on, instead of just throwing up our hands and saying this is too hard a problem."

Homing In on the Crisis

Population is stable in most of the developed world. In 29 countries, including the United States, Canada, Europe, Japan, Taiwan, Singapore, Hong Kong, South Korea, New Zealand, Australia, as well as a few countries in Eastern Europe, families average two children. In an additional 41 countries with almost *half the world's population,* it is almost under control: more than 60 percent of couples use contraceptives, and families average less than three children.

Population experts know exactly where to direct their efforts: 97 percent of world population growth will occur in Africa, Asia and Latin America. Since 1950 the developing world has grown from 1.7 billion to 4.1 billion. By 2000 it will approach 5 billion, out of a world population of 6.26 billion.

But the developing world is too large for generalizations; some countries are more successful than others. In Mexico, for example, the percentage of couples on birth control increased from 13 percent in 1973 to 53 percent in 1987 (one assumes it has increased since, but 1987 is the last year for which Population Action International has figures).

If women bore only the number of children they desired, says the United Nations Population Fund, births would decrease by one quarter in Africa and by about one third in Asia and Latin America. Educating women is critical: poorly educated women in Brazil average 6.5 children; those with secondary education average 2.5 children. In Liberia, women who have attended secondary school are 10 times *more* likely to practice family planning than women with no education.

Today family planning is beginning to reduce fertility rates, even in Asia and Africa:

- In 15 years family size in Thailand decreased from 6.5 to 3.5 children. Thailand's fertility rate stands at 2.2 percent.
- In Indonesia contraceptive use has increased from 19 percent of couples in 1976 to 50 percent in 1992.
- In Zimbabwe, 43 percent of couples use contraceptives—one of the highest percentages on the African continent.

Population in Africa

There is long-standing consensus that the most difficult area in terms of population is Africa. Statistics tell the story:

- In Africa 77 percent of couples *who do not want any more children* nevertheless do *not* practice contraception. (In Asia it is 57 percent and in Latin America 43 percent.) Only about half of women in developing countries have access to family planning.

- In 1990 women in 40 sub-Saharan African countries had 5.8 to 8.3 children.
- The contraception rate is less than 6 percent in Cameroon.

But now most African women want smaller families, and 42 governments provide direct support for family planning. Six more offer indirect support. As noted, Zimbabwe has a relatively high rate of contraceptive use. So has Mauritius. Birthrates are declining in Ghana, Botswana and Kenya.

The United Nations estimate of the cost to achieve a stable world population is about the same as Population Action International's— the UN says $9 billion a year by 2000, about twice the $4.5 billion now spent annually.

But population control also demands creativity and input from local women, along with money. In that department, the Dominican Republic takes the prize.

Beauty salons in Santo Domingo are among the few places where women gather privately outside the home—and therefore are an ideal location for family planning. Beauticians are trained in family planning and reproduction. Since 1988 almost 200 beauticians have provided more than 5,000 women with contraceptives. Maria Estella Guzman Suazo says her customers "are happy to come here for their birth-control pills. It's convenient and more private than going to see the doctor."

In the poorest countries, where hair salons are few, and in the cities, women's markets and other female-dominated institutions exist. Alternative delivery of family-planning services to women is still a real possibility.

In Zimbabwe, bicycle-riding women involved in family planning make house calls on women and their families in the countryside.

Lima, Peru's Asociación Desarrollo de la Mujer provides women with leadership training, business skills and credit and family-planning services all at the same center (it gives new meaning to one-stop shopping). The organization's motto, voiced by former director Gabriella Canepa, is "There are three things that women need—self-esteem, economic power and reproductive freedom."

Similarly, women in Egypt, India, Kenya, Mali, Mexico and Senegal get family-planning and business-skills training through projects started by the alumni of the Centre for Development and Population Activities in Washington, D.C.

The Media's Role in Family Planning

In the mid-1970's the Peruvian soap opera *Simplemente María* transformed viewers' behavior. The heroine, Maria, migrates to Lima to work as a maid for a wealthy family. Because of her expertise with a Singer sewing machine, she breaks out of poverty and climbs the socioeconomic ladder. Young women signed up for sewing classes in droves, and sales of Singer machines soared. The same thing happened when the soap ran in other Latin countries.

If the soaps can do this much for sewing machines, what can they do for family planning?

This is what population experts began asking themselves. There are 2 billion radios in the world, roughly one for every three people, and growing numbers of TVs. In places where most people cannot read, TV and radio soap operas, popular music and phone-in talk shows can teach family planning.

- A Mexican soap opera brought thousands of people to family-planning clinics.
- In Nigeria family-planning themes were part of a TV drama series.
- In Egypt TV dramas offered family-planning information.
- In Turkey 55 percent of adult TV viewers watched a special family-planning series.
- In 1986 Johns Hopkins University Population Communication Services turned to popular music to get its message across.
- Mexican singer Tatiana encourages young people to "Wait." Her songs are number-one hits in Mexico.
- Nigerian singer Onyeka Onwenu also sings about sex and responsibility.
- Philippine singer Lea Salonga, who later starred in *Miss Saigon,* sings about family planning. Her songs and videos with the Menudo singers top the Filipino hit parade.

Dr. Phyllis T. Piotrow, director of the Center for Communication Programs at Johns Hopkins School of Hygiene and Public Health, says communication about public health must follow the "four P's"—personal, popular, pervasive and persuasive.

The first international conference on Entertainment for Social Change was held in California in 1989. Almost 200 people from entertainment, health, family planning and the media from 30 countries shared ideas about linking entertainment and education.

Reinventing Volunteering

Traditionally, America's housewives were the backbone of organizations seeking justice in an unjust world. In the '50's, '60's, even into the '70's, women from all income groups put volunteering high on their list of priorities. But as women joined the work force, volunteering suffered. The "me generation" took the blame: selfish yuppies, even women, were out to take care of "number one."

Perhaps there was a bit of truth to it: women starting out in the business world of the 1970's had to prove their competence. Many say they had to work twice as hard as male colleagues. Family, marriage and friendship suffered, too. Devotion to career, for a time, became the exclusive relationship.

But in the 1990's the desire to contribute has reemerged at home and in the office. Women are concerned about a long list of issues, and working women are confident enough on the job to embrace a new priority—service. Young women peer out from Esprit ads declaring how they would change the world.

New Volunteers

But the desire to serve often must accommodate a full-time work (or school) schedule. Organizations that rely on volunteers must reinvent themselves to fit the needs of a new breed of women.

The new volunteer wants flexibility: "There is no such thing as a typical volunteer," says Richard F. Schubert, president and chief executive officer of the Points of Light Foundation in Washington, D.C. "Service agencies are responding to this by providing flexible times and events for after-hours service."

Meeting times must change, too, says Judy Maggrett, executive director of the General Federation of Women's Clubs. "It's not reasonable to have a meeting in the middle of the day. Women are working."

Volunteer opportunities must change because the majority of volunteers are working people, says Susanne Favretto, formerly with the National Volunteer Center in Arlington, Virginia, which is now part of the Points of Light Foundation. "Volunteers are working people . . . volunteering after hours, 6 till 9 P.M., and weekend volunteering has become a big thing. . . . A lot of volunteers are working women, but men are also catching up."

The new volunteer wants meaningful work: "The new volunteer is less willing to type letters, stuff envelopes and lick stamps," says Leigh Wintz, former executive director of the General Federation of Women's Clubs.

"People want to feel that they are addressing the problems they see every day," says Favretto. "To address the real issues that surround them on the way to work each day, like homelessness."

The new volunteer wants opportunity to build skills or make contacts: Volunteers are looking to gain new skills or practice old ones. "Volunteering builds skills, provides leadership training and opportunities to network," says Maggrett. "It's an advantage for the résumé."

Nancy Lukitsch, a principal at the management-consulting firm McKinsey and Company, would probably agree. A board member of the March of Dimes since 1986, she says board membership can be profitable—she gained a client as a result.

The ranks of the new volunteer include yuppies, school kids, corporate types, seniors and socialites-turned-activists.

"There is a developing sense among youth that there are significant problems that need to be solved in American society and that they need to put their idealism into practice," says Ira Harkavy, director of community partnerships at the University of Pennsylvania. "And there is a growing interest in universities in how their studies may be linked to service—how they can put their minds to helping solve the most pressing problems of their times."

About two thirds of university and college campuses in the United States have community service offices. In 1992, 140,000 students in more than 300 schools gave of their time each week to work on community service projects.

When the Campus Outreach Opportunity League held its first national conference on community service in 1983, 30 people attended. In 1992, 2,000 people came to the conference.

New York Cares

Harvard Law graduate Suzette Brooks and some old college chums got together to start New York Cares, a clearinghouse that schedules volunteer work to fit the hectic careers of bankers, lawyers and executives. "We began in reaction against the slick benefits that we'd all gotten invited to 50 million times," she says.

Brooks's new breed of volunteer was in great demand. "Most of the traditional volunteers they see are teenagers, housewives or retired people," she says. "We can't give the time those groups give, but the quality of our time is, well, excellent."

New York Cares's more than 3,000 volunteers have worked in homeless shelters, welfare hotels, soup kitchens and in more than 200 agencies. Some volunteer every six months, others twice a week. "Volunteering has become desirable, or finally acceptable," says Brooks. "There are a lot of young professionals who feel they are focusing much too much on themselves, their career . . . their clients. They want to give something."

Not to Be Outdone by New Yorkers: D.C. Cares

"We're trying to make volunteering accessible," says Jeffrey Keitelman, a lawyer who modeled **D.C. Cares** after the New York group. It helps working people schedule volunteer time "to build homes for the homeless, deliver meals to the elderly, comfort AIDS patients, cuddle boarder babies or tutor children." It has attracted 2,500 volunteers at more than 70 agencies.

Washington, D.C., held its first "friend-raising" telethon and volunteer fair in July 1991; 5,000 people signed up for community-service jobs.

Reinventing the Junior League

The ranks of the new volunteers include women of limited means and heiresses who are committed to action. Both are making a difference. Susan Gatten, former president of the San Francisco Junior League, transformed its objective from socializing to AIDS activism. "I'm not the Eleanor Roosevelt or Florence Nightingale type," says Gatten, "but I couldn't just stand by and watch. I decided to do what I do best—organize and educate."

Missy Staples Thompson, the Peavey grain heiress, resigned

from the Minneapolis Junior League and the Symphony Orchestra Board to start a company helping low-income families finance homes. In the Hispanic section of St. Paul, she buys and renovates boarded-up town houses.

"Everybody has to do something, whether you have time or money or know-how or space," says former First Lady Barbara Bush. "Today you can no longer say, 'The drug problem worries me' or 'Crime worries me' or 'Illiteracy worries me.' If it worries you, then you've got to do something about it."

Corporate Volunteers

To encourage employees to volunteer, the San Francisco head-quarters of Esprit de Corps will match donated volunteer time with up to 10 hours off a month. "In the '80's we gave our employees French lessons, sent them on river trips—all those personal things," says Susie Tompkins, co-founder and creative director of Esprit. "Now we're giving them character-building opportunities."

Esprit's advertising addresses social issues, rather than clothes. "The wave of the '90's is to do good things," says Tompkins.

Doing well by doing good is becoming more popular in corporate America. Some companies have volunteer departments with their own budgets and staffs. Others permit volunteering on company time.

- NCNB Corporation urges employees to take paid time to tutor in the schools, work in food lines or help out during state emergencies.
- Every other Thursday about 25 employees of the Hard Rock Cafe in New Orleans come in early to make 200 lunches for the homeless.
- After three years at Wells Fargo Bank, any employee can apply for a six-month leave to work for a nonprofit organization.

Corporations gave $5.9 billion worth of charitable gifts, 1.9 percent of pretax profits, to charities in 1990, a mediocre showing. Companies that are good public citizens contribute 5 percent—and exceptional firms give 10 percent.

In the Schools

At Chadwick School, a prestigious private school in Southern California, 95 percent of the 290 high school students participate in the school's voluntary community program. Students average one to one and one half volunteer hours each week.

"At Somerset Elementary School in Chevy Chase, Maryland, kindergartners play bingo with senior citizens, the first graders help the homeless and second graders are setting up a recycling center," says a *Washingtonian* magazine story. The Maryland State Board of Education considered making 75 hours of community service a requirement for high school graduation.

Seniors

Forty-one percent of people over 60 volunteered within the past year; one fourth would like to give more time, according to a study by Marriot Senior Living Services and the U.S. Administration on Aging. An added 37 percent said they would consider volunteering if asked.

"The most important thing is to provide an opportunity for seniors to use their talents," says Ann Helgeland, director of the Davidson County Retired Senior Volunteer Program in Tennessee.

The proportion of volunteers over the age of 65 increased from 8 percent in 1974 to almost 13 percent in 1989.

Delma Dockett, an 80-plus great-great-grandmother, teaches children the Mexican hat dance at the Capital Children's Museum in Washington, D.C. Dockett took up volunteering almost 20 years ago, after her husband died. Until then, she says, she hadn't given much thought to it. She also works for Meals on Wheels.

Elizabeth Dole, former secretary of both transportation and labor, is the first woman to head the Red Cross since founder Clara Barton. She oversees 2,700 chapters, a $1 billion budget, a staff of 23,000 and 1.1 million volunteers. "Volunteers . . . are the heart and soul of the Red Cross," says Dole, "and the best way I can let volunteers know of their importance is to be one of them. . . . Therefore, during my first year as president, I will accept no salary."

Of all the chapters in this book, this is the most awesome in scope, the most difficult to get a handle on. Knowing full well that we cannot treat this subject adequately, we have, nevertheless, tried to address certain objectives. They are:

1. Shift the discussion from dramatizing the world's problems to collecting information about solutions.

Many dedicated people believe the only way to raise consciousness, money and political support is by dramatizing the horror of their cause, thereby illustrating how worthy it is of people's support. The experts who help in fund-raising reinforce the syndrome again and again. As a result, the people who are doing the most good in the world are using negative energy to fuel their efforts.

Furthermore, when well-meaning charities constantly resort to picturing starving children in Africa, for example, it gives a distorted view of the continent in the West, minimizing its great culture and the important work the African people have achieved in solving problems on their own.

So long as the world's activists, tireless and pure-hearted though they are, keep focusing on problems, they will never evolve the database that will identify what works and put "Save the World" groups out of business.

We all know it will take money and commitment to solve the world's problems. But we need another element, too—good information. There are lots of studies. But when solutions are found, they are buried under analytical descriptions of problems. We actually need more than information; we need high-level intelligence—data that has been interpreted and finely honed into *knowledge*.

2. Isolate some principles that work in many, though not all, situations.

As noted earlier, author Tom Peters did just that for the business community.

An *In Search of*-type study of successful strategies in human rights, homeless advocacy, grass-roots and international development and other social issues would be a provocative, educational and perhaps inspiring way to show people what works and keep them from making the same mistake twice. As one friend often says, "To hell with the old mistakes, I want to make *new* mistakes."

3. Emphasize empowerment.

Everyone agrees social transformation must empower people to become independent, rather than encourage dependence.

The call of compassion must be tempered with the desire for concrete results. This holds special importance for women. The desire to comfort, feed and nurture a baby is whole and complete unto itself. When you are dealing with adults and refuse to treat them like children, it is a different matter. What supports people is to help them access their own power. Otherwise, one is not changing the world but mounting a relief effort, which is valuable indeed, but meant to remain in effect for a limited time. Long-term social transformation is an organic process; it is about power, self-reliance and prosperity.

The women described in this chapter work under difficult circumstances, yet find the love within to recommit themselves day after day. That love often comes from the people they are serving and the reward of having made a difference in people's lives. May their example inspire us to join them—or at least support them with our political, economic and emotional power.

11.
Women
in the New World Order

There has been more dramatic change in the world in the last three years than any of us has otherwise experienced in a lifetime.

The collapse of communism, the rise of the Pacific Rim and the revolution in telecommunications have turned the world upside down, and a New World Order is indeed emerging. The old arrangements are behind us; the new arrangements are just being formed. The old postwar order was two superpowers, each with an array of countries grouped around them, while nonaligned countries played one superpower off against the other. That changed with the emergence of Gorbachev, the collapse of communism and the worldwide cooperative response to the aggression of Saddam Hussein in the Persian Gulf.

The new relationship between the United States and Russia takes the spotlight off nuclear weapons, espionage and military adventurism, arenas where men typically dominate. That sets the stage for more women to assume political power as they have in Scandinavia and Northern Europe and will soon in North America.

The New World Order is a creative association of democratic states—all over the world. The global spread of democracy from Poland to Taiwan and even in Romania and South Korea could hardly have been imagined just a few years ago.

The United States is now the lone superpower in the New World Order, but it must act cooperatively with other major powers: the summits of the Group of Seven—the United States, Britain, Ger-

many, Japan, France, Italy and Canada—have replaced the importance of the two superpower summits of the old world order, and they
will increasingly work with all the democracies of the world.

The shared values of the New World Order have become clear:
multiparty democracy, freedom of choice, free trade, privatization
and prosperity based on the marketplace. Only a few places, like
North Korea and Burma, have not yet embraced these now almost
universal values, but in time they will.

This run to democracy around the world opens more doors for
women to participate in governance and politics. The politics in Eastern Europe have already brought several key women to positions of
leadership. In the mature democracies of Scandinavia, which long ago
abandoned military adventurism, women's political equality is well
established.

Around the world the list of female presidents and prime ministers grows, a welcome spur to U.S. women, who are the first to
concede that, for an "advanced" country that prides itself on "equality," the United States is hardly setting the pace for women in political
leadership. That honor goes to northern Europe. Even as the order
and relationships of countries undergo profound change, the older
democracies are setting the new directions.

- The world's first popularly elected female head of state is Vigdis
  Finnbogadottir, president of Iceland since 1980. Divorced with
  an adopted daughter, she is the only single mother to lead a
  nation. Extraordinarily popular, she won the last election with 95
  percent of the vote. Iceland is run by four people: the president,
  the prime minister, the president of the parliament and the chief
  justice. Three of the four are women.
- Edith Cresson, who held several ministerial posts in François
  Mitterrand's Socialist government, became France's first woman
  prime minister in 1991.
- Prime Minister Gro Harlem Brundtland is back in power for the
  third time in Norway, "the world's most feminized democracy."
  Eight members of PM Brundtland's 18-member Cabinet are
  women. She gained international stature chairing the UN's Commission on the Environment and Development and faces fall
  1993 elections.
- But Finland is giving Norway a lot of competition. In 1991
  Finnish women won 40 percent of the seats in the Parliament,
  and a woman is expected to be elected president soon.

- In Sweden, often overshadowed by the female power of its neighbors, 38 percent of parliament seats are held by women, a critical mass by any measure and downright revolutionary next to the U.S. Congress's 10 percent (in 1993).
- And how about Margaret Thatcher, who, though out of office since 1991, is not letting us forget her role in reshaping Britain.
- Archconservative Thatcher must have watched in dismay as ultraliberal Mary Robinson was elected Ireland's president in what amounted to a political earthquake.

Conventional wisdom holds women have to be more conservative, more militant, than men to attain and hold power—the Indira Gandhi/Golda Meir profile. Some dismissed Margaret Thatcher as reflecting that old mold. Now the mold is shattering. If anything, the spotlight is on women who are somewhat left of center.

France

When President Mitterrand appointed Edith Cresson prime minister, he called her the most qualified person to lead France through the new challenges of single-market Europe. On her first day in office Cresson's boss was not disappointed. The prime minister laid out an impressive agenda: 1) confront Japan's economic challenge; 2) upgrade France's economy to match Germany's, thereby achieving a new balance of economic power in Europe. Her time as prime minister was short of one year. She resigned in the spring of 1992 after the Socialists lost badly in the regional elections. Cresson had served as Mitterrand's minister for European affairs, but quit in October 1990 to work in private industry. Earlier she served as minister of agriculture and of trade. In 1975 she was the first woman admitted to the all-male Socialist party executive committee. As prime minister, her job was to oversee France's domestic affairs and its vast government bureaucracy.

The Cresson appointment was aimed to enhance the Socialists' standing with France's 20 million women voters—who constitute the majority, 53 percent, of the electorate. Despite their numbers, women hold only 6 percent of the seats in the National Assembly.

Cresson is the epitome of Gallic competence and self-confidence. She comes across as a woman who knows herself well: although a very sharp dresser, she is no fashion slave. She has developed a personal style—which includes being a bit outspoken—and is not about to change it. Nor is she about to be intimidated by anyone, least of all Japanese males. Regardless of one's trade policy—and Mme. Cresson is too protectionist for our taste—one has to delight in how she stands up to the Japanese. Any woman who has endured the chauvinism of Japanese businessmen must feel a vicarious thrill watching Edith Cresson give those guys a taste of their own medicine.

"Sometimes I feel men are being condescending, but that amuses rather than irritates me," says Cresson, who says she is "not a feminist in the normal sense [whatever that means]. Men," she concludes, "are only irreplaceable in one area—one's private life."

The New Ireland Welcomes Mrs. Thatcher's Antithesis

"Ireland is a country whose time has come. There is a new energy—new self-confidence. . . . We're making our mark internationally in industry, the Arts and Sport," read a campaign poster for Mary Robinson, feminist lawyer with a Harvard master's degree. "And, in a country on the move, the weak and the vulnerable tend to be left behind—forgotten. That's why we need a President who stands up for justice for all . . . something I have been doing all my working life."

On that simple, articulate platform Mary Robinson won 52.8 percent of the vote, to become Ireland's first woman president. Her stunning victory came through tireless campaigning, not much money and a tangible level of integrity.

Ireland's oddsmakers gave Robinson 100 to 1. Ireland's main political party, Fianna Fáil, outspent her 10 to 1. But Robinson campaigned for six months; her opponents were on the road for less than two. "Robinson visited every city, town and village of any significance in Ireland up to three times." Even in a time of "modern image politics," concluded *The Financial Times,* "there is no substitute for old-fashioned campaigning."

In conservative, Roman Catholic and politically male-dominated Ireland, Robinson spoke out in favor of women's rights and liberalization of laws against contraception, divorce and homosexuality. To the shock of traditional politicians, people listened.

She attributes her success to the women of Ireland; "instead of rocking the cradle," she says, they "rocked the system." *The Financial Times* agrees. Most of all, the prestigious paper concludes, it was "a victory for Irish women."

The president has no political power and is required to stay out of politics. But Robinson, says *New York Times* columnist Anthony

Lewis, leads "by force of character" and "achieves popular moral leadership." He describes her as "phenomenally successful," with an 80 percent approval rating.

In November 1992 Irish women won 20 of the 165 seats available in the Irish parliament, the Dail, up from 13 in the last legislature. "The jump to the Big 20 represents a huge psychological boost in one of the most male-dominated professions," said Mary Cummings in *The Irish Times.*

"Women in all parties point to the election of Mary Robinson as president in 1990 as the catalyst for the surge of women in politics," wrote James Claity in *The New York Times.*

Those Norwegian Women

If you question Norway's status as "the most feminized democracy in the world," consider this: not only are the prime minister and almost half the cabinet female, **the country's three major political parties are all run by women:**

- Prime Minister Gro Brundtland led the Labor party for more than 10 years.
- Kaci Kullmann Five is the head of the Conservative party.
- Anne Enger Lahnstein leads the agrarian Center party.

To put it another way, the top three politicians in Norway are mothers. They have four, two and three children, respectively.

The idea that women must take part fully and equally in politics is widespread in Norway. Dr. Brundtland (she is a Harvard-trained physician) and her Labor party adopted a rule almost a decade ago requiring that "no fewer than 40 percent and no more than 60 percent of its candidates must be women." Other parties followed. Notice that we haven't seen the Democrats or the Republicans suggesting such a system. With all the women in politics in Norway, there is today little political debate over questions of sexual equality.

After a recent television debate regarding Norway and the European Community (Norway is not a member) in which Prime Minister Brundtland appeared with Mrs. Lahnstein and Mrs. Five, political researcher Bernt Aardal said, "You no longer think: these are three women talking. Where are the men?" He also noticed that "they all call each other by the first name. The men would never have been so informal." It was another case of women integrating their personal values into the previously male-dominated arena they were changing.

In the last election the Conservatives tried to gain from the fact that Gro Brundtland's husband, Arne Olav, had once been a member of their party.

"Do as Gro did," they said. "Choose a Conservative." Dr. Brundtland's quick response: "Do as Arne Olav did," she said. "Choose Gro."

Until Finland caught up, Norway had the largest proportion of women in politics of any democracy: 59 of its 165 members of parliament are women.

The Fabulous Finns

In Finland, the 1991 election, which threw out the Social Democratic party after 25 years, gave 40 percent of the seats in the parliament to women, about the same percentage as Norway.

The average age of the new parliament is less than 40. "I think we are going to have fun," said the newly elected 23-year-old Minna Karhunen, the youngest member elected to the 200-member parliament. Eeva-Liisa Tuominen, head of the government's Council of Equality, said, "We will no longer bow down to the men. The time has come for real political change in this country."

Six of Finnish prime minister Esko Aho's 17-member cabinet are female. Finland's president, Mauno Koivisto, is very much a male, but Eva Kuuskoski-Vikatmaa, a powerful figure in the Center party, will run for president in 1994. In addition, Finland now boasts Europe's only female defense minister: Elisabeth Rehn.

That is a "first" the Norwegians seem to almost resent. Asked why Norway's defense minister's post went to a male, Prime Minister Brundtland replied somewhat humorlessly, "it is not obvious to Norwegians that defense is more important than justice."

It would be true Nordic irony if the Defense Ministry were to become the low-status job in the cabinet.

Indeed, women's rise to power in Norway is not without cynical observers.

"Men are moving out of politics and women are taking positions that men no longer want," claims sociologist Andreas Hompland, because men believe "real power" lies elsewhere. The salaries of politicians have declined significantly for the last 15 years, he says.

"Younger men during the seventies and eighties were more attracted to jobs in private firms," says Hompland. "While political office is falling in status and income," he concludes, "politics is becoming more dominated by women."

Many disagree with Hompland, and few—male or female—would consider PM Brundtland a lightweight.

Comments like Hompland's try to undermine women's achievements, says Hege Skgeie, a researcher at Oslo's Institute for Social Research. The struggle for equality and economic expansion in Norway "have integrated women into politics and achieved recognition that they have a legitimate position on the political agenda," she says.

Brundtland's main opposition is from the Conservatives. The new party leader, Kaci Kullman Five, a former trade minister, "promises to bring a breath of fresh air to a party that has become demoralized over the past five years under three elderly male leaders," concludes London's *Financial Times* It appears that she already has livened things up. The party hit an all-time low in early 1991, when only 14.4 percent of voters identified themselves as Conservatives. Once her election was expected, the percentage rose to 22.5.

Whatever Norway's political future, it is safe to assume it will include a woman at the helm for some time.

Elsewhere in Europe

Elsewhere in Europe, women are attaining prominence.

Carmen Romero, wife of Spain's premier Felipe González, is a left-leaning MP who promotes women's issues and favors liberalizing abortion, a controversial position in Europe's largest Roman Catholic country.

The European describes Ana Aznar, wife of Spain's Popular party leader José Maria Aznar, as "Spain's answer to Hillary Clinton." As her husband prepared for the 1993 elections, Ana appeared on magazine covers and gave her opinions on a range of issues.

"The Popular party hopes to present José and Ana as Spain's answer to Bill and Hillary, and to cast current prime minister Felipe González as a Bush-style has-been who, after 10 years in power, lacks fresh ideas," *The European* reported.

In Germany the newspapers call her the most powerful woman in the country. Birgit Breuel is the head of Treuhand, the agency that is managing and privatizing all the companies that were in what used to be East Germany. She oversees more than 9,000 companies with about 4 million employees.

In Eastern Europe women are seizing the opportunities of change.

Marju Lauristin is the deputy speaker of the Estonian parliament. She was an early leader and one of the founders of the Popular Front of Estonia, and is well known for her role in persuading Estonians that they could break with Moscow.

Lithuania's female former prime minister, Kazimiera-Danute Prunskiene, was a leader in negotiating agreement with Moscow for Lithuania's independence. President Vytautas Landsbergis made the fiery speeches, but Prunskiene got the deal done.

These two women, Prunskiene and Lauristin, in Estonia and Lithuania were largely responsible for putting the struggle of the Baltics on the world's political agenda.

In the summer of 1992, Hanna Suchocka was elected Poland's first female prime minister. Polish leaders needed someone who, in the words of *The Financial Times*, was "untainted by the endless compromises and intrigues of Polish politics." She fit the bill. After seven difficult months, she could boast a 76 percent approval rating.

Suchocka kickstarted Poland's privatization scheme and increased Poland's stock in international business. The International Monetary Fund released $1.7 billion in aid that was on hold because of the country's budget problems. Multinational companies have pledged more than $2 billion in investments.

Under her leadership, "Poland looks to be the first former Soviet satellite to turn the economic corner," *Business Week* reported. "Growth is likely to be 2 percent to 3 percent in 1993."

In Hungary, Klara Ungarn, 35, is a member of Parliament representing the Federation of Young Democrats. Her party holds 21 seats in the Hungarian Parliament and is aiming higher. "We will control the government in 10 years," she said two years ago. "But not before." Unlike some power-hungry politicians, she shows the maturity needed to polish her craft. She says that women in these newly democratic countries "need time to learn the profession of politics. Being in the opposition is very different from running the government."

In 1992 Blaga Dimitrova, at the age of 70, became vice president of Bulgaria. Dismissed by many because of her gender, age and profession (she's a poet), she ran for office and won.

"All my life I was fighting against power, and now at the end of it I am in the unusual position of being in power," she says. "My daily life now is about hard work and exhaustion. People can't realize that democracy is not an act; it is a process, and the big changes can't come overnight. . . . The most painful feeling for me is the impossibility of helping everyone."

Turkey

One hardly thinks of Turkey as European, but this Mideast country seeks admittance to the European Common Market, even as the conservative forces of Islam grow stronger within it.

That European influence became even more apparent in June 1993, when Turkey elected its first woman prime minister, Tansu Ciller, 47. Political observers were shocked when the True Path party, which boasts much conservative Islamic support, turned to a woman, albeit the former finance minister, after party leader Suleyman Demirel became president following Turgut Özal's death.

But before prime minister Ciller, another important Turkish woman had paved the way. Semra Özal, wife of the late Turkish president Turgut Özal, is a force pushing toward the European, rather than the Muslim, side of Turkey's complex social, religious and cultural equation.

Mrs. Özal won a 1991 bid to lead the Istanbul branch of Turkey's Motherland party. In a warm show of spouse support, President Özal appeared on state television to attack those who opposed her candidacy. Her victory represents a challenge to male-dominated Muslim society. Semra Özal is closely identified with secular forces trying to help women attain greater rights.

- In 1986 she established the Foundation for the Strengthening and Recognition of the Turkish Women to teach women how to take advantage of their rights according to Turkey's constitution.
- She helped women in rural areas to convert religious marriages into civil contracts that grant women some rights to inheritance and child custody.

"I'm different from other presidents' wives," she says. "I don't sit in the corner and do as protocol dictates."

All three major parties in Turkey—Motherland, the rightist True Path party and the Social Democratic populist party—are seeking the female vote. "We now have a quota system like in Scandinavian countries—20 percent of party posts go to women," said the male general secretary of the Social Democrats.

"For the first time women have become an election issue," said Tansu Ciller before becoming prime minister.

Some believe Semra Özal wants to be president after her husband, who died of heart problems in April 1993. If they are right, there could be some interesting times ahead for Turkey: will two women someday run against each other for top office in this conservative country?

Russia

Russian women are increasingly active in campaigns, demonstrations and rallies. They are growing intolerant of the injustice routinely dished out to women in the former Soviet system. Some favor a women's political party.

A Moscow political club for women headed by journalist Larisa Kuznetsova and political scientist Tatyana Ivanova aims to:

- prepare women for political action,
- encourage leadership qualities,
- attain positions of power,
- win guarantees of minimum representation of women in elective and public organizations.

Women may have one ally in former president Gorbachev. In a 1990 address to the Communist Party Congress, he denounced the overwork and underappreciation accorded Soviet women.

"I think we should be ashamed of ourselves now that we see women take an active part in big politics in many countries," he said. "Just take a look at this assembly—how many women are there among the delegates?"

When the Soviet Union was still the Soviet Union, journalist Galina Semyonva, at age 54, was elected to the Politburo of the Central Committee of the Communist party, the party's top governing body. Her appointment was a rare achievement for a woman.

"All of us should think hard about what society owes women and about how to save life itself by saving the women," she says. "We need politics to harmonize relations in society, and we need women in politics," says Semyonva. "Women have an aphorism: we were invited to the feast, that is, politics, but we were offered only half a helping . . . but in our timidity we took only a fourth."

Middle East

One of the most visible women in the world today is Hanan Ashrawi, the official spokesperson for the Palestinian delegation to the Middle East peace talks. A professor of English at Bir Zeit, Ashrawi says her role is a great victory for women in general and in particular for Arab and Palestinian women. "I came buttressed by a clear feminist vision and agenda," she says. "My role legitimizes women's struggles; I can speak out on behalf of all women whose voices have not been heard."

On being a role model for Palestinian women, Ashrawi says Palestinian women tell her, " 'You give us a sense of pride. You give us a voice.' They tell their husbands or their brothers or fathers, 'You see what Hanan is doing. We can do that.' "

Asia's Female Power

In Asia, where women are traditionally expected to be timid and passive, there is, instead, a growing trend toward female leadership. Two Moslem countries in Asia have elected women leaders, unimaginable a few years ago.

In the Philippines, Bangladesh and for a time in Pakistan, democratic female leaders have replaced dictatorship and military rule. Corazon Aquino electrified her followers and endeavored to deal with intractable social issues that her male opposition leaders wouldn't touch with a 10-foot pole.

Another Filipino woman, Miriam Defensor-Santiago, came from out of the blue and almost won the 1992 presidential election, running on a clean-government platform.

In February 1991, while the world was preoccupied by the Persian Gulf War, Khaleda Zia's Bangladesh Nationalist party won the most seats. Supported by business interests, she became the first woman prime minister of this conservative Muslim country, and it was the first peaceful transfer of power in the bloody history of Bangladesh. (Her primary political opponent, Sheik Hasina, is also a woman.)

Bangladesh has made a new start politically and economically, and Prime Minister Zia has made no small plans. She has set out to safeguard the sovereignty of the country, to ensure the continuation and full flowering of democracy and to have a corruption-free administration. "Last, but not least," she says, "is economic and social uplift by promoting self-reliance, production and employment, checking population growth, ensuring the five basic needs (food, clothing, shelter, medical care and education), protecting the environment and bringing women into the mainstream of development."

Benazir Bhutto, the ousted prime minister of Pakistan, was the first woman to head an Islamic country. But in 1990 the president removed her from power and charged her government with corruption. Bhutto's husband, Asif Ali Zardari—*The Financial Times* says he is known as "Mr. Ten Per Cent"—is the reason for her downfall, many believe. (So much for arranged marriages.)

"If there was corruption, why did no one bring me the facts?" she asks. "I'm the only prime minister whose relatives did not take an industrial unit . . . while the ones who looted the country are pointing their fingers at me."

Even if the husband is as guilty as his reputation suggests, Bhutto may still have a point. Maybe her government was less corruption-ridden than others. Still, it gave her enemies the opportunity they needed. And enemies she had. "Business was suspicious of her socialist platform," writes Christina Lamb in *The Financial Times,* "and much of the influential religious community was against the idea of a woman leader."

Bhutto remains popular within Pakistan and in the West. But would she win another election? Would such an election have a chance at fairness? At this point it is only speculation. The opposition remains firmly in control.

Bhutto is not the only woman in Pakistani politics. Abida Hussain has a more than 20-year track record in local and national politics. She chaired a local district council, served in the Pakistani National Assembly and is often called "the most accomplished woman" in Pakistani politics. She is now Pakistani ambassador to the United States.

Japan

Japanese prime minister Sousuke Uno was forced to resign after publicity about an extramarital affair. It was shocking: not the affair, not the publicity, but the resignation. In a country where men behave pretty much as they please, a male leader's apparent lack of respect toward women brought his downfall.

So when his successor, Prime Minister Toshiki Kaifu, appointed two women to his cabinet, Japanese women were encouraged. For years Japanese women have voted in greater numbers than men—and Kaifu clearly realized he needed women to win. Immediately after the elections, however, in a stunning betrayal, he forced the women out of his cabinet.

"I wish Japan had an organization like America's National Organization for Women," says Keiko Higuchi, a professor of women's studies at Kasei University in Tokyo. "We need an organization like that to support women politicians and help them get elected. It is important for women to get organized, because no matter how much noise we make, nothing will change in Japan until women are more involved in politics."

But even without a NOW chapter, change is coming, albeit slowly:

- In 1989 a record 146 Japanese women ran for the upper house of Japan's parliament.
- "Women's influence is going to be very big from now on," says Takako Doi, female former head of the Socialists, Japan's leading opposition party.
- The highest-ranking Japanese in an international agency is a woman. In 1991 Sadako Ogata, a university dean of foreign studies, became the first woman to serve as United Nations High Commissioner for Refugees.

"What can one small woman do for the 17 million people in this world who are refugees from war, persecution or man-made disaster?" asked *The Financial Times.* "Quite a lot," said the *FT,* "if that woman's name is Sadako Ogata." Her first task was to organize protection for Iraqi citizens from their own rulers in the wake of the Gulf War.

Sounding her own sense of the New World Order, Ogata said that the international community "expects the UN to do much more." "The big wars have probably gone," she says, "but there are going to be a lot of internal wars and unrest in which the UN is expected to carry out peacemaking, peacekeeping and humanitarian work."

In the cause of humanity, Ogata embarrassed the male-dominated United Nations and world leaders by requesting drastic action to evacuate the Bosnian town of Srebrenica. She suspended all relief efforts to Bosnia to dramatize frustration and inability to carry out her task. Criticized by many leaders for these actions (including Secretary General Boutros Boutros-Ghali), she nevertheless won high marks from world refugee groups.

"She did precisely the right thing," says Roger Winter, director of the U.S. Committee for Refugees, a nonprofit group based in Washington, D.C.

At age 65, she is the embodiment of the Wisewoman, fully empowered, completely unintimidated by the patriarchy. The world needs millions more of her—and will have them as female baby boomers take power.

Japan's new political party—the women-friendly Japan New Party (JNP)—is the only party gaining support in scandal-ridden Japanese politics. Former TV anchorwoman Yuriko Koife won one of the party's four seats in the parliament in July 1992.

Koike maintains that the marriage of former foreign service officer Masako Owada to the crown prince is "an inspiration for women in the party. In an age when a career woman in a Calvin Klein suit is . . . the crown princess," says Koike, "it is ridiculous that Japanese women should walk three steps behind men."

Known as the "clean party," the JNP offers a conservative, anticorruption alternative to the dominant Liberal Democratic Party (LDP). It also favors importing foreign rice, reducing Tokyo's power and setting a 20 percent quota for women as party candidates. The party has set up a school for potential female candidates.

In 1991 Makiko Hamada ran for the governorship of Tokyo. Though she received only one percent of the vote, that was better than most independents. She now plans to start a political party—the New Democrats. She believes many Japanese housewives are frustrated that no one in power represents their interests—and that their sentiment could be funneled into a movement.

When attorney Harue Kitamura defeated an incumbent to become mayor of Ashiya City in April of 1991, she became the first woman mayor in all of Japan. After serving as a school-board member for 12 years, she was urged to run by other women concerned about the quality of education in Ashiya City. She had never before been involved in politics.

The Japanese media now talk of the dawning of an *"Onna no Jidai,"* an Era of Women.

Women in the Americas

In 1990 Violeta Chamorro surprised the world by defeating Daniel Ortega in free elections to lead war-ravaged Nicaragua, a rural agricultural country with a population of 4 million. She became the first democratically elected official in the 170 years since Nicaragua won its independence from Spain. Chamorro was not above blaming the Sandinistas for a lot of the problems she faced: Nicaragua was $13 billion in debt. Managua, the capital, was never rebuilt after a 1972 earthquake.

"The future of this country is trade, not aid," says her foreign minister, Enrique Dreyfus, "but to get there we have to have aid." Chamorro got the United States to contribute $200 million a year beginning in 1991.

Violeta's late husband, Pedro Joaquín Chamórro, editor of *La Prensa,* fought the right-wing Somoza dictatorship until he was assassinated in 1978. The outrage people felt at his death helped the Sandinistas take over in July 1979. Doña Violeta, as she is known to her fellow citizens, briefly served in the Daniel Ortega government. But she became disillusioned with the Sandinistas and took over *La Prensa* to carry on the struggle. Today a poverty-stricken Nicaragua has freedom of the press. Chamorro stabilized and privatized the banking system, passed laws to attract foreign trade and investment and stabilized Nicaragua's currency, the córdoba.

At 63, Doña Violeta, mother of four, has settled into her role as "La Presidenta" and commander in chief. She says, "I feel calm and at ease. I face it as a mother and grandmother."

What she has had to face lately are her old antagonists, the Sandinistas, with whom she has had to share power.

"The Sandinistas, the largest political force in the country, again have de facto control over Nicaragua," reported *Time* magazine in early 1993. Violeta announced wage freezes and a 20 percent currency devaluation—and added three more Sandinistas to her cabinet.

Brazil

In Brazil, known for its Portuguese brand of machismo, women are moving into political leadership, building from the bottom up:

- Beginning in 1988 the mayor of São Paulo—a city of at least 18 million people—was Luiza Erundina de Souza. Her election was a major achievement in Brazilian political history. Not only was she the first woman to be elected mayor, she was the candidate of the leftist Workers party in conservative São Paulo, the home of most of Brazil's industry. After a very rocky start, she now has wide support. She describes herself as "a truthful, authentic per-

son—and a radical when faced with injustice and disrespect."
Unlike most politicians, Luiza Erundina sought to end her political career with less power than when she began: "That will mean
that I shared power with the organized sectors of society, initiat-
ing a process that will be irreversible." She left office in 1992.

• Telma de Souza is the mayor of Santos, one of the most important cities in the state of São Paulo.

• Congresswoman Rita Camata, 30, from the state of Espirito
Santo, is the youngest woman ever elected to the Federal Assembly.

• Esther de Figueriredo Ferraz, former minister of education, was
the first woman dean of a university in all of Latin America.

• Congresswoman Sandra Cavalcanti, reelected numerous times to
the Federal Assembly, once ran for governor of Rio de Janeiro.

Zélia Cardoso de Mello, Brazil's first economic minister under
the presidency of Fernando Collor de Mello, held the most important
post after the presidency, the first woman to do so. Reportedly inspired by Margaret Thatcher, she was in charge of an ambitious plan
to reduce Brazil's bureaucracy and state industry. Alas, Brazil re-
sisted, and she resigned after two years.

Panama

Mayin Correa became mayor of Panama City in the spring of
1991. She was a city councilor from 1978 to 1984 and later a member
of the National Assembly. She was forced into exile by Manuel
Noriega for two years, returning to "a heroine's welcome" after the
1989 U.S. invasion. She begins each day at 7:00 A.M. with a two-hour
radio program. A "firestorm of energy," she then goes from event to
event, putting in 18-hour days. Correa, 57, was a girl from the country, orphaned at 6. Today she is one of the most powerful politicians
in Panama. People say she wants to be president. The publisher of the
newspaper *La Prensa,* Roberto Eisenmann, says, "She sees herself as
the Margaret Thatcher of the future." On her morning radio show,
she harangues just about everybody. "The problem is that nobody in
this country works—nobody!" she says. "Everyone knows that I
work. So they say I've got political ambitions."

Guatemala

Rigoberta Menchu, a 33-year-old Quiche Indian, won the 1992 Nobel Peace Prize for her work in promoting human rights. She fled Guatemala in 1981 after her family was killed, and continues to work for Native Americans and the rights of indigenous people throughout the hemisphere. Menchu will use her prize money in the quest for peace in Guatemala.

Canada

Former Canadian defense minister Kim Campbell became Canada's first woman prime minister in June 1993, replacing Brian Mulroney, who, in February 1993, had announced he would resign as prime minister of Canada.

Campbell, a 46-year-old lawyer and former university lecturer from British Columbia, has been called tough and outspoken. Though not liberal enough for some left-leaning feminists, she is colorful, controversial and trilingual (English, French and Russian). She plays the cello and piano.

In 1990 Canada's New Democratic Party (NDP) became Ontario's first socialist government—by a large majority. The NDP appointed 11 women cabinet ministers, out of 26, a record for both the province and the country. The female ministers include the head of Meals on Wheels, the director of a battered-women's shelter, a nurse and a workers' compensation claims adjudicator. Women will hold 31 of the party's 73 seats in the parliament—a lot higher than the 14 percent female representation countrywide.

"The proof is in the pudding for women voters," says David Agnew, principal secretary to Ontario premier Bob Rae. "If we deliver on the policies that are relevant to them, they will reward us or punish us accordingly."

In November 1991 the NDP became the first party in Canada to mandate that 50 percent of the list of nominations for the House of Commons be women.

Which party in the United States will be the first to do so?

Thatcher

In 1979 Margaret Thatcher's election as prime minister was revolutionary. Yet for the children of the 1980's, her presence at 10 Downing Street became the norm. When the conservatives who ousted her had to decide on her replacement, a British child was heard to ask, "But, Daddy, can a *man* be prime minister?"

Indeed, Thatcher proved more brilliant, capable and powerful than almost any man. Internationally she earned greater respect than any prime minister since Churchill. At home she was the only prime minister in 160 years to win three consecutive elections.

Yet liberal women dismissed her because of her conservative politics. She was no friend to women, they argue. And not once did she appoint a woman to her cabinet. These are certainly legitimate criticisms.

But even those who despise Thatcher's politics can learn from her qualities as an individual leader—and apply them to their own political agenda:

- She never waffled on the issues. She defined her position precisely and stuck to it to the end (sometimes the bitter end).
- She spoke brilliantly—and extemporaneously.
- Criticism never bothered her in the least. Indeed, she loved a good fight. And never, never lost her cool.

She was also known to publicly humiliate cabinet ministers and others who had the nerve to disagree with her, or to banish them entirely. It is her strengths women can learn from, and her strengths reflected leadership, not conservatism per se. Any leftist could translate her best qualities—and gain politically.

She sometimes worked 19 hours a day, seven days a week. While many leaders seem to age in power, Thatcher seemed to look better each year. Unemployment fell, private ownership rose, the economy grew, she launched a global privatization trend and Great Britain defeated Argentina in the Falklands. She slashed taxes and reversed the direction of socialism in Great Britain.

She left the country much stronger than when she entered office. "Nothing can dim the glitter of her career," said *The Financial Times.*

Peggy Noonan, speechwriter to Ronald Reagan and George Bush and author of the best-selling *What I Saw at the Revolution,* put it well: "She was a great woman who did us great good. She made the system more open to women by her very presence."

Indeed she did. On December 16, 1991, Britain for the first time appointed a woman to run its top-secret MI5 counterespionage service. On the same day the defense ministry announced that the British air force was giving women pilots the chance to fly combat jets for the first time.

These events were topped in the spring of 1992 when Betty Boothroyd was elected by the British House of Commons as the first woman speaker in its 615-year history.

Shaping the New World Order

The global spread of democracy—the big story as we address the new millennium—is the context for opportunity for women in government and politics in the 1990's.

When China joins the democratic ranks in the last half of the decade—as it will after the old men die—it will mean that 90 percent of the world will be ruled by democracies. It reached 50 percent only three years ago.

Democracy creates opportunities. A growing number of world leaders arc women, and women throughout the world are becoming an increasingly powerful voice.

Already, women leaders from Gro Brundtland to Violeta Chamorro have rejected outright the notion of modeling themselves or their policies on male political images of the past. Like the women business leaders described in the chapter on work, they are integrating their values as individuals—and as women—into the stands they take on the environment, the free press, trade, child care and the whole range of domestic and international issues.

In time the New World Order will come to stand for something very different from what it means today. It will mark the beginnings of the integration of women into a New Order, a new global power structure that celebrates the positive traits of both male and female.

Women have opportunities as never before—as never before imagined—to serve, to shape the New World Order.

Conclusion

Women have pushed themselves beyond the evolutionary limits that once defined them and willingly taken over roles that were once the exclusive domain of the male sex.

In 1964 men did not sit around and say, "We've done pretty well at work, in business, on the golf course and on the military battlefield. But we're not complete human beings. We can't have children, we don't really get too deeply into relationships and it would probably do us good to learn to be more caring and spiritual."

But women, in their way, did.

On one day over the past 20 years or so, one woman out of the millions who did the same said, "I am a good mother, wife and friend. I support and care for people. I am a sharp dresser and a good cook. But there has to be *more* to life than this. I want to make a difference. **I want to make something of myself. I want to be part of the world at large."**

A spark of desire went off within an individual woman, and a process began. While juggling children and classwork, a job and marriage (and sometimes cursing the day she decided to "be somebody"), she stayed the course. Today, years later, she is a lawyer or fashion designer, a physician or teacher, a systems analyst or a marketing executive. She has made something of herself and she is *still* a great mother, wife and friend.

Now she possesses skills in the outer-directed, worldly part of life as well as the inner, more personal and spiritual side. It is with this combination of skills—logic and intuition, emotion and intelligence—that she is equipped to change the world. Women today are powerful and whole—more balanced, more complete, than most of their male colleagues.

This Book's Main Points

What now? That is the question we asked in the introduction to this book. We are prepared to offer our vision, but first a recap of this book's main ideas.

A critical mass of women and like-minded men have embraced "women's liberation." It has become a *self-sustaining* movement that may at times experience setbacks, but its direction is unstoppable. Women are transforming the world—even though *all women* are not yet fully liberated.

Pursuing new routes to power via statewide elective office, women will make up 10 to 15 governors by the late 1990's, and a woman, probably as yet unknown to the public at large, will ascend to the U.S. presidency by 2008—at the latest.

Engaging in sports, women will find the wherewithal to develop the new leadership qualities they need in both politics and business, including persistence, courage and discipline—and good sportswomanship. Winning is *not* everything; playing and giving your all is what counts.

A metaphor for women's growing political and economic power is the outright rejection by the women of organized religion that God is somehow male.

The concrete economic beginnings of what Riane Eisler, author of *The Chalice and the Blade,* calls the "partnership" society may be present in the collaborative-couples trend—women and men who choose not to be separated by the nine-to-five workday, but pool their creative talents into a satisfying new enterprise.

Having paid their dues for 15 to 20 years of hard work, sexual harassment and the wage gap, older baby-boom women are poised to win top leadership posts in both corporate culture and independently owned small to midsize businesses. But they will not do so as carbon copies of the businessmen they follow—they bring with them their own leadership style hammered out and tested over the years. But that leadership will also be tempered by the call of balance, family and recreation.

The women headed toward business and political leadership will be the first generation to openly confront and widely discuss menopause—and the added health risks it brings. With the help of female health activists, this new group will safeguard its health and well-being and enjoy in their pinnacle career years the added energy of "postmenopausal zest."

Women will no longer "follow" fashion; fashion—and retailing—will have to start following women: the clothing of the 1990's bears the stamp of female designers—comfortable, simple, elegant. Larger sizes and more convenient ways to shop by television, fax and computer will make it easier to connect good-looking fashions and busy lifestyles. Thanks to customers and women designers, the anorexic, excessive 1980's have given way to the natural, easy and beautiful 1990's.

Women are changing the world, and now women and men as equal parents are seeking to change the family, to resecure it as the basis of society, the strong core of all social institutions. But they cannot succeed without the help of family-friendly companies and government policies.

Before the Judeo-Christian tradition, there was the Great Goddess. The female body that brings forth life was associated with the Good Earth and its crops, and was worshiped. Today the Great Goddess is reawakening in the modern woman, politically and economically powerful like the Greek Athena, yet balanced with the mercy of the Chinese Kuan-yin.

When humanity reaches out to people in need, the feminine principle of caring and compassion is at work. Today women have graduated from yesterday's underappreciated volunteer roles to assume leadership as social activists dealing with issues from world population to affordable housing.

The ugliest, most painful remnant of male domination is violence and abuse of women the world over, carried out with the power of what Eisler calls "the Blade"—power enforced by violence or its threat and abhorrent to all civilized human beings.

Women's growing political and economic power—as well as their prominence within the legal and medical establishment—shall be marshaled against the rapist and the abusers. With the help of supportive men, those who harm will become the ultimate social pariahs.

Women's greatest allies in achieving social transformation are the voices of new women leaders emerging in Northern Europe, parts of Asia, Eastern Europe and locally in South America and Africa. The presence of strong women leaders at the global level reinforces women's value and competence. The New World Order is also a "New Order of Women."

Our Daughters, Ourselves

But to what end are women's recent successes if the generation that follows is not nurtured to assume leadership and carry forward a new social order where women and men are beginning to be truly equal? It is time that successful professional women shift gears and begin the second part of their lives—mentoring, teaching and supporting young women, teens and girls. They are the future, and they desperately need positive role models.

Professional women should be replacing rock-music and TV stars, actresses and models as the role models for young women— especially teens. Sex education should be taught in conjunction with career education and with successful women serving as guest speakers.

Teenage girls are terribly vulnerable: to pregnancy, drugs and alcohol, violence, eating disorders, smoking—and today AIDS. Simply getting off to a bad start academically can destroy a young woman's self-confidence and set the stage for a lifetime of under-achievement.

The reason is that teenage girls are running low on self-esteem, the critical foundation of healthy behavior. This is where secure adult women can help.

The percentage of girls with high self-esteem decreased 23 percent between elementary and middle school, a study of 3,000 girls and boys by the American Association of University.Women found. Only 29 percent of high school girls were happy with themselves, compared with 46 percent of boys.

The report concluded that adults, family and school have more of an impact on teenagers' self-esteem than do peers.

Carol Gilligan, a Harvard University education professor and author of *In a Different Voice,* says girls have aggressive confidence around age 11. But by age 16, their self-assurance decreases. Gilligan believes women teachers may actually be undermining young women without realizing it. But, she asserts, these same teachers *could* become a great *source of validation* for girls.

Professional women can amplify and reinforce the positive influence of female teachers.

New networks and alliances ought to be forged between teachers usually isolated from the business world and businesswomen usually isolated from the schools—especially before or after they have their own children.

This generation of women, for the most part, had no mentors. They know how difficult it is to succeed without them. For the professional woman who wants to work with girls, there are two basic choices: 1) work with one of the established organizations Girl Scouts, Girls, Inc. (formerly Girls Clubs) or Big Sisters. From career education to sports to academics, each offers excellent programs and wants and needs professional women volunteers—or 2) take the more entrepreneurial route, starting a program or finding a grass-roots group that reflects your goals.

Take Our Daughters to Work Day

April 28, 1993, was "Take Our Daughters to Work Day," a chance for girls age 9 to 15 to experience a real work day. The idea, proposed by the Ms. Foundation, was first planned for New York City but soon took off nationwide. About 500,000 girls were expected to participate. Well over a million, perhaps 1.5 million, actually did.

- Baptist Hospital of Miami was one of the first organizations to design a program.
- One hundred twenty girls spent the day with Merrill Lynch on the stock trading floor.
- US Air showed 12 middle school girls the airline industry by flying them between Washington, D.C., and Pittsburgh.
- Nine West, Ortho Pharmaceutical and Liz Claiborne, Inc., were among the many companies that participated.

"There is evidence that when daughters see an example of a competent, self-supporting mother, they incorporate it into their view of what's possible for themselves," says Dr. Deborah Phillips, a psychologist at the University of Virginia.

"Even if my daughter decided not to work outside the home,"

says Kathy McCullough, a Northwest Airlines pilot, "at least she knows . . . that she has the option to be anything she wants to be." Darcie, McCullough's eight-year-old daughter, went to Japan with her mom on a recent flight.

One Woman's Dynamic Approach

In 1990 researcher Cheryl Bartholomew of George Mason University in Fairfax, Virginia, designed and taught a one-semester class called "Horizons 2000" at Fairfax High School in Virginia. Its objective: to build and reinforce girls' self-esteem. Based on six years of research conducted from public schools nationwide, it features videotapes of successful women, guided fantasy and mentoring.

Each girl meets a professional woman in a career matching her interests. Bartholomew will track her students through college and beyond to test the course's success; 100 percent of students said it "helped build their confidence and commitment to pursue a career." In the fall of 1991 Bartholomew's class was added to three Virginia schools: Thomas Jefferson High School in Annandale, George Washington Junior High in Alexandria and Jenny Dean Elementary in Manassas.

A Call to Leadership

In the introduction of this book, we asked, What comes next?

Having described chapter by chapter the ways in which women are transforming almost every walk of life, we offer our vision.

We believe the answer is threefold: 1) the full participation of women in society at the highest levels of creativity and leadership in each area from politics to religion to the arts to business; 2) the integration of female values and thought into institutions from the family to sports to spirituality; and 3) the shaping of a genuine New World Order where positive traits of women and men fuse into a new partnership and are reflected in the remaking of social structures and their subsequent governance.

We live in a world of problems and opportunities that is in constant flux. While the new organizations described in this book thrive, the patriarchal power structure is falling apart—and each segment is then *blaming* the other for its parallel demise.

"It's all the fault of you Republicans."

"No, actually it's all the fault of you Democrats."

"Let's get a real take-charge kind of guy in here to get the job done."

It won't work.

Because what is needed is a new vision and a new social order. People have been *yearning* to get beyond the tired old labels of Left versus Right, to create policies that are socially liberal *and* financially responsible, social programs that really empower people to become independent of government resources.

We believe that the women who have honed their skills and experience in a "man's world"—along with their like-minded male colleagues—are going to have to assert the leadership for a new social agenda that is caring, concrete and cost-effective.

But these new opportunities for women in leadership are not going to be automatic.

Individual women are going to have to be willing to "go for it." One of the key objectives of *Megatrends for Women* is to persuade women to do just that.

It requires courage and hope. You are not going to be a leader and you are not going to change the world if you sit around thinking, **I'm never going to have any power. I'm never going to lead.**

You have to be optimistic enough to anticipate opportunity. It is not going to happen overnight. You must create a five- to seven-year plan to prepare for the leadership opportunity that will present itself in 1998 or 2002. That might mean working now to

• Develop fund-raising and/or marketing skills.
• Study the issues.
• Start speaking out.

If you think you do not have the power position today to do what should be done, start where you are and do it anyway. Experiment, gather data, see what works and why. Create the database and track record today that will be your blueprint for leadership tomorrow.

It is time to shift the contemporary discussion about the women's movement from the past (the extent to which women have been oppressed) to the *future*—what women are doing with what freedom and power they do possess.

Are women prepared to move beyond the repression and victimization of the past and into the dynamic action of the future? So far, women have effectively utilized the negativity of their oppression to build awareness that it must stop. But negative energy does not have the power to transform; it can only point out evils and raise consciousness about them.

Clearly, it is demoralizing when a movement's countervailing forces seem overwhelming and omnipotent. But the recent history of the 20th century demonstrates anew that nothing stands in the way of an idea whose time has come: the end of apartheid, the fall of Eastern Europe, the rise of democracy in the former Soviet Union. Look at what was the Soviet Union: talk about countervailing forces! How about the KGB, the Communist party and totalitarianism? Yet democracy burst through and, the world prays, will suffer no counterrevolutionary setbacks.

Are women now prepared to shift gears and reach within to find the positive energy that will build what must replace millennia of oppression?

The beginning of the achievement of women's liberation may be the symbolic shift from consciousness-raising to fund-raising.

The shift from "Look how horrible this is!" to "And here is *exactly* what we propose to do about it: will you give us your support?"

The pioneering women described in *Megatrends for Women* have rediscovered that the source of female values is caring and *love*. But they are not content with that knowledge. They are committed to moving beyond it to *reintegrate* caring and love with the *skills* they have acquired and honed in "a man's world"—of politicking, athletics, business competence, medicine, law.

The result is love in action. With it women are transforming the world.

We have not yet reached the modern "partnership society" that Riane Eisler envisioned in *The Chalice and the Blade*, described earlier.

Fifty years from now, when that ideal is realized in the developed world and actualized in much of the developing world, it will be clear in retrospect that the *turning point*, the time when the critical mass for social transformation was present, occurred in the decade of the 1990's.

Between now and then comes the real work. The new "women's movement," which will transform the world we live in, has begun.

Notes

Preface

x Household health decisions made by women from *Marketing to Women*. Women and their percent of expenditures reported in *Lear's*, March 1993, pp. 93, 103, 107. Women truck buyers from "Automakers come a long way," *USA Today*, January 27, 1992.

Introduction

xxi–xxii The numbers of democratic countries and dates are from Francis Fukuyama's *The End of History and the Last Man* (Free Press) pp. 48–50.

1. Women in Politics: The Road to the U.S. Presidency

3 Woods quote from "Illinois' Braun tops female candidates," *Denver Post*, November 4, 1992.

4 Voter Research and Surveys information reported in *Glamour*, February 1993, p. 83.

5 The *U.S. News & World Report* poll appeared in the April 27, 1992, issue, p. 37.

7 Numbers and percentages of women in state legislatures from the Center for the American Woman in Politics (CAWP), Eagleton Institute of Politics, Rutgers University.

Landrieu's prediction from "Women in Politics Gain," *New York Times,* February 25, 1991. Trudell quote from "NOW Women Elect 2000 Project," *National NOW Times,* December 1991.

8 Data on Jackie Speier and Sproul quote from *San Francisco* magazine, June 1989, p. 11.

Information on Nancy Kopp and her quote from "Montgomery's Del. Kopp A Possibility for the Podium," *Washington Post,* March 17, 1991.

9 Numbers on women mayors from CAWP and the U.S. Conference of Mayors.

Data on Deedee Corradini and Miller quote from *Time,* November 18, 1991, p. 24, and from "Non-Mormon Woman Favored for Salt Lake Mayor," *Washington Post,* October 27, 1991.

Kelly quote from "Dixon Shares Winning Formula With Women Municipal Leaders," *Washington Post,* March 10, 1990; other Dixon data from various sources, including "100 Days Later, New D.C. Mayor Still Riding High," *USA Today,* April 8, 1991, and *Ebony* magazine, February 1992, p. 29.

10 Whitmire quote from *Savvy Woman,* November 1990, p. 13.

Murray quote and information from "Uncertainty a Certainty," *Washington Post,* September 14, 1993, and "Racial, Gender Diversity," *Denver Post,* November 6, 1992.

10–11 Cooperation between O'Connor, Copley, and Kroc, and O'Connor quote from *Time,* March 19, 1990, p. 21, and from the mayor's office.

11–12 Numbers of women running for office from CAWP.

11 Mandel quote from "Gains Seen for Women," *New York Times,* October 29, 1990.

Black women in office from "USA Snapshot," *USA Today,* May 15, 1991.

That half of women won, and education-officials data, from CAWP; lieutenant-governor data from "Where Women Won," *Washington Post,* November 16, 1990.

12 Iowa data from "1990 Elections—A Year of Wins for Women!" issued by National Women's Political Caucus.

Woods quote from interview with authors.

Ellen Malcolm quotes and data from "Feminists Vow to Seek Political Changes," *Washington Post,* October 17, 1991, and "1992 Seen as

Promising for Female Candidates," *Washington Post,* October 21, 1991.

12–13 Nominations and elections of women from CAWP. Roukema quote from *Newsweek,* April 30, 1990, p. 20.

13–14 Women in office as lieutenant governor, attorney general, state treasurer, secretary of state from CAWP.

14 Mandel quote from "Sisterhood Is Political," *New York Times,* May 24, 1992.

Harriett Woods quote from interview with authors.

14–16 Gov. Roberts quotes and background from "Ms. Roberts Goes to the Statehouse," *Christian Science Monitor,* February 15, 1991, and her office.

15 Sharon Rodine quoted in *Boston Globe,* November 8, 1990.

16 The 1981 State of Connecticut Register and Manual was dedicated to Ella Grasso.

17 Percentages of women in governors' cabinets from NWPC.

Statistics on governors and lieutenant governors from CAWP and "1990 Elections—A Year of Wins for Women!" by NWPC.

17–18 Description of Gov. Kunin and her quote and Nelson quote from "Now Is the Time for Women," *Christian Science Monitor,* June 25, 1990, and her office.

18–19 Brough and Mandel quotes from "Women Debate Term Limits," *USA Today,* January 18, 1991.

19 Jordan quote from *Time,* June 3, 1991, p. 9.

States with term limits from "Women Debate Term Limits," *USA Today,* January 18, 1991, and "Limits on Terms," *Denver Post,* November 14, 1992.

Redistricting data from CAWP and IMPAC 2000.

Information on retirements from "House Is Ready to Shift Gears," November 19, 1992, and the Fund for the Feminist Majority.

19–20 Lake's polls and 100 seats available from *Working Woman,* February 1992, p. 66.

20 O'Brien quote from "1992 Seen as Promising for Female Candidates," *Washington Post,* October 21, 1991.

Craver-commissioned Hart poll from "Women's Anger About Hill-Thomas Hearings," *Wall Street Journal,* January 6, 1992.

20–21 Bullets on female candidates outspent by males from CAWP and "Hispanic Elected in L.A. County," *Washington Post,* February 21, 1991.

21 Feinstein quote from "California Women: 'It's Our Turn,' " *USA Today,* February 2, 1990. Fund-raising data from "Women Seeking Office," *Christian Science Monitor,* October 22, 1991.

Schroeder quote from "Why Most Officials Are Still Men," *Christian Science Monitor,* February 15, 1991.

22 Smeal quote from "Feminists Vow to Seek Political Changes," *Washington Post,* October 17, 1991.

Mandel quote from "1992 Holds Promise for Female Candidates," *USA Today,* October 23, 1991.

NOW membership from "Women's Anger About Hill-Thomas Hearings," *Wall Street Journal,* January 6, 1992.

The Women's Campaign Fund from "Women Seeking Office," *Christian Science Monitor,* October 22, 1991.

Harriman statement from *Time,* October 28, 1991, p. 24.

23 Republican women who crossed party lines from "High Note from the Heartland," *Washington Post,* March 26, 1992.

Mason and Friedan quotes from "Arlen Specter's Rude Awakening," *Washington Post,* October 18, 1991.

Woods quote from "From Women, an Outpouring of Anger," *Washington Post,* October 9, 1991.

Craver quote from "Feminists Vow to Seek Political Changes," *Washington Post,* October 17, 1991.

23-24 Bullets on fund-raising by women's groups, and EMILY's List and Minnesota Million, from "Women's Anger About Hill-Thomas Hearings," *Wall Street Journal,* January 6, 1992; NWPC; EMILY's List and the Women's Campaign Fund.

24 Eu quote from "California Women: 'It's Our Turn,' " *USA Today,* February 2, 1990.

1987 NWPC survey from "Women in Politics," *New York Times,* August 13, 1987.

25 Celinda Lake poll reported in *Working Woman,* February 1992, p. 66.

Women legislators in statehouses: CAWP study reported in "Survey: Female Legislators Press Feminist Issues," *Washington Post,* November 17, 1991.

Jane Danowitz quote from *Glamour,* November 1990, p. 92.

Gov. Roberts quote from "Ms. Roberts Goes to the Statehouse," *Christian Science Monitor,* February 15, 1991.

Gag rule elimination and Clinton's statement reported by NARAL.

CAWP abortion study was entitled *Election 1989: The Abortion Issue in New Jersey and Virginia.*

Tambornino's actions reported in *Glamour,* February 1991, p. 80.

25–26 Michelman quote from "Overturning 'Roe': Threat or Benefit," *USA Today,* January 7, 1992. Abortion status from NARAL.

26 Yorkin quote from "Big Boost for Feminists," *Washington Post,* October 3, 1991.

Danowitz quote from "Female Ranks in Elected Jobs," *New York Times,* November 8, 1992.

Women voters in 1988 and 1992 elections from the U.S. Census Bureau.

That women make up 54 percent of the electorate in proportion to their percentage of the adult population from NWPC.

27 Poll that saw women as "incorruptible outsiders" reported in *The Economist,* November 23, 1991, p. 25.

Divall quote from "Women's Anger about Hill-Thomas Hearings," *Wall Street Journal,* January 6, 1992.

Lake quote from "When Politics Lose, Women Win," *Washington Post,* December 29, 1991.

Results of 1987 leadership poll reported in "Women in Politics," *New York Times,* August 13, 1987.

27–28 Celinda Lake poll described in *Working Woman,* February 1992, p. 66. Danowitz quote from "Why Most Public Officials Are Still Men," *Christian Science Monitor,* February 15, 1991.

28 Gov. Roberts quote from "Ms. Roberts Goes to the Statehouse," *Christian Science Monitor,* February 15, 1991.

28–29 Risks of women in air force and navy from "Clearing the Legal Way For Women in Combat," by William P. Lawrence, *Washington Post,* July 28, 1991, and from Women in Military Service for America Memorial Foundation, Inc.

29 Women in the military from the Department of Defense. Highest percentage on active duty in the world from "Parenthood and Policy," *Washington Post,* February 19, 1991.

Harris quote from "War Puts U.S. Servicewomen Closer than Ever to Combat," *New York Times,* January 22, 1991.

Sanders quote from "Females on the Front Lines," *USA Today,* December 13, 1990.

Saudi "characterization" of women from *Time,* February 25, 1991, p. 36.

Kuwaiti women soldiers reported in Style section, *Washington Post,* February 26, 1991.

30 Schroeder quote from "A 200-year-old Revolutionary Idea," *USA Today*, May 30, 1991.

Davis quoted in *Newsweek*, September 10, 1991, p. 22.

Newsweek poll on women in combat from the August 5, 1991, issue, p. 27.

Commission's recommendations from "Panel: Ban Women," *Washington Post*, November 4, 1992, and *U.S. News & World Report*, November 16, 1992, p. 17. Aspin's action reported in various articles including "Female Top Guns," *Denver Post*, April 29, 1993.

30–31 Canada's new combat laws, and women in combat in Norway, Denmark, the Netherlands and Belgium from "Canada's Leap to Equality in Combat," *Washington Post*, September 26, 1989.

31 Foote quotes from "War Reveals Women's Advances," *Washington Post*, March 1, 1991.

Korb quote from *Newsweek*, August 5, 1991, p. 22.

Kennett quote from *Newsweek*, August 5, 1991, p. 25.

32 Richards quote from "Not One of the Boys," *Atlanta Journal and Constitution*, August 23, 1989.

Data on Richards's appointments from her office.

Christian quote and numbers of letters received from *Vogue*, August 1991, p. 244.

32–33 Boxer's fund-raising success from her office.

33 Data on Feinstein funds from "Women Seeking Office," *Christian Science Monitor*, October 22, 1991, and from her office.

Lake's analysis of California politics from "California Sets the Pace," *Boston Globe*, April 5, 1990.

Woods and Malcolm quotes from "Female Ranks in Elected Jobs," *New York Times*, November 8, 1992. *Time* story appeared May 20, 1991, p. 20.

2. The Sporting Life

35 Studies on benefits of sports (in order) are from *Self* magazine, September 1990, p. 22; *Working Woman*, June 1989, p. 138; and "The Wilson Report: Moms, Dads, Daughters and Sports," 1988, sponsored by Wilson Sporting Goods with Women's Sports Foundation.

35–36 Mariah Burton Nelson, *Are We Winning Yet?* (Random House), p. 49. Weiss quote from *Working Woman*, June 1989, p. 138.

37 *Sports Illustrated* Sports Poll 1991. Percentages of Women in most popular sports from the National Sporting Goods Association

(NSGA) press release, June 1991. New participants from "Women and the Sporting Life," *Washington Post,* June 18, 1991, and National Golf Association.

Numbers of high school and college athletes from the National Federation of State High Schools Associations and from interviews with Drs. R. Vivian Acosta and Jean Carpenter, Brooklyn College, and their report, "Women in Intercollegiate Sport 1977–1990."

Katie Zubricky from *Women's Sports & Fitness,* January/February 1991, p. 59.

Number of girl golfers from the National Golf Foundation. Kitty Porterfield is described in Nelson, *Are We Winning Yet?* pp. 26–37. Klein statistic from *Women's Sports & Fitness,* October 1992, p. 15. Ruth Rothfarb from *Women's Sports & Fitness,* September 1990, p. 57.

37–38 Petrucci quote from *Women's Sports & Fitness,* May/June 1992, p. 13.

38 Activities of older women reported in *Melpomene Journal,* Fall 1990, p. 16.

Wagstaff quote from "Daredevil Pilots New Course," *USA Today,* October 2, 1991. Her second win reported in *Women's Sports & Fitness,* March 1993, p. 22.

Marshall from *Women's Sports & Fitness,* April 1990, p. 74.

Numbers of U.S. rugby clubs from *Women's Sports & Fitness,* September 1991, p. 14.

Numbers of British and French clubs from "Women Tackle Rigors of the World Cup," *The European,* May 5–7, 1991, as is the Almond quote.

38–39 Brooklyn and L.A. boxing and LaMotta quote from *Self,* January 1992, p. 44, and from *Women's Sports & Fitness,* July/August 1991, p. 58.

39 Fishing stats from NSGA press release cited above.

Bowling information from the Women's International Bowling Congress.

Numbers of volleyball players and NCAA programs from NSGA.

Numbers of women in the various sports from NSGA press release cited above.

40 Boston's 1966 response to Gibb reported in *Runner's World,* April 1990, p. 31. 1993 stats from Boston Marathon.

New York stats from N.Y. Road Runners Club of America. Benoit Samuelson and previous male marathoners from *Women's Sports & Fitness,* January/February 1992, p. 24.

Number of 1991 biathlons from *Women's Sports & Fitness,* July/ August, 1991, p. A1.

Women of Iron from *City Sports,* August 1991, p. 22; and *Women's Sports & Fitness,* January/February 1993, p 20.

Lori Norwood from *Women's Sports & Fitness,* May/June 1991, p. 68.

40–41   Stats on tennis wins from *Tennis,* July 1991, p. 58; *Women's Sports & Fitness,* January/February 1992, p. 24; "Seles is Slims Champion," *Washington Post,* November 25, 1991; "Martina Nets Milestone Win No. 158," *USA Today,* February 17, 1991; and *Women's Sports & Fitness,* March 1990, p. 25. Tennis prize money stats from *Ms.,* January/February 1991, p. 43; *Tennis,* June 1991, p. 36; and from "Capriati: Teen, Tennis Lives Collide," *USA Today,* March 30, 1992.

41   Nelson quotes from p. 48 and p. 56.

Nelson quote, "Male athletic superiority . . . ," from pp. 47–48. Pat Harris story, "Pat Harris Doesn't Need to Be One of the Boys to Coach Them," *Washington Post,* December 18, 1990, and from 1991 interview.

42   Notorangelo from Nelson, pp. 55–56.

Newby-Fraser triumph cited in *Women's Sports & Fitness,* January/ February, 1989, p. 50, and the magazine's March 1993 issue p. 44.

Baker stat from *Glamour,* May 1991, p. 248.

43   Olivares quote from Nelson, p. 56.

Griffith Joyner's and Lewis's times from Indianapolis-based Athletics Congress/USA.

Whipp and Ward from "Two Experts Say Women Who Run May Overtake Men," *New York Times,* January 7, 1992, as is Lebow quote.

43–44   Whipp quote from "Champion Female Runners Are Gaining on Men," *Washington Post,* January 2, 1992.

44   Trason 1989 victory and Trapp's finish cited in *Runner's World,* June 1990, p. 109, and *Women's Sports & Fitness,* April 1990, p. 62, and in Nelson, p. 54.

Trason 1991 win and description from *City Sports,* August 1991, p. 25. Her 1992 victory is reported in *Women's Sports & Fitness,* October 1992, p. 15.

Stats on women swimmers from *Women's Sports & Fitness,* January/ February 1992, p. 24, and from Nelson, p. 55.

44–45   Nelson and McAllister quotes from Nelson, p. 55.

45   Butcher quote and description from *Women's Sports & Fitness,* February 1987, p. 22; *Sports Illustrated,* February 11, 1991, p. 190; "Mas-

ter Musher," *USA Today,* March 12, 1992; *Outdoor Life,* February 1991, p. 18; and *Current Biography,* June 1991, p. 14.

Description of Swenson win and his quotes from *Sports Illustrated,* February 11, 1991, p. 190, and March 25, 1991, p. 86.

Arthaud win and quote from "Arthaud's Record Win," *The European,* November 23, 1990, and "Solo Sailor on the Waves of Freedom," *Washington Post,* December 8, 1990.

45–46 Autissier win and quote from "Autissier Lands a Blow for Women with Solo Success," *The European,* May 3–5, 1991.

46 Kratzig from "Action Guide," *Women's Sports & Fitness,* November/ December 1991.

NCAA riflery from *Sports Illustrated,* April 9, 1990, p. 106 and 1992 results from NCAA.

Billiards and Davis statement from "Queens of the Green Baize," *The European,* January 4, 1991.

46–47 Statistics on high school athletes (girls and boys) and girls in most popular sports from National Federation of State High Schools Association's Handbook, 1990–1991.

47 DeFrantz quote from *Women's Sports & Fitness,* April 1991, p. 57.

Little League Softball and Nancy Winnard from Nelson, p. 18; *Ms.,* September/October 1991, p. 44; and "Little League is Big Business," *The Sporting News,* June 19, 1989.

47–48 Numbers of college women in sports and most popular sports from interview with Drs. Acosta and Carpenter, their report cited above, and from their research published in *Academe,* January/February 1991, p. 23.

48 Data on athletic scholarships from *Glamour,* September 1991, p. 119.

Bullets on Title IX and Collins statement from "Women in Sports," *USA Today,* February 10, 1993; "Only One School Meets Gender Equity Goal," *Washington Post,* June 21, 1992, and *Self,* October 1992, p. 78.

Percentages of athletes who graduate from "Tracking Scholarships for Female Athletes," *Washington Post,* January 15, 1991, and "Women Fare Better at Diploma Time," *USA Today,* June 20, 1991.

49 Sara Lee grant from *Women's Sports & Fitness,* March 1991, p. 14.

Audiences for women's college basketball cited in "USA Snapshot," *USA Today,* January 29, 1991.

Griffin's statement and quote from "CBS Gives Women's Game a Try," *USA Today,* January 4, 1991.

Stats on Olympic team members from U.S. Olympic Committee. Quote about Joyner-Kersee from *Women's Sports & Fitness,* January/

February 1993, p. 30. New Olympic events and male-only events cited in *Women's Sports & Fitness,* July/August 1991, p. 68, in the April 1992 issue, p. 16, and the October 1992 issue, p. 15.

DeFrantz quote reported in *Women's Sports & Fitness,* April 1991, p. 57.

50 Numbers of women basketball players overseas and Levy quote from *Ms.,* January/February 1991, p. 45.

50–51 Fastpitch Association information was reported in *Women's Sports & Fitness,* January/February 1993, p. 19. Lopiano quote is from "Panelists: Encourage Girls Early," *USA Today,* February 4, 1993.

51 Rheaume information from "NHL Team Set to Sign Woman," *USA Today,* September 24, 1992; *Time,* October 5, 1992, p. 24; and "Female Goalie Makes Debut," *New York Times,* September 24, 1992.

Chesterton and Twain quotes were cited in *Vogue,* August 1990, p. 191.

51–52 All women's golf stats, unless otherwise noted, from National Golf Foundation. Percentages of women who feel "unwelcome" from "Analysis of Research on Women's Golf" by Coopers & Lybrand, October 1991.

52 Data on John Jacobs's Practical Golf Schools from "Golf, Women and Office Politics," *Boston Globe,* June 19, 1991.

Futch quote from *Business Week,* March 27, 1989, p. 76.

Percentage who take up golf for business from Coopers & Lybrand, cited above. NGF survey reported in "Women Have New Link into Old Boys Network, " *USA Today,* April 9, 1992.

Robsham anecdote from *Business Week,* December 24, 1990, p. 56.

Thompson quote from "Women Teeing Up in a Business Game," *Washington Post,* May 16, 1991.

52–53 Dean quote from "Golf, Women and Office Politics," *Boston Globe,* June 19, 1991.

53 Mazda clinic and Black quote from: "Women Teeing Up in a Business Game," *Washington Post,* May 16, 1991.

Bohn quote cited in "Golf, Women and Office Politics," *Boston Globe,* June 19, 1991.

Beyer quote from "Business Golf For Women," an advertising section in *Savvy Woman,* June 1990.

Jacobi quoted in "LPGA Is Trying to Fill the Holes in Its Game," *Washington Post,* June 23, 1991.

Blalock statement from "Golf, Women and Office Politics," *Boston Globe,* June 19, 1991.

Cole quoted in "Women Teeing Up in a Business Game," *Washington Post,* May 16, 1991.

Inkster triumph from *Women's Sports & Fitness,* April 1991, p. 76.

54 Women coaches in 1972 vs. 1991 from Drs. Acosta and Carpenter, report cited above and interview.

Hasbrook study and Delano, Hasbrook, Van Derveer, and Kroger quotes from *Women's Sports & Fitness,* September 1990, p. 40. Kane statement from interview.

55 NCAA programs headed by women from "Sweet's Job Surpasses Her Dreams," *USA Today,* January 14, 1992; *Glamour,* September 1991, p. 119; "New Regis Soccer Coach," *Rocky Mountain News,* January 31, 1992; and *Women's Sports & Fitness,* September 1991, p. 17.

Van Derveer quote from *Women's Sports & Fitness,* September 1990, p. 40.

Glamour's plea and Van Derveer quote from *Glamour,* September 1991, p. 119.

Sweet data from "New President Judy Sweet," *Washington Post,* January 11, 1992.

Sweet quote from "Sweet's Job Surpasses Her Dreams," *USA Today,* January 14, 1992.

56 Weddington's duties described in *Savvy Woman,* July/August 1990, p. 16. Bogdan from *Women's Sports & Fitness,* May/June 1992, p. 108.

Female trainers and Lowry quote from "Female Trainers Ready," *USA Today,* November 11, 1992.

56–57 Junko Tabei data and her quotes from "At the Peak of Her Profession," *Washington Post,* April 8, 1991.

57 All Krone stats from *The Daily Racing Form* in New Jersey.

Moran quote from "She Is Riding Her Way to Top," *New York Newsday,* December 17, 1987.

Shoemaker quote about Krone from *Connoisseur,* July 1990, p. 84.

Description of Shoemaker from "Keeping Score," *The Sporting News,* October 17, 1988, and "Shoemaker 'Rides' to Meet the Media," *USA Today,* October 2, 1991.

Gilman is described in *Women's Sports & Fitness,* July/August 1991, p. 67; October 1990, p. 57; March 1992 Action Guide; September 1992, p. 48.

57–58 AWE description and quotes from *Trilogy,* May/June 1991, p. 95; "Women's Ski Team Lands at South Pole," *USA Today,* January 15, 1993; and "Endurance on the Ice," *Denver Post,* April 4, 1993.

58 Percentage of adventure travel estimated in "Adventure Travel—Mind-expanding Vacations," *Boston Globe,* June 23, 1991.

Hubbard and McCoy quoted in *Outside Business,* September 1989, p. 45.

Giammatteo quote from *Women's Sports & Fitness,* April 1991, p. 51.

59 Quotes from Sturgess and Halty from "Fitness Vacations," *Washington Post* Health section, June 25, 1991.

Elissa Slanger quote from "Women's Way Ski Seminar," 1991–1992 brochure.

59–60 Spangler and Jones quotes and description of Okemo program from *Cooking Light,* January/February 1992, p. 14, and *Women's Sports & Fitness,* November/December 1990, p. 12.

60 Savath quote and program description from "Telluride Women's Week," 1991–92 brochure.

Athletic expenditures of women and men from "Aiming Sports Apparel at Women," *New York Times,* February 8, 1992. "Only one width" from "If the Shoe Fits, It's Rare," *Washington Post* Health section, October 1, 1991.

Hubbard quote from *Outside Business,* September 1990, p. 45. Edwards quote and company sales figure from *Women's Sports & Fitness,* November/December 1990, p. 48, and from Sacramento headquarters.

60–61 Button and Moore quotes from *Women's Sports & Fitness,* November/December 1990, p. 48.

61 Percentage of Nike goods sold to women from "Aiming Sports Apparel at Women," *New York Times,* February 8, 1992. 45,000 responses cited in *Forbes,* March 30, 1992, p. 96.

Park quote and description of Berkeley–based Title 9 Sports from *Outside Business,* September 1990, p. 45. Revenue increase from *Success,* April 1993, p. 21.

Whiteaker quote from *Women's Sports & Fitness,* November/December 1990, p. 46.

61–62 Susan Schafer's experience is cited in Nelson's *Are We Winning Yet?* p. 165.

62 Lombardi's retraction cited in Nelson, p. 187.

Donovan program cited in Nelson, p. 165.

LaFrance quote from *Women's Sports & Fitness,* April 1990, p. 76.

62–63 Donna Coombs anecdote from interview with authors.

63 St. James data and quote from *Vogue,* June 1989, p. 162, and a Woman's Sports Foundation advertisement in *Women's Sports & Fitness,* January/February 1991.

Stoick quote from *Women's Sports & Fitness*, May/June 1992, p. 82.

63-64 Sue Cobb story from interview with authors and from *The Edge of Everest* (Stackpole Books) by Sue Cobb.

3. Women at Work: Opportunity, Leadership and Balance

66 The Feminist Majority study was publicized in various media, including "Study Finds Few Women Hold Top Executive Jobs," *Washington Post,* August 26, 1991.

67 Korn was quoted in *Lear's,* March 1990, p. 25.

Korn's and Herzlinger's predictions appeared in "Experience, Demographics in Their Favor," *USA Today,* June 1, 1990.

67-68 The Cognetics/NFWBO study is entitled "Woman-Owned Businesses, The New Economic Force."

68-69 *All* future job projections to 2005 are from Outlook: 1990-2005: "Occupational Employment," *Monthly Labor Review,* November 1991, published by the Bureau of Labor Statistics.

70 Barad description and quote from "Mattel President," *USA Today,* August 10, 1992; *Working Woman,* January 1993, p. 49; and *Fortune,* April 19, 1993, p. 193. Josefen data from *Business Week,* May 4, 1992, p. 145.

SBA projections on future women's business ownership are widely quoted. Sometimes an SBA source says women will own 50 percent of businesses by 2000, but we have found it difficult to get them to go beyond 40 percent—officially.

Entrepreneurial Woman list was publicized in " 'California Mentality' Puts State in 10 Best for Women-owned Firms," *San Diego Union,* August 11, 1991.

70-71 Statistics on the increase in women-owned business and revenues between 1977 and 1988 are from SBA and appeared in various sources including "Women Start Firms Faster than You Can Say 'Glass Ceiling,' " *USA Today,* May 6, 1991.

71 The Avon/New Work Decision study was cited in *Lear's,* April 1991, p. 29.

The Harris-Lange and the Fitzpatrick quotes from "Women Starting Small Businesses Twice as Fast as Men," *Washington Post,* September 2, 1991.

Moldt statement and quote from *Nation's Business,* July 1992, p. 16.

72 Estimates on size of child-care industry based in part on *American Demographics,* September 1989, p. 20, as well as interviews with the Census Bureau and the Children's Defense Fund.

Pre-K Today estimate cited in *American Demographics,* September 1989, p. 20.

Susan Schmidt anecdote and quote from *Success,* April 1989, p. 44, and author's interview.

72–73 Story of Special Care and Griswold quote from *Forbes,* December 24, 1990, p. 144, and author's interview.

73 Estimate of health-care industry size based on figures from Health Care Financing Administration.

1990 statistics on job growth in health care from "Against Trends, Health-Care Jobs Rise," *New York Times,* January 13, 1991.

BLS figures on nurses and medical assistants from *Monthly Labor Review* cited earlier.

SRI projections cited in *Fortune,* February 24, 1992, p. 54.

Pharmacist salaries from "The 25 Hottest Careers (Even in Tough Times)," *Working Woman,* July 1991, pp. 57–65.

73–74 Personick, Curran and Ginzberg quotes from "Against Trends, Health-Care Jobs Rise," *New York Times,* January 13, 1991.

74 Behnke anecdote and quotes from *Working Woman,* February 1990, p. 53, and from author's interview.

Number of female accountants from BLS; financial managers from "For Women, Uneven Strides in Workplace," *Washington Post,* December 21, 1992. Korn quote from *Lear's,* March 1990, p. 25.

Estimate of women traders from "Women Traders Make Headway," *Wall Street Journal,* September 3, 1991.

75 Robert Half data appeared in *Working Woman,* July 1992, p. 45.

Challenger quote from *Savvy Woman,* August 1989, p. 33.

Merck portfolio size from "Experience, Demographics in Their Favor," *USA Today,* June 1, 1990, and interview.

Siebert's anniversary reported in *Fortune,* December 14, 1992, p. 177.

The survey of MBA salaries from *Business Week,* October 29, 1990, p. 57.

Data on Shearson and Garzarelli from *Working Woman,* August 1991, pp. 49–51.

Quote by woman Rosener studied from *Harvard Business Review,* November/December 1990, p. 124.

Artemis from *Business Week,* February 12, 1990, p. 66, and author interview.

75–76 Morningstar study reported in "Mutual Funds Take Stock in Female Managers," *USA Today,* March 23, 1992.

76 Beth Terrana described in *Fortune,* March 9, 1992; "Women Turn Bias to Their Advantage," *USA Today,* March 23, 1992; and *Working Woman,* January 1993, p. 45.

Bramwell data from *USA Today,* and *Working Woman* cited above.

Description of Biggs based on "The Global Strategy of Fiona Biggs," *New York Times,* October 28, 1990; interview; *Money,* January 1993, p. 132; and *Working Woman,* August 1992, p. 20.

Dudley profile in *Fortune,* May 17, 1993, p. 34. Harris information from *Working Woman,* January 1993, p. 46.

Falcone quote from *USA Today,* cited above.

77 Baer's *New York Times* piece "The Feminist Disdain for Nursing" appeared February 23, 1991.

Need for nurses based on BLS's *Monthly Labor Review* cited earlier.

78 Average nursing salary and top RN salaries cited in *American Journal of Nursing* Salary Survey, March 1992.

Nurse anesthetist salary from *Working Woman,* 1991, Top Jobs issue cited earlier.

Incomes for nurses, professors and directors from *American Journal of Nursing* issue cited earlier and from American Association of Colleges of Nursing's 1991–1992 Faculty Salaries.

79 Zanders quote from *Ms.,* June 1988, p. 78.

The October 26, 1992, issue of *Newsweek* described nurse practitioners on p. 106.

Nurses with higher education and Hinshaw quote from "Nursing Research," *USA Today,* August 4, 1992.

80 Professor retirements by 2000 from *Savvy Woman,* August 1989, p. 34.

Rochester teacher salaries from Tom Gillette, chief negotiator for Rochester Teachers Association.

Salaries of principals from the National Association of Secondary School Principals in "Senior High Principal Pay: $61,768 Average," *USA Today,* February 14, 1992.

Need for secretaries, including legal and medical, from BLS.

81 That secretaries in major cities can earn $50,000 based on *Nine to Five* newsletter.

Survey of professional secretaries cited in *Today's Secretary: A Summary Report by Professional Secretaries International*, 1991.

81–82 Hancock description from "IBM Puts Female Executive Closer to the Top," *USA Today*, November 27, 1992, and *Business Week*, April 5, 1993, p. 21. Bartz information from *Working Woman*, July 1992, p. 14.

   82 Sims data from *Business Week*, January 11, 1993, p. 120. Mehan's "breakthrough" from *Working Woman*, December 1992, p. 21.

       Good described in *Business Month*, April 1989, p. 44.

       Braun is described in "A Key Officer is Picked for Western Digital," *New York Times*, July 31, 1990.

       Survey of high-tech firms cited in "Tech's Faded Promise; Women Execs Crash into Glass Ceiling," *USA Today*, July 13, 1990.

       Wage gap for computer scientists from BLS document.

       Need for computer analysts, scientists and programmers is in *Monthly Labor Review* cited earlier.

82–83 Barbara Jones story and quote from author interview; she is Patricia Aburdene's sister.

   83 Department of Education study reported in "Women + College Math = Better Pay," *USA Today*, June 10, 1991.

83–84 Tech program reported in Northwest Airlines magazine, April 1992, pp. 100–103.

   84 Actuary information from *Working Woman*, July 1992, p. 46, and *U.S. News & World Report*, October 26, 1992, p. 106.

       Culinary Institute enrollments today and in 1970 reported in "Where Women Are Chief Cooks and Bottle Washers and More," *New York Times*, January 16, 1991.

       Description of San Francisco restaurant scene, and Blue, Goldstein, Nicoletti and Waters quotes, from *New York Times* story cited above.

84–85 James Beard Awards reported in "Women Chefs," *USA Today*, May 5, 1992.

   85 Mrs. Gooch's Natural Foods and Gooch quote from *East West*, August 1990, p. 43, and author interviews.

85–86 Jackson quotes and My Own Meals information from interviews with authors; *Self*, March 1992, p. 129; and *Success*, April 1989, p. 44.

   86 Percentage of new primary-care physicians that are women reported in "Salaries Up, Supply Down in Family Practice," *Washington Post* Health section, September 3, 1991.

86–87 Need for new lawyers is a BLS stat from *Monthly Labor Review* cited earlier.

87 *National Law Journal* survey results were published in the January 27, 1992, issue and in "Percentage of Minorities, Women at Elite Law Firms Varies by City," *Wall Street Journal*, January 22, 1992.

Salaries of bankruptcy and environmental attorneys from *Working Woman*, 1991 List of Top 25 Jobs cited earlier.

Employment attorney information from *Working Woman*, July 1992, p. 46.

88 Statistic on women firefighters from "Few Women Follow Virginia's Trailblazing Firefighter," *Washington Post*, December 25, 1990.

Female pilots at United reported in *Business Week*, November 9, 1992, p. 78.

Number of women in law enforcement from BLS and from "Few Women Follow Virginia's Trailblazing Firefighter," *Washington Post*, December 25, 1990.

Women in sports reported in "Female Reporters See Renewed Resistance," *New York Times*, October 3, 1990.

Female postal carriers and bus drivers from "For Women, Uneven Strides," *Washington Post*, December 21, 1992.

88–89 Watson quotes from *Time*, November 26, 1990, p. 80, and *Time*, February 17, 1992, p. 71. Los Angeles "use-of-force" data, Luna and Belknap quotes are also from the *Time* article.

89 Data on women in construction from "For Women, Uneven Strides," *Washington Post*, December 21, 1992, and "Manhattan to California: Scant Success for California Efforts to Put Women in Construction Jobs," *New York Times*, February 15, 1991.

Women managers/executives in construction from the Women's Bureau, Department of Labor, reported in "Grace Pastiak's 'Web of Inclusion,'" *New York Times*, May 5, 1991.

Julia Stasch story from author interview and from "Putting Up Office Tower, Women Break Sex Barrier," *New York Times*, August 25, 1990; *Working Woman*, April 1992, pp. 29–30; *Time*, September 23, 1991, p. 215; and *Business Week*, January 25, 1993, p. 102.

90 Evans was profiled in "Denver Lands a Problem-Solver," *Rocky Mountain News*, October 25, 1992.

Alsop quote and anecdote reported in "Obstacles to Success Self-imposed," *USA Today*, August 10, 1990; and "It's Official," *Denver Post*, March 31, 1993.

91 D'Harnoncourt information from *Newsweek*, May 11, 1992, p. 74.

Roberts description from *Lear's*, February 1993, p. 55.

Goodman quotes from "Beauty and the Broadcast," *New York Times*, January 26, 1992.

92 Salhany information from *Working Woman*, January 1993, p. 49, and *Mirabella*, September 1992, p. 80.

Lillian Gish quote from "Are Women Directors an Endangered Species?" *New York Times*, March 17, 1991.

Weber statistic from *U.S. News & World Report*, March 16, 1992, p. 8.

92–93 Statistics on number of films women have made from "Hollywood's New Directions," *Time*, October 14, 1991.

93 Ephron quote from "Hollywood Is Talking," *Newsweek*, March 2, 1992.

Coolidge quote from "Hollywood's New Directions," *Time*, October 14, 1991.

Lansing profile from *Mirabella*, September 1992, p. 72, *Working Woman* April 1993, p. 16, and *U.S. News and World Report*, November 16, 1992, p. 25.

The *New York Times* article quoted was written by Caryn James. It appeared in the *Denver Post*, January 17, 1993, under the title "Oscar Finds Series of Weak Women's Role's."

Heller quote from her book, p. 235.

94 *New York Times* quote from "Women Deflate Some Adland Images," November 17, 1991.

Lori Spano quote from "Women Deflate Some Adland Images," *New York Times*, November 17, 1991.

Beers description from *Glamour*, December 1992, p. 115.

95–97 Sexual harassment section based almost exclusively on a superb article, "Sexual Harassment After the Headlines," in *Training*, March, 1992, pp. 23–31. We also drew on *Newsweek*, October 21, 1991, p. 34; *Business Week*, November 9, 1992, p. 78; and *Glamour*, December, 1992, p. 117.

98 Peter Drucker statement from "The Pyramid and the Web," *New York Times*, May 27, 1990.

Yancey quotes from "Women Lead Way in Management Style," *Rocky Mountain News*, January 11, 1991.

99, 101 Rosener's research was sponsored by the International Women's Forum and appeared in *Harvard Business Review*, November/December, 1990, p. 119.

102 Moldt quotes from *Nation's Business,* July 1990, p. 16.

Goya information and Stewart quote from *Business Month,* April 1989, p. 44.

103 Apple Computer information and quote from *Business Month,* April 1989, p. 39.

Hall quote from *Entrepreneurial Woman,* March 1991, p. 59.

103–104 Helgesen quotes from *The Female Advantage: Women's Ways of Leadership* (Doubleday). "Motherhood . . ." from p. 31; "in center of things," and "Iced tea glasses . . ." description of Web style from Helgesen, pp. 44–45, and from "The Pyramid and the Web," *New York Times,* May 27, 1990.

104 Drucker quote from *Business Week,* March 26, 1990, pp. 66–74, as are statements by Bennis and Harvard professor.

105–106 Information and Pastiak quotes from "Grace Pastiak's 'Web of Inclusion,' " *New York Times,* May 5, 1991, which is our source for many of the "downside" examples.

106 Rosener quotes from *Harvard Business Review,* November/December 1990, p. 119.

106–107 Landmark/CMD description and statements from interview with author and company materials.

107 Center for Values Research cited in Helgesen, p. 31.

108 Whitehead quotes from "Work Losing Romanticized Aura of the '80's," *Washington Post,* May 12, 1991.

How many workers spent 49 hours a week or more at work from "Tales from the Digital Treadmill," *New York Times,* June 3, 1990.

Hochschild data cited in *Newsweek,* July 31, 1989, p. 65.

Robinson quote and results of his study from *Wall Street Journal,* August 5, 1991.

"Yiffies" from *Fortune,* August 27, 1990, p. 42.

109 Nemeth quotes from *Nation's Business,* July 1990, p. 16. Sales from *Working Woman,* May 1993, pp. 62, 64.

Badore and Grogan cited in Helgesen, pp. 22, 26.

109–110 Schwartz's article was "Management Women and the New Facts of Life," *Harvard Business Review,* January/February 1989, pp. 65–76.

110 Rogers and Schroeder quotes from "The 'Mommy Track': Feminists Outraged by 2-Tier Treatment," *International Herald Tribune,* March 9, 1989.

Half poll and Du Pont survey cited in *U.S. News & World Report,* June 17, 1991.

110–111 Regan, Howard, Blake, and Persico quotes from *Fortune*, August 27, 1990, p. 42.

Silicon Valley psychotherapist quote from *Savvy Woman*, May 1990, p. 62.

111–112 Kurtzig and Coleman quotes from *Savvy Woman*, May 1990, p. 62.

112 Moberg quote from *Business Week*, March 20, 1989, p. 126.

Goya's part-time phase described in "Saying No to the Mommy Track," *New York Times*, January 28, 1990.

Appignani information from *Business Week*, November 25, 1991, p. 236.

112–113 McKirdy quotes from *Working Woman*, April 1991, p. 44.

113 Schor's analysis is described in "Cut Workday but Not Wages," *USA Today*, February 12, 1992. Kellogg quote and corporate example from Schor's book, pp. 154–56.

114 Wayne quote from "Debunking 5 Wage Myths," *Rocky Mountain News*, March 22, 1990.

115 O'Neill figure from *Washington Times*, December 16, 1990.

National Law Journal study cited in *Savvy Woman*, July/August 1990, p. 50.

Business Week survey from *Business Week*, October 29, 1990, p. 57.

Reed-Crisp quote from "The Pay Lag Persists, Whatever the Reasons," *New York Times*, May 5, 1991.

115–116 Korn quote from *Lear's*, March 1990, p. 25.

116 Soder quote from *Savvy Woman*, July/August 1990, p. 51.

4. To Hell with Sexism: Women in Religion

120 Church of England female deacons, Carey quotes and Vatican's response from *Newsweek*, November 23, 1992, p. 72; "Carey Retracts 'Heresy' Declaration," *The Times* (London), September 10, 1991; and "Anglicans OK Women as Priests," *Denver Post*, November 12, 1992.

McManus quote from *Newsweek*, February 13, 1989, p. 58.

Dreyfus is quoted in "Women Continue to Push for Bigger Roles," *Chicago Tribune*, May 13, 1990.

120–121 Women-Church information and Hunt statements from *The Christian Century*, May 10, 1989, p. 492; "Religious Women's Crusade," *Boston Globe*, March 1, 1990; *Newsweek*, February 13, 1989, p. 58; interviews with Hunt, and *Waterwheel* (Water's newsletter), Summer 1990.

121 Koller-Fox quotes from interview.

121–122 Eisenstein and Sasso quotes from "Bat Mitzvah Pioneer Looks to Her 2d," *New York Times,* March 19, 1992.

122 Schneiders quote from *U.S. Catholic,* May 1990, p. 20.

122–123 Schüssler Fiorenza quotes *In Memory of Her:* "Biblical revelation . . . actors," p. 30, and "power and authority," p. 36.

123 White is quoted in *World Press Review,* January 1988, p. 57.

Interview with Hestenes reported in *Christianity Today,* March 4, 1988, p. 34.

124 Daly is quoted in *National Catholic Reporter,* May 18, 1990, p. 16.

Thiering quote from *World Press Review,* January 1988, p. 57.

Ochs quote appeared in "Women Challenge Old Theology," *Christian Science Monitor,* April 13, 1990.

124–125 Schneiders quotes from an interview with her published in *U.S. Catholic,* May 1990, p. 20.

125 Schüssler Fiorenza statements from "Women Challenge Old Theology," *Christian Science Monitor,* April 13, 1990, and *U.S. Catholic,* May 1990, p. 20.

Schneiders quote from *U.S. Catholic,* May 1990, p. 20.

125–126 Cady Stanton and Trible quotes from "Genesis from Eve's Point of View," *Washington Post,* March 26, 1989.

126 Rejection by Suffrage Association from Schüssler Fiorenza, p. 8.

Soriah quoted in *World Press Review,* January 1988, p. 57.

The Women's Commission of the Ecumenical Association is described by Rosemary Radford Ruether in "Third World Feminism Is on the Move," *National Catholic Reporter,* February 2, 1990.

126–127 Young Kim described in *The Christian Century,* May 2, 1990, p. 452.

127 Women and Islam from "Benazir Bhutto and Islamic Law," *Christian Science Monitor,* February 6, 1989. Al-Ammari quote appeared in "Riddle of Riyadh," *Wall Street Journal,* November 9, 1989.

Ranke-Heinemann's book was reviewed by Peter Steinfels in "Against Those Old Male Celibates," *New York Times,* January 11, 1991. O'Connor's reaction described in "Cardinal and Doubleday Are at Odds," *New York Times,* December 5, 1990.

127–128 Christians for Biblical Equality statement and description from *Christianity Today,* August 18, 1989, p. 38; "Women Served as Priests," *Grand Rapids Press,* November 9, 1991.

128 Bullets on ordained women from spokespersons from the various denominations. The National Council of Churches findings appeared in "Women Ministers in 1986 and 1977."

African Methodist Episcopal ministers from "Black Women's Bumpy Path to Church Leadership," *New York Times,* July 29, 1990.

129 Parker quoted in "Women, Older Students Are Changing the Face of Protestant Clergy," *Atlanta Journal and Constitution,* August 19, 1989.

Weiss quoted in "Woman Rabbi Finds Life's Prayer Answered," *Washington Post,* November 2, 1989.

129–130 Anglican rector quote from an interview. Woman pastor in Memphis and Wiebe quote from *U.S. Catholic,* March 1988, p. 32.

130 Berling is quoted in *National Catholic Reporter,* April 22, 1988, p. 7.

Riley statement from interview.

Oehler quoted in "Women Continue to Push for Bigger Roles," *Chicago Tribune,* May 13, 1990.

Lyons is written about in "Helen Lyons, 79, Dies," *New York Times,* August 15, 1989.

131 Greenberg quote from an article she wrote in *Washington Post,* "The Education of a 'Lady Rabbi,'" July 2, 1989.

131–132 Bishop Harris information and quotes from various articles including "Women, Blacks Feel Acceptance" and "Woman Consecrated as Episcopal Bishop," which appeared in *Boston Globe,* February 12, 1989; "Black Women's Bumpy Path to Church Leadership," *New York Times,* July 29, 1990; *New Choices,* July 1989, p. 39; *U.S. News & World Report,* June 19, 1989, p. 56.

132 Holmes is profiled in "Woman Bishop Consecrated," *Washington Post,* November 20, 1992.

Quinn quoted in "Women Continue to Push for Bigger Roles," *Chicago Tribune,* May 13, 1990.

Keller quoted in *U.S. Catholic,* March 1988, p. 32.

Brown Zikmund quote reported in "Women Challenge Old Theology," *Christian Science Monitor,* April 13, 1990.

Harris is quoted in "Episcopal Bishop Urges Women Take Leadership Roles," *Boston Globe,* April 29, 1991.

133 Hennessey quote from *National Catholic Reporter,* April 22, 1988, p. 7.

Wooden quoted in *U.S. Catholic,* March 1988, p. 32.

Smith quote reported in *McCall's,* December 1989, p. 91.

Grade-school teacher quote from *National Catholic Reporter,* April 27, 1990, p. 14.

Language revisions reported in *The Christian Century,* April 22, 1987, p. 376, and April 15, 1987, p. 352; "Women Clerics Still Unwelcome," *Chicago Tribune,* June 30, 1989; and *Time,* October 26, 1992, p. 72.

133–134 Cohen quote from "For Area Jewish Women, Passover Is Time to Reflect," *Washington Post,* April 18, 1992.

134 An interview with Schneiders appeared in *U.S. Catholic,* May 1990, p. 20.

Kane's quote reported in "Religious Women's Crusade," *Boston Globe,* March 1, 1990.

Stone-Horst is quoted in "Women Continue to Push for Bigger Roles," *Chicago Tribune,* May 13, 1990.

Schneiders quotes from her interview in *U.S. Catholic,* May 1990, p. 20.

135 Hermes article appeared in *U.S. Catholic,* August 1989, p. 28.

Catholic woman's quote from *National Catholic Reporter,* April 27, 1990, p. 14.

Bishops' drafts from the Center of Concern, "Bishops Decry Sexism," *Boston Globe,* April 3, 1990, and "America's Catholic Bishops," *New York Times,* April 3, 1990.

Rosemary Radford Ruether's letter appeared in *National Catholic Reporter,* May 18, 1990, p. 16.

135–136 Fourth draft information and Fiedler quote from "Bishops' Draft," *Washington Post,* September 6, 1992, and "Bishops Reject Vatican Stance," *Denver Post,* November 19, 1992.

136 Center of Concern statement from "Split Catholic Bishops Shun Proposals," *New York Times,* September 14, 1990.

Niesen quote from *Time,* November 23, 1992, p. 57.

Catholics favoring women priests from "Catholics Are at Odds with Bishops," *New York Times,* June 19, 1992.

136–137 Sipe statement and abuse information from "Catholic Crisis: Abuse by Priests," *USA Today,* February 1, 1993; and "Opening the Door," in the paper's December 14, 1992, issue.

137 DeRycke's statement from "Catholic Women Seek to Open,"
    Washington Post, November 11, 1990. Numbers on priests reported
    in *Economist,* December 15, 1990, p. 41.

    Bonnike statement from "Catholic Group Calls for Reform," *Chi-
    cago Tribune,* February 28, 1990.

    Gallup poll from "Priests as Husbands," *New York Times,* June 13,
    1992.

    Ohio church action cited in *National Catholic Reporter* (*NCR*),
    March 30, 1990, p. 5.

138 Pope's statement from *NCR,* November 18, 1988, p. 2. Reid and
    Repikoff quotes appeared in *NCR,* August 24, 1990, p. 4.

    The Burgmaier statement found in "Let Women Come in from the
    Cold," *National Catholic Reporter,* December 8, 1989.

    Wallace statement and Kane quote from "Catholic Women Seek to
    Open," *Washington Post,* November 11, 1990.

139 Vaughn quote appeared in *Glamour,* March 1993, p. 201.

139–140 "Tradition gets a twist" section based on information from an
    interview with Rossi, "Women Served as Priests," *Grand Rapids
    Press,* November 9, 1991. Rossi's work appeared in the *Journal of
    Feminist Studies in Religion,* vol. 7, no. 1. Kroeger, Otranto, Kara-
    ban and Fitzpatrick quotes from the *Grand Rapids Press* article.

5. The Menopause Megatrend

141 Gail Sheehy's excellent article was "The Silent Passage: Meno-
    pause," *Vanity Fair,* October 1991, which was also the source for
    the Mansfield and Bush quotes on p. 143 and for the ages at which
    women undergo menopause after hysterectomies.

143 Menopause before 40 information from *Newsweek,* cited below,
    p. 67.

144 The *Newsweek* story appeared August 6, 1990, p. 66, and is the
    source for the Utian quote on this page.

    Attendance at 1992 meeting and Census prediction from *American
    Demographics,* March 1993, p. 44.

144–145 Utian quote from *Newsweek* story cited above.

145 National Osteoporosis Foundation estimates cited in Sheehy.

    Estimates of hip fracture costs from the March 1990 *Journal of
    Clinical Orthopedics & Related Research,* pp. 163–66.

    New Zealand study reported in "Study: Calcium Prevents Bone
    Loss," *Denver Post,* February 18, 1993.

145–146 Matthews study cited in *Newsweek,* which is also the source for the McKinlay results and quote.

147 Bernau quote from "False Security," *Rocky Mountain News,* August 9, 1991.

Brigham and Women's Hospital study reported in "Women Needed for NIH Study," *USA Today,* September 18, 1992.

GAO study reported in "Women Often Slighted in Drug Studies," *USA Today,* October 30, 1992.

147–148 "Explanations" of women's exclusions from clinical trials cited in *Business Week,* July 16, 1990, p. 33.

148 Blumenthal quote from "Women's Health Issues Excluded from Research," *USA Today,* December 27, 1990.

148–149 *The New England Journal of Medicine,* and the Brigham and Women's study were reported in various media, including "Women Face Treatment Gap in Heart Disease," *Wall Street Journal,* June 26, 1991.

Colorado Hospital Association report from "False Security," *Rocky Mountain News,* August 9, 1991.

Seattle study and quote from researchers from "Study Finds a Gender Gap in the Treatment of Heart Attacks," *New York Times,* November 13, 1991.

Wenger quote from "Women Don't Get Equal Heart Care," *New York Times,* July 25, 1991, as is the Ayanian quote.

149–150 Healy quote from *New England Journal of Medicine* cited in *Washington Post* story above.

150 Women's Health Initiative description and Shalala quote from "U.S. Launches Vast Study of Woman's Health," *USA Today,* October 29, 1991; "U.S. Health Study to Involve 160,000 Women," *New York Times,* March 31, 1993; and "NIH Has Coordinator," *Washington Post* Health section, October 6, 1992.

Schroeder's bill described in "Unisex Research," *Denver Post,* August 4, 1991.

151 Gotto quote from "Estrogen After Menopause Cuts Heart Attack Risk," *New York Times,* September 12, 1991.

Marino story and quotes from "False Security," *Rocky Mountain News,* August 9, 1991.

151–152 Altman's story, "Men, Women and Heart Disease: More Than a Question of Sexism," appeared in *New York Times,* August 6, 1991.

152 Kirschstein quote from "Gender Bias in Health Care Is No Myth," *Washington Post* Health section, July 30, 1991.

Percent of women who take estrogen reported in *American Demographics*, March 1993, p. 47.

153 Benefit of adding progestin to estrogen reported in "Menopause Study Favors Drug Mixture," *Washington Post*, April 15, 1993.

153–154 Barrett-Connor and Friedman quote from "Estrogen Therapy: More Data, Less Certainty," *Washington Post* Health section, September 4, 1990.

154 Sales of Premarin cited in "Doubt Remains About Estrogen," *Wall Street Journal*, September 12, 1991; and *American Demographics*, March 1993, p. 47.

154–155 Dr. Lert recommends calcium oronate or calcium glutonate and reports that one symptom of menopause is a decrease in the production of hydrochloric acid (HCL) in the stomach, needed for the absorption of calcium. One telltale sign that a menopausal or post-menopausal woman is low on HCL is if she begins to belch after a fairly simple meal when she did not do so before. One way to absorb more calcium is to replace the acid with the old folk remedy of a teaspoon of apple cider vinegar in a glass of water sipped during a meal.

Dr. Lert suggests asking a nutritionist or chiropractor about glandular extracts (proto-morphogeno) of the uterus and ovaries, which are *not* available over the counter at health food stores. Considering that synthetic estrogen comes from pregnant cows, a bovine ovary extract is not *that* strange. She thinks the best company making these supplements is Standard Process Labs in Palmyra, Wisconsin, and recommends only their product. The company has an 800 number that refers people to a nearby chiropractor or nutritionist who can dispense it. A growing number of gynecologists are also recommending these supplements that are derived from animals.

For an additional discussion, see "Menopause Naturally," *Natural Health*, March/April 1992, p. 75.

155–156 Sheehy, Mead and Stevenson quotes from Sheehy, cited earlier.

156 Numbers of letters to the White House cited in "Breast Cancer, A Special Terror," *Boston Globe*, November 4, 1991.

Maguire quote from *Boston Globe*, cited above.

157 Donoghue quote from "Turning Disease into a Cause," *New York Times*, January 7, 1991.

All figures on breast cancer and AIDS research from the National Institutes of Health.

Langer quote from *Boston Globe,* cited above.

158 Boston and Sacramento demonstrations cited in "Health and Fitness" notes, *Vogue,* August 1991, p. 178.

Boston demonstration from *Boston Globe,* cited above, and in "A No-Show at the Women's Health Rally," *Boston Globe,* November 4, 1991.

158–159 CAN ACT demonstration is described in "Activists Mobilize for Healthcare," *New Directions for Women,* July/August 1991.

159 Rosenberg quote from *Boston Globe,* November 4, 1991, cited above.

State laws concerning mammography coverage from the American College of Obstetricians and Gynecologists and the American Cancer Society.

New Blue Cross/Blue Shield policy reported in "Blue Cross Agrees to Fund Breast Cancer Experiment," *Washington Post,* November 13, 1990.

159–160 Pinn statement, budget and study reported in "A Better Prognosis," *USA Today,* September 24, 1992.

160 Increase in early-stage tumors cited in "Quandary Created by Gain in Detecting Breast Cancer," *New York Times,* July 21, 1991.

160–161 Section "Good News About Breast Cancer" is based on the landmark story "Saving Your Breasts" in the October 1991 issue of *Self.* Editor in chief Alexandra Penney worked with guest editor Evelyn Lauder, who spearheaded the drive to build a state-of-the-art breast cancer facility at Memorial Sloan-Kettering Cancer Center in New York. In that story, we read the words "cure" and "20"-year survival rate for the first time.

161 Norton quote from *Self* article, cited above.

Percent of mastectomies and those who should be able to have breast conservation from "Curbing Breast Removal," *USA Today,* October 20, 1992.

Blakeslee article appeared in *New York Times,* March 15, 1992.

New NCI figure, based on expanding pool to 85 from "Chances of Breast Cancer Is Figured," *New York Times,* September 27, 1992.

Kelly statement from Blakeslee story, cited above.

162 Size of tumors and age at which mammography can detect them from *Self,* October 1991, as is NIH estimate of potential lowered death rates.

The 1993 studies, American Cancer Society recommendation and Lawrence quote are from "Mammograms During 40's Urged," *Denver Post,* February 3, 1993.

163 Langer quote from "Quandary Created by Gain in Detecting Breast Cancer," *New York Times,* July 21, 1991.

Camp quote from "In Providing Mammograms, Questions of Cost and Care," *New York Times,* August 16, 1991.

Bates quote from *FDA Consumer,* September 1991, pp. 15–20.

164 Fugh-Beerman quote from "Powerful Hormone to Be Tested in War to Prevent Breast Cancer," *New York Times,* September 18, 1991.

Benefits of tamoxifen from "Breast Cancer Drug's Benefit," *Washington Post,* October 23, 1992.

Pradi gene cited in *Self* story above.

164–165 King quote on Pap smear–type test is from "Gene Linked to Breast Cancer," *USA Today,* July 31, 1991.

165–167 The implant issue was of course widely covered in the media but we thought the best coverage was in the *Wall Street Journal* and offer these citations in particular: "The Implant Circus" (editorial), February 18, 1992, and "Breast Implant Debate Is Pitting Women Against Other Women," February 14, 1992.

165 Plastic surgeon survey of implant recipients cited in *Newsweek,* November 25, 1991, p. 65.

165–166 Information about implant recipients in Public Citizen's Health Research Study from "Women Assail, Praise Silicone at Hearing," *Washington Post,* November 13, 1991, and the FDA.

166–167 Dow 1993 confession reported in "Silicone Gel Found to Be an Irritant," *Denver Post,* March 20, 1993.

167 Uterine and cervical cancer deaths and diagnosis from National Cancer Institute. Richart quote from "The Importance of Pap Tests," *Washington Post* Health section, July 24, 1990, which is also the source for the "90 percent of deaths could be prevented" statistic.

The 1983 study is cited in "The Importance of Pap Tests," *Washington Post* Health section, July 24, 1990.

The University of Washington study is from "The Importance of Pap Smears," cited above.

168 "Infrequent Pap Smears Raise Risk of Cancer," *Washington Post* Health section, January 2, 1990.

AMA concerns are cited in "The Controversial Pap Test: It Could Save Your Life," *FDA Consumer,* September 1989, which is also the source for the regulations cited in bullet form on page 168, and for the Creasman quote.

169 Ovarian cancer diagnoses and deaths from the National Cancer Institute.

169–170 The section on ovarian cancer, including Dudzinski, Piver, Young and Alberts quotes, based on "Fighting Ovarian Cancer," *Washington Post* Health section, May 30, 1990, as is the profile (or lack thereof) of typical victim.

170–171 All numbers on AIDS from the Centers for Disease Control.

171 That AIDs is the leading killer of young women in New York is from a study published in *Lancet* and reported in "U.N. Sees 1990's AIDS Toll Soar for Women and Young," *New York Times,* July 28, 1990.

Women are the fastest growing AIDS group from *Self,* October 1992, p. 98. One in seven statistic from *Glamour,* November 1992, p. 30.

171–172 Women's increased vulnerability to AIDS, ability of some people in early and late stages to infect more easily, and the legacy of the Belgian engineer from "The AIDS Epidemic's Forgotten Side," *Washington Post,* November 17, 1991. The *Post* story on the women's group, including the anonymous quote, was "Women with HIV: Angry and Often Unsuspecting," November 18, 1991.

172–173 Birth-control section on Norplant based in large part on "5-year Contraceptive Implant Seems Headed for Wide Use," *New York Times,* November 29, 1991, which is also the source for the Kotecki quote and the reports from physicians about patients' reactions.

173 Paquin school information and Law quote from *Newsweek,* February 15, 1993, p. 37.

Judge Broadman's action reported in above *New York Times* article and woman's withdrawal of agreement cited in *Time,* March 23, 1992, p. 54.

Depo Provera data from "FDA Approves Depo Provera," *Washington Post,* October 30, 1992, and "Making Birth Control Easier," *New York Times,* November 8, 1992. New birth control pill trials reported in "New Birth Control Pill," *USA Today,* December 23, 1992.

174 American Fertility Society report from *Lear's,* January 1993, p. 37.

175 Brinsden quote from "Off the Shelf Babies for Childless Couples," *Sunday Times* (London), December 15, 1991.

Newsweek article on fertility services appeared in the June 29, 1992, issue, p. 38.

American Fertility Society data is from "When Grandmother Is the Mother, Until Birth," *New York Times,* August 5, 1991, which is also the source for the Righetti family surrogacy and the quotes from Drs. Katz and Jonsen.

175–176 Sherling information from "53-Year-Old Grandmother Has Test-Tube Twins," *Boston Globe*, November 12, 1992. Wesolowski data appeared in "One Birth Makes Woman Both Mom and Grandma," *Rocky Mountain News*, December 30, 1992; and "A Mother's Gift," *New York Times*, February 16, 1993. Cooper is quoted in the *Rocky Mountain Times* article.

176 Percentage of new primary-care physicians is cited in "Salaries Up, Supply Down in Family Practice," *Washington Post* Health section, September 3, 1991.

Percentage of females in American College of Obstetricians and Gynecologists, residents, and medical students from "Women Still Behind in Medicine," *New York Times,* September 10, 1991.

Statistics on doctors who began residencies and ob/gyns by 2000 from *Glamour*, February 1993, p. 50.

177 Older medical-school graduate cited in "American Topics," *International Herald Tribune,* June 6, 1992.

Paragraph on lack of women as medical school deans, and as AMA CEO's or in American College of Obstetricians and Gynecologists is from source cited directly above.

178 Nursing studies cited in "Beyond Tender Loving Care, Nurses Are a Force in Research," *New York Times,* August 13, 1991.

Number of nurse researchers from "Nursing Research," *USA Today*, August 4, 1992.

The George Washington University study cited in *U.S. News & World Report,* August 5, 1992, p. 44, which is the source for their poll.

179 The Morrissey statement is from *Newsweek,* August 12, 1991, p. 57.

San Diego's and Gainesville's menopause programs/centers cited in *Newsweek,* August 6, 1990, pp. 66–68.

179–180 Groertzen, Dan and Harrison statements appeared in "Doctors Consider a Specialty Focusing on Women's Health," *New York Times*, November 7, 1992. American Hospital Association data reported in *American Demographics*, March 1993, p. 48. Rynne quote is from "Hospitals Court Women," *New York Times*, October 18, 1992.

180 Examples of women's centers from *Glamour,* March 1992, pp. 52–55. Stuenkel quote from *Newsweek,* August 12, 1991, p. 57.

181 Norton quote from 1991 *Self* story cited earlier.

6. Collaborative Couples

183 Rodham Clinton's ranking by *National Law Journal* reported in "Hillary a Star in Her Own Right," *Denver Post*, November 9, 1992.

Schneiders quote from *Newsweek*, April 26, 1993, p. 34.

Washington Post statements appeared in "Hillary Clinton's Inner Politics," May 6, 1993.

184 Lee and Davis information from "Married with Spacesuits," *Boston Globe*, August 9, 1992, and "Shuttle Soars," *Washington Post*, September 13, 1992. The Fraser's were profiled in "Working at Home," *San Diego Union*, August 25, 1991. Zagat data from *Business Week*, October 28, 1991, p. 98. Ilitch information from "He's Marketing, She's Finance," *New York Times*, December 6, 1992. Gordon data from *Working Woman*, May 1993, p. 54.

186–187 Schrage and Oldenberg quotes from "Getting it Together: The Promise of Collaboration in an Egocentric Society," *Washington Post*, March 12, 1991.

187 Campbell quotes from "Married . . . With Business," *Black Enterprise*, April 1990.

187–188 Rosenfeld quote from *The Art Biz*, Alice Goldfarb Marquis (Chicago: Contemporary Books), 1991.

188 Dose quote from "Unlimited Partners," *New Age Journal*, March/April 1989.

188–189 Michael Dorris and Louise Erdrich quotes from "A Novel Relationship," *Boston Globe*, April 3, 1991.

190 Will and Michele Beemer quotes from "Building Blocks," *Continental Profiles*, July 1991, and interview with the authors.

191–193 All Roger and Nana Sullivan quotes from interviews. Nana Sullivan is John Naisbitt's daughter.

193 Treadway quote from "Inside the Nation's Best-Run S. & L.," *New York Times*, September 9, 1990.

193–194 Herb and Marion Sandler quotes from "Inside the Nation's Best-Run S. & L.," *New York Times*, September 9, 1990.

195 Sam Edelman quote from *New Age Journal*, March 1989.

Nicola Pelly and Harry Parnass quoted from "Stylemaking Couples," *Chatelaine*, June 1988.

196–197 Tom and Gun Denhart quotes from "The Bold New Force In Kids' Wear," *Working Woman*, November 1989.

197 Edelman quotes from "Unlimited Partners," *New Age Journal*, March/April 1989.

198 Rosen quote from "The American Dream," *Inc.*, April 1990.

199–200 Jeanlozes quotes from "Unlimited Partners," *New Age Journal*, March/April 1989.

200 Business Enterprise Awards quote from a full-page ad in *The New York Times*, March 6, 1992.

201 Campbell quote from "Married . . . With Business," *Black Enterprise*, April 1990.

Pelly quote from "Stylemaking Couples," *Chatelaine*, June 1988.

203 Estridges quotes from "Hard Times for Ken and Jennifer," *Boston Globe*, April 2, 1991.

203–204 Marta Vago quotes and information from *Glamour*, April 1991.

205 Criswell quote from *In Love & Business*, Sharon Nelton (New York: John Wiley & Sons).

7. Fashion: Top Down to Bottom Up

208 Citations from *The Encyclopaedia of Fashion*, pp. 68, 187.

208–209 Quote from *20,000 Years of Fashion*, p. 429.

209 Karan quote reported in *Current Biography*, August 1990, p. 25.

Data on women designers and apparel market from *Forbes*, May 11, 1992, p. 118.

210–211 Data on incomes from the U.S. Census Bureau.

211 Retail sales figures reported in "January Sales of Retail Goods Were Up," *Wall Street Journal*, July 2, 1991.

Business Week quote from the January 18, 1993, issue, p. 38.

Wall Street Journal article cited and Millstein quote from "Working Women Vary Their Styles," July 2, 1991. Women who buy on sale from *American Demographics*, July 1991, p. 11.

Robinson statement cited in *American Demographics*, February 1989, p. 50.

212 Ford Model Agency from an interview.

Sinderbrand quote from *Newsweek*, April 4, 1988, p. 54.

Karan's quote from "Donna Karan," *Los Angeles Times*, June 24, 1990.

213 Paglia is quoted in "Yes, But Can She Make Them Swoon?" *New York Times*, May 26, 1991.

214 Banks statement from "Fantasy Gives Ground To Midrange Apparel," *Wall Street Journal*, January 23, 1991.

Glamour poll reported in the magazine's March 1989 issue, p. 207.

Wintour was quoted in *Business Week,* November 26, 1990, p. 137.

215 Cooper's quote appeared in "Fantasy Gives Ground To Midrange Apparel," *Wall Street Journal,* January 23, 1991.

Mirabella's circulation and growth rate from "Can Four Magazines Stay in Fashion?" *New York Times,* January 27, 1992, and *Mirabella* spokesperson.

Wells quote appeared in *Advertising Age,* March 11, 1991, pp. 5–6.

216 *Encyclopaedia of Fashion* quote found on p. 70.

Value of Chanel empire from *Forbes,* April 3, 1989, p. 104. Quote attributed to Chanel from *New Yorker,* February 27, 1989, p. 71.

Sales data on Miller and Jovine reported in *Forbes,* May 11, 1992, p. 116, Vittadini from *Working Woman,* May 1993.

216–217 Karan quotes from "Donna Karan: Sensual Flair for Executives," *Los Angeles Times,* June 16, 1989, and *Savvy Woman,* September 1989, p. 63.

Mellen quoted in *Manhattan, Inc.,* October 1989, p. 63.

217 Rykiel quote from "The Fashionable Spell of Sonia Rykiel," *Chicago Tribune,* November 2, 1988.

217–218 Claiborne statements reported in *Current Biography,* June 1989, p. 6. Additional Claiborne information from various sources including the company, and *Working Woman,* April 1992, p. 68. Bronston statements from *Forbes,* January 7, 1991, p. 139, and *Fortune,* September 9, 1991, p. 32.

218 List of most admired companies from *Fortune,* February 10, 1992, pp. 40–46.

218–219 Millstein quotes from *Manhattan, Inc.,* October 1989, p. 63. Karan information and quotes from *People,* December 25, 1989, p. 105; "Donna Karan," *Los Angeles Times,* June 24, 1990; "The Easy Style of New York," *The European,* April 5, 1991; *Business Week,* December 16, 1991, p. 122; *Time,* November 11, 1991, p. 69; *Forbes,* May 11, 1992, p. 116. *Forbes* statistic cited in October 1, 1990, issue, p. 261. Burstein quote from "The Easy Style of New York," *The European,* April 5, 1991.

219 Sales estimates from *Working Woman,* May 1993, p. 53; *Business Week*, September 28, 1992, p. 84; and *Time,* December 21, 1992, p. 54.

Karan in Europe from "U.S. Designers with All the Answers," *The European,* March 15, 1991, and company spokesperson.

220 Allard and Scandiffio quotes from *Savvy Woman,* October 1988, p. 51. Sales reported in Forbes, May 11, 1992, p. 116.

Rykiel quote and data from "The Fashionable Spell of Sonia Rykiel," *Chicago Tribune,* November 2, 1988, and from Sonia Rykiel Company spokesperson.

Kawakubo information from "Rei Kawakubo," *Asahi Shimbun Japan Access,* March 23, 1992.

220–221 Escada data from various sources, including *Lear's,* March 1991, p. 100; *Forbes,* September 16, 1991, p. 65; "High Fashion Escada Expands World-Wide," *Wall Street Journal,* April 15, 1992; "Escada Style," *The European,* April 15–18, 1993; and *Forbes,* December 7, 1992.

221–222 Bergé and Pinto are quoted in *Business Week,* April 22, 1991, p. 108. Mori, Klein and Ruttenstein statements, and secondary line sales figures, from *Time,* November 11, 1991, p. 69.

222 *Working Woman* survey reported in "USA Snapshot," *USA Today,* September 11, 1992.

Kors data and quote from *Fortune,* May 6, 1991, p. 9.

Karan quotes appeared in *Newsweek,* April 24, 1989, p. 84, and *Current Biography,* August 1990, p. 25.

Sales of DKNY in 1992 reported in *Time*, December 21, 1992, p. 57.

223 Card quotes are from her book *The Ms. Money Book* (E. P. Dutton), pp. 5, 6, 150, 143.

Verdan is quoted in "The Easy Style of New York," *The European,* April 5, 1991.

223–224 Cho statements from an interview, *New Choices for the Best Years,* August 1990, p. 80.

224 Bullets on the image industry from "Firms Help Clients," *Chicago Tribune,* August 20, 1990; *Forbes,* November 25, 1991, p. 212; and *Psychology Today,* January 1988, p. 51.

Pertschuk quote cited in *Working Woman,* November 1990, p. 144. Holland is quoted in *Glamour,* June 1991, p. 72.

Karan is quoted in *Manhattan, Inc.,* October 1989, p. 63.

Glamour survey reported in the May 1992 issue, p. 187.

225 Information on and quotes by young female designers from various sources, including *Harper's Bazaar,* August 1990, p. 70; *Nation's Business,* April 1990, p. 14; *Vogue,* October 1990, p. 131; *Savvy Woman,* August 1989, p. 77; *Mirabella,* October 1991, p. 168; and *Working Woman,* May 1993, p. 53.

226 Powell quote appeared in "In Clothes, Bigger Gets Better," *Washington Post,* August 17, 1991.

Large-size women over age 40 from *Forbes*, March 16, 1992, p. 116.

226–227 Radmin quotes and information on the Forgotten Woman from *Working Woman,* August 1991, p. 28; and from *Forgotten Woman.*

227 Store listings, Eden quote, apparel sales and growth cited in "In Clothes, Bigger Gets Better," *Washington Post,* August 17, 1991; *Forbes,* March 16, 1992, p. 116, and the March 29, 1993, issue, p. 44; and *Glamour,* February 1993, p. 150.

The *Forbes* report and Nelson quote appeared in the 1992 issue cited above.

227–228 *BBW* subscribers, statement and Shaw quote from *Big Beautiful Woman,* and the November 1991 issue of the magazine.

228 Ford Model Agency information from its New York office.

Fullem and Baylin quotes from "In Clothes, Bigger Gets Better," *Washington Post,* August 17, 1991.

229 White Plains quote and statistics measuring declines in mall shopping (including age groups) from *American Demographics,* October 1991, pp. 16, 48, and *Business Week,* November 26, 1990, p. 134.

229–230 *Wall Street Journal* article "Developed to Reinvigorate" appeared November 16, 1992. *The Future of Retailing* is described in *Future Survey,* September 1992. Number of shopping centers and Clayton statement from "42% of Denver Area Malls Likely to Fail," *Rocky Mountain News,* August 6, 1992.

230–231 Numbers of malls cited in "USA Snapshot," *USA Today,* July 23, 1991. The *American Demographics* story appeared in the April 1990 issue, on p. 37; it also included a description of Levitt's article, statistic on discretionary incomes and data on Donnelley Marketing study. Gordon was quoted in *Advertising Age,* January 21, 1991, p. 39. Statistic on discretionary incomes and data on Donnelly Marketing study.

231–232 Factory outlet and customer data, and statements by Frankfort, Morton, Dunham, and Carson from "Outlet Malls, No Longer Outcasts," *Washington Post,* December 17, 1991; Frankfort and Dunham interviews; *Lear's,* November 1991, p. 104.

232 Number of 1991 Reading, Pennsylvania, shoppers from customer coordinator, Vanity Fair factory outlet, Reading.

232–233 Segel, and TV shopping executive quotes, from *Insight,* May 7, 1990, p. 51.

Other shopping channel data and Holliday quote from QVC interviews.

233 Sherwood information and quote from interview.

Mail-order and shop-at-home citations from Direct Marketing Association. Walker is quoted in "Catalogers' Outlook Grows Brighter," *USA Today,* October 17, 1990.

Mail order as a percent of the women's apparel market reported in *Forbes,* December 7, 1992, p. 100.

234 Toll-free panty hose number cited in *Working Woman,* March 1990, p. 65.

Dixon quote from "Weekend Walker's Cry," *New York Times,* April 4, 1992.

234–235 Pendley, Beres, Campagnoli, Monyake and Addison statements, and mall information, from "Doing the Mall Stroll," *Washington Post,* October 12, 1991, and the *Saturday Evening Post,* September 1989, p. 55.

236 Theaters cited in *Advertising Age,* January 21, 1991, p. 39.

Gap sales reported in *Fortune,* December 2, 1991.

8. The Family Revival

Unless otherwise noted, statistics in this chapter are from the U.S. Census Bureau.

237 Hall quote from " 'Parent Power' Is on the Rise," *Christian Science Monitor,* May 6, 1991.

238 Percentage of traditional families reported in "Making Time for the Families," *Washington Post,* January 9, 1991.

239 Epstein quote from "Homeowners', Wed Couples' Numbers Dwindle," *USA Today,* June 11, 1991.

Waite is quoted in "Change in the American Family," *New York Times,* January 30, 1991.

239–240 Children being raised by a single-parent, poverty, and child-support statistics from Census Bureau, *Newsweek* special issue, Winter/Spring 1990, p. 16, and the January 13, 1992, issue, p. 48.

240 Burt is quoted in *Newsweek* special issue, Winter/Spring 1990, p. 24.

By 2010 estimate reported in *American Demographics,* December 1990, p. 24.

Children born to unwed mothers age 30 to 34 and education levels from the National Center for Health Statistics (NCHS).

Mattes is quoted in "A Baby Doesn't Mean Marriage Anymore," *USA Today,* December 4, 1991.

241 Weddings involving someone who had already been married, that half of unmarried-couple households marry, and women who have lived with someone from NCHS. Marriage rate lowest in ten years from *U.S. News & World Report*, October 19, 1992, p. 54.

Experts and Wilson statements reported in "Americans Spending Less Time Married," *Washington Post*, August 26, 1991.

U.S. News & World Report, December 16, 1991, p. 80.

242 Grandmother and Lee quotes from "More Children Are Being Raised by Their Grandparents," *Grand Rapids Press*, November 14, 1991.

Divorce data and *Newsweek* story from the January 13, 1992, issue, p. 49, and NCHS.

Lasch is quoted in *New Perspectives Quarterly*, Winter 1990, p. 45.

242–243 Mattox and Dafoe quotes appeared in "More Choose to Stay Home with Children," *USA Today*, May 10, 1991. Robert Half survey reported in "USA Snapshot," *USA Today*, November 20, 1990.

243 Robinson data from "Trading Fat Paychecks for Free Time," *Wall Street Journal*, August 5, 1991.

Yankelovich Clancy Shulman data reported in *Fortune*, February 10, 1992, p. 101. Gallup poll appeared in the *American Demographics* article cited, December 1991, p. 17.

244 Barnett and Rivers statements and most studies cited in "Good News" section from *Working Woman*, February 1992, p. 62.

244–245 Reisman quote and *Working Mother* survey appeared in the magazine's April 1993 issue, p. 58.

245 O'Connor's quote appeared in *New Perspectives Quarterly*, Winter 1990, p. 4.

Working men statistics from the Bureau of Labor Statistics.

Levine statement and Robert Half survey from *American Demographics*, February 1991, p. 52.

245–246 Catalyst survey, Smith, Sotsky, and Reynolds quotes, and leave information from "More Men Taking the Daddy Track," *Washington Post*, November 6, 1990, and *Business Week*, April 15, 1991, p. 90. Lotus information from the company. Du Pont survey appeared in "The Daddy Track," *Wall Street Journal*, April 30, 1991.

246–247 Weisner and Kelly quotes, and polls from "Even in the Frenzy of the 90's, Dinner Time," *New York Times*, December 5, 1990.

247 The neo–baby boom section including Easterlin statement based on *Fortune*, February 10, 1992, p. 101.

248 Rodham Clinton quote appeared in *Working Mother*, September 1992, p. 38.

248–249 Burkin and Marshall quotes from "The Trials of Being a Mother in Law," *Boston Globe*, May 23, 1991. Fenning is quoted in "Working Part Time Without Paying the Penalty," *New York Times*, August 3, 1990.

249 Pillsbury Madison & Sutro policy and Craston quote from "Part-Time Partners," *Washington Post*, December 15, 1992.

Larson quotes reported in " 'Today' Anchor Larson Prefers Tomorrow with Family," *Denver Post*, April 21, 1993.

249–250 Christensen, Brodman and Bregger quotes from "More Choose to Stay Home with Children," *USA Today*, May 10, 1991. An interview with O'Connor appeared in *New Perspectives Quarterly*, Winter 1990, p. 4.

250 Nanny information from various sources, including *Newsweek*, January 27, 1992, p. 50.

251–252 Miller quote from an interview. Quotes and information on Grey, Risse, Ades and Felton from "Expanding the Office and Staying at Home," *Washington Post*, February 26, 1991.

252 Franchising moms data and quotes from "More Working Mothers Opt for Flexibility," *Wall Street Journal*, January 31, 1991.

253–254 Companies listed and Bush quotes from various sources, including *Home Office Computing*, June 1990, p. 88; "Increasingly in Area, Home Is Where the Workplace Is," *Washington Post*, April 22, 1991. Gordon statement from interview. Benefits of telecommuting reported in *Newsweek*, April 24, 1989, p. 58.

254 Lasch quote from *New Perspectives Quarterly*, Winter 1990, p. 45.

Christensen is quoted in "More Choose to Stay Home with Children," *USA Today*, May 10, 1991.

254–255 Spriggs and Tyler data from "Managers Navigate Unchartered Waters," *Wall Street Journal*, December 7, 1992. King quote from *Glamour*, February 1993, p. 95.

255–256 Family-Friendly Index data and quotes in these two sections from "Small Strides, Relatively Speaking" and "Pro-Family, Pro-Business," *Washington Post*, November 15, 1991; "Companies Get C for Sensitivity," *USA Today*, November 15, 1991; *Business Week*, November 25, 1991, p. 234; *Newsweek*, November 25, 1991, p. 48; *Working Woman*, January 1992, p. 27; and *Glamour*, February 1993, p. 198.

257 Wipfler quotes appeared in " 'Parent Power' Is on the Rise," *Christian Science Monitor*, May 6, 1991.

Presser statement from *American Demographics,* February 1991, p. 51.

Dreyer statement from an interview.

Vann statement appeared in "More Care for the Corporate Kids," *New York Times,* June 9, 1991.

258–259 Collaboration with IBM, Childs quote, and Minneapolis companies reported in "Companies Team Up to Improve Quality of Their Employees' Child-Care Choices," *Wall Street Journal,* October 17, 1991. Rittenburg and Rose were quoted in *American Demographics,* February 1991, p. 53.

American Business Collaboration was described in various articles, including "A Corporate Collaboration," *New York Times,* September 27, 1992, "Six Area Firms Launch Day Care," *Washington Post,* September 11, 1992, and *Business Week,* February 8, 1993, p. 105.

Working Mother and Reisman statements from *Working Mother,* November 1992, p. 80.

Washington D.C.–area child-care pledge and similar programs reported in "Four Large Firms in Area to Sponsor Child Care," *Washington Post,* December 19, 1993.

Child-care activity by small businesses reported in "Firms Offer Parents Help Caring for Kids," *Wall Street Journal,* September 5, 1991.

259–260 Innovation honor-roll section and quotes from "More Care for the Corporate Kids," *New York Times,* June 9, 1991; *Newsweek,* November 25, 1991, p. 49; *Business Week,* November 25, 1991, p. 234; "Pro-Family, Pro-Business," *Washington Post,* November 15, 1991.

260–261 Older day-care workers information and quotes from "Companies Team Up to Improve Quality of Their Employees' Child-Care Choices," *Wall Street Journal,* October 17, 1991; "At Day Care, a Meeting of Generations," *Washington Post,* January 27, 1992.

261–262 Number of adult day-care centers reported in *Newsweek,* July 2, 1990, p. 56. Scharlach data and Thursz quote appeared in "Elder Care Takes Time," *USA Today,* February 4, 1991. Average age of caregivers, Kuriansky statement, and study reported in *USA Today* appeared in "The Growing Burden of Caring for Elderly Parents," September 3, 1991. *Newsweek* data cited in the July 16, 1990, issue, p. 48, which also includes Kuriansky quote and AARP percentage. Leibold is quoted in "Day Care Program Bridges Generations," *Christian Science Monitor,* April 15, 1991. Boudreaux quote from an interview.

262 Work/Family Directions described in *Working Woman*, January 1993, p. 30.

262–263 Corporations accept gay families section and benefits provided based on *Working Woman*, December 1991, p. 13, *Fortune*, December 16, 1991, p. 50; and "Gays Make Gains in Health Care" *USA Today*, April 23, 1993.

264 Popenoe from " 'Parent Power' Is on the Rise," *Christian Science Monitor*, May 6, 1991.

State action reported in "3 States Proceed With Measures on Family Leave," *Washington Post*, December 31, 1991.

264–265 Family leave data and Families and Work Institute statement from *Nation's Business*, April 1993, p. 26; "Effect of Family-Leave Bill," *USA Today*, February 3, 1993; and *U.S. News & World Report*, February 15, 1993, p. 28.

9. The Goddess Reawakening

267 Interest in Freya reported in "God as Woman Wins Converts," *The European*, May 31–June 2, 1991.

Earth Day ritual reported in "When God Was a Woman," *Time*, May 6, 1991.

267–268 Auerbach quoted in "Is Goddess Worship Finally Going to Put Men in Their Place?" *Wall Street Journal*, June 7, 1990.

268 Beasley quoted in "God as Woman," *The European*, May 31–June 2, 1991.

Time's description appeared in "When God Was a Woman," May 6, 1991.

269 500,000 estimate from "God as Woman," *The European*, May 31–June 2, 1991; the 100,000 estimate from "When God Was a Woman," *Time*, May 6, 1991.

Fox quote from *Elle*, August 1991, p. 62.

Sage Women circulation, Los Angeles and San Francisco groups and Starr Goode from *Wall Street Journal*, cited above.

The *Wall Street Journal* statement appeared in "Is Goddess Worship Finally Going to Put Men in Their Place?" June 7, 1990.

269–270 Data on "Cakes" course, Luck quote, Borrowes-Toabe, Drake quote, and "Our Mother" quote all from "In Goddesses They Trust," *Boston Globe*, July 9, 1990.

270 Gadon's three-part heresy and new historical view from her book, *The Once and Future Goddess* (Harper & Row), pp. xi–xv.

271 Robb quote from her story "In Goddesses They Trust," *Boston Globe,* July 9, 1990.

274 Shakti-Shiva saying cited in Gadon, p. 19.

275 North American goddess figures from "Sacred and Legendary Women of Native North America" by Nancy Zak in *The Goddess Re-Awakening,* compiled by Shirley Nicholson (Theosophical Publishing House), pp. 232–42.

276 Discussion of Gimbutas draws extensively from Eisler's *The Chalice and the Blade* (Harper & Row) and in part from "The Goddess Theory," *Los Angeles Times Magazine,* June 11, 1989; "Raiders of the Lost Goddess," *East West,* December 1990; and "Did Goddess Worship Mark Ancient Age of Peace?" *Washington Post,* January 7, 1990.

277–278 Gimbutas quote cited in Eisler, p. 48.

Discussion of Gimbutas's critics and her response to them appears in *Los Angeles Times Magazine,* cited above.

Gimbutas quote from "Did Goddess Worship Mark Ancient Age of Peace?" *Washington Post,* January 7, 1990.

278 Gimbutas quote cited in Eisler, p. 51.

Eisler quote from her book, p. xvii.

Gimbutas quote "The Kurgan ideology . . ." from Eisler, p. 48.

"Weapons . . . etc." from *Los Angeles Times Magazine,* cited above.

Eisler quote from her book, p. 59.

279 Eisler's discussion of the Goddess and the Garden of Eden appears pp. 88–89.

Consolidation of power and male-dominant values discussed in many sources, including Gadon, p. xiv, and Eisler, pp. 124–34.

Gadon quote from her book, p. 199.

Mary and Apocrypha from Gadon, p. 194.

280 Crusaders restoring veneration of Virgin, *Golden Legend,* and zenith of Virgin's power from Gadon, pp. 203, 194.

Gadon quote, cathedral sites, "cakes and wine" from Gadon, pp. 194–95.

Gadon quote and discussion of virgin/whore sexuality from Gadon, p. 208.

280–281 Descriptions of Isis, Demeter and Artemis based on Gadon, pp. 194–99.

281 Eisler's discussion of witch trials as backlash appears on pp. 139–42.

Gadon quote from her book, p. 211, as is "constellation of beliefs" quote, p. 113.

Estimate of witches destroyed and quote from Starhawk, *Spiral Dance*, p. 20.

"Constellation of beliefs . . ." from Gadon, p. 113.

Description of tortures from *Spiral Dance*, p. 20.

Village beauties and villages with one or no women from *Spiral Dance*, p. 21.

282 Feast of Assumption and Titian painting cited in Gadon, p. 204.

Vatican's backoff of co-equal status of Mary cited in Gadon, p. 206, and in *Time*, December 30, 1991, p. 66.

Time story is also the source for the Warner quote, the list of the Virgin's recent sightings and the Schneiders quote.

284 Bruteau quote from "The Unknown Goddess" by Beatrice Bruteau in *The Goddess Re-Awakening*, p. 71.

285–286 Discussion of "masculine" and "feminine" characteristics and Stone quote from Merlin Stone's introduction to *The Goddess Re-Awakening*, pp. 7–9.

287 Oda quote from *The Heart of the Goddess* by Hallie Iglehart Austin (Wingbow Press), p. 146.

Bruteau quote from Nicholson, p. 76.

287–288 Napoli and Saul article appeared in *New Directions for Women*, July/August 1991.

10. Save the World: Women as Social Activists

291 Sen quote from "Public Action to Remedy Hunger," The Hunger Project, August 2, 1990.

Long quote from interview with authors.

Bush quote appeared in *Newsweek*, July 10, 1989, p. 36.

291–292 Winfrey information from "Kid Abuse Oprah's New Capitol Cause" and "Child Abuse: Big Secret of Shame," *USA Today*, November 13, 1991. Documentary data from "Hot Line Heats Up," *USA Today*, September 8, 1992.

292 Foley information and quote from *The Washingtonian*, October 1991, p. 67.

James information from "Voluntary Action Leadership," published by the National Volunteer Center, Summer 1991, p. 11.

Hopkinson quotes from October 1991, p. 81.

292–293 Do information and Iwanaga-Penrose quote from "She Teaches Good Old U.S. Assertiveness—to Refugees," *Los Angeles Times,* November 11, 1991.

293 Kelly and Bruenderman quotes from "Super Mom Has Taken 200 Children into Her Home Over the Years," *Grand Rapids Press,* November 10, 1991.

Muhammad quotes from "From Mom's Grief, Crusade Emerges Against Black-on-Black Violence," *Washington Post,* February 11, 1991, and from interview.

Flood information from "Voluntary Action Leadership," published by the National Volunteer Center, Summer 1991, p. 12.

293–294 Varela quotes from "Aiding the Poor Receives Its Reward," *New York Times,* August 20, 1990.

294 Brown quotes from "Neighborhood Reclaimed Its Street," *Washington Post,* November 19, 1990.

Silbert and Delancey Street information from *Parade,* March 15, 1992, pp. 4–6.

295 Data on women's philanthropy from National Network of Women's Funds and from *Business Week,* January 29, 1990, which is also the source for the Person and Ransom quotes.

295–296 Inayatullah quote from "A 'Marshall Plan' for the Environment," *New York Times,* May 3, 1990.

296 Global Assembly data from InterAction, Washington, D.C.

Starke information and quote from "An Upbeat Look at the Earth," *Los Angeles Times,* July 16, 1990.

296–297 Data on Wangari Maathai from "Foresters Without Diplomas" by Maathai in *Ms.,* March/April 1991; *Time,* April 29, 1991, and from *Women: The Key to Ending Hunger* (The Hunger Project) by Margaret Snyder, p. 8.

298 Drucker quoted in *Working Woman,* October 1989, p. 122.

298–299 Dec-Tam information from interview and from *Working Woman,* October 1989, p. 122.

299 Scruggs-Leftwich data quote from *Success,* January/February 1991, p. 30.

299–300 Houghton data and quote from *Working Woman,* October 1989, p. 122; from South Shore Bank interviews and literature; and "Chicago Bank Redefines Role," *USA Today,* January 8, 1993.

300 Conte information from interview.

300–301 Information on Gleaners from *Newsweek*, July 10, 1989, p. 56, and from interviews.

301 Berkeley Cares description in *The Economist*, October 12, 1991, p. 28.

SHARE information from *New Age Journal*, August/September 1990, p. 18, and from SHARE interview and literature.

301–302 WDC described in "Female Solutions to Housing Need," *Christian Science Monitor*, November 6, 1990.

302 Nelson quotes from "Chicago Program Helps Women on Welfare Return to Work," *Christian Science Monitor*, December 13, 1990, and from interviews.

Gray quotes from "Slum-buster," *Dallas Morning News*, August 17, 1987.

303 Updates and additional information from the National Center for Neighborhood Enterprise.

First Williams quote from "The President and Choice," *Wall Street Journal*, May 3, 1991.

Second Williams quote from "Get the Hostages Out," *Agenda*, Fall 1991.

Michelle Easton quote from "Choice: An Idea that Just Won't Go Away," *Agenda*, Spring 1991.

304 J. Patrick Rooney quotes from "Education's Golden Rule," *Wall Street Journal*, August 2, 1991.

Turner attribution from "The President and Choice," *Wall Street Journal*, May 3, 1991.

Clint Bolick quotes from "Choice: An Idea That Just Won't Go Away," *Agenda*, Spring 1991.

Polly Williams quotes from "Education's Golden Rule," *Wall Street Journal*, August 2, 1991.

305 Tracy quotes from "It Is Time to Give Choice a Chance," *Boston Globe*, May 26, 1991.

Chubb and Moe quotes from "Education Choice Tide Rising," *Washington Times*, August 30, 1990.

306 That 25 percent of women will be abused, from the American Medical Association and reported in "Doctors Urged to Check Women for Abuse Signs," *Boston Globe*, June 17, 1992, which is also the source for the FBI murder stat and the 1992 AMA report of 4 million battered women.

State requirements on child abuse from *Time*, June 29, 1992, p. 57.

Spillar quote from *The Feminist Majority Report*, December 1992, p. 9.

307 Smeal quote from "Inquiry: Women Are Refusing to Be Victims Anymore," *USA Today,* April 15, 1991.

Surgeon General statements reported in "Doctors Urged to Check Women," *Boston Globe,* June 17, 1992, and "Panel Cites Attacks on Women," *Washington Post,* October 3, 1992.

Paragraph on domestic violence citing American Medical Association and battering from Fund for the Feminist Majority fact sheet.

307–308 Sugg and Schwartz statements from "AMA Urges Questioning," *Washington Post,* June 17, 1992. Goldfarb quote appeared in *Time,* June 29, 1992, p. 57.

308 Crime Victims Research and Treatment Center's study cited in various media, including "Rapes More Common, New Study Claims," *USA Today,* April 23, 1992.

Percent of rapes reported in *Lear's,* March 1993, p. 46.

309 The Fund for the Feminist Majority issues the estimate of acquaintance rape. The Crime Victims study cited above says only 22 percent of rape perpetrators were strangers. That puts the percentage of acquaintance rapes at 78.

Smeal statement and *one* percent of rapists are convicted from the *USA Today* Inquiry story cited above.

310 States with violence against women laws reported in "Victims' Rights," *New York Times,* November 8, 1992.

IMPACT/Model Mugging from interviews and from "Women Learn to Shake Off Fear," *Washington Post,* November 20, 1989; "Women Find Self-Defense Courses in Short Supply," *Washington Post,* November 8, 1990; and "Mugging in the Classroom," *The Northwest Current,* June 1–14, 1989.

310–311 LaMotta knockout from *Self,* January 1992, p. 44.

311 Reecher quote from *Glamour,* February 1992, p. 63.

Heise article appeared in the March/April 1989 volume of *World Watch,* pp. 12–21.

311–312 Lockhart information from *Glamour,* October 1991, p. 102, and from interviews.

312 Caven quote from *Glamour,* February 1992, p. 20; Philadelphia center from *U.S. News & World Report,* September 30, 1991, p. 26.

312–313 Bosnian rapes and murders reported in "Muslims Killing Rape Victims," *Denver Post,* February 10, 1993.

313 Lori Heise quote from "When Women Are Prey," *Washington Post,* December 8, 1991.

Female genital mutilation data from Fran P. Hosken, Women's International Network, Lexington, Massachusetts.

314 Bullets on roles women play in the Third World are cited in "Building the Future with Women," a brochure of UNIFEM, the United Nation Development Fund for Women and in Snyder's *Women: The Key to Ending Hunger,* cited above.

The examples of SEWA and the Grameen Bank are cited in Snyder, p. 15.

FINCA data from interview and literature, Foundation for International Community Assistance, Alexandria, Va.

314–315 Trickle Up from interviews and organization's literature.

315 Ocloo is described in *Ms.,* May/June 1991, p. 16, and in *The Africa Prize for Leadership,* a publication of The Hunger Project.

315–316 Barry information from *Business Week,* June 3, 1991, p. 104.

316 Camp and Potts quotes from "Plan Is Offered for Stable Birth Rate," *New York Times,* February 26, 1990.

316–317 Data on population from *1990 Report on Progress Towards Population Stabilization,* published by Population Action International, or directly from the organization, unless otherwise noted.

317 Information in paragraph beginning "Population experts know" from *Population Issues Briefing Kit 1991,* published by United Nations Population Fund.

Mexico contraceptive use from "Plan Is Offered for Stable Birth Rate," *New York Times,* February 26, 1990.

Educated women in Brazil and Liberia and their family size from *Population Issues,* cited above.

Bullets on successful family planning by country: Thailand from "UN Reports Slowdown in World Population," *Christian Science Monitor,* May 15, 1991.

Indonesia's 1976 rate from "Plan Is Offered for Stable Birth Rate," *New York Times,* February 26, 1990; 1992 rate from Population Action International.

Zimbabwe from *The State of World Population 1991,* published by the United Nation's Population Fund, p. 19.

Percentages who want no more children yet do not practice birth control, and only half have access to family planning from *Population Issues* cited, p. 2.

318 Sub-Saharan birth rates from *Population Issues,* p. 5.

Contraception in Cameroon from "Plan Is Offered for Stable Birth Rate," *New York Times,* February 26, 1990.

Other African birthrates decline, African government support and UN estimate from *Population Issues,* pp. 5–6.

Suazo quote from *Ms.,* July/August 1991, p. 10.

Zimbabwe, Lima, and CEDPA accounts from InterAction, Washington, D.C.

319 *Simplemente Maria* from *Proceedings from The Enter-Educate Conference: Entertainment for Social Change,* published by Johns Hopkins University Center, p. 14.

Examples from Mexico, Nigeria, Egypt and Turkey from *Population Issues,* p. 18.

Examples of popular singers with family planning message from *Entertainment for Social Change,* cited above, pp. 20–23.

Piotrow material from *Entertainment for Social Change,* p. 13.

320–321 Schubert and both Maggrett quotes from interviews.

Favretto quotes from interview.

321 Wintz quote from *Lear's,* September 1990, p. 42.

Lukitsch statement from *Working Woman,* November 1991, p. 83.

Harkavy quote and description of campus community service from "Activism Makes 'Cool' Comeback," *Denver Post,* April 11, 1993.

322 Brooks quotes from *Savvy Woman,* February 1989, p. 58.

Additional New York Cares data from the organization. D.C. Cares data and Keitelman quote from *The Washingtonian,* November 1991, p. 67.

322–323 Gatten quote and Thompson data from *Savvy Woman,* February 1989, p. 58.

323 Barbara Bush quote from *Newsweek,* July 10, 1989, p. 44.

Tompkins quotes from *Working Woman,* September 1991, p. 67.

NCNB, Hard Rock Cafe and Wells Fargo examples from *Newsweek,* July 10, 1989, p. 38.

Total 1990 corporate contributions cited in *American Demographics,* September 1991, p. 38.

323–324 Chadwick School from interview.

324 Somerset School from *The Washingtonian,* November 1991, p. 68.

Marriot study cited in "Giving of Yourself," *Washington Post,* June 3, 1991.

Helgeland quote and increase of volunteers over age 65 from *American Demographics,* June 1991, p. 54.

Information on Dockett from "A One-Woman Volunteer Brigade," *Washington Post,* November 2, 1989.

Dole quote from "Personalities," *Washington Post,* February 5, 1991.

11. Women in the New World Order

330 Cresson quote from "Mitterrand Bets on Woman PM," *The European,* May 17, 1991.

First Robinson quotes from *Financial Times,* December 6, 1990.

Financial Times quotes from December 6, 1990, issue.

Second Robinson quote from "New President Sees a 'New Ireland'; Could She Be a Startling Beginning?" *New York Times,* December 27, 1990.

330–331 Lewis statement appeared in "Mary Robinson: Symbol and Witness," *International Herald Tribune,* January 16, 1993. Election data, Cummings and Clarity quotes from "Irishwoman on the March," *New York Times,* November 30, 1992.

331 Heads of Norwegian parties from *Economist,* March 23, 1991, p. 56.

331–332 Aardal and Brundtland quotes from "Who's in Charge Here? Chances Are It's a Woman," *New York Times,* May 22, 1991.

332 Karhunen and Tuominen quotes from "Finnish Parliament: Average Age Under 40," *New York Times,* March 20, 1991.

Brundtland quote from *Chatelaine,* October 1988.

332–333 Hompland quote from "Petticoat Politicians Run into Trouble," *The European,* December 5, 1991.

333 *Financial Times* quote from April 22, 1991, issue.

The European article on Aznar, "Opposition Trusts in Hillary Factor," appeared in the February 11–14, 1993, issue.

334 *Financial Times* quote on Poland from "Poland's Reigning Queen," the March 1, 1993, edition. Actions by Suchocka and *Business Week* quote from the magazine's December 28, 1992, issue, p. 55.

Ungarn quotes from "Challenge in the East," *Time* magazine's special issue on women, Fall 1990.

334–335 Dimitrova reported in *Ms.,* July/August 1992, p. 17.

335 Semra Özal quote from "Fast-Living First Lady Tilts at Turkish Islam," *Sunday Times,* December 23, 1990.

336 Ciller quote from "Fast-Living First Lady Tilts at Turkish Islam," *Sunday Times,* December 23, 1990.

Semyonva quotes from *Soviet Life*, March 1991, p. 16.

337 Ashrawi quotes from "The Feminist Behind the Spokeswoman—A Candid Talk with Hanan Ashrawi," *Ms.*, March/April 1992.

Role model quote reported in "Hanan Ashrawi a Fresh Voice," *Denver Post*, December 4, 1992.

337–338 Zia quote from "Fresh Priorities," *Far Eastern Economic Review*, December 12, 1991.

338 Bhutto and Lamb quotes from *Financial Times*, October 15, 1990.

339 Higuchi quotes from "Kaifu Drops Women From Cabinet, Defies Factions' Leaders," *Washington Post*, February 28, 1990.

Doi quote from "Women in Japan Get Political," *Los Angeles Times*, January 23, 1990.

The *Financial Times* and Ogata quotes from "One Woman's Crusade for the World's Dispossessed," *Financial Times*, February 8, 1992.

339–340 Ogata's sanctions and Winter quote from "Japanese Diplomat Puts Refugees before Politics," *New York Times*, April 7, 1993. Description of JNP and Koike quotes from " 'Clean' Party Gains as Japan's Leaders Falter," *Christian Science Monitor*, April 6, 1993.

340 Information on Harue Kitamura from "Japan: Record Breakers," *Ms.*, July/August 1991.

341 Violeta Chamorro quote from "Managua Mama," *W*, July 22, 1991.

Time magazine quote from the January 25, 1993, issue, p. 19.

341–342 Erundina quote from "Brazil: São Paulo's Radical Mayor," *Ms.*, May/June 1991.

342 Eisenmann and Correa quotes from "Panama City Mayor Broadcasts Politics," *Washington Post*, June 19, 1991.

343 Menchu description from *The Feminist Majority Report*, December 1992, p. 11.

Campbell information from "Canadians Turn to Woman for Top Post," *Rocky Mountain News*, March 27, 1993.

NDP information from *Chatelaine*, April 1989, p. 4.

344 Child's quote from "Thatcher Backs Major in Contest to Become Next Prime Minister," *Washington Post*, November 27, 1990.

Financial Times quote from November 23, 1990, issue.

Noonan quote from *New York Times Magazine*, December 16, 1990.

Conclusion

350–351 American Association of University Women study and Gilligan data from "Girls' Toughest Time," *Washington Post,* January 11, 1991; *Science News,* March 23, 1991, p. 184.

351–352 Take Our Daughters to Work Day section based on *Working Mother*, April 1993, pp. 30, 32, 40; and "Girls to Join Workforce," *USA Today*, April 26, 1993.

352 Bartholomew's "Horizons 2000" class described in "The Self-Esteem Slide," *Washington Post,* June 27, 1991.

Index

About the Authors

PATRICIA ABURDENE and JOHN NAISBITT have been collaborators since before the 1982 publication of *Megatrends*. They co-authored *Reinventing the Corporation* in 1985 and *Megatrends 2000* in 1990. Their books have sold more than 14 million copies worldwide. Each year, their lectures reach tens of thousands of business leaders and opinion makers around the globe. The authors live in Telluride, Colorado, and Cambridge, Massachusetts, and maintain an office in Washington, D.C.